The Poetry of

Giovanni Meli

(A Bilingual Anthology)

Legas

Pueti d'Arba Sicula / Poets of Arba Sicula

Volume XIV

This series is intended as a showcase for Sicilian poetry. Since poetry is the best mirror of a nation's soul, these volumes offer English-speaking people an opportunity to know and understand the Sicilian people better. The following is a list of all the volumes published so far. All volumes are available through Legas, P. O. Box 149, Mineola, New York 11501 USA

Giovanni Meli

The Poetry of

Giovanni Meli

A Bilingual Anthology (Sicilian/English)

Edited, Introduced and Translated into English Verse by
GAETANO CIPOLLA

With Illustrations by Diane Miller, William Ronalds
and Beppe Vesco

LEGAS

Meli, Giovanni, (1740-1815)
The Poetry of Giovanni Meli: a Bilingual Anthology (Sicilian/English)
ISBN 978-1-939693-09-9

Library of Congress Control Number: 2015934340

Acknowledgements

The publisher gratefully acknowledges a grant from Arba Sicula which made it possible, in part, to publish this book.

The author owes a debt of gratitude to Professor Emeritus Charles Giordano for his careful proofreading of the English translation and for his many valuable suggestions. Many thanks also to Professor Emeritus Joseph Tusiani for his advice and encouragement.

P. O. Box 149
Mineola, NY 11501
USA

3 Wood Aster Bay
Ottawa, ONTARIO
K2R ID3

Legaspublishing.com

To my wife Florence

Indici / Table of Contents

FAVULI MORALI/Moral Fables

Introduction

HISTORICAL BACKGROUND

Giovanni Meli (1740-1815) is undoubtedly the most accomplished poet who ever wrote in Sicilian; a language that had already distinguished itself, under Frederick II, as the first poetic idiom of Italy. While there has been considerable disagreement over Meli's specific place in the history of Italian literature (was he an Arcadian poet? How open was he to revolutionary ideas?), he is regarded today as one of the most important literary figures of his time. In spite of the fact that the use of his native language made his poetry nearly inaccessible to a majority of Italians, Meli occupies a place of prominence among Italian poets of the 18th century. Mario Apollonio goes even farther in his assessment of Meli by claiming that his is among the loftiest and purest poetry in 18th century Europe."

Meli's European dimension is easily demonstrable. While it is true that the god of the poet was Sicily (as Luigi Settembrini put it in his *Lezioni di letteratura italiana*), and that Meli was "the perfect Sicilian poet" (as his French translator Gustave Chetenet wrote in the preface to an anthology of his poems published in Paris in 1892), it would be erroneous to think of Meli as a Sicilian poet" if by that we mean a person whose intellectual concerns were entirely of a regional or provincial nature. Indeed, as Giorgio Santangelo has shown, particularly in his most recent work (*La "Siepe" Sicilia*, Palermo: Flaccovio, 1985) as well as in his masterful introduction to Meli's *Opere* (Rizzoli: Milano, 1965), this Sicilian poet's spiritual world cannot be comprehended unless it is framed against the background of the history of ideas in Europe. Modern research has proved conclusively that Sicily, especially during the second half of the 18th century, was not the backward island completely cut off from civilization that thinkers such a Giovanni Gentile had supposed it was. While Sicilian society was still in large part very conservative and backward-looking, a small group of intellectuals had started a dialogue not only with their counterparts on the Italian mainland, but also with those philosophers in France and in England whose works had created a new intellectual climate culminating in the French Revolution and the birth of the modern era. Bacon, Descartes, Leibnitz, Wolff and Rousseau were read avidly in Palermo. In 1728, at Messina, Tommaso Campailla had published a long poem in octaves entitled *L'Adamo ovvero, il mondo creato*, a popularization of Descartes' philosophical system, and Tommaso Natale in 1756 had tried to do the same thing for the next hegemonic philosophical system by writing a verse treatise entitled *La filosofia leibniziana*. Economic and social problems were the subject of many a study conducted with more modern techniques. Numerous treatises in physics, astronomy, agriculture, and volcanic phenomena, to name but a few of the many new fields of interest, give evidence of the new spirit that animated the intellectuals of the island. New schools were opened, not to duplicate the work of the ecclesiastical institutions already in place, but to foster the creation of a new breed of educated person. New methods of scientific investigation were being employed. Meli himself, who as we will see was a practicing physician and a chemistry professor, published a pamphlet describing the extraordinary effects of a spider's poison. The importance of Meli's contribution was not in the content of the pamphlet but rather in the manner in which he approached his investigation. His findings were based exclusively on the direct and verifiable observation of reality, without recourse to traditional explanations or unverifiable theories. This procedure — central to the modern scientific approach — reveals an important component of Meli's personality, that is, his life-long belief in experience as the most reliable of teachers.

The lessons of the Enlightenment had not gone unheeded in Sicily. Diderot, Boileau, Voltaire, Fenelon, Young, Locke, Hume, Pope and other major writers were well-known in Palermo, albeit to a relatively small group of intellectuals and aristocrats.

The rule of two successive Viceroys offers us clear evidence of the spread of the principles of the Enlightenment: they were Domenico Caracciolo, Viceroy of Sicily from 1781 to 1786 and Francesco D'Aquino, Prince of Caramanico, who ruled the island from 1786 to 1795. Caracciolo who had lived in Paris and had been nurtured on the ideas of the French "Lumiéres," attempted during his short government to introduce a number of reforms designed to free Sicily of its feudal shackles and to bring it out of its centuries-old backwardness. He sought (1) to restore the authority of the state over an aristocracy that had come to regard its feudal powers as divinely-given rights, (2) to revive the depressed economy of the island, and (3) to improve the lot of the poor classes. Caracciolo's actions scored some successes in curbing the power of the barons — one of his greatest was the abolition of the Inquisition in 1782 — however, the Viceroy's attempts at reforms eventually clashed with the Sicilian Parliament — the political arm of the Sicilian aristocracy — and he was forced to give up the fight, returning to Naples as King Ferdinand IV's Minister of Foreign Affairs.

His successor, chosen by Caracciolo himself, though animated by the same anti-feudalistic, enlightened principles, was a more realistic and prudent man who was able to win the support of the Sicilian barons, instituting a number of those reforms that had been the cause of the rift between the Parliament and his predecessor. The Prince of Caramanico ruled Sicily for 19 years and was responsible for many important changes in the political, economic and social life of the island. In May of 1789, for example, even before the French legislators promulgated similar reforms, Francesco D'Aquino passed an ordinance abolishing slavery, guaranteeing personal freedoms, granting the right to a legal defense and civil equality of citizens, as we learn from Giuseppe Quatriglio's *Mille anni in Sicilia: dagli Arabi ai Borboni*, (Palermo: Ediprint, 1985). His government continued to work towards a more liberal and progressive rule even after the events of the French Revolution which were seen in Sicily as a tremendous threat to the established authority of the king. The events of France caused a harsh and repressive reaction in the island and many of the gains made by the masses were lost. The Jacobins were particularly feared. In fact, the name was used synonymously with "scoundrel" and murderer". Francesco Paolo Di Blasi, the Palermitan lawyer whose idealism and passion for social justice and for the rights of the individual was wonderfully portrayed in Leonardo Sciascia's *Consiglio d'Egitto*, was beheaded for ill-conceived and vague Jacobin revolution intended to institute a Sicilian Republic patterned on the French model.

The negative reaction towards the French Revolution was not typical only of the monarchical forces within Sicily, which understandably could not embrace the republican ideals of the Jacobins with open arms, but it was typical also of the small group of intellectuals who considered themselves free thinkers, men who adhered to most of the principles of the Enlightenment, with the exception of the idea of revolution. Another belief which acted as a damper on the spread of revolutionary republican ideas espoused by the French Revolution was the myth, among the intellectuals, of the Sicilian "nationhood," that is, of Sicily as an autonomous political entity which identified itself with its Parliament and with the feudal rights of its barons. The intellectuals' conviction that all reforms had to be channeled through the system, that is, maintaining the monarchy in place which in turn would be a guarantee of the Sicilian nation's microcosmic feudal system, created strong negative sentiments toward any idea that threatened the political *status quo*. Hence the antipathy towards the French, in which undoubtedly old memories of the Sicilian Vespers of 1282 played a part, and the sympathy towards the English system of reforms which eventually was responsible for the formulation of Lord Bentinck's Constitution, adopted by the Sicilian Parliament in 1812.

One very important psychological attitude common among Sicilian intellectuals of Meli's time, which remains a constant point of reference even today, was their tendency to consider any new idea not deeply grounded on reason and on a solid appreciation of reality as utopian and delirious. A very strong vein of skepticism has always been the patrimony of Sicilians. This is probably why the philosophy of John Locke, the founder of Empiricism, was found to be very congenial by Sicilian intellectuals. His Essay on Human Understanding was widely read in Palermo. The writings of David Hume were equally well-known, as well as those of the French thinkers who subscribed to Empiricism and further developed its tenets, namely Diderot, Voltaire, Condillac, D'Alembert and Helvetius. These philosophers, who exerted a very strong influence on Meli, represent his European dimension.

The Sicilian intellectuals' skepticism played an important role in shaping their reactions to political and social problems, and that role is best illustrated by considering their responses to the French Revolution. The Parisian events of 1789 found few supporters, if any, among Sicilian intellectuals. Most of them, including Meli, condemned them as an abomination. Sebastiano Ayala, to name but one of the many critics defined it as "a frightening and horrible monster," which had tried to play a hoax on people with the legislation of the rights of man (Santangelo, *La "Siepe" Sicilia*, p. 129). Their failure to understand the principles that had animated the reign of terror was equivalent to their failure to carry to their logical conclusions their assessments of Sicilian realities. The obstacles that stood in the way of a freer society, a fairer division of wealth and better standards of living for the lower classes resided in large measure in the feudalistic institutions of Sicily. The intellectuals understood this. So did Caracciolo and D'Aquino, whose efforts were directed primarily against the barons.

Belief in the myth of the enlightened monarch caused the intellectuals to fail to carry their assessment a step further, and embrace the republican ideals of the Jacobins which would have done away with the monarchy and its appendage (the feudal barons). They failed to go that far because the system had been in place for so long (since the 14th century) that any alternative, especially if it came from the outside, was viewed with suspicion. The task of overhauling the system, and undoubtedly it must have crossed their minds, would have appeared as totally beyond reality, a delirium. Their common sense, their widespread skepticism, their reliance on empirical data and the weight of four centuries of rigid feudal domination spoke eloquently on behalf of the status quo regarding political institutions. It is perhaps axiomatic that sane, sober-minded men are almost never found at the center of revolutions. The Sicilian intellectual of this time had his feet on solid ground, and relied on experience and on history. A few visionaries at this juncture might have changed the course of Sicilian events.

It could not be said, however, that these men wanted reforms with less intensity, or that they felt the need to renew Sicilian society with any less urgency. Their desire to improve the standards of living of the poor classes was genuine. However, the means through which they chose to pursue their aims (through concessions granted by an enlightened monarchy) failed to take into account the greed of the barons and the self-interests of the many groups which would suffer economic losses through the introduction of those reforms. Their desires were bound to be thwarted and frustrated. In his longing to bring about reforms and his skepticism, Giovanni Meli was a product of his time, indeed, we may say that he was the perfect embodiment of the dichotomies that troubled the Sicilian intellectual of the second half of the 18th century and the beginning of the 19th century. His *Don Chisciotti e Sanciu Panza* is the meeting point between the principles of the Enlightenment and the ideals of a deeply conservative society.

HIS LIFE AND WORKS

Giovanni Meli was born in Palermo on March 6, 1740. His family was not wealthy. His father, Antonio, was a goldsmith; his mother Vincenza Torriquos, was of Spanish origin. Having received a traditional education seven years in the Jesuits' Collegio Massimo, which he later characterized as worthless, he felt the need to study on his own. He began reading Latin and Italian classics as well as the authors of the French Encyclopaedia when he was 16 years old. More at the urging of his mother than of his own volition, young Meli began attending the lectures of the most renowned physicians of his time at the Accademia degli Studi, which became the University of Palermo in 1805. His mother intended to prepare him for the medical profession in the hope that he might help alleviate the family's financial difficulties. While attending to his medical training, Meli devoted himself to writing verse in the manner of Metastasio, Rolli and Frugoni, the foremost representatives of the Arcadian movement in Italy. His facile pen earned him a place in several poetic academies which flourished in the capital. His first poetic season saw him writing entirely in Italian, but after the poem "La Ragione," a compendium of his vast scientific and philosophical readings Meli wrote primarily in Sicilian. The search for a more vivid linguistic medium with which to give expression to his inner world culminated in the *La Fata Galanti*, (*The Gallant Fairy*) a Bernesque poem in eight cantos, written in octaves and inspired primarily by Ariosto's *Orlando Furioso*. *La Fata Galanti* was his first substantial experiment with an "Illustrious Sicilian" idiom. The poem was recited in 1761-2 at the meetings of the "Accademia della Galante Conversazione," and earned him the admiration of fellow poets, as well as the protection of the Prince of Campofranco who invited the "pueticchiu," as Meli referred to himself on account of his young age, to live as a member of his household.

Many of Meli's traits are contained in this poem: his penchant for philosophical and literary satire, his concern for social problems, his personal aspiration for a life of peace and tranquility in the bosom of mother nature, and his vocation as a painter of idyllic and bucolic scenes. Particularly important are the passages in which Meli, under the guidance of Fantasy, passes in review the most famous philosophical systems from Leibnitz' vantage point. Indeed, this part may be considered as a celebration of Leibnitz' deism. The poem is also important to understand the literary apprenticeship of the poet. In it he imagines that with the aid of his Fantasy he is visiting the shops of the greatest ancient and modern poets, whose wares are set on display for every one to compare. The largest and the most impressively decorated tents are those of Metastasio, Ariosto, Anacreon, Pindar, and Homer, among many others. His dislike of Baroque poetry is made evident by the epithet he hurled against the 17th century. He called it "un seculu strammu" (a weird century), adding that it would have become mute if hyperbole and metaphor had been withdrawn from it. (Canto II, 34).

Named medical officer for the town of Cinisi, (30 kms. from Palermo) Meli moved there in 1767. He had received his license to practice medicine in 1764. As was the custom of the time, he began wearing the typical short tunic with the collar of a clergyman and was called "Abbate" (Abbot) from that time onward, even though he did not receive Minor Orders until 1814, one year before his death. He remained in Cinisi for five years, and it is there that he wrote part of his *La Buccolica*, most of his Elegies and *L'origini di lu munnu*.

The Origin of the World, first translated into English verse by the present writer, (New York: Arba Sicula, 1985), consists of 75 octaves written between 1768 and 1770. It was published in 1781, but it had circulated in manuscript form among Meli's friends since shortly after its completion. The satire represented Meli's contribution to the hotly debated philosophical issues revolving around the views of Vincenzo Miceli, a thinker from Monreale who had attempted to reconcile Spinoza's pantheism with Catholic theology. Meli, who regarded with skepticism any system which claimed absolute validity for itself, ridiculed Miceli and his followers likening, them to "Aesop's blackbirds who dressed themselves with the feathers of other birds." (*Le Lettere di G.M.* ed. Giovanna Micali, Palermo: Trimarchi, 1919, p. 13). Miceli's adversaries in the controversy were not spared either. The poem, which Francesco De Sanctis and other critics praised as Meli's satirical masterpiece, "a real jewel," as Francesco

Orestano said, — is in reality a caricature of the various conjectures that man had advanced to explain the origin of the universe. Miceli's system corresponds with the final part of the poem in which Jove — who had been seeking the advice of his family of gods on how best to make the world and had listened patiently to their absurd notions—decides that he is the only substance that exists in the universe void and, therefore, he is the world. He asks his children to dismember him so that his limbs could become nature. His thigh becomes Italy, and his head, of course, becomes Sicily. With his usual, subtly ironic smile Meli concludes the poem with a prayer to Jove to remain stiff upon the ground (for any sudden movement would prove fatal to Italy).

If Miceli's conjecture was the target of Meli's satire, all others are shown in their weakness and absurdity. The biblical account is not mentioned for fear of the censors, a fear that was responsible also for the deletion of octaves 12-20 from the first edition of the work. Jove and his family behave in low burlesque style in these octaves assuming postures and speech that are less than godly.

In this satire, Meli poked fun at the materialists, who denied the existence of the soul, the will, and of consciousness, and at the idealists who believed that only what exists in the mind is real. His satire, as Paolo Emiliani Giudici wrote, is pungent without ferocity. He corrects but does not insult. (*Storia della letteratura italiana*, Firenze, 1857, p. 15.) But it is inventive, delightful, earthy, humorous, fully charged with slyness at times bordering on the blasphemous. The opening line of the poem announces both the subject matter and the tone with which it is going to be treated: "Jeu cantu li murriti di li dei" (I sing of the tumescences of gods). To speak of the gods' swollen condition in preparation for the act of creation is an irreverent but also mischievous tone which is maintained throughout the poem, often with hilarious effects.

Before his departure for Cinisi, Meli had written four poems, one for each of the seasons. *La Buccolica* grew around these four poems. In the final edition of Meli's works, *La Buccolica* contained two sonnets, five eclogues and ten idylls. The changing of the seasons was a very popular topic in the European literature of the 18th century. Thomson (The Seasons), Saint Lambert ("Les Saisons"), Gessner ("Idyllen"), as well as the Prince of Campofranco, Meli's protector, had been inspired by the same subject. The *Buccolica* has been regarded as Meli's masterpiece by most critics, especially by those who consider him an Arcadian poet. Attilio Momigliano regarded this volume as the "only genuine bucolic work that Italian literature has ever produced." (*Storia della letteratura italiana*, Messina-Milano, 1958, p. 346) Generally speaking, the collection may be considered a celebration of love, seen as a primordial and regenerating force in the world. Love is the dominant theme of the work. Its celebration is interwoven with the changing of the seasons: delicate and tender hues in the spring, harsh and violent tones in the summer to reflect the harshness of the Sicilian sun. In autumn, feelings of warmth and melancholia permeate the poems, replaced by coldness, fear and dark forebodings in winter. The *Buccolica* must not be seen as just another volume of Arcadian poetry in which shepherds and nymphs are shown gamboling amorously in an effort to escape the corrupt and tumultuous world of the city. Meli's education as a scientist and the lessons of the Enlightenment allowed him to look at the world with attitudes that were unknown to the poets of Arcadia. Meli brought to his poetry a greater sincerity and a fresher imagination which revived and rekindled the old and worn-out clichés of the shepherd-loving poets of the previous age. Whereas the poets of Arcadia had sung of a return to the simplicity of nature as a reaction against the eccentricities and convolutedness of the Baroque Age, Meli's return to nature was predicated on a fresher reappraisal, not only of nature as a wise, benevolent, and providing mother, but also of the innate qualities of man which by nature tended towards what was good. If man were freed of the corrupting influences of the cities, happiness could still be found in the bosom of Mother Nature. In such attitudes, of course, one can recognize J. J. Rousseau's pervasive influence on Meli. Rousseau's works, perhaps more than those of any other author, have left an indelible mark on his opus.

The first sonnet, which serves as an introduction to the collection and is emblematic of Meli's life-long aspiration to live in peace and quiet in harmonious communion with nature, opens on a grandiose vista of Sicilian landscapes. The poet addresses the mountains of Sicily, its meadows, its crystalline lakes, its silvery waterfalls, its dark caves and its barren countryside as though they were living and pulsating creatures which inspire tenderness as well as apprehension, and asks them to welcome him in their midst. While nature is presented in its dual realities as threatening and welcoming, the poet characterizes himself as "l'amico di la paci e di la quieti" (The friend of peace and of tranquility). The search for such rare moments of communion between man and nature constitutes Meli's life-long struggle, and represents the nucleus out of which Meli derived his most original poetry, according to Giorgio Santangelo. (See his Introduction to Meli's *Opere*.)

It's interesting to point out the absence of any references to man or beast from the list of elements the poet addressed, except of course, for the reference to the "passaru sulitariu" (the solitary sparrow) a Petrarchan reminiscence, which was to become one of Leopardi's most famous poems. The poet asks to be received by nature and claims a privileged space for himself as though his natural disposition gave him a special dispensation to be part of it and to take up the role of intermediary between it and the world of men. He will take on the role of the singer of nature as the second sonnet makes abundantly clear.

In the second sonnet, which cannot be separated from the first as was done in some editions of Meli's work (see *I lirici del Settecento*, a cura di Mario Fubini), the poet addresses Pan, the pastoral divinity, lord of the wolves, who explicitly invests him not only as a singer of "the countryside, the herds and shepherds," but as the natural heir to the father of bucolic poetry, the Sicilian Greek, Theocritus. Thus Meli claims for himself a very specific line of descent through Pan, and Theocritus. He will be the new Theocritus who will bring back the glory of the Sicilian Muses.

Since the poems in the *Buccolica* were written in different stages of Meli's career — in the second edition of 1814 six more poems were added — the work may be regarded as a compendium of the most pervasive and time-resistant traits that contributed to his poetic personality. The open character of the collection which allowed him to add poems makes it possible for us to see the evolution of the poet through the years. In fact, the addition of the six poems to the 1814 edition allows us to see how Meli's concern for social and economic issues became stronger with the passing of time. Given his wide reading and considering the intellectual climate of the times, it is not surprising that his poems should contain strong social commentary on the plight of the poor classes of Sicily, and particularly on the plight of agriculture in the island. Social justice, economic fairness, an end to the abuses of one class against another, greater rewards for the peasants who alone are the producers of the wealth of nations, are themes that will return even more insistently in the *Don Chisciotti e Sanciu Panza.*

I have chosen to include five poems, one per season, except for Autumn which has two poems. The poems are translated into English here for the first time, except for the Polemuni poem which appeared in *Moral Fables and Other Poems.* These are the poems: from Spring, Idyll I, Dameta; from Summer, Idyll III, Daphnis; from Autunn, Idyll VI Martinu, and Idyll VII, Polemuni; and from Winter, Idyll VIII.

Idyll I opens to a pastoral scene that recalls a Virgilian eclogue at a moment when the shadows of night are falling and the animals are returning to their shelter accompanied by dogs and shepherds. From a hill, Dameta, with Dori next to him, begins a tender song which is basically a hymn to love, understood as a force of nature that cannot and should not be denied. Dameta asks his beloved to give in to the impulses of love for in so doing she would obey the supreme law that governs the universe. Dameta's song, which recalls the rarefied sensuality of Meli's best known odes, also testifies to Meli's scientific understanding of the forces that drive the attraction between man and woman.

Idyll III has Daphnis as protagonist. Mercury's son, who was a disciple of Pan, regarded as the father of bucolic poetry, was a master of playing the reed pipe. The Idyll relates a nocturnal scene dominated by the appearance of the white, resplendent Moon that Daphnis addresses with a sorrowful invocation so that somehow she could intercede with the woman he loves and change her coldness of heart. The poem again portrays love as a force that is capable of overcoming all obstacles, even between social classes. In reminding the Moon how she (as Diana or Selene) fell in love with the shepherd Endymion, Daphnis undescores the great power of love that can unite god and men.

Idyll VI, Martinu, is a celebration of nature. The poem is constructed on the concept that man who moves away from nature loses his sense of direction and behaves as a robot, obeying the bad habits to which city life has accustomed him. It is a contrast between city life and country life in which mother nature speaks eloquently about the gifts she has bestowed on man. Nature demonstrates how deviating from the universal law of "Amari e farsi amari" (To love and to make all love you) is a prescription for unhappiness. Nature passes in review the wondrous gifts that she has provided for mankind, from the majesty of the the mountains and the seas, to the precious stones and resources of the earth, and from the fruits and myriad animals that populate the earth, to the gifts of the senses given to man.

But in spite of this, man is easily distracted by illusory goods and follows false idols. Meli's pessimism once again is reiterated when at the end of the poem Martinu returns to the life he had led before, a victim of habit. As Giorgio Santangelo wrote, "In Martinu circulates a breath of cosmic grandeur, a foreboding of the poetry of the infinite, that are not present in Meli's other works, and at the same time a moral engagement that redeems Arcadian literature from the conventional poetry about shepherds that marked so much of Italian literature of the second half of the 18th century." (p. 76)

Coursing through many of the poems of the *Buccolica,* there is a sense of restlessness and dissatisfaction with the world that few Arcadians probably ever felt. Meli's attitudes towards the world and the scope of his concerns can be considered as foreshadowing the Romantic Movement. There is a sense of skepticism in some of the poems that some critics have regarded as pre-Leopardian. Typical of this vein is "Idiliu VII, Polemuni," which Meli probably wrote in a moment of despair during his sojourn in Cinisi. The poem, relates the story of a man who has lost everything, his love, his boat, his friends and who sits by the sea complaining about his bitter fate. In his touching soliloquy he questions the very meaning of life. The waves themselves are moved by his complaint, so much so that they try to intercede with Destiny and when their prayers are unanswered, they grow mountainous and stormy and fall upon Polemuni, swallowing him. Meli's comment is:

> Pri l'infelici e li disgraziati
> qualchi vota è pietà si l'ammazzati."

(For wretched and unhappy human beings;
sometimes to kill them is much more humane).

Idyll VIII is a representation of the winter season embodied in the figure of Montano, an octogenarian who has learned from his vast experience to live following the rhythm of the seasons. Sitting in the middle of his hut, surrounded by his family, he shares what he has learned though his "eighty winters" not only to survive the rigors of the weather but to enjoy the fruits of his labor. Winter is for him a time to rest and to use what he has accumulated through his work. Ths winter offers opportunities for socialization, for spending time with friends and relatives for rituals such as the annual slaughtering of the pig, which provides an oppotunity for neighbors to join the festivities. Finally, Uraniu sings offering his love and simple gifts to Nice, who is shivering from the cold.

The pessimism that we saw in Polemuni and some of the other Idylls is present in the three elegies entitled "Lu chiantu d'Eraclitu" (The Crying of Heraclitus) and "Su lu stissu suggettu" (On the Same Subject), written during the poet's stay in Cinisi. It is not difficult to see why many critics have seen in these poems a precursor of Leopardi. We need to read but a short passage of the first "The Crying of Heraclitus" (All three elegies are included in this anthology) to realize how Meli and Leopardi were kindred spirits, as G. A. Cesareo wrote:

Ah, wretched man! In what abyss you fell
by breathing in this atmosphere of life!
How dearly you have paid just to exist!
O worthless mixture of the humblest clay
where barbarous uncertainty's supreme,
spreading its poison over every sore!
And this is man? Ah, stupid nothingness,
absorb my being and my name as well!
Have we sufficient tears to weep for man?

Another poem in which Meli expressed his bitterly skeptical views about life is entitled "Lu specchiu di lu disingannu, o sia, la cugghiuniata" (The Mirror of Disillusionment, that is, Mockery). This poem, also included in this anthology, was recited originally during the days of Carnival in the home of Baron Lombardo in 1779. In a volume of Meli's poetry, published in 1783, this poem had the title of "Eraclito," confirming the thematic thread I have been following. The poem was published in Pisa in 1805. This work is a systematic destruction of all those values and qualities that man holds dearest. One by one, the myths that man lives by are revealed as nothing but a hoax, a great mockery. Luigi Pirandello, who knew the work of his fellow Sicilian very well, as I have shown elsewhere (See my "Pirandello: "Don Quijote or Don Chisciotti?" in *QUADERNI D'ITALIANISTICA*, vol. Vl, pp. 111-16) objected strongly to the tag of "sincere Arcadian" which critics like Zendrini and Carducci had pinned on Meli. In his essay on "Umorismo," Pirandello spoke of Meli as a humorist: "Isn't there veritable humor in much of Meli's poetry? To demonstrate it we need only quote La Cutuliata":

Tic tic. . . what was it? Mockery!

Quoting from memory, Pirandello got the title wrong and substituted "Cutuliata" for "Cugghiuniata". He may have also opted to use "cutuliata" because it a less offensive term. The playwright was, however, very accurate as to the contents of the poem. Indeed, it is a perfect embodiment of the "sentimento del contrario" with which Pirandello defined his concept of humor. l suspect that Pirandello owes much more to Meli than has been so far acknowledged, for the Palermitan poet, in this and in many of his other works, fulfills most of the requirements of a Pirandellian humorist. As a humorist, Meli proceeds to peel away all of the delusions, all of the intellectual fabrications of man to leave him naked and alone in a godless and mocking universe. The little demon which Pirandello held responsible for breaking up every image to show its opposite, that special function of reflection which allowed the Pirandellian humorist to see the two faces of a coin, to see the surface and what is beneath the surface, must have been at work in Meli too.

Throughout Meli's poetic career, however, seldom did the bitterness of "Disillusionment" become so pervasive and all encompassing. However, it would be entirely wrong to think of Meli as a lugubrious and bitter man. Indeed, the picture that emerges from a reading of his work is rather the opposite, so much so that Meli on several occasions felt the need to caution the reader not to be misled by his apparent joviality and amiability. A sonnet which was to be a preface to the 1814 edition of his *Opere* addressed itself to the contrast between appearances and reality. In this poem Meli warns the reader who should happen to read his playful rhymes not to be deceived into thinking him a happy man:

> "How wrong can human judgment be! Not always
> are one's true feelings in a song expressed!"

Meli succeeded in masking his serious temperament with an outgoing personality. According to Agostino Gallo, his friend and first biographer, Meli was affable and witty, humble and generous with his friends and with everyone. It seems that he was at times even too embarrassed to ask for his physician's fees. The image that best characterizes Meli is perhaps the one that he himself created. He compared himself to an oyster, always attached to the rock where it was born, bearing on its back the vehemence of the waves and of the storms.

Meli was endowed with a very rich imagination and it was this virtue that enabled him to accept the difficulties of life. He used his imagination to escape into the world of poetry, the world of artistic creation. His verses, even the bitterest, were equivalent to a cathartic release. His muse was a safe harbor for his storm-tossed sail. She liberated him from the corrupt valley and brought him into the bosom of nature, as he wrote in the ode "A la Musa."

The happiest season of Meli's life began when he returned from Cinisi to Palermo. Dr. Gianconte, a well-known physician having to travel abroad, invited Meli to take over his medical practice. Thus dawned a period of great success: loves, honor, and money were his to enjoy. Already famous, Meli became the favorite of Palermitan aristocracy. The ladies of the nobility vied to have him as a guest at their elegant parties. The most celebrated gallant and erotic odes, written for the likes of Baroness Martinez, Duchess Lucia Migliaccio, the Marquise Regiovanni, Lady Marianna Mantegna, and others, belong to this period. In these poems he sang the beauties of women, that half of the human race without whom he could not live, as he was to say to a monk who had invited him to live in a cloister in his mature years. His consummate artistry and absolute command of his linguistic medium contributed to the creation of the most delicate, erotic odes of his time. In a rarefied atmosphere of sighs and restrained sensuality, of words that are whispered more than spoken, the poet celebrated various parts of the beloved's figure —

"Lu labbru," (The Lips); "Li capiddi," (The Hair); "La vuci," (The Voice); "La vucca," (The Mouth); and "L'occhi," (The Eyes) to name a few of his most famous poems. These topics were hardly original and belonged to a rich tradition dating back to the Sicilian School of poetry and culminating with the Arcadian movement, but Meli, whose language shed here the coarseness of every day speech contributed to renewing the imagery of Arcadia and to making it appear fresh and new. Typical of Meli's ability was the ode "Lu labbru" created around the worn-out cliché of the beloved's lips storing the sweetest honey. Meli succeeded in giving it new loveliness and delicacy by using diminutives and a complex pattern of rhyme. This ode, translated into German by J. Herder, bears the curious distinction of being the only Italian poem to have been translated into Finnish.

Equally famous is "L'occhi," (The Eyes) inspired by Lucia Migliaccio, Duchess of Floridia, who was to become the morganatic wife of King Ferdinand, and with whom the poet may have had a romantic interlude. Goethe, who visited Palermo in 1787, liked the poem so much he translated the first eight lines into German, entitling it "Sizilianisches Lied" (Sicilian Song).

Poems such as these, whose validity rests on the poet's technical abilities, on the musicality of their rhythm, on the allusiveness of the message, and the apparent simplicity of the language, which carries instead the weight of a long literary tradition, are a challenge to any translator.

"La vucca" (The Mouth) is a little jewel in which Meli has staged a silent drama whose characters are the beloved's most attractive features: her hair, her eyes, her eyebrows. The poet has, however, a great weakness for the mouth on which his gaze rests longingly, causing the eyes to feel a tinge of jealousy and resentment.

The sensuality that exudes from these poems and from many of the others in the collection, goes beyond the Arcadian poets' exercises with their Venuses and little Cupids floating in the air. In reading these poems, one feels the longing of the poet to touch the beloved tresses, to linger with a kiss on her skin, to caress her. In terms of inventiveness, freshness of images, and technical ability, these Melian poems can stand side by side with those of such masters as Chiabrera, Rolli, Frugoni, and Metastasio. This anthology contains most of the Odes, except some that may be occasional rhymes.

It is undoubtedly symptomatic of Meli's divided self that at the same time that he was composing his Anacreontic odes, he was also writing his *Satire, Capitoli* and *Epigrammi*. As a physician who had access to the homes of the aristocracy, and as a celebrated poet, Meli had first hand knowledge of how the wealthy lived. He also saw how the poor people of Palermo lived, and his enlightened sense of justice was offended. In satires such as "La Moda" (Fashions), "Lu Cagghiostrisimu" (Cagliostrism), and "Lu Cafeaos," (The Coffeehouse) he chastised the wealthy for their vanity, their endless intrigues, their fatuous love affairs, and their corruption. But the attitudes that prevail in these poems are not those of an ardent zealot. Meli himself stated in "Lu Cafeaos" that he had always been a friend to man and that he had never written out of spite, but only to warn him when he went astray. Meli was never moved by personal animosity against any one. His attitudes towards man, in the satires and elsewhere in his opus, are those of one who understands the nature of delusions, who laughs, and feels compassion at the same time. He was not a true satirist. Indeed, as Pirandello insightfully saw, he was a humorist, as we will see more precisely when we discuss his *Don Chisciotti e Sanciu Panza*.

But when the sufferings became too strong, when the injustices of the world became too unbearable and he was no longer able to laugh at man's folly, he offered this advice: give yourself to the god Bacchus. Oblivion can't be far behind. This Dionysian vein cannot be ignored in Meli. The praise of wine had been a literary subject of some popularity since the 17th century. (See for example Francesco Redi's "Bacco in Toscana," and in Sicily Domenico Tempio's "Ditirammu" and Giuseppe Leonardi's "Cuntu supra di lu vinu"). Meli himself sang of it on various occasions: "Li Baccanti," "Innu a Baccu," "In lodi di lu vinu," and in a long episode of the *Don Chisciotti e Sanciu Panza*. But the poem in which, according to Alessio Di Giovanni, he reached the pinnacle of his expressive powers," (*La vita e l'opera di G. M.*, Firenze, 1934) was his "Ditirammu: Sarudda," the most famous drinking song in Sicily, still recited at weddings and parties in Palermo, according to Lorenzo Messinese (*Poesie di G. M.*, Messina, 1973, p. 1). In this song Meli temporarily put aside the whispering of his erotic odes to grovel in a tavern together with some less than elegant drinking companions whose names — Andrew the Flop, Tommy the Blind, Lame Tony, Crazy Joe and Con-man Blaise — are hardly reassuring. The leader of this little group of drunkards is Sarudda who functions as Meli's alter ego, especially when he chastises old Palermo for its corruption and pretensions as a city of glamour when in fact it is morally and economically bankrupt, and when he sings the curative powers of Sicilian wines. Particularly hilarious is Sarudda's, and Meli's, listing of the illnesses that wine can cure. Sarudda's attitudes reflect Meli's characteristic stance when confronted with things that he could neither change nor control in any way. After his denunciation of the city's ills, Sarudda resorts to wine to drown his frustrations: To the devil with such melancholic thoughts, he exclaims, promising himself to live like monks who sing and dance and eat with their heads inside a sack. Sarudda-Meli, at times, may have sought to drown his awareness of the evils of the world in wine-caused oblivion.

The "Ditirammu" is a volcanic eruption of sounds and concepts that goes from learned reflections to mere games of associations and word play. Its immediate impression on the reader is of an explosion of sounds that wane only to begin again in an infernal cacophony. The meter is very irregular; lines of various lengths are placed one after another at random. Rhyme is irregularly distributed throughout the poem, both internally and externally, together with assonances and consonances that contribute to giving the poem its irrepressible sense of motion and energy.

The "Ditirammu" was written at about the same time as the episode in the *Don Chisciotti* in which a young man, suffering from a case of unrequited love, received from a wise old man of the town the same advice Sarudda dispenses freely: drown your sorrows in wine. It can make a happy man even of the most miserable of beings. The two works were born out of the same substratum of pessimism that tended to become increasingly more bitter with the passing of time.

Meli's interests were many, as we have seen, and he expressed his inner world in many different ways and with different voices. Those voices are present in all their modulations in a work that has been neglected for too long. I am referring to his most ambitious project, the *Don Chisciotti e Sanciu Panza*, a mock-heroic poem of 12 cantos and a "Vision," written between 1785 and 1786 and published for the first time in 1787, which I translated into

English. (See *Don Chisciotti and Sanciu Panza*, Toronto: The Canadian Society for Italian Studies, 1986, reprinted in a revised edition with Legas in 2005). Canto V of this work is included in this volume.

Don Chisciotti and Sanciu Panza is a poem that reflects, perhaps more fully than any other of his works, the author's personality and the conflicts of his time. It can be studied from a number of perspectives: as an historical document embodying the dynamic relationship between the ideas of the Enlightenment and the deeply conservative ideals of tradition-bound Sicilian society, as a record of social customs and traditions of a society that until recently had not changed appreciably, as an important moment in the struggle between social classes, and as a literary work of considerable scope and depth which shares in a tradition having deep roots in the Italian spirit and which has produced such poets as Pulci, Ariosto, Tassoni, and Berni, to name a few of the best known.

Why did Meli choose the two characters of Don Quijote and Sancho Panza? While the motivations for creating poetry are seldom clear cut or readily apparent, we may be certain that when Giovanni Meli conceived his ambitious project he was well aware of the possible risks involved in the choice. Undoubtedly the two characters living symbols of the opposing forces within man fulfilled deep-seated psychological needs of the Sicilian poet. Meli knew very well that his work would be judged from the perspective of the Cervantian masterpiece. His selection of the Spanish characters was an open invitation to compare the two works. In retrospect, Meli's choice may have to be considered an act of hubris punished by silence, neglect and often unjust dismissal of his poem. Those critics who have measured the Sicilian Don Chisciotti by his Spanish counterpart, (E. Giudici, Settembrini, De Sanctis and Cesareo) that is, who have regarded him as a mere continuation or extension of the *Don Quijote* — an imitation of an inimitable work — have done a great disservice to Meli and have failed to understand Meli's goals. Meli was too consummate an artist not to have realized that imitation was doomed to failure from the beginning. His *Don Chisciotti* was conceived in a different manner and had different goals to pursue on his return to earth. While the Sicilian knight had the same physiognomy as his predecessor, he lived in a different time and spoke with a different voice. The character of Sanciu Panza underwent an even greater metamorphosis, the most obvious manifestation of which was his elevation to the rank of his master. The Sicilian poem is entitled *Don Chisciotti e Sanciu Panza*. The Spanish novel was entitled *El ingenioso hidalgo Don Quijote de la Mancha*. Sancho's name did not appear in it. This shifting of emphasis is in reality more important than it seems, as we shall see shortly. The two works must not be seen as an original and an imitation, but rather as two different manifestations of the same archetype. Don Quijote and Sancho Panza constitute an archetypal couple: an inseparable and separate union of opposites. Don Quijote could not exist alone, as Cervantes learned after his hero's first solo adventure. Miguel De Unamuno, commenting on Don Quijote's acquisition of Sancho as his squire, said:

> Now Don Quijote is complete. He had need of Sancho. He needed him so as

to be able to talk, that is, to think aloud with frankness and listen to the sound of his own voice in the world." (From *Our Lord Don Quijote*, Bollingen Series LXXXV, - 3 Princeton: Princeton Univ. Press 1967, pp. 53-54).

We have been conditioned to think of Sancho Panza as an extension of Don Quijote, an appendage, if you will, — that is, an embodiment of the knight's less developed psychological components. — This complementary role of Sancho may in fact be nothing more than a bias of Cervantes' own peculiar psychological and philosophical attitudes, or perhaps a bias of the critics who have considered the archetypal couple a natural reaction, since in every couple there must be a dominant aspect, "un maggior corno," as Dante said referring to that "greater horn" of the flames engulfing that other manifestation of the archetypal couple as Ulysses and Diomedes in Canto XXVI of the *Inferno*. Unanumo considered Don Quijote the dominant half of the couple. But neither Unamuno's nor Cervantes' need to be the sole viable interpretations of the archetype.

Archetypes are experienced in a manner that is not independent from the psychological conditions present in the person. As we know, archetypes are always polyvalent and their contents are never static, fixed or unchangeable. Indeed, the content is fluid, and contradictory and blurred, a feature that manifests itself even after the couple has been projected onto two separate identities. Is there not a bit of Don Quijote in Sancho Panza and vice versa? In fact, we might ask whether Sancho in Cervantes' novel is not more Quijotic than Don Quijote himself. Knowingly, he chooses to follow a madman in search of glory while Don Quijote follows his own inner call. Thus when a poet experiences an archetype, he does so through all those personal factors that make up his distinctive self. The contents of the archetype being, however, fluid, he is apt to re-arrange the proportions assigned to each half of the couple to fit his needs.

Meli, in this context, need not be seen as an imitator of Cervantes, but rather as a poet in whom the archetype was activated. *Don Chisciotti and Sanciu Panza* were as alive in him as they had been in Cervantes. But, the antithetical couple was experienced in a different manner. The fact that Sanciu became for Meli the "maggior corno," that is, the dominant half of the couple, represents a shifting of the components to suit his psychological and philosophical stance toward the world. This re-arrangement was Meli's peculiar and unique reaction to the archetype, brought about by all those psychological, historical, and sociological factors that contributed to making him the man he was. The difference between Meli and Cervantes was that the scale containing the two halves of the archetype was weighted more on the side of skepticism for the Sicilian poet. Meli, to use a term dear to Unamuno, would seem to be a proponent of Sanchopanzism.

Although skepticism was a predominant attitude in him, it cannot be said that he was incapable of being moved by optimism. Nor would it be true to say that his empiricist's attitudes prevented him from harboring idealistic beliefs. Indeed, the poet was continuously torn between these two divergent attitudes throughout his life; in fact, this is the most evident characteristic of his poetry.

As an enlightened man who believed in the dignity of human beings and as a physician who saw how the different classes of Sicily lived (there were primarily the rich and the poor without any middle classes), Meli fervently longed to see the suffering of peasants and shepherds alleviated. He believed in and advocated many reforms designed to bring Sicily out of its backwardness. In 1801 he wrote a treatise entitled "Riflessioni sullo stato presente del Regno di Sicilia intorno alla agricoltura e alla pastorizia" ("Reflections on the Present State of Agriculture and Stock-Breeding in the Kingdom of Sicily") in which the poverty, sickness and malnutrition of the poor people of Sicily were deplored most bitterly. Many of the points contained in the treatise had already been made in his *Don Chisciotti e Sanciu Panza*.

The fact that he joined the movement of the Masons reflected his commitment to humanitarian and social ideals. As we know, this international organization was guided by philanthropic objectives. It is significant that Meli became a member of this organization sometime between 1781 and 1785; that is, at the time when the fervor for reforms was at its highest thanks to the political action of the enlightened Viceroy, Domenico Caracciolo. (See Eugenio di Carlo, "Spigolature Meliane," in *Studi su G. M.* p. 432).

Meli's social ideals are clearly expressed throughout the work. We need no special lens to see where Meli's heart was. The rich, the powerful, and the titled are constantly denigrated, while the peasants, the shepherds, in short, those who are the producers of wealth are exalted. Social justice, an end to the perennial exploitation of the working classes by the parasitic noblemen, the right for every person to work, the establishment of an international tribunal to settle cases, the abolition of wars, were ideas to which Meli subscribed whole-heartedly, and are the ideals which animate his Don Chisciotti (As we can read in canto XII, octaves 60-67).

Thus Meli can be defined as an empiricist with idealistic tendencies, a realist with a penchant for dreaming, a skeptical man who harbored optimistic views, a man who relied on facts but tended to be governed by principles. *Don Chisciotti and Sanciu Panza* was an embodiment of such a conflict. In a letter written in 1804 to Filippo Rehfues, he described the conflict in vivid terms. He confirmed that his life-long preoccupation had been

"to think of the most plausible ways to arrange and order the society of men so that the just would not be overcome by the unjust, the honest would find ways of living without being oppressed or humbled, virtue would be given the consideration due to it, and the laws would not be used for vile trafficking. The employment of countless loafers, charlatans and delinquents by the justice system is ruinous for the state and for the individual as well, and prevents those who are entrusted with its administration from ridding themselves of the yoke of such parasites. But then, realizing my humble condition as a private and the imbecility of my spirit, I would consider myself completely mad, promising myself never again to venture beyond the sphere of my desires or thoughts: a moment after, having moved away from such resolutions, I would return to my first deliriums, then I'd see the errors of my ways and I'd repent again. Now this state of perpetual contradiction within myself prompted me to mask with the allegory of *Don Chisciotti e Sanciu* the periods of my deliriums and the lucid intervals of good sense." (*Le Lettere*, p. 130). (My translation).

Prof. Gaetano Cipolla

P.O. Box 149

Mineola, NY 11501

Email @

gcipolla @optonline.net

Grocery List

If on the one hand Meli fervently hoped he could help the poor people of Sicily, on the other hand, he felt that all efforts were inevitably futile. His humanitarian ideals — embodied by Don Chisciotti — conflicted externally with the attitudes of an entrenched and intransigent nobility, unwilling to give up any of its privileges and, internally, with that realistic, skeptical part of himself that considered the task of changing the social fabric of the island a foolish and hopeless attempt. On Don Chisciotti Meli projected his yearnings for human justice, liberty and a more equitable division of wealth among the peoples of the world. But, at the same time, these yearnings had to be represented as the dreams of a delirious fool. Sanciu Panza, on the other hand, represented Meli's own skeptical attitudes toward Don Chisciotti's deliriums.

Don Chisciotti and Sanciu Panza is a humoristic poem in the Pirandellian sense, that is, as an embodiment of the "sentimento del contrario." Meli embodies the Janus figure within himself. Each of the two heroes is the incarnation of opposite tendencies. Indeed, each hero contains within himself his own contrary, the other side of the coin. Don Chisciotti is a humoristic character. Sanciu described him well when in Canto V, 28, (which I have included in this anthology because it is well representative of the work), he said:

> A certain malady possessed him, though:
> being on earth, he thought he was in heaven;
> being a beggar, he believed he was a lord;
> not having eaten, full. In short: out of his gourd!"

Don Chisciotti was a would-be hero, a fruiting tree that could never produce a fig or a pear; his good intentions were always undermined by his faulty reading of the physical evidence before him. His senses were constantly deceiving him. He was himself the negation of his desires. His death was a perfect expression of the humoristic mode. The man who presumed to set straight the world died of a hernia while attempting to straighten an old and odd-shaped rowan tree. His death was more Quijotic than that of his predecessor who, as you recall, died in his own bed in a very peaceful way after recovering his senses.

Sanciu too was created in a humoristic way. Whereas Don Chisciotti was a mass of undigested learning, a conglomeration of unassimilated notions without a unifying principle, Sanciu was an ignorant man who grew to become a natural philosopher, another Aesop. Experience and suffering changed him from a poor illiterate peasant into a highly esteemed, wise, and prudent man. This metamorphosis is but one of the most obvious humoristic touches.

Critics have attempted to associate Meli with one or the other of his characters. The truth is that Meli was both Don Chisciotti and Sanciu Panza and it would not be too hard to identify those utterances that Meli would have acknowledged as his own. If one were to separate the sane utterances of Don Chisciotti from those that are patently insane, one would have a compendium of Melian wisdom. But, Sanciu, too, is Meli. Indeed, he represents the prevailing attitude within the poet. He is, as we have seen, the tabula rasa that experience and the example of Don Chisciotti have filled. He is the empiricist, the sensationalist, the skeptic, the man who does not believe in witches, and the materialist who believes in the need to work.

It is symptomatic that it is Sanciu, and not Don Chisciotti, who returns after his death. He is the Melian hero. In the battle between idealism and materialism the latter won. Sanciu who had suffered during his life on earth was rewarded by being allowed to enter the Elysian Fields to spend his time with the greatest philosophers: Plato, Aristotle, and Aesop. Meli's particular admiration for Aesop, whom he regarded as the wisest natural philosopher, is especially evident in his last, and according to many critics, his most memorable work: *Favuli morali*, a collection of 89 verse fables, written during the last years of his life and published for the first time in 1814, except for Fables LXIII and LXIV, which had already appeared in the 1787 edition.

As was the case for the *Buccolica, L'origini di lu munnu*, and "Ditirammu. Sarudda," each of which found critics who extolled it as Meli's masterpiece, the *Moral Fables* have evoked enthusiastic appraisals from the majority of critics. Attilio Momigliano did not hesitate in calling the work, "The loftiest collection of fables in Italian literature." For Giulio Natali, Meli ranked very high not only among Italian dialectal fabulists, but among the ancient and modern fabulists world-wide. The authors of the article on Meli in *Settecento: Storia e Testi*, (Bari: Laterza, 1973, p. 392) consider the *Fables* Meli's absolute masterpiece and the masterpiece of the genre in the 18th century.

"In reading the fables," the authors said, "you can recall Aesop with La Fontaine, Gasparo Gozzi, Pignotti and others (whom the poet knew well), but Meli's fables are unmistakable for their lyric realism which is filtered through a language that is affectionate and without harshness, which is also a clue to the serenity of judgment that he had achieved." (My translation).

A number of critics believe that the fable as a genre was more congenial to the requirements of Meli's timid and trouble-shy personality. Meli chose the fable presumably to voice his true feelings about the corruption he saw in the courts, in the government, and in the social fabric of Sicily, without having to worry about repercussions and persecutions from those whom he would attack. Francesco Biondolillo, while acknowledging Meli's considerable lyric, bucolic, and satiric gifts, concluded that,

> "As a fabulist (he) was a lot greater both because in the brevity of the tale he was best able to engage his inventive and imaginative powers, and because behind the screen of the fable he was best able to express his soul and his thoughts, coloring the one and the other with the grace and the wit proper to his temperament." (My translation). ("Meli favolista," in *Studi*, p. 181).

Meli's presumed timidity need not be considered a major factor in the choice of the fable as a means of expression. He devoted the last years of his life to this genre because it had been growing in popularity and in critical esteem. In fact, the period that goes from 1700 to 1820 saw a renaissance of the fable in Sicily, as well as outside. On the island many collections were published by Venerando Gangi, Giuseppe Maraffino, and Domenico Tempio, to name three of the best known practitioners of the genre. The fact that some fabulists employed their tales of animals for specific political ends (I am thinking of the political fables published in 1813 by Giuseppe Maraffino in support of the Jacobin movement in Sicily) should be understood as another indication of the validity of the fable as a means of expression. Meli was aware of the increasing importance of the genre and chose it as his medium because he saw it as an effective tool for reaching a wider audience composed of different social classes. In fact, in a brief note written as a preface to his *Fables*, Meli acknowledged his debt to the fabulists of the past — particularly to Aesop and La Fontaine — and indicated that he had also intended to follow in the footsteps of the English writer Addison whose tales, published in *The Spectator,* had given readers of different social classes "extreme pleasure and profit".

There are other reasons for minimizing the "timidity factor" in the choice of the fable: primary among them is the fact that Meli does not spare anyone his criticism. No amount of misreading can change what he has to say about the noblemen, the lawyers, the priests, the government, and the mighty. They are hardly his favorite people, as we have already seen. Meli always stands by the side of the poor and the oppressed and he does not hesitate to point out where the errors are.

The 89 fables (I added the long fable included in *Don Chisciotti and Sanciu Panza*, bringing the number to 90), can be considered the work in which the poet's life-long search for wisdom finds its maturest expression. In them he celebrated the wisdom of the animals who live according to their natural instincts without harming others gratuitously. Man, on the other hand, is portrayed as corrupted by civilization. In the long verse preface, in which the poet speaks his mind in a more forth-right manner than he does in the fables themselves, Meli takes a very dim view of human nature and of that quality that distinguishes man from beasts: human reason. Speaking through his alter ego, an old man who is introduced as a direct descendant of Aesop, who translates the old moth-eaten manuscript found by the poet, Meli has harsh and bitter words to say about mankind. The old Translator, who provides a loose cornice that holds the 89 fables together, claims that Mother Nature, having distributed instincts and talents to every species, realized there were no instincts left for man, so she collected some residues from the other animals and gave them to him. Owing to such instincts there live on earth such creatures as Fox-men, Wolf-men, Mole-men, Dog-men, Cat-men, Strong-box-men and even such hybrids as Automatic-men who when their mistresses or wives or servants pull a string, move and perform on command as automatons. Such hybrid creatures embody qualities that Meli found particularly abhorrent.

The Old translator can find few redeeming qualities in man. He asks in bitterness and disillusionment:

> What species, say, what race
> of brutes or animals
> knows someone who's so mad
> that he works hard to bring
> abuse and woeful tears
> upon those who're his peers?

The art of killing is one on which man has penned more than one tome. And as for human reason, that gift that man alone supposedly possesses, the old man complains that there is little left. The human race has fallen on bad times. In a fierce indictment of reason as the primary cause of self-deception, which anticipates Pirandello's life-long concern, Meli has his old fellow say that reason is relative to the individual and even to an individual state. Hence communication becomes impossible. The posters on which the declarations of war are written are full of reasons; the endless legal suits that extort sentences and gold from men's purses, are reasons one and all; human passions often spring camouflaged by wise masks and good intentions, but ultimately they have their roots in treachery. The picture that the old man paints in the preface is extremely pessimistic and corresponds to Meli's own assessment of contemporary society. Undoubtedly, the hardships and the financial difficulties experienced by the poet in the last years of his life took their toll on him and contributed to his choice of darker, more somber colors. Only the animals who obey natural law are free of blame.

Throughout the fables, however, Meli adopts the same direct approach only in a few cases. Fable LXIII, which was published in 1787 as a "Capitolo," and as part of a threesome that included Fable LXIV and the story of the little mouse caught in a trap which became part of *Don Chisciotti and Sanciu Panza* (Canto X, Oct. 43), is atypically direct in its indictment of man's vices and evil nature. The fable is a conversation between two wolves who, resenting the reputation that man has pinned on them as rapacious beasts of prey, proceed to indict him for being an ungrateful, voracious, and cruel creature, who kills animals out of sport and not necessity, and preys on every being that lives in the air, in the sea, and on the ground. The wolves' bitter conclusion is that man is twice the wolf." Similarly atypical is Fable LXXXIII, in which a tiger reproaches man not for all the evil things he does to other species or to his own, but for the evils that he harbors in the secret recesses of his mind and for the vicarious pleasures that he derives from reading about atrocious deeds of the past or watching blood-soaked spectacles in theatres. Coincidentally, the two fables are also atypical in that they were both written in *terza rima*, the only two in the collection, which suggests that Fable LXXXIII may have been written at about the same time, that is, before 1787, although I cannot confirm this at present.

This approach represents the exception rather than the rule. Meli does not accuse from the ivory tower of moral righteousness. His fables may be an act of condemnation, but they are, as well, an act of acceptance of the shortcomings of man. The attitude that prevails throughout is the one displayed in the justly famous first fable about a little mouse who has gone astray:

> A little mouse who was lightheaded, brash,
> had gone the way of wine to vinegar,
> living in sheer debauchery with dash,
> along with bosom pals who were his par.

What we have here is a picture of two mice, one young and foolish, who knows only one aspect of life — his pleasures, his bosom buddies, his discotheques and bars, we'd say today,— and an old mouse who has seen everything: the brashness of youth and the wisdom of old age at odds. But, there is no animosity towards the brash young fellow. There is understanding and there is the regret that wisdom is not one of his qualities, but there is no open denunciation of his foolishness. The message, the moral teaching according to which brashness and debauchery, coupled with the arrogance of youth, can have dire consequences, emerges out of the events as they unfold.

Meli did not indulge in the explicit moralizing which can be found in many of his fellow fabulists, including La Fontaine. This is one of the distinguishing features of his fables. Animals meet, exchange words, perform their wise or foolish ceremonies, and we watch with an amused bittersweet smile upon our lips. The moral lesson that they teach is contained in their actions, in their vivid exchanges, in their essential movements, where nothing is ever out of place, no detail is ever superfluous, no deed insignificant. Consider, if you will the second fable, "The Crabs" and compare it with La Fontaine's "L'ecrevisse et sa fille" (The Crab and her Daughter), which deals with a similar theme. Both fables contain nearly the same number of lines. But, La Fontaine devoted 26 of them to comment on the philosophical and moral issues involved and barely 8 lines to telling the story. In addition, the French master seems not to have focused precisely on which moral lesson he wished to highlight. He spoke of sailors who lean backwards to go forwards, of philosophers who reach their goal by going backwardly and of a general who wins battles because of his ability to feign the opposite of his intent. These applications of the moral lesson go beyond the example offered in the fable, for the crab is not aware that there is anything wrong with the way she walks and does not feign anything. In other words, the moral lesson offered by La Fontaine was an intellectual formulation after the fact which was somewhat extraneous to the action of the fable.

Meli, on the other hand, did not address himself to the moral lesson in any explicit fashion. There is nothing extraneous in his descriptions and in the quick-paced exchanges between the well-intentioned, but inevitably myopic father crab and the inexperienced crablets. The father is drawn swiftly and with a sure stroke as a misguided figure of authority who cannot tolerate scrutiny from anyone, who resorts to that authority to impose his will on those who are weaker and smaller than he is; he is a well-meaning, but shortsighted boor who thinks earnestly that he is performing his duties as a father. Meli singled out the clear lesson of the story, which is that you must teach by examples, not by words, and made every detail subordinate to this simple truth. By making the father interested in the education of his youngsters, Meli added another dimension to the character of the crab. In fact, Meli exposes the true nature of the father crab as a sanctimonious figure who is not necessarily hypocritical as much as he is deluded and deceived by his inability to see himself for what he really is. Meli here is the humorist again who strips the mask of good intentions from the father and reveals him to be a victim of his myopia. The fact that the father continues to repeat his maxims forever shows that he is not aware of his shortcomings, while we and the author have established a sort of complicity that puts us above the crab and the human attitudes that he embodies. We know what the author knows. We see what the crab is too blind to see: a typical humoristic narrative device!

But we are not moved to laughter by the crabs' performance of their endless and futile pantomime, which seems to foreshadow a scene from the theatre of the absurd. Readers are rarely moved to a hearty, full-throated laughter in reading Meli's little gems. That is so because Meli never laughs at his protagonists, nor does he inveigh against them for their foolishness, vanity, pride, or meanness. Indeed, whenever his tone threatens to become too somber, whenever his tale threatens to become too tragic, he curls his lips at the corners of his mouth and a little ironic smile appears, dissolving the gloominess that had been building up, destroying the seriousness of his intent. The poet seems to be endowed with the uncanny ability to step outside of himself and to look at his own involvement and takes measures to establish a greater distance between himself and the spectacle that he is observing. And this, as we know, is another typical narrative ploy of the humorist who never occupies the same space as his characters.

Meli did not shout at the top of his lungs against the social injustices that he saw everyday, the corruption of the courts, the exploitation of the poor, the abuses of the nobility, or the ineptitude of the government. He felt no need to shout, knowing full well that his voice would have been drowned by the silence of the desert. But he was not ready to stop speaking the truth; perhaps he was speaking to himself, perhaps only to those few who have good hearing.

And those who listen carefully can hear as Meli punctures the balloons of hypocrisy (LXII, "The Bat and the Mice"), vanity (LIV, "The Fly"; LXXXIX, "The Fly and the Lion"), ingratitude (V, "The Mouse and the Hedgehog"; XXVIII, "The Dogs"; XXXVI, "The Old Woman and the Hog"; LXVI, "The Beaver and Other Animals"), ambition (XIII, "The Dogs and the Statue"), stubborness (LI, "The Donkey and the Bees"), stupidity (LXXII, "The Donkeys' Race") intolerance (LII, "The White Raven and the Black Ravens"), selfishness (VIII, "The Cat, the Stranger, and the Abbot"), greed (XVII, "Aesop and the Skylark") and cowardliness (LVIII, "The Stag, the Hound, and the Bull").

Vincenzo De Maria, in the introduction to *Le bestie gli uomini le favole*, (Catania: Tringale Editore, 1978) used a marvelous image to describe Meli's deceivingly light touch. He said: "La sua penna è come un fioretto che penetra di punta e par che neppure s'avverta per la sottigliezza della lama" (His pen is like a foil that pierces with its tip and owing to the thinness of the blade is barely felt). We might add, however, that the heart of a giant can be more easily pierced by a thin and pointed blade than by an unwieldy and heavy sword. And Meli's foil was sharp enough to penetrate even an armature of steel.

Precisely because of this lightness of touch, Meli's political engagement has not been fully recognized. A careful examination of the 89 fables reveals that over one third of them is a commentary on political and social problems confronting the people of Sicily. This is indeed surprising, particularly because Meli has usually been characterized as a compromising and conservative fellow by a number of critics. Meli does not hesitate to speak his mind on any subject. In fact, few problems confronting Sicilian society escape his keen observation.

He applied his training as an empirical scientist to the observation of reality, whether it was a physical phenomenon or the interactions between two social classes. His descriptions denote a sharp and far reaching vision, unclouded by any sentimentality and convincing to the utmost. Let us look for example at the description of the system of justice as practiced in Sicily during Meli's time. Fable LXXXIII, "The Marine Code," is as precise a rendering of the system's failures as any social treatise on the same subject. The fable, which relates the difficulties encountered by a group of sardines who were accused of slaughtering a large tuna because they had been found near the consumed carcass, is a lucid account of the social mechanisms which contributed to the creation of an unjust and unethical system based on the principle that might makes right. The sardines (the common people) are victimized by a triumvirate of adversaries represented by an unjust taxation system, by the crabs (the judges and lawyers) who perform a service of legitimization of the power held by the largest fish (the rich noblemen and politicians) so that it becomes hereditary. This fable is an indictment (1) of the fiscal policies of Sicily, (2) of the judges who, being more concerned with safeguarding their investments and patrimonies, act in collusion with the mighty to keep power in the hands of a few, and shroud their ceremonies under a cloak, linguistic and procedural, which appears mysterious, nay, unfathomable to the uninitiated, and (3) of the rich who are simply characterized as bullies who rely on the law according to which the large fish eats the little one. The crabs, as the supreme legal authorities, are characterized as "deities" and the lawyers and the people who back the crabs as official priests in a religion based on injustice and unfairness.

In "The Dogs' Alliance" (Fable LXXXII), the greed of a few members of a pack destroys the fibers of a society of dogs that had been extremely successful in attacking stronger and larger beasts through coordinated, collaborative efforts. A once thriving community disintegrated and became extinct because the individuals who were charged to make the laws were also the first and greatest transgressors. The ones who suffer in this kind of society are the weak and those who obey the laws to the letter.

Private pleasures vs the public good is a theme that returns often in Meli's fables. In "The Hornet and the Bee" (Fable LX), a hornet, who wishes to be free from society's restrictions and a bee, who thinks that true freedom can exist only within the bosom of organized society, are contrasted. The bee exclaims at last:

> If we lose sight of the good
> of the community,
> then either devil's home,
> or call it anarchy!

Disunity before a common foe spells out disaster for a herd of he-goats (Fable XXXIX). They are slaughtered one by one because they, instead of formulating a plan of attack against their common enemy, waste precious time in self recrimination and reproaches against one another. Meli comments bitterly:

The last ones learned too late, at their expense,
that when a common foe is waging war,
with private hatreds we should all dispense.
When present —dangers knock upon our door,
the swiftest and most daring resolutions
the only good means are to save a nation.

In Fable XLVIII, Meli revisits the theme of disunity and combines it with the lack of leadership and the lack of proper planning exercised by the pseudo scientists of his time who tried to apply some half-baked notions to solving the many problems besetting Sicilian society. Such men were like the monkey builders of the fable who begin their edifice from the top.

Those folk who threaten to destroy the fibers of society with their greed, their vanity, and intolerance are the butt of Meli's ironic attentions. A particular place is reserved to those who are deceitful. Politicians are indicted for their seemingly innate ability to feign the object of their desires in Fable XII. In Fable LXXIX, cunning, malice, and deceitfulness are listed as the qualities prized most in a realm of foxes, that is, in this world. But, the symbol par excellence of deceitfulness was the cat. His dislike of cats was almost visceral. In Fable LXIII, a mouse who is trying to instill in her little mice fear of the sweet looking, but deadly beast tells them,

Don't trust such hypocrites! Don't be naive!
Of such tame looks and manners be on guard!
Their eyes seem closed, but all things they perceive.
They are bloodthirsty, restless, and rock hard,
traitorous, thieving, heartless, indiscreet
selfish and greedy, and without regard.

In Fable VII, the cat is made the symbol of egotism and self interest, similar to his master, a selfish monk. In Fable XIV, referring to the cat's traditional image as a voracious and hungry beast, (I must say that in Sicily cats don't occupy today, and I suppose also in Meli's time, the same status as loved pets as they do in the United States) he paints a delightful picture of a cat who goes gallivanting the whole night and then during the day sleeps through the loud and continued hammering in a blacksmith's shop. However, when he hears the sound of dishes and lips, at dinner time, he awakens. Meli comments wryly and with his familiar smile:

Therefore, the noise that lips and dishes make
is strong enough both cats and men to wake.

In Fable XXXII, the spider who offers his services to keep the cave of the bear free of bothersome little insect, is a representation of minor officials, petty bureaucrats, who enforce rules and regulations only when the weak and poor are before them. The mighty, however, are free to come and go as they please. Speaking through the bear, Meli complains,

> This net smells of inequities
> It does control the small, but can't disarm
> the larger ones who cause much greater harm.
> So I conclude: All or no one. I say
> it's a dishonor and a cowardice
> upon the weak and lowly to hold sway."

In Fable LXXXV, Meli, who had regarded the French revolution as an abomination, went as far as to suggest that there is a limit to the abuse that the oppressed will take before retaliating:

> Don't be too confident
> When teasing those who're meek,
> who walk with their brows bent.
> Your future may turn bleak.
> So then remain alert.
> Recall the cricket's hurt.

This warning echoes a similar one issued in Fable X:

> Do not tease folks too much
> who suffer and stay still.
> You may find one who's such
> to make you pay the bill.

It is obvious that Meli was a man of the opposition, a "contestatore," that is, one who could not keep silent before the spectacle of an oppressed Sicily. His denunciation may lack the fire and brim stone of the zealot, but could we say that his words are less effective for it? I don't believe so. Could the resignation and the bitterness of a people that has endured oppression for many centuries be expressed more effectively than in Fable LXXVI?

> "Run, quick...the thieves!" said Chiron to his ass,
> who was quite burdened with a heavy pack.
> The donkey answered him: "These thieves, alas,
> will they increase the load upon my back?"
> "Oh, no, the load you'll bear will not surpass
> the one you're carrying right now." "Well, Jack,
> you'd better run, for I care not a whit
> which one of you will make me bite the bit."

The wisdom that Meli displays in his fables as a fruit of his vast experience is expressed in a more systematic way in a poem published in 1814, that is, a year before his death, entitled "Avvertimenti morali e politici" (Moral and Political Advice), included in this anthology. The word "political" is used in its original etymological meaning relating to social living, rather than politics. In fact, one of the recommendations he gives is not to worry about such political things as the finances of the government.

In this poem, Meli lays out the fundamental principles of his moral philosophy. He outlines, through the words of an ancient Greek wise man the norms that man should use to live a happy life. The advice Meli gives represents a sort of *vademecum* for all Sicilians, a guide to behavior that most good Sicilians espouse, written without animosity or the fierceness of a moralist. The advice he gives was clearly the result of learning through experience and it reminds me of the trajectory to wisdom undergone by Sanciu Panza, who started as a *tabula rasa* and became a philosopher. "Experience, study and suffering" were his teachers.

A word about the translation. It is an axiomatic that a translator is never truly satisfied with his work and that, given the opportunity, he will continue to polish his translation. Most translators, however, do not have the chance to revise their translations once they are sent to press. I consider myself fortunate for the opportunity to revise my work. The text of *Moral Fables*, however, because of its difficult rhyme scheme, has remained essentially the same but a number of important changes have been made. Describing one's work runs the risk of becoming a confession of sins, minor and major, committed knowingly and unknowingly. The dangers are many and unavoidable. Those dangers are increased exponentially when the translator insists on retaining the original meters and rhyme schemes. I don't think that I really had a choice in the matter, once I decided to translate the fables. They had to be translated with rhymes, because rhymes are an essential aspect of the fables and I knew that to do justice to them I had to follow Meli's example.

The same can be said with the *Odes* translated here for the first time. They too had to be translated maintaining wherever possible Meli's rhyme scheme. Meli is such a master at this and achieves such lightness through external and internal rhyming that it was impossible to reproduce it exactly without creating distortions and unnatural rythms. I added rhymes whenever possible, keeping in mind not to distort the original meaning.

I approached my work as a kind of problem solving. Translators are at heart a pragmatic lot who solve seemingly impossible problems. Translation demands all the creativity and ingenuity that they possess and more. Whether my own resources were sufficient to the task is not for me to say. Dryden once said that translating poetry into poetry was an act of sympathy. I can say that in my case, translating Meli into English has been something more than that. I have felt as an advocate pleading a special case: Giovanni Meli's poetry as an embodiment of an aspect of the Sicilian soul we share.

L'origini di lu munnu

The Origin of the World

Original Illustrations by
Diane Himmelbaum

ARGUMENTU	Summary
Spiega lu primu statu di li Dei, *prima chi fussi fattu l'Universu,* *li soi primi pinseri e primi idei,* *pri stabiliri li cosi cu versu.* *Dopu varii pariri chiù plebei,* *Giovi si fa stirari pri traversu,* *e da ddi soi stinnicchi e cosi tali* *ni risulta lu munnu cu l'armali.*	*First I explain the Gods' primeval state,* *before creation of the universe.* *Then come the Gods' ideas, their first thoughts* *on how to set up things more properly.* *After surveying some plebeian views,* *Jove asks that he be stretched transversally* *and from that stretching and things of that sort* *the world with all the animals was wrought.*

I

Jeu cantu li murriti di li Dei,
chi vulennu sbiarisi cu nui,
crearu un Munnu chinu di nichei,
d'omini pazzi, eccettu 'un si sa cui;
jeu di li soi, e Tiziu di li mei. . .
Basta, ni trizziamu tutti dui;
e li Dei da lu celu a sti cuntisi
sinni piscianu certu di li risi.

I

I sing of the capriciousness of Gods
who, wanting to be entertained by us,
produced a world replete with vexing things
and crazy men—with some exceptions though!—
I may be one and What's-his-name another!
Enough! The teasing is reciprocal.
But from the sky, on seeing how we fight,
the Gods must pee themselves from sheer delight.

II

Ora stu Munnu a cui lu dugnu? A tia
ti l'arrigalu, mora l'avarizia,
Neli Duci, pirchì fusti cu mia
n'estrattu e quinta essenza d'amicizia.
Jeu t'amu tantu, ca nun lu dirria,
timennu ch''un pinsassiru a malizia
s''un fussi ch'avi un annu, e forsi chiui,
ch''un ni videmu ntra nuautri dui.

II

To whom should I donate this World of mine?
I will give it to you, my Neli Duci—[1]
Let avarice be dead!—You've been for me
an extract and quintessence of true friendship.
I love you so that I would not have said it,
for fear that people might begin to think
malicious thoughts, had it not been a year
since we last saw each other, maybe more.

III

Chistu servi a pruvari ca si duna
lu platonicu amuri tra dui oggetti;
però ci voli sta condiziununa:
ch'annu ad essiri o masculi perfetti,
o donni tutti dui, né già chist'una
basta a livari tutti li sospetti;
ma ci vonnu cu chista st'autri dui:
luntani, e senza intressu, comu nui.

III

This serves to prove that true Platonic love
between two objects can exist. However,
a very large condition must be met:
they must be perfect males, or women both.
But having met this one is not enough
to take away suspicions, for two others
are added to the first: like us, they must
live far apart and share no money interest.

IV

E quannu veni poi l'occasioni
di faricci a l'amicu qualchi beni,
si parra; s'introduci, si proponi,
si loda, si difenni, si susteni,
lasciannu affattu dd'affettazioni
chi ntra li suli labbra si tratteni,
ma dannu qualchi signu chiattu e tunnu,
esempli grazia, rigalari un munnu.

V

Accettalu, 'un è pocu complimentu;
e a pinsarlu chiù grossu mi cunfunnu;
jeu nun fazzu spirtizzi, nè spaventu,
cu diri li toi preggi sinu a funnu;
pirchì doppu chi fannu juramentu,
li poeti criduti nun ci sunnu,
ed eu cu chiù ragiuni, anchi mi chiamu
suspettu, comu amicu...'ncominciamu.

VI

A tempu chi lu tempu 'un era tempu,
lu Munnu era una cosa impercettibili
chi jia granciuliannu a tempu a tempu,
ntra la sfera unni stannu li possibili;
nun c'era allura stu tardu, o pirtempu,
nun c'eranu occhi, nè cosi visibili,
ma senz'essiri c'era lu gran Nenti,
nudu, crudu, spirutu, orvu e scuntenti.

VII

Nun c'eranu perciò senza lu Munnu
oggetti chi alienanu e trattennu;
Giovi stissu facia lu vacabunnu
senz'arti, senza parti, e jia scurrennu
ntra un vacuu senza tettu e senza funnu;
illimitatu, orribili e stupennu;
e un avennu nè casi nè pagghiara,
unni junceva armava cufulara.

VIII

E pirchì la famigghia jia 'ngrussannu,
ch'avia ottu figghi granni e tri a nurrizza,
e la ventri a Giununi jeva unciannu,

IV

And when the opportunity arises
to do a good deed for your friend, you'll talk,
you'll introduce things, and you'll make proposals,
you'll praise, defend, and you'll support him then,
leaving aside all empty promises
that represent air passing through the lips,
giving instead a token that is real,
a World, that is, that he can touch and feel.

V

Accept it then! It's no small compliment.
My mind would reel to think a greater one.
When I recount your wondrous qualities
I'm not performing an amazing feat,
for poets, having sworn before the world,
are not believed and thus, with greater cause,
on the sincerity that's in my heart
I would cast serious doubts. So let me start!

VI

Upon the time when time was yet not time,[2]
the world was something imperceptible
which kept advancing slowly like a crab
within the sphere where possibles are stored.
To be on time or late meant nothing then.
There were no eyes nor things that could be seen,
but Void existing without life: vast, dumb,
naked and raw, malnourished, blind, and glum.

VII

And since there was no world, there were no things
that could amuse or entertain a soul.
Great Jove himself loafed aimlessly about[3]
just like a bum inside this vacuum
astonishing, horrendous, without bounds,
without a ceiling and without an end.
Not having homes, not even a hay stack,
He made a hearth wherever he'd unpack.

VIII

But since his family was growing large—
eight children all full grown and three still nursing—
and Juno's womb was swelling visibly,[4]

39

sicchè traseva già ntra la franchizza,
a santa crozza jiaci machinannu,
pri situarli a tutti cu grannizza,
"Pirchì un patri ci metti di cuscenza,
si a collocari li soi figghi 'un pensa".

IX
Benchì iddu 'un era tantu scrupulusu,
cu tuttu ciò 'un vulìa 'nsignarli mali,
"Ch'un patri, ancorchì fussi vizziusu,
li figghi sempri li disìa morali".
A Marti lu sapìa pricipitusu,
Mercuriu latru, Veneri carnali,
'nzumma lu patri Giovi era mbrugghiatu
cu tanti birbi chi vidiasi allatu.

X
Perciò si metti a machinari fissu
pri situarli, e daricci anchi spassu;
pigghia un pinseri, ed ora lassa chissu;
n'afferra n'autru, poi lu caccia arrassu;
fa reguli e pitinni cu lu jissu,
fa circuli e figuri cu cumpassu,
nun vidi, 'un senti chiù, già è tuttu astrattu
cu l'occhi stralunati, comu un gattu.

XI
All'urtimata poi dda saggia menti,
chi a tutti l'autri sempri è stata avanti,
determina, pri stari allegramenti,
di dari corpu a chidd'umbri vacanti,
e fari un gran teatru di viventi
di milli umuri tutti stravaganti,
chi, standu assemi, comu li furmiculi,
furmassiru cumeddii ridiculi.

XII
Stu pinseri ci quatra; e nun putennu
chiù trattiniri l'alligrizza interna,
si leva a pilucca e va currennu
comu un 'mbriacu dintra a taverna;
sauta a cuncumeddu, e va sbattennu
li manu in ogni sua tempula eterna;
di ccà... di ddà...s'aggira comu strummula;

(which gave him title to a tax exemption)[5]
Jove's holy brain began to work in earnest
to find a good position for each one,
because a father's conscience won't be soothed
until he's found a job for all his brood.

IX
Although he was not very scrupulous,
he did not want them to be poorly taught:
"A Father, even though he may have vices,[6]
expects his children to be ethical."
He knew that Mars was quick to take offense,
Venus was oversexed, and Mercury[7]
a thief. In short, Jove was really most upset:
those rascals always gave him cause to fret.[9]

X
So he began a single-minded search
to find a job for them and make them happy.
He had a thought but dropped it presently;
he thought another, soon discarding it.
He drew some rules and cabalistic signs
with chalk, then forms and circles with a compass.
With wild cat eyes, absorbed so thoroughly,
he could no longer hear or even see.

XI
But finally, that ever prudent mind
that has been far ahead of all the rest,
resolved, his life to live in merriment,
to give a body to those empty shades
making a theater of living souls,
each one eccentric in a thousand ways,
who, living close together like the ants,
the gods would entertain with songs and dance.

XII
This thought completely answered all his needs,
so much he could not hold his joy inside,
and thus he took his wig off and he ran
as someone who'd been drinking in a tavern;
He jumped and kicked his heels and with his hands
continued smacking each eternal temple,
just like a top from here to there he spun

X. So Jove began a single-minded search...

e poi cafudda na cazzicatùmmula.

and with a somersault he topped his fun.

XIII

Li figghi ci jucavanu a la cucca,
cridemu ch'era già nisciutu pazzu,
chi sotannu e ghittannu la pilucca,
sbattia li manu comu un babbanazzu.
Giovi però ch''un avìa pilu 'nbucca,
si vota allura comu un liunazzu:
Ch''un c'è megghiu crianza? Vastasuni!
Vi vegnu a pigghiu a càuci e a timpuluni.

XIII

His children, thinking Jove had lost his mind
because he jumped and hurled his wig about,
clapping his hands just like a simpleton,
began to play the owl's game with him.[10]
But Jove, who always called a spade a spade,
turned like a mean old lion and he said:
"Is that how you behave? Ill-mannered putts!
I'll smack your faces and I'll kick your butts!

XIV

Ieu 'ngrazia di vuautri signuri
m'aju sgangatu li corna a pinsari
ed ora mi faciti li dutturi!
Chi bellu modu di niguziari!
Sapiti cui sugn'eu?...lu meu riguri
nun stati, culazzuni, a provocari;
ah!... talè ardiri!... trizziari a mia!
si muzzica lu jiditu, e tistia.

XIV

I've nearly racked my brains on your behalf,
my learned gentlemen, and now you dare
to act like pompous Ph.D.'s. What gall!
A very pleasant way to act, indeed!
You know not who I am? You clods, you oafs!
Do not provoke the harshness of my wrath!
Imagine... making fun of me!" he said,
and, biting on his finger, shook his head.

XV

Comu li picciutteddi di li scoli,
chi lu so Mastru vidennu distrattu,
ci abballanu e ci fannu caprioli;
e mentri pri darreri scuntrafattu
qualch'unu d'iddi imitari lu voli,
iddu si vota, e lu trova ntra dd'attu,
cu vucca aperta, cu ghidita a corna,
testa cu testa in attu chi lu scorna:

XV

As children who begin to dance and jump
when they see that their teacher seems to act
in a distracted way, while one attempts
to imitate the Master, aping him,
then suddenly the teacher turns around
and catches him at it, with mouth agape,
and fingers raised as horns[11] in a child's game,
as head approaches head that bows in shame.

XVI

cussì li figghi di lu summu Giovi
si vidinu d'un subitu allampari:
cui appuzza l'occhi 'nterra, e nun si movi,
n'autru s'arraspa in attu di pinsari,
cui dormi comu un ghiru quannu chiovi,
n'autru fa scusa di jiri a pisciari,
l'ultimu finalmenti a lu so latu
pigghia tabbaccu menzu 'nsunnacchiatu.

XVI

So were the children of the Highest Jove,
who felt the stunning power of his words.
Some quickly bowed their heads and dared not move;
One scratched his head as though engrossed in thought;
Another slept most soundly like a log,
and one begged leave to go relieve himself.
And finally the last one at his side
sniffed some tobacco somewhat sleepy-eyed.

XVII

Giovi si vota, lu guarda, e tistia.

XVII

Jove turned, and looked at him, and shook his head.

Believing that he had but lost his mind,
because he jumped and hurled his wig and clapped
his hands, as if he were a simpleton,
the children played the owl's game on him.

Chiddu sodu ci proi la tabbacchera:
Ammiru la tustizza di vossia!
ci dici Giovi, ma cu brusca cera.
Ch'aviti, Gnuri, parrati cu mia?
rispunni chiddu cu n'aria sincera.
E Giovi: Cu sta vostra santitati,
nni vurrissivu corpa di pitrati.

XVIII
La cosa jeva a lungu: ma Giununi
si misi ntra lu menzu: Via 'un c'è nenti.
Chi cosa fu? S'arrùsica prumuni!
A sti picciotti sempri li turmenti.
Chi pesti! D'ogni cosa fa' un catùni!
Sempri stizzatu contra st'innoccenti?
Ah... tuccau a mia sta retica vintura!
e quannu speddi? E quannu sarrà l'ura?

XIX
Cussì dicennu, si torci lu mussu,
fa lu cucchiaru e metti a picchiari.
Giovi a ddu chiantu si fa russu russu,
e li sigghiuzzi si senti acchianari.
Anchi allura curra stu malu 'nflussu,
(è cosa veramenti di notari)
ch'un omu duru chiù di na culonna
allaschisci a li chianti d'una donna.

XX
Tiramu avanti. Ntra maritu e mogghi
facilmenti s'accommoda na sciarra;
lu maritu ci cunta quattru 'mbrogghi,
ci fa quattru carizzi pri caparra;
idda si munci comu avissi dogghi,
fa la 'ncagnata, sigghiuzzannu parra...
'Nzumma 'ntempu di quantu vi lu dicu,
Erodes a Pilatu già c'è amicu.

XXI
Si accosta intantu l'ura di manciari;
li figghi si arricogghinu affamati;
Apollini si metti a badagghiari,
Veneri avi li visceri 'nfasciati,
ch'è debuli ed in pedi 'un ci pò stari;

His son, unflinching, offered him a pinch.
"I marvel at your brazen impudence,"
said Jove, but with an angry countenance.
"What is the matter, Sir? Addressing me?"
he answered with an air that seemed sincere.
"Your saintliness" Jove was right quick to say,
"will earn the stoning you deserve one day."

XVIII
The row would have gone on for long, it seemed,
but Juno intervened: "All right, come on. . .
What was this all about? Why growl so much?
Poor children! You are always on their backs!
You pest! For every little thing you growl.
Must you be always vexed with these poor lambs?!
What awful destiny has come my way!
When will it finish? When will come that day?"

XIX
Having said this, she pouted, made a face,
twisted her lips, and then began to sob.
When Jove saw Juno cry, his face grew red
and he began to feel sobs welling up.
This ill effect was true both then and now—
and it is truly something to behold—
although he may be harder than a nail,
before a woman's tears a man will fail.

XX
But let's go on! Disputes are settled fast
between a husband and his wife: indeed
the man will tell his wife some far-fetched story,
giving her some caresses on account;
the wife will act aggrieved, she'll talk and sob,
moaning as though she felt some labor pains,
and in the time it took to end this tale,
Pilate in Herod a close friend will hail!

XXI
It was, meanwhile, quite near to dinner time
and all the famished children gathered home.
Apollo[12] was the first to start to yawn
and Venus had her stomach tied in knots.
She was so weak she hardly could stand up;

Marti avi li diavuli acchianati,
grida, strilla e 'un ci va un capiddu a versu
s'un s'ammucca un pagnottu pri traversu.

Mars had a devil gnawing at his sides,
screaming and squealing, acting like an oaf,
and would not stop until he ate a loaf.

XXII

Ma però Giovi; seriu cu l'occhiali,
veni, e mustra a la cera un gran riguri;
la varva, lu vastuni e lu vracali
pri incutiri rispettu e chiù timuri;
ma pirchì Giovi è veru gioviali,
nun sapi conservari lu rancuri,
ed in chi è gravi ed uncia comu buffa,
ed in chi poi guarda a se stissu e sbruffa.

XXII

But then came Jove and with his glasses on
he looked the picture of severity.
His beard, his rod and even his old truss
commanded much respect and greater fear.
But Jove, because he's really jovial,
could not keep rancor in his heart for long.
One moment he was in a mood most foul,
but when he saw himself with glee he'd howl.

XXIII

Quannu iddu ridi, scaccanianu tutti,
quann'iddu è seriu c'è un silenziu granni;
su in fini di manciari e già li frutti
sta spartennu Giununi a lu chiù granni;
di vinu sinni vippiru na vutti,
e tutti sinni jianu canni canni;
e accussì ntra li brinnisi e li vuci,
s'imbriacaru tutti duci duci.

XXIII

And when he laughed, all laughed without control;
when he was grim, there was great silence there.
The meal was near the end and Juno
had served the fruit to her first born already.[13]
They probably consumed a keg of wine
and they were as contented as could be.
And so between the screaming and the toasts,
they got high inadvertently almost.

XXIV

Sbarazzata la tavula e livati
li tuvagghi di supra e li cucchiari,
Giovi ripigghia a serietati,
dicennu: S"à pinsatu a lu manciari,
ora pinsamu cu maturitati
comu s'avi stu Munnu a fabricari.
Ci dici Marti: Chi cos'è stu Munnu?
Giovi: Sarrà. . . nun so . . . lu vurria tunnu.

XXIV

As soon as they had cleared the dinner table,
putting the spoons and tablecloth away,
Jove started speaking in a serious tone,
saying, "Since we have given thought to food,
let us consider with maturity
how we can now create this world." Mars said:
"What is this thing, 'the world' you want to found?"
Jove answered: "I don't know . . . I'd like it round!"

XXV

Ripigghia Apollu: Chi sarrà a la fini?
E Giovi: Chistu stissu aju a pinsari,
giacchì di vinu li testi sù chini;
ora è tempu, picciotti, d'inventari:
circamu ntra li specii peregrini,
comu corpu a lu nenti si pò dari;
ogn'unu dica la sua apinioni,
pri poi mettirla in esecuzioni.

XXV

Apollo said: "What could it be, I wonder!"
"That's what I need to figure out," said Jove.
"Now that our heads are full of wine, my boys,
it's time to start inventing. So let's look
among the rarer species and let's see
if we can give a body to the void.
I'm asking now that you express your views;
later we'll try to put them into use."

45

XXVI

Rispunni allura Marti prosuntusu:
Oh via! mi cridia ch'era sta gran cosa!
Pri chistu, Gnuri miu, siti confusu?
Ora ccà 'un ci sugn'eu? Vossia riposa:
vuliti fattu un Munnu machinusu
di nenti affattu? Recipe una dosa
di nenti, e di poi nàutra supra chidda,
e supra chidda nàutra supra d'idda.

XXVII

Rispunni Giovi già 'mbistialutu;
Oh lu gran ciriveddu veramenti!
Oh lu gran sceccu quasatu e vistutu!
Lu nenti, juntu a nenti, resta nenti.
Ripigghia allura Apollu, ch'è chiù astutu:
Ma si lu sulu nenti n'è presenti,
fincemunni di Munnu già provisti
cu suli idei, e siamu idealisti.

XXVIII

O s'avi a fari o no? Giovi ripigghia:
S''un s'avi a fari, trasi zoccu ài dittu;
si s'avi a fari, resti d'una trigghia;
e stu cunsigghiu 'un reggi, nè va drittu.
'Nzumma, picciotti, 'un jucamu a canigghia:
vogghiu ch'esista, e non in menti o in scrittu,
pirchì esistendu sulu in fantasia,
non esisti lu Munnu, ma l'idia.

XXIX

Mercuriu, comu figghiu chiù anzianu,
ci dici: Patri miu, s'eu ben discernu,
duvemu ricercari si luntanu
fussi lu Munnu, esistenti *ab eternu*;
chi forsi a nui sia incognitu ed arcanu,
ch'avemu di lu nenti lu governu;
pò essiri . . . cui sa? fussi ammucciatu
ntra 'n'abissu di nenti sprofunnatu.

XXX

Comu! *ab eternu* esistiri lu Munnu,
esclama Giovi, oh armali memorannu!
Senza circari e firriari 'ntunnu,

XXVI

Mars answered with his usual bravado:
"Come, come, this thing can't be so difficult![14]
My Lord, you're fretting really over nothing.
Am I not here? Just leave it up to me.
You want a complex world made out of nothing?
Do this: just take a dose of nothing first
and after that you add another dose:
and finally a third one just to close."

XXVII

Jove was already fuming and replied:
"You truly are the king of all bird brains!
A great big dunce dressed up with coat and tie!
Nothing to nothing joined remains still nothing."
But then Apollo, who was more astute,
began to speak: "If nothing's all there is,
pretend already that the world exists
as pure idea and we'd be idealists."[15]

XXVIII

"Must it be made or mustn't it?" said Jove.
"If it must not, what you just said applies,
but if it must, yours is a foolish thought.
So, your advice does not make sense; it's wrong.
Come on, now boys, let's stop these foolish games!
I want the world to be, not in the mind
or written, for, if it's a fantasy,
the thought exists, the world will never be."

XXIX

Now Mercury, the eldest son, spoke up:[16]
"If I correctly comprehend, my father,
our task is to discover if the world
existed *ab eternum* far from us.
Perhaps, since we are masters of the void,
the world remains unknown, mysterious.
Who knows? It could be hidden deep, I guess,
within the great abyss of nothingness."

XXX

"What's that? The world existing "ab eternum"?"
exclaimed now Jove: "O memorable beast!
Even if we did not go out to look for it,

46

l'avirrìamu presenti tuttu l'annu;
chi lu nenti 'un'à 'gnuni, 'un'avi funnu,
pri cui a jiri l'avissimu circannu;
e poi senza ragiun sufficienti
poi imagginari mai cosa esistenti?

XXXI
Chistu è lu mancu, pò avirla in se stissu,
dissi Mercuriu. E Giovi: Concepiri
chistu 'un si pò. Ma, patri, cu permissu,
st'oggezioni nun la stati a diri,
chi anchi ferisci a vui; megghiu è di chissu
diri chi l'avirrèvanu a vidiri,
si mai esistissi, pirchì o ammanca o crisci,
lu nenti nun è cosa chi impedisci.

XXXII
Senza pinsarlu eternu, dici Marti,
pò essiri lu Casu o l'Accidenti,
chi avissi fattu e unitu tanti parti,
pri cui ni fussi lu Munnu esistenti;
cussì succedi, 'mmiscannu li carti,
chi senza mettirci artifiziu nenti,
o vennu d'ogni mercia, o tutti a schera,
e succedi lu goffu o la primera.

XXXIII
Rispunni Giovi: Bella asinitati!
Dintra un mazzu di carti sù comprisi
li varii merci, e tutti dda ficcati
esistinu, unni può farli divisi
lu casu, o uniti, quannu li 'mmiscati,
non già crearli; chistu nun s'intisi;
e poi, figghioli, Casu ed Accidenti
sù cucini carnali di lu Nenti.

XXXIV
Parentisi: ccà pari a prima vista
qualchi sfacciata contradizioni:
cioè, mentri chi povera e sprovista
la Deità di tuttu si supponi,
si finci non ostanti assai provista
di robba chi a lu nenti si ci apponi,
e vinu e carti e cosi di manciari. . .

the world would be around us all the time,
because the void does not possess an end,
nor hiding places where we'd have to search.
And furthermore, without sufficient cause,[17]
can it exist at all, this world of yours?"

XXXI
"That is the least, the cause could be inside itself,"
said Mercury, but Jove dismissed him so:
"That is beyond conception." "Father, please,
such an objection undermines your case.
It's better than your saying that we'd see it
if it were in existence, for two things are true:
something will either grow or it will fade:
the void can't offer obstacles or aid."[18]

XXXII
"Without considering the world eternal,"
said Mars, "mere Accident or Chance, perhaps,
made up and joined so many parts as one
through which somehow the world came into being.
That is what happens when, in shuffling cards,
without performing any sleight of hand,
you deal sequential cards or of one suit
giving you flush or even a high straight."

XXXIII
Jove answered him: "That's really asinine!
The different suits are all included
within a deck of cards and they exist.
Chance may divide the cards or yet unite them
when they are shuffled, but it can't create them.
That's something quite beyond my comprehension!
But Accident and Chance, I will confess,
are both bloodrelatives of Nothingness."

XXXIV
Parenthesis: it seems that at first glance
there is a brazen contradiction here,
that while the Gods supposedly are poor,
that is, possessing not a thing at all,
nevertheless, I show them quite well stocked
with things that surely contradict the Void:
I mean the wine, and cards, and things to eat.

47

Now Juno spoke:
"As for myself, I'd bake a great round bread..."

Ma chistu è a modu nostru di spiegari.

But that's my way to make things more concrete.

XXXV
Anzi chi eu trovu tri Oturi di menti,
chi commentandu beni stu gran passu,
l'unu fa Giovi strologu eccellenti,
chi tuttu prevedìa, ancorchì d'arrassu;
e l'idei di li cosi avìa presenti,
ma confusi, in disordini e fracassu;
ed alcuni di chiù necessitati
l'avìa purtatu a la realitati.

XXXV
In fact, among three authors of renown
who glossed this point at length, I find
that one made Jove a great astrologer
who had foreseen all things, if from afar,
possessing concepts of all things to come,
although in a confused, chaotic way.
But those for which there was some urgency,
he had already made reality.

XXXVI
St'opinioni, pri quantu discernu,
mi pari veramenti chi zuppìa,
unn'eu chiù tostu accordu ntra l'internu
cu l'autri dui l'opinioni mia;
chisti l'eternità rota, e lu pernu
supponnu Giovi, unn'idda si firrìa;
pri tantu Giovi vidi chiaramenti
lu passatu e futuru pri presenti.

XXXVI
As far as I am able to discern,
I think that this opinion is lame;
that's why, deep in my heart, I go along
with the belief held by the other two.
Eternity's a wheel, they thought, and Jove
was just the axis round which it rotates.
And for this reason Jove can clearly look
into the past and future like a book.

XXXVII
Ed iddu, pirchì è veru gioviali,
pri divertirsi un pocu di li figghi;
si finci loccu, stolidu e minnali,
pri sèntiri li soi strammi cunsigghi.
St'opinioni, eu criu, ch'avi chiù sali,
e servi ad evitari li bisbigghi,
chi a li scoli farrìa l'eternitati
intornu a prescienza e libertati.

XXXVII
And he, because he's truly jovial,
to have a little fun with his offspring
pretends to be a dolt, a silly fool,
so as to listen to their weird advice.
This view which makes more sense will serve, I think,
to put a stop to all the arguments
about foreknowledge and true liberty
schools will engage in for eternity.

XXXVIII
Ma sti cosi 'un si divinu spianari,
ca servinu pri sbiiu a li Dutturi;
pirchì autru 'un voli diri argumentari,
chi viaggiari ntra paisi oscuri;
ne li vonnu illustrati, ca ci pari
chi mancanu di meritu e valuri,
unn'eu mi rinniria troppu odiusu,
na finestra grapennucci o un purtusu.

XXXVIII
These matters though must not be made
too plain, for scholars need them as diversions.
Because to argue signifies no more
than travelling within dark continents
and scholars would not care to see them lit,
for they would lose in merit and in worth.
If on these matters I dared shine a light,
to them I would be a most odious sight!

XXXIX
Chiudemu sta parentisi. Giununi

XXXIX
Let's close parenthesis! Now Juno spoke, [19]

spiega cu l'autri la sua opinioni,
e dici: Jeu farrìa un gran guastidduni,
specia di pani di munizioni,
ci mittiria materia a munsidduni,
tutta in confusu senza eccezioni,
e di qualunqui specii, anzi mi basta
d'una specii sula estisa e vasta.

and she like all the others gave her views:
"If it were up to me, I'd bake a bread
quite large like those made for the troops. I'd pile
on it a heap of matter like a mountain,
thrown in at random and of any kind;
One kind alone might well be all we need,
provided it were vast in magnitude.

XL

Fattu stu gran pastizzu scammaratu,
lu farrìa cu un cuteddu feddi feddi;
doppu lu fiddirìa di l'àutru latu,
tuttu già riducennulu a tasseddi;
chiddi di 'mmenzu sù fatti a quatratu,
a li lati c'è cubbi e cubbiceddi,
e dannu motu a tutti quantu sunnu,
li vidiriti firriari intunnu.

XL

Once I had baked this great and lean pastiche,
I would proceed to slice it with a knife,
then I would slice it from the other side
until I had cut wedges all around.
The central ones would be cut up as squares,
and those along the sides in cubic shapes,
both large and small, and moving them with pace
you'd see them as they whirled around in space.

XLI

Cussì jocu di focu a la romana
avi li gran rutuni concertati
cu carrittigghi di manera strana,
chi sbrugghiannusi giranu 'mbrugghiati;
unu gira di supra e nàutru acchiana
cu nàutru 'mmenzu e nàutri dui a li lati;
e ntra tantu disordini e sconcertu
gira la rota granni e fa un concertu.

XLI

It's very similar to Roman fireworks
which have some awesome wheels arranged this way,
with wheeling rockets that are strangely made,
tangling themselves with disentangling turns.
When one wheel turns above, another rises
with one more flanked by two along its sides.
But through the noise and great disharmony,
the large wheel turns in wondrous harmony.

XLII

Cussì, cu lu girari, ddi quadrati
vennu a smanciari l'anguli d'intornu,
chi tutti sinni vannu sprannuzzati,
comu vuscagghi sutta di lu tornu,
vinennu li figuri variati,
acuti, cubbi e tunni di cuntornu;
ed eccu di la varia figura,
di li varii elementi la natura.

XLII

So as the squares begin to turn around,
the corners one by one are rounded off
and scattered all about as happens with
the shavings when a "lathe's applied to wood,
producing figures of diverse contours,
some shaped as cubes, some round, some with sharp
      edges.
And there you have it, plain for all to see,
how elements and shapes will come to be!"

XLIII

'Nterrumpi Giovi: Oh pesta, quantu parri!
Chi diascacci scacci, babbanazza,
chi carrittigghi! tricchi tracchi e carri!
Chi guastidduni? Locca, tu sì pazza!

XLIII

Jove cut her short: "My word! How you can talk!
What are you giving me, you silly goose!
What rockets and what carts, what wheels and reels
and great round soldier's bread! You must be mad!

E nun lu vidi ca 'mprincipiu sgarri?
Nun farrìa guastidduni e guastiddazza,
s'avissi la materia a lu miu 'mparu,
ma ci ammanca lu funnu a lu panaru.

But don't you see, you fool, you went astray
when you began? Wouldn't I have baked round breads
and even square ones if I'd had the dough?
There is no bottom to the pail, you know!"

XLIV

Ora eu farrìa na cosa curiusa,
dissi Mercuriu: Un mostru bestiali,
ch'avissi un motu ed una forza infusa
in tutta la sustanza sua brutali,
e Menti ancora ed Anima diffusa
in tutti li soi membri a signu tali
ch'ogn'unu sia un viventi, e a middi e a middi
tutti vivanu in iddu, ed iddu in iddi.

"Now, I would make a curious, new thing,
a brutish monster," said then Mercury,[20]
"endowing it with motion of its own,
possessing power in its brutal substance,
and having Mind and Soul in every limb
so that each one of them would be alive
and by the thousands they'd inhabit him
and live in Him and likewise He in them."

XLV

Bravu, ripigghia Giovi, egregiamenti!
Ma stu motu e sta vita, chi diciti,
vi pari forsi na cosa di nenti?
Chistu è lu gruppu chi nun sciugghiriti.
Appressu... all'àutri ... cui avi sennu e menti
spieghi l'idei chiù chiari e chiù graditi:
ci voli flemma assai cu sti 'gnuranti)
cui avi a diri àutra cosa vegna avanti.

"Well done, I grant you!" was Jove's quick reply.[21]
"But do you think that such a motion, life,
are things that you can find so easily?
This is the knot that you will never solve!
Next one!. . . Let others who have wit and brains
express their clearest and most pleasing thoughts;
—with such dumb fools one must be calm indeed!—
Let those with other things to say proceed!"

XLVI

Veniri s'immizzigghia un pocu, e dici:
Papa, stu meu sistema 'un mi dispiaci:
si pigghia un ovu friscu di pirnici
o di gaddu o qualunqu'àutru vi piaci,
ci dicemu: Carvuni, inchiostru, pici,
e àutri paroli niuri efficaci,
e cu chistu linguaggiu girbuniscu
s'imprena l'ovu fattu a basiliscu.

"Daddy," said Venus somewhat languidly,
"this system I've devised does not displease me:
we take a partridge egg that's fresh or else
a rooster's egg or any egg you like;
we say to it aloud: coal, pitch, and ink,
and other black and efficacious words;
and once such magic words we mix and match
out of the egg a basilisk will hatch.[22]

XLVII

Poi st'ovu cu l'essenzi di tant'ova
lu mittirìa, ciatànnulu, a cuvari;
ed eccu supra l'annu chi si trova
ddà dintra un Munniceddu cu lu mari;
Cussì di tempu in tempu sempri nova
qualchi cosa si vidi arriminari,
ed a proporzioni chi chiù crisci,
lu Munnu si multiplica e ciurisci.

I'd put this egg with many other eggs
and start the hatching process with my breath;
behold, within a year a little world
complete with sea would start to grow inside.
And so, from time to time, some novel thing
would surely start to stir and move about.
And in a way commensurate with its growth rate
the world would multiply and procreate.

51

XLIV. "Now I would make a curious new thing,"
said Mercury: "I'd make a brutish fiend..."

XLVIII

Cussì mi rigord'iu, comu fuss'ora,
chi essennu ancora nica, mi spassava
cu un cannulicchiu nicu nicu ancora,
chi ntra la sapunata l'abbagnava,
e poi ciusciannu ni nisceva fora
na bella lampa, chi si dilatava
cu lu simplici ciatu; da stu jocu
viju chi fari un Munnu custa pocu.

XLIX

Multiplicanu l'omini, e si avanza
cu dda sua stissa regula e misura
la terra pr'abitari, e la sustanza
atta e bastanti ad ogni criatura;
anzi, fatta Sibilla, in luntananza
supra li spaddi di l'età futura,
viju crisciri apposta pri la Spagna
l'America, ch'è quasi na cuccagna.

L

Rispunni Giovi: 'Un ci sbattiti spissu
cu sta cuva e cu st'ova, marioli,
pirchì (sia dittu cu vostru permissu)
la lingua batti unni lu denti doli.
Passanu avanti; stu sistema stissu
s'impugna iddu medesimu, e 'un ci voli
gran duttrina a cunusciri abbastanza,
quantu è sollenni la sua repugnanza.

LI

Apollu, chi si vanta indovinari,
raccunta un sonnu, e dici: A mia, Signuri,
parìa, durmennu, aviri a suprastari
a una ciàccula immenza di splenduri:
fissa immenzu a li spazii avvampari
vidìasi, e dari all'umbri li figuri;
giranu supra e attornu luminusi
machini ancora grandi e spaziusi.

LII

Una di chisti 'mmesti supra un latu
la ciaccula di 'mmenzu, e fa sotari
di dda materia un pezzu, chi sgangatu

XLVIII

So clearly I recall—as if it were right now—
when as a little girl I had such fun
with nothing but a tiny tiny straw.
I used to dip it in the soapy suds
and then, by blowing gently in the tube
a nice big bubble would expand and grow.
If as a guide this little game you take
you'll see a world won't cost that much to make...[23]

XLX

Should mankind multiply? Well, then, we'll let
the land on which he lives increase as well
in speed and measure proper to his growth,
with sustenance that's adequate for all.
In fact, having just made myself a Sybil,[24]
beyond the shoulders of the future age
I see America, land of Cockaigne,
starting to grow just for the sake of Spain."

L

Jove said: "Let's not keep harping on such things
as eggs and hatchings, scoundrels that you are!
Because (and let me say this with your leave)
the mind returns to things it loves the most.
But let's proceed. Your very system seems
to undermine itself so there's no need
to be great scholars and to realize
how truly awesome its repugnance is."

LI

Apollo, boasting his divining gift, [25]
began to tell a dream and said: "My Lord,
it seemed to me that while I slept I saw
a wondrous torch that was immensely bright,
ablaze right in the center of our space,
giving a body and consistency to shadows.
Revolving all around it in plain sight,
other machines all luminous and bright.[26]

LII

One such machine collided with the torch
that was in center space and chipped a piece
of matter from its side. The piece, now free,

si vidi cu gran furia arrivulari;
mentri chi curri liquidu e squagghiatu,
si senti da dui forzi dominari;
l'ammuttuni chi fora lu spincìa,
lu so tuttu omogeneu l'attraìa.

LIII

Da sti forzi cuntrarii cummattuta,
nun sapi a cui obbediri ntra ssa lutta:
cerca scappari, e da una è trattinuta;
cerca turnari, ma l'àutra l'ammutta;
cosa fa? Senza avirni dispiaciuta
nessuna di li dui, sfui pri sutta;
e mentri sti dui forzi opposti sunnu,
passa pri 'mmenzu, e ci firrìa ntunnu.

LIV

Cussì 'mmenzu a dui turbini spiranti
cu forzi uguali da l'opposti lati,
li pagghi e sicchi pampini a l'istanti
si restrincinu tutti ammunsiddati,
poi mettinu a furmari tutti quanti
li vortici e li circuli ordinati;
ed eccu chi ntra l'aria firriannu,
di lu sistema miu la prova fannu.

LV

Poi di stu pezzu in giru già astutata
la vampa pri la furia di la scossa,
na materia ristau vitrificata,
chi s'addensa, s'attunna, e ancora smossa
s'aggira di vapuri atturniata;
raffriddatasi poi, eccu s'ingrossa
dda negghia, e appocu appocu tutta intera
cadi in acqua, e ricopri la gran sfera.

LVI

St'acqui da lu Livanti a lu Punenti
muvennusi cu moti regulari,
vi formanu la reuma, o sia currenti,
cu lu flussu e riflussu di lu mari;
lu quali, strascinannu sedimenti,
appocu appocu li va a cumulari
tutti ntra certi lati, e agghiunci in iddi

was sent rebounding at great speed through space.
But while it ran in liquid form, all fused,
it felt the pull of two opposing mights:
the shove propelling matter outwardly,
its homogeneous parts pulled inwardly.

LIII

The torch, now torn by these contrasting forces,
could not decide which one it should obey.
It tried to flee but was held back by one;
the other pushed it when it tried to turn.
What could it do? It fled straight downwardly;
and while these forces were still struggling hard,
not giving either one the upper ground,
it passed between them and it whirled around.

LIV

As when the chaff and dry vine leaves are caught
between two whirlwinds having equal force
from two opposing sides, and in an instant
they are all gathered into a large heap,
and they proceed in order to create
great vortices and circles into space
so then by whirling round up in the air,
the proof of my good system they declare.

LV

As for the piece that had been broken off, [27]
the fury of the crash had snuffed the flame,
leaving some of the matter vitrified,
which then condensed, becoming like a ball,
which as it turned, was bathed by vapor fumes.
Then as it started to cool down, the fog
became more dense and slowly fell as rain
which covered the enormous sphere's terrain.

LVI

These waters, moving then with ordered flow
from East to West, gave rise to streams, that is,
to currents running deep within the sea,
and to the ocean's tides that ebb and flow.
The sea which carries sediment to shore,
a little at a time made heaps of it
in certain spots and added grasses, bones

"Daddy," said Venus somewhat languidly,
"This system I've devised does not displease me:
We take a partridge egg that's fresh, or else,
a rooster's egg, or any egg you like…"

reschi di pisci, ossa, ervi e crucchiuliddi.

of fish and tiny shells and skeletons.

LVII
Chisti lu tempu poi li forma un massu,
si fannu munti granni e spaziusi,
l'acqua abbassannu va di passu in passu,
sprofunnata ntra grutti e ntra purtusi;
chiù chi l'acqua declina e si fa arrassu,
chiù apparinu li munti machinusi;
già appocu appocu la terra cumpari,
e nasci da lu funnu di lu mari.

LVII
Time then transformed these things into a rock.
Great spacious mountains were created thus.
The level of the water slowly fell,
as it receded deep down caves and holes.
The more the sea declined and moved away,
the more imposing mountains did appear.
Slowly the earth was there for all to see,
emerging from the bottom of the sea."

LVIII
Chiù vulia diri, ma mpazientatu
Giovi l'interrumpìu: Beni, t'accordu,
ci dici, chi pozz'essiri 'nfruntatu
lu suli da un cometa, e, ntra dd'abbordu,
un pezzu nni pozz'essiri sgangatu,
e resti in aria, e un Munnu sia di lordu
cu l'atmosfera, chi in arrifriddari
caschi disciolta in acqua e formi un mari.

LVIII
He wanted to say more but Jove cut in
impatiently and said: "I grant you that
the Sun can be hit squarely by a comet
and in the crash a piece could be cut off
and stay in space; I grant you that a world
has to include, of course, an atmosphere
which would, then liquefy, as it cooled down,
and form a sea when it fell down as rain.

LIX
Ma dimmi poi: Stu suli, sti cometi,
chi tu supponi prima di lu Munnu,
su tuttu o parti di l'àutri pianeti?
d'unni foru sgangati? cosa sunnu?
'Nzumma li primi primi e consueti
d'unni scupparu? d'unn'appiru funnu?
Senza sfirniciariti, va dici:
Cui pò fari la tigna, fa la pici.

LIX
But tell me: all these comets and this sun,
which you suppose to antedate the world,
are they a part or are they the whole planets?
From what were they cut off? And what are they?
And finally whence came the very first,
the ones that are best known? Come now, speak up!
You need not strain yourself too hard, my son!
A man who can make stars, can make a sun!

LX
Lu stissu dicu all'àutri; ora, picciotti,
nun mi sustàti chiù, ca sugnu stancu;
già l'aju vistu quantu siti dotti,
da sti discursi di pedi di vancu;
vui, li lasagni li vuliti cotti
e ministrati ntra lu piattu e mancu
viditi la sullenni repugnanza
chi c'è ntra lu gran Nenti e la sustanza!

LX
The same I say to all. But now, my boys,
don't bother me again for I am tired.
I've had a measure of your scholarship
from your discourses that have no head or tail.
You'd like to have your cake and eat it, too,
apparently, and you can't even see
the great repugnance that exists between
the awesome Void and substance that is seen.

LXI
La sustanzia è unica, e sugn'Eu.

LXI
Essentially contrasting the great Void,[28]

Apollo, boasting of his divining gifts,
began to tell a dream and said: "My Lord..."

essenzialmenti opposta a lu gran nenti;
pirchì è veru impossibili ch'ora Eu
mentri sugnu ed esistu fussi nenti;
pirtantu siti vui, pirchì sugn'Eu,
cioè, quannu distintu da lu nenti
vogghiu me stissu a mia rappresentari,
multiplicu lu miu modificari.

there's only one true substance: I am it.
For, it is quite impossible that I,
while I exist and am, should yet not be.
And as for you, you are because I am,
that is, when I want to distinguish me
from nothingness, I simply modify
my own identity and multiply.

LXII

Scummettu un occhiu ca nun mi sintiti;
del restu mi sent'Iu, m'importa un ficu;
verrannu un tempu l'omini eruditi
a diri chistu stissu ch'Eu vi dicu;
nun sarrannu mai intisi, e chi vuliti
quann'è comprisu in mia tuttu l'intricu?
S'ultra lu nenti sulu ci sugn'Iu,
Iu intennu tuttu, ed è l'Essiri miu.

LXII

I'll bet an arm you cannot hear a thing.
It matters not, since I can hear myself.
In time, some learned men will come to say
exactly what I have just said to you.
They won't be heard... But what would you expect,
when the whole maze exists inside of me?
If I in this great Void exist alone,
I understand all things for they're my own.

LXIII

Via dunqui almu e curaggiu, picciuttazzi:
stiratimi sta gamma, ch'Eu vi stennu;
e vidiriti poi, 'gnurantunazzi,
un prodigiu ridiculu e stupennu.
Cussì dittu, li figghi, comu pazzi,
dda gamma s'afferranu currennu,
e tirannu e stirannu, finalmenti,
si forma lu chiù bellu continenti.

LXIII

Come now, my boys, have courage, show some heart!
Stretch out this leg of mine. As you will see
I will display for you, you witless fools,
a comic and stupendous miracle."
Once he'd said this, his sons as in a frenzy
took hold of that great leg of his and ran.
They pulled and stretched and when at last all cleared
the fairest of the Continents appeared.

LXIV

Eccu l'Italia, chi fu l'anca dritta
di Giovi, e fu rigina di la terra;
la saluta e si leva la birritta
Saturnu, e poi cuntenti si l'afferra:
Marti puru, susennusi a l'addritta,
jura acquistarla cu l'armi e la guerra;
ma Giovi, pri livari ogn'àutra liti
dici all'àutri: Stiràti e nn'avirriti.

LXIV

Behold there Italy who ruled as queen
on earth.[28] She was once the right thigh of Jove.
Saturn took off his cap saluting her;
then happily he seized for himself.
Mars, too, who quickly rising to his feet, [29]
swore to possess her through the force of arms;
but Jove, intending to avert a war,
said to the others: "Pull and you'll get more!"

LXV

Veneri e Apollu, tutti dui a l'oricchi
si ci lassanu comu dui 'mmistini;
la prima tantu fa cu ddi manicchi,
chi ci la scodda, cadi, e dà li rini;
l'àutru, pigghiatu ancora a sticchi e nicchi,

LXV

Both Venus and Apollo like two mastiffs
attacked Jove's ears. Despite her dainty hands,
The former pulled so hard she tore an ear
and fell down on her back; the latter one,
not wanting to appear less valorous,

"Come now, my boys, have courage, show some heart.
Stretch out this leg of mine. As you will see,
I will display for you, you witless fools,
a comic and stupendous prodigy."

ci scodda l'àutra, ed eccu chi a la fini
caduti sti grand'isuli d'in celu.
l'una si chiamau Cipru e l'àutra Delu.

unglued the other ear and when they fell
out of the sky, they formed two islands in the sea:
Cyprus and Delos were their names respectively.[30]

LXVI

Sicutaru cussì a squartariari
l'àutri figghi lu patri, anzi lu Munnu:
lu nasu crisciù in Alpi, a separari
l'una Gallia da l'àutra, chi c'è 'ntunnu:
la sua saliva si conversi in mari,
salata ancora sinu a lu profunnu;
e da l'àutri fratturi e pezzi rutti
sinni ficiru scogghi, isuli e grutti.

LXVI

The other sons continued quartering
the father, nay, the World, limb after limb:
the nose became the Alps, to separate
this Gaul from the surrounding other;
From his saliva was the sea derived,
still salty even in its deepest parts;
the other torn and fractured limbs became
some reefs, or islands, or caves with no name.

LXVII

Ma la testa? (ora cca vennu li liti);
jeu dicu; è la Sicilia; ma un Romanu
dici ch'è Roma; dicinu li Sciti
ch'è la Scizia; e accussì di manu in manu
quantu c'è regni, tantu sintiriti
essirci testi... Jamu chianu chianu:
la testa è una; addunca senza sbagghi
è la Sicilia, e c'è ntra li midagghi.

LXVII

What of the head? (That's where disputes begin!)
I say the head is Sicily; a Roman
will say it's Rome, and Scythians will say
it's Scythia. Therefore the heads will be
as many as the realms upon this earth.
So let's proceed with calm and logic here:
the head is one and so without ado,
it's Sicily, and medals show this too.[31]

LXVIII

Ci viditi na testa cu tri pedi
chi a prima vista vi fa strinziari:
si vuliti, sta cosa nun mi sedi
a quattru pedi la duvìanu fari.
Ma s'è accussì, criu; ch'accussì richiedi;
l'àutru pedi si potti sdillucari;
anzi rumpiri affattu; chi fu allura
quannu l'Istmu di Riggiu iu in malura.

LXVIII

You see a head with three feet in these medals
which gives you shivers when at first you see her.[32]
I must confess I'm not too fond of it.
I think they should have made her with four feet,
but since it's so, that's how it had to be.
Perhaps, the other foot was badly sprained;
or maybe it was sheared right off that day
when Reggio's isthmus fell in disarray.

LXIX

E lu peju qual'è? Chi ntra ssa testa
ci sunnu purci, lindini e pidocchi;
na pittinata ci vurrìa ogni festa;
ma a mia nun m'apparteni, chiuiu l'occhi;
si Giovi arraspa, la cosa è funesta;
la Sicilia cu tutti li crafogghi
si subissa; pirchì la sua manuzza
è un regnu chi nni 'ncoppula e sammuzza.

LXIX

What is the worst of it? The worst is that
the head contains lice, fleas, and eggs of lice,
and should be combed on every Holy day.
But that's not my concern, I'll shut my eyes.
But if Jove scratched an itch, it would be fatal.
Poor Sicily, already full of holes,
would sink. Jove's little hand's a realm
that our small world can crush and overwhelm.

Behold: that is how Jove became the world,
with trees and grasses and with things like that,
which once were hair and now have all become
great forests full of sheep and other beasts.

LXX

Ed eccu accussì Giovi fattu Munnu
cu l'àrvuli, cu l'ervi e cosi tali,
ch'un tempu eranu pila, ed ora sunnu
voschi chini di pecuri e d'armali.
Tutti li figghi lu firrìanu 'ntunnu,
gudennusillu ntra jochi e ntra sciali;
e da una pia modificazioni
vinni la prima generazioni.

LXXI

Foru li Semidei; oh chi scuvata
felici chi fu chista! Oh fussi allura
natu ntra dda bellissima vintrata!
E chi ti fici, chi, matri Natura,
ca mi sarvasti ntra sta mal'annata!...
Ma no, chi dicu? Sarrìa mortu a st'ura.
L'eroi nasceru da li Semidei,
e da l'eroi l'àutri omini plebei.

LXXII

Appocu appocu lu stissu timuri
ci insigna a fari spinciri li mura;
nascinu li città ntra ddi chianuri
da li mucchi di petri e crita dura.
lu scantu fu lu so legislaturi:
contra la forza forma liggi e jura;
e mentri d'àutru carcera la fidi;
s'incatina iddu stissu, e 'un si nn'avvidi.

LXXIII

Finalmenti eccu Giovi Munnu, ed eccu
lu Munnu Giovi, nui Giuviceddi ancora;
parti di Giovi l'àrvulu, lu sceccu,
l'omu, l'armali, lu turcu, la mora,
lu tauru, la pecura, lu beccu;
e quantu insumma esisti dintra e fora,
manciamu a Giovi, evacuamu a Giovi,
spissu in specie di rìganu e d'anciovi.

LXXIV

Rinnemucci la fama a li Poeti,
chi s''annu pri bugiardi e munsignari;
non pri nenti sti savii e sti profeti

LXX

And so that is how Jove became the World
with trees and grasses and with things like that,
which once were hair and now they have become
great forests full of sheep and other beasts.
All of his sons enjoy his gifts in games
and dissipation as they whirl him 'round.
And from what was a "pious" modification[33]
there issued forth the primal generation.

LXXI

They were the Demigods. A happy brood!
O how I wish that I had been born then
from such a beautiful and happy litter.
What did I do to you, o Mother Earth,
that you reserved me for so lean a year?
What am I saying? I'd be dead by now!
The Demigods begat the Heroes' race
and from the Heroes common man arose.

LXXII

As time went on, fear taught these men
how to erect great walls around themselves.
And so from heaps of stone and dried up clay
great cities rose along the hills and dales.
Fear was a legislator unto them.
It set up laws and rights against brute force,
and while it chains the faith of other men,
it's not aware it locks itself into a pen.

LXXIII

Behold now Jove-turned-World, and finally
behold the world as Jove and each of us
a little Jove: the tree is part of Jove,
so too are men and beasts, and Turks and bulls,
and Moorish women, sheep, he-goats. In short,
whatever is alive inside and out,
eats Jove and then evacuates as Jove,
oft as oregano and as anchovie.

LXXIV

Let us restore the poets' reputation
who are believed to be deceitful liars.
It's not for naught that these wise men,

a Giovi l'ànnu fattu trasmutari	these prophets gave so many forms to Jove:
in tanti formi: in cignu, in arieti	they made a swan of him, an Aries, too,
(simbulu di lu so modificari),	(the sign that symbolized his transformations)
in aquila, in serpenti, in focu, in toru,	an eagle and a snake, a bull, a fire,
in satiru, in pasturi, in pioggia d'oru.	faun, golden rain, and shepherd with a lyre.[34]

LXXV	LXXV
E certu ch'è un piaciri essiri tutti	It's certainly a pleasure for us all
non chiù fangu, non petri, mancu crita;	to be no longer mud[35] or even clay[36]
ma estenzioni, numeri produtti	or stones,[37] but numbers and extensions made
di l'eterna Sustanza ed infinita;	by the eternal never-ending Substance.
ma s'iddu si ritira, ohimè! nn'agghiutti;	But if he should withdraw we all will drown;
si movi un'anca, l'Italia è la zita;	Italy would be lost if he should move
prigamu a Giovi cu tuttu lu ciatu,	a thigh. With all our breath so let us pray
chi stassi sempri tisu e stinnicchiatu.	that Jove may lie here stiff through all our days.

Notes

1. **Neli Dolce**: Emmanuele Dolce., "an incomparable friend," as Meli called him in one of his letters; other than he was a notary, not much is known about him.

2. **Upon the time . . . sad**: Meli begins his Creation presenting an almost tangible image of Chaos.

3. **Great Jove...Void**: Unable to imagine what a god does without the universe, Meli jokingly portrays Jove as an unemployed god who goes roaming about the void.

4. **Juno**: Jove's wife and sister, also known as Hera.

5. **So ... exemption**: In Sicily, during Meli's time, the father of twelve children enjoyed certain tax privileges.

6. **Even if he were vice-ridden**: A veiled reference to Jove who had a reputation as the most promiscuous of the gods who fathered numberless illegitimate offspring.

7. **Mars... Venus...Mercury**: Respectively, the god of war and strife; the goddess of love and beauty, presented here only as the goddess of sex; and the god who was known as the Master Thief who stole, among other things, Apollo's herds.

8. These nine stanzas were deleted by Meli from the first edition of 1787 because, as can be seen, Jove and the other gods were presented in vulgar and even blasphemous tones. Jove was not only the highest of the pagan gods, but he was represented here as the symbol of divinity. His actions, especially as described in these lines, can hardly be called "godly". The deletion of these stanzas was dictated by Meli's cautious attitude towards the possibility of censure.

9. **The owl's game**: A game in which two young men try to knock the cap off the head of a third player who places himself between the other two. The selected player tries defending himself by raising and lowering his head to avoid being hit while kicking at the other two and by touching the ground with his hands which suspends the game temporarily. The winner is the one who succeeds in knocking the cap off.

10. **With fingers raised as horns**: a vulgar gesture, done by keeping the index and pinky extended while folding the middle and ring fingers, which in Italy signifies "cuckhold".

11. **Apollo**: The god of music and light.

12. **Her first born**: Mercury.

13. **Come now... another dose**: Meli commented on Mars' scheme for creation by pointing out that the human mind, left to its natural powers, could not comprehend the mystery of creation. The Greeks themselves, he added, were never able to conceive how something could be extracted from nothing. They believed firmly with Lucretius who stated in his *De Rerum Natura* that "nothing can ever be created by divine power out of nothing."

14. **Let us... idealists**: Meli was poking fun at the philosophers of Materialism who denied the existence of such

intangible things as "the soul," "will," and "consciousness" and affirmed that only matter and motion existed. The poet was also ridiculing the idealists who believed that only what exists in the mind is real.

15.   Mercury was expressing the view, often repeated by philosophers—Empedocles, Democritus—that matter itself was eternal and that at a given point in time it must have taken its present form.

16.   **Without sufficient reason... exist**: A reference to the doctrine developed by Leibnitz and Wolff, according to which an extrinsic reason must be present for all existing things and animals. Only God was excluded from having a "sufficient reason" to exist. Thus when Mercury says, "it wounds you, too" he is thinking of Leibnitz' exception. In fact, Jove is the exception to the rule to which he alluded.

17.   The view that the universe was born from the accidental joining and mixing of atoms in space was embraced by such ancient philosophers as Democritus, Epicurus, and Lucretius. Juno's explanation of how the world came into being was in reality a parody of the system developed by the French thinker René Descartes.

18.   **I'd make a brutish fiend** ... : an allusion to Anaxagoras and to Plato's pantheism, as explained by Virgil in the VI Book of the *Aeneid*, according to Meli's own annotation.

19.   The idea that the world was originally derived from an egg was attributed to Orpheus by Plutarch and Macrobius.

20.   A **basilisk**: A fantastic animal which, according to a widely known legend, was hatched, after seven years of incubation, from a rooster's egg.

21.   Modern Indians, according to Meli's note, believed that the world had grown from an egg which a god had taken out of his mouth through a tube.

22.   **A Sybil**: The Sybils were prophetesses who interpreted the will of the gods.

23.   **I see... Spain**: A reference to the discovery of the American continent and its exploitation by the Spaniards.

24.   **Apollo**: A multi-talented god, Apollo was the son of Jove and Latona. He was identified with the sun: ("He had to oversee a great and splendid torch.") and he announced the will of Jove through oracles pronounced by his priestess at Delphi.

25.   **Around it... and bright**: A reference to comets.

26.   Apollo's solution of the problem of creation consists of relating the theories of Buffon, a French naturalist who called his imaginings "romanzi fisici." In contrast to Baffon's "Physical Tales," Meli entitled his work *Romanzi filosofici circa l'origini di lu munnu...* that is, *Philosophical Tales About the Origin of the World.*

27.   **The piece. . .'round**: The Earth.

28.   **Essentially ... modifications**: Meli was referring to the Portuguese philosopher B. Spinoza who maintained that in nature there was one individual substance which was endowed with an infinite number of attributes. On this one substance-God-all things depended. Everything in this world was but a modification of the one substance that is God.

29.   Italy was originally sacred to Saturn according to Meli's note. It was known as Saturnia.

30   A reference to the Romans who became the masters of Italy. The Romans claimed descent from Mars because the god and Rhea Silvia were the parents of Romulus and Remus, the legendary founders of Rome.

31.   **Cyprus ... Delos**: Born from the foam of the seas, Venus was wafted to Cyprus which became sacred to her. She was often called the Cyprian. Apollo was born on the island of Delos.

32.   The poet is referring to the "Trinacria," the well-known emblem of Sicily.

33.   **"pious"**: Since Spinoza had claimed that all things are modifications of the one eternal substance, Meli called "pious" the modifications which concerned the birth of the demigods.

34.   **They made ... golden rain**: Meli is referring to the various incarnations of Jove. As a swan, Jove loved Leda, as a bull, he ravished Europa; and as a golden shower, he impregnated Danae... etcetera.

35.   **No longer mud**: An allusion to Diodoro Siculo's opinion according to which men were born from the heated mud of the banks of the Nile.

36.   **Clay**: An allusion to the biblical account of the creation of Adam from clay.

37.   **Stones**: An allusion to the myth of Deucalion and Pyrrha, the survivors of the Flood who cast stones (the bones of Mother Earth) behind their backs and when the stones fell to the ground, they took human shape.

Selezioni di *La Buccolica*

Selections from Bucolic Poetry

LA BUCCOLICA

Sonettu I

Muntagnoli interrutti da vaddati,
rocchi di lippu e arèddara vistuti,
caduti d'acqua chiari inargintati,
    vattàli murmuranti e stagni muti;
vàusi e cunzarri scuri ed imbuscati,
sterili junchi e jinestri ciuruti,
trunchi da lunghi età malisbarrati,
grutti e lambichi d'acqua già impitruti,
    pàssari sulitari chi chianciti,
Ecu, ch'ascuti tuttu, e poi ripeti,
almi abbrazzati stritti da li viti,
    vapuri taciturni, umbri segreti,
ritiri tranquillissimi, accugghiti
l'amicu di la paci e la quieti.

Sonettu II

Pani, chi ntra li sagri grutti oscuri,
unni s'adura la tua effigi santa,
parrasti un jornu e mi dicisti: "Canta
li campagni, l'armenti e li pasturi";
    e la sampugna, ingrata a lu to amuri,
chi fu la Ninfa superba, e poi fu pianta,
mi pruisti, dicennu: "Cu tia vanta
lu sulu Grecu Siculu st'onuri";
    giacchì tantu gradisci li mei rimi,
addurmenta li lupi ntra li tani,
e di l'agneddi acceèttanni li primi;
    scaccia l'ambizziusi e li profani,
e si qualcunu la tua bili 'un timi,
fallu vivu manciari da li cani.

Bucolic Poems

Sonnet I

Low mountains interrupted by wide valleys,
rock faces covered up with musk and ivy,
waterfalls flowing with clear, silver waters,
    whispering streams and stagnant, silent pools,
cliffs and dark quarries hidden by the brush,
sterile bamboo trunks and broom in flower,
ancient tree trunks that time has worn right out,
caverns and dripping water turned to stone,
    weeping and solitary sparrows, Echo[1]
who listens to all things and then repeats,
elm trees held in a tight embrace by vines,
    taciturn vapors, and dark secret shadows,
most peaceful place of refuge, welcome, please
the friend of peace and of tranquillity.

Sonnet II

Pan,[2] who inside the dark and sacred caves
wherein your holy image is adored,
you spoke one day and said to me: "Do sing
the countryside, the shepherds and the herds."
    And the reed pipe, ungrateful to your love,
who was a proud nymph first and then a plant,
you handed me, and said: "The only one
who boasts this honor's the Sicilian Greek.[3]"
    As you appreciate my rhymes so much
make the wolves sleep inside their lairs,
and do accept the first born of the lambs;
    chase the ambitious and profane away,
and if someone your anger does not fear,
let him be eaten by the dogs alive.

---

1. Echo was the daughter of Gaea. She was in love with Narcissus, who did not return her love. She was changed into stone but had the power of speech.
2. Pan was the son of Hermes and Dryope. He is the Greek god of flocks and shepherds, forests and wild life, and fertility. Part man, part goat. He loved the nymph Syrinx who was transformed into a bamboo from which he fashioned the reed pipe.
3. The Sicilian Greek is a reference to Theocritus, the father of bucolic poetry. He was born in Siracusa.

PRIMAVERA
IDILIU I
DAMETA

Già cadevanu granni da li munti l'umbri,
spruzzannu supra li campagni
la suttili acquazzina; d'ogni latu
si vidianu fumari in luntananza
li rustici capanni; a guardii a guardii
turnavanu li pecuri a li mandri:
parti scinnianu da li costi, e parti,
sfilannu da li macchi e rampicannu
attornu di li concavi vaddati,
vinianu allegri ntra l'aperti chiani.

E prima d'iddi e poi, gravi e severi,
li grici cani, cu la lunga giubba, marciavanu
guardigni, a passi lenti,
la sfiluccata cuda strascinannu.

Siquitavanu appressu li pasturi,
tinennu stritti sutta di lu vrazzu
la virga e lu saccuni, mentr'intenti
e la vucca e li manu eranu tutti
ad animari flauti e sampugni.

Mugghiavanu li vacchi pri chiamari
li vitidduzzi, è già distingui ogn'una
lu propriu sangu, e si l'agguccia allatu
timennu chi lu lupu, latru astutu,
pri fari li soi straggi
s' approfitti di l'umbri e di la notti,
comu solinu fari li malvaggi.

Tàcinu l'ocidduzzi ntra li rami:
sula la cucucciuta, ch'era stata
la prima a lu sbigghiarsi, ultim'ancora
va circannu risettu pri li chiani,
ed ora, l'ali soi parpagghiannu,
si suspenni tra l'aria, ora s'abbassa,
ripitennu la solita canzuna.

Ma assai chiù varia, chiù suavi e grata
lu rusignolu in funnu a lu vadduni
la sua ripigghia, chi d'intornu intornu
l'aria, la terra e tutti li viventi
penetra, tocca, e spusa all'armunia
l'amabili piaciri e la ducizza.

Dameta intantu allatu a la sua Dori

Spring
Idyll I
Dameta

Large shadows were already falling down
the mountains, spreading a fine dew throughout
the countryside. From everywhere around
and in the distance one could see smoke
rising above the rustic huts; the flocks of sheep,
in clusters, headed back to their corrals.
While some descended from the hills,
another group emerged out of the bushes,
climbing around out of the concave dales,
moving quite gingerly onto the open plains.

In front of them and back, long-haired gray dogs,
looking severe and grave, kept pace with them
with measured step and vigilant demeanor,
dragging their scraggly tails behind them.

The shepherds followed then behind the dogs,
holding their canes and knapsack under arm,
and with their mouths and hands
they were intent in giving breath
to their flutes and reed pipes.

The cows were bellowing to summon back
their calves, already each has singled out
her own offspring, and keeps it close to her,
afraid the wolf, a cunning thief, might take
advantage of the shadows of the night,
as scoundrels always do,
to execute its massacres.

Sweet birds sit silently upon the branches;
Only the skylark, which had been the first
to wake, was last in seeking shelter in the valley.
And alternates between gliding in midair,
suspended on slow moving wings,
or lowering its flight as it
repeats its usual refrain.

But much more varied, sweet and pleasing
the nightingale deep in the gorge resumes
its own song, penetrating, touching all
the air, the land and every living soul
while marrying the pleasure and the sweetness
of its refrain to harmony.

Meanwhile Dameta was sitting on a hill

sidia ntra na collina, in cui na rocca
spurgìa supra la valli, e duminava
la valli istissa e li campagni intornu
e li costi luntani e li chianuri.
Penetratu lu cori di piaciri
pri tanti granni e maistusi oggetti,
chi tutti si vinìanu all'occhi soi,
iddi propria, quasi ad offeriri,
ma supra tuttu scossu e traspurtatu
da l'amabili oggettu ch'avìa accantu,
senz'aspittari autr'armunia chi chidda
chi respirava intornu la natura,
teneru e gratu incominciau lu cantu.

Dameta Canta:

Sti silenzii, sta virdura
sti muntagni, sti vallati
l'ha criatu la natura
pri li cori innamurati.
Lu susurru di li frunni,
di lu ciumi lu lamentu,
l'aria, l'ecu chi rispunni,
tuttu spira sentimentu.
Dda farfalla accussì vaga,
lu muggitu di li tori,
l'innoccenza, chi vi appaga,
tutti parranu a lu cori.
Stu frischettu insinuanti
chiudi un gruppu di piaciri,
accarizza l'alma amanti,
e ci arrobba li suspiri.
Ccà l'armuzza li soi porti
apri tutti a lu dilettu:
sulu è indignu di sta sorti
cui nun chiudi amuri in pettu;
sulu è reu cui pò guardari
duru e immobili sta scena;
ma lu stissu nun amari
è delittu insemi e pena.
Donna bella senza amuri
è na rosa fatta in cira,
senza vezzi, senza oduri,
chi nun veggeta nè spira.

next to his Dori underneath a hanging cliff
that dominated the whole dale below
and every field in all directions,
even the distant coastlines and the plains.
His heart was filled with pleasure at the sight
of all the wondrous and majestic views
that almost seemed to be an offering,
that came to be displayed before his eyes,
but most of all he was enthralled and moved
by the fair subject that stood next to him,
and without waiting for a melody
other than what evoked nature herself,
he gladly started singing tenderly:

Dameta Sings:

"This quietude, this plant life,
these high mountains and these dales,
were by nature all created
for the hearts that are in love.
The soft whispering of leaves,
the lament that rivers make,
air and echo that replies,
all things sentiment awake.
That most lovely butterfly,
the low bellowing of bulls,
innocence that satisfies,
all things here speak to the heart.
This pervading little breeze
a few pleasures does include,
it caresses loving hearts
and steals sighs away from them.
Here your sweet soul opens wide
its own gate to all delights.
Only those who love don't feel
are unworthy of this fate.
Only guilty souls can gaze
at this scene unmoved and cold.
But not loving is itself
at once crime and penalty.
A fair woman without love
is a rose made out of wax,
without charms and without smell
who won't grow or even breathe.

68

Tu nun parri, o Dori mia?
Stu silenziu mi spaventa;
è possibili ch'in tia
qualchi affettu nun si senta?
    O chi l'alma 'mbriacata
di la duci voluttati,
dintra un'estasi biata
li soi sensi ha confinati?
    Lu to cori senza focu
comu cridiri purrìa,
si, guardànnuti pri pocu,
vennu vampi all'alma mia?
    Vampi, ohimè! chi l'occhiu esala,
ch'eu li vivu, ch'eu l'anelu,
comu vivi la cicala
la ruggiada di lu celu.
    Sti toi languidi pupiddi
mi convincinu abbastanza
chi l'amuri parra in iddi,
chi c'è focu in abbundanza.
    Oh! chi fussiru in concertu
l'occhi toi cu li labbruzzi!
oh! nni fussi fattu certu
cu paroli almenu muzzi!
    Fussi almenu stu gentili
graziusu to russuri
tistimoniu fidili,
veru interpetri d'amuri!
    Dimmi: Forsi fa paura
a lu cori to severu
un affettu di natura?
un amuri finu e veru?
    Ah!, mia cara Pasturedda,
li Dei giusti ed immortali
t'avirrìanu fattu bedda,
si l'amuri fussi un mali?
    È l'amuri un puru raggiu
chi lu celu fa scappari,
e ch'avviva pri viaggiu
suli, luna, terra e mari.
    Iddu duna a li suspiri
la ducizza chiù esquisita,
ed aspergi di piaciri
li miserii di la vita.

You don't speak, my dearest Dori?
This your silence frightens me,
is it possible that you
nothing feel inside your heart?
    Has your soul been overwhelmed
by the sweetness of the pleasure
in a blessed ecstasy
that your senses has confined?
    How can I believe your heart
has no burning flame inside?
If I look at you an instant,
I feel burning in my soul?
    Fire, alas, the eye exhales
which I yearn for and I drink,
as cicadas drink the dew
that rains down out of the sky.
    As I see your languid eyes
I'm convinced sufficiently
that love speaks with clarity
that much passion therein lies.
    Oh! If only your sweet lips
were in tune with your bright eyes!
Oh! If I could be assured
even with half-spoken words!
    Oh! If only your sweet blushing
were a faithful indication,
a reliant, true interpreter
of the love you feel for me!
    To a heart that's so severe
is a natural affection,
a love that is fine and true,
such a frightening affair?
    Ah! My dearest shepherdess,
the just and immortal gods
would have given you such beauty
if to love was a bad thing?
    A pure beam the sky allows
to escape, Love, as it goes,
is what gives life to the Sun,
to the Moon, the earth and sea.
    Love is what gives to our sighs
its exquisite tenderness
and what sprinkles pleasure on
the harsh miseries of life.

Giovanni Meli

Mugghia l'aria, e a so dispettu
lu pasturi a li capanni
strinci a se l'amatu oggettu,
e si scorda di l' affanni.

Quann'unitu a lu liuni Febbu
tuttu sicca ed ardi,
lu pasturi ntra un macchiuni
pasci l'alma cu li sguardi.

Quannu tutti l'elementi
poi cospiranu a favuri,
oh! ch'amabili momenti!
oh! delizii d'amuri!

Quannu provi la ducizza
di dui cori amanti amati,
chiancirai l'insipidizza
di li tempi già passati;

e sti pianti, sti ciuriddi,
chi pri tia su stati muti,
a lu cori ogn'unu d'iddi
ti dirrà: jorna e saluti!,

ch'a lu focu di l'affetti
ogn'irvuzza chiacchiarìa;
un commerciu di diletti
s'aprirà ntra d'iddi e tia.

Cedi, o Dori, miu cunfortu,
a sta liggi chiù suprema;
ah! nun fari stu gran tortu
a la tua biddizza estrema.

Si spusassi cu l'amuri
di natura ssi tesori,
l'anni virdi ed immaturi
ti dirrevanu a lu cori:

"Godi, o Dori, e fa gudiri
stu momentu chi t'è datu;
nun è nostru l'avveniri,
è pirdutu lu passatu".

The wind howls and in disdain
in their huts, the shepherd holds
his beloved object close,
and his troubles he forsakes.

When the Lion joins with Phoebus[1]
everything dries out and burns,
so the shepherd in the bushes
feeds his soul just with his eyes.

But when all the elements
do conspire in support,
oh! what charming moments come!
Oh what pleasures love then brings!

When you come to feel the sweetness
of two loving hearts in love,
you'll regret the tastelessness
of the times that have gone by.

And these plants, these little flowers
that have silent been for you,
to your heart each will declare:
"A long life and health to you!"

In the glow of sweet affections
every blade of grass now whispers;
a communion of delights
between them and you is born.

Yield, my Dori, my dear comfort
to this law that reigns supreme.
This disservice do not do
to a beauty so extreme.

If these treasures you would wed
to the love of nature, then
your unripe and verdant years
would speak like this to your heart:

"Oh enjoy this moment, Dori,
and give joy to others too,
for the future is not ours,
and the past's already lost."

---

1. A reference to the Sun (Phoebus) when it is in the constellation of the Lion (Leo), that is, during the hottest period of the summer when the Sicilian countryside is parched.

ESTÀ
IDILIU III
DAFNI

Summer
Idyll III
Daphnis

Guidava lu pateticu so carru
ntra li gravi silenzii la notti:
l'umbri, abbrazzati a la gran matri antica,
s'agnunavanu friddi e taciturni
sutta li grutti e l'arvuli, scanzannu
di la nascenti luna la chiarìa.

Di li mortali supra li palpèbri
sidìa l'amicu sonnu, ed aggravava
li sensi di suavi stupidizza,
mentri chi di balsamicu ristoru
lu riposu spargìa li membri stanchi.

Ntra la profunda, placida quieti
scutìa di tantu in tantu na campana
lu voi, chi ruminava ntra li grutti
l'ervi pasciuti a la vicina valli.

Sulu, ohimè! lu riposu universali,
tantu duci e graditu a cui rispira,
Dafni ritrova chiù chi morti amaru:
Dafni gratu a li Musi, a lu cui cantu
Pani spissu affacciau da li ruvetti
la testa, ed affilau l'acuti oricchi;
Dafni, ohimè! sulu vigghia, chi chiantata
avi in pettu la spina di l'amuri.

E cu li soi lamenti armuniusi
esercitava a pedi d'un cipressu
l'Ecu, spiritu nudu, chi va errannu
di grutta in grutta tra macigni e rocchi,
ch'impietusita a li soi peni amari
li ripeti fidili e li tramanna
a li vàusi vicini in chisti accenti:

Dafni canta:

O bianca, lucidissima
luna, chi senza velu
sulcannu vai pri l'aria
li campi di lu celu,
    tu dissipi li tènebri
cu la serena facci,

Night her pathetic cart was driving in
the heavy and most dismal silences;
shadows, embracing the mighty ancient Mother,
were huddling, taciturn and cold, beneath
the trees and in the grottoes, to avoid
the glimmer that precedes the rising Moon.

Amiable sleep was sitting on the eyelids
of mortals and induced upon their senses
a gentle grogginess, as welcome rest
provided a good measure of relief
to their exhausted limbs.

In the profound and tranquil quietude,
once in a while, an ox made its bell sound
while ruminating in the cave upon
the grasses it consumed in the near valley.

The universal period of rest,
so sweet and welcome to all human beings,
for Daphnis[1] was more bitter than death is.
Daphnis, beloved of the Muses[2], whose
singing prompted Pan[3] to often lean
through the thorn bushes, cocking his sharp ears.
The wretched Daphnis wakes alone because
the thorn of love is stuck inside his chest.

And with his sad, harmonious lamentations,
sung underneath a cypress tree, he moved
Echo, a naked spirit who roamed through
from cave to cave, among big rocks and boulders,
who, feeling sorry for his bitter woes,
repeated them most faithfully,
spreading them to the nearby cliffs as follows:

Daphnis Sings:

"O white, resplendent Moon,
who without shade do fly
crossing the limpid air
through meadows in the sky!
    You dissipate the darkness
with your untroubled face.

71

li stiddi impallidiscinu
appena chi tu affacci.

   Li placidi silenzii,
all'umidu to raggiu,
di la natura parranu
l'amabili linguaggiu.

   A tia l'amanti teneru,
cu palpiti segreti,
la dulurusa storia
mestissimu ripeti.

   E mentri amari lagrimi
la dogghia sua produci,
tu spruzzi a la mestizzia
lu sentimentu duci.

   Quannu una negghia pallida
ti vidi pri davanti,
su li suspiri flebbili
di lu miu cori amanti.

   Pri mia la bedda e splendida
tua facci si sculura;
jiu, jiu lu miserabili,
'ngramagghiu la natura.

   Pri mia li friddi vàusi
supra l'alpestri munti
d'orruri e di mestizzia
si coprinu la frunti.

   Cu lamintusu strepitu
l'acqui, a lu miu duluri
chiancennu, si sdirrupanu
dintra li vaddi oscuri.

   Pri la pietà suspiranu
di li mei crudi peni,
trimannu ntra li pampini,
li zefiretti ameni.

   La notti malinconica
si parti o s'avvicina,
pietusa metti a chioviri
lagrimi d'acquazzina.

   A lu dulenti esempiu
di l'alma mia rispunni
zefiru, luna ed aria
notti, macigni ed unni.

   Ma l'unica insensibili,
lu cori, ohimè! chiù duru,

The stars turn pale at once
as soon as you will rise.

   The tranquil silences
under your humid ray,
the loving language use
that nature too employs.

   To you the tender lover
his own vexatious tales
with secret palpitations
most woefully unveils.

   While his unhappiness
produces bitter tears,
upon his sad distress,
sweet sentiments you spread.

   When a pale cloud you see
appear before your eyes,
know they're the feeble sighs
of my own loving heart.

   Your splendid and bright face
because of me grows dim.
I, I'm the wretched one,
who makes all nature grim.

   For me the frigid cliffs
upon the alpine heights
with horror and with sadness
their foreheads bow contrite.

   With sorrowful laments
the streams, at my chagrin,
cry out and plunge headlong
into obscure ravines.

   Out of compassion sigh,
on seeing how I grieve,
the pleasing gentle breezes
through branches and through leaves.

   The melancholic night,
when ending or when new,
in sheer compassion starts
to rain tears made of dew.

   The sorrowful example
of my soul's cruel plight
by Moon, breeze, rocks, and air
is echoed and by night.

   The only one immune,
alas, the hardest heart

è chidda pri cui spasimu,	is she that I adore,
è l'unica ch' aduru.	the one for whom I smart.
Na rocca, un truncu, un ruvulu,	A cliff, a trunk, an oak,
pri sorti mia fatali,	for my ill-omened fate
pigghiau la bedda imagini	a woman's image took
di donna senza uguali.	who has no peer or mate.
Cun idda nun mi giuvanu	With her my tears and pains
li chianti e li duluri,	are of no use at all,
nè pozzu amuri esiggiri,	nor can I love demand
pagannula d'amuri.	by paying her with love.
Giacchì l'affetti inclinanu	Since feelings all incline
a un insensatu oggettu,	to senseless things, fair goddess,
o vaga Dia, di màrmura	please change this heart of mine
fammi lu cori in pettu.	to marble in my chest.
Lu simili a lu simili	In nature all like things
sempri natura unisci;	together always dwell;
'mmenzu a li duri vàusi	among the hardest cliffs
dura la quercia crisci:	oak trees grow hard as well.
sta liggi inviiulabili	This permanent edict
di l'ordini immortali	of the immortal scheme
sulu pri mia si limita?	is null alone for me?
Pri mia nun è chiù tali?	For me it's not the same?
O bianca Dia, rigordati	White Goddess,[4] do recall
chi ntra li silvi erranti	that erring in this grove
d'un pastureddu amabili	a lovable young shepherd
fusti tu ancora amanti,	you took once as your love,
e chi oziusu e inutili	and that your bow became
l'arcu pri tia si fici,	an idle, useless thing.
nè l'echi chiù 'ntunavanu	No echoes then declaimed
"Diana cacciatrici".	'Diana, the Huntress.'
Nè chiù di cervi e daini	Nor did your grey, bloodhounds
li toi livreri e bracchi	follow the scent of deer
lu rastu sequitavanu	and fawns, exhausted and
tutti anelanti e stracchi,	all breathless any more,
ma allegri festeggiavanu,	but cheerfully they ran
di lu pasturi attornu,	around the shepherd then,
quasi pri annunziariti	as though to let you know
lu gratu so ritornu.	that he had just returned.
Cu quantu to rammaricu	Oh! what regret you felt,
juncevati importuna	how you found importune,
chidd'ura di curreggiri	when it was time to steer
lu carru di la luna!	the right course for the Moon!
Duvennuti dividiri	When you had to take leave
da la tua gioia estrema,	of your extreme great joy

73

forsi t'avisti a pentiri	perhaps you did regret
d'essiri dia suprema.	that you a goddess were.
Cunsidira, cunsidira	Consider, please, consider
da lu to cori, o Dia,	o Goddess, with great care,
lu statu miserabili,	the miserable state,
la cruda pena mia.	the cruel pain I bear.
O casta, ma sensibili	O chaste, and yet receptive
ad una ciamma vera,	to a flame that's sincere.
sentimi, accogghi l'umili	My humble plea accept,
giustissima prighera:	my rightful prayer hear.
"Si mai gradita vittima	'If ever soul devoutly
l'alma devota offrìu,	a welcome victim offered
Dia, ddu cori mutacci,	o goddess, change her heart
o canciami lu miu".	or else then change my own.'
Dissi l'afflittu Dafni; e l'aspri trunchi	The wretched Daphnis spoke, and the hard
'ntisiru dintra insolitu trimuri;	tree trunks felt a strange quivering inside,
scossi lu munti la ferrigna basi;	the mountain shuddered from its iron base;
la terra di nov'umbri si cuprìu;	the earth was covered with some new-formed shadows,
l'umidu raggiu di la bianca luna	the humid beam of the resplendent Moon
'ntisi d'iddu pietati e impallidìu.	compassion felt for him and then turned pale.

---

1. Daphnis was a son of Hermes (Mercury) and of a Sicilian nymph. The god Pan taught him to play the flute and the Muses inspired him with the love of poetry.
2. The nine Muses lived on Mount Pindus and represented the various arts.
3. Pan: Cfr. Sonnet II of *Buccolica*.
4. The White Goddess is a reference to the goddess Diana, (Artemis) who represents the Moon. She was the patroness of hunting and of chastity. Meli here makes reference to the myth wherein she saw the shepherd Endymion as he slept and fell madly in love with him and made love to him during his sleep.

L'AUTUNNU
IDILIU VI
MARTINU

The Fall
Idyll VI
Martinu

L'omu chi nesci fora di la 'mmesta
cu scotiri li guidi e la tutela
di la saggia Natura,
perdi la tramuntana e si smarrisci;
e quantu chiù s'è d'idd'alluntanatu
tantu chiù spersu si ritrova, e senti
(quannu di l'idei vani
taci pri pocu lu tumultu riu)
richiamarisi ddà d'unni partiu.

L'illudirà pr'un tempu la citati,
li pompi, li spettaculi, lu lussu,
li commodi e li gran magnificenzi;
ma poi multiplicati
senti l'interni passioni, e chisti
crisciri cu lu crisciri di l'anni,
e di lu cori so farsi tiranni.

Mentri da chisti è devoratu, chiama
la Natura, ma indarnu;
l'abiti ci annu stritti li catini
di cui nun sapi sciogghirsi, e fratantu
pr'illudiri a se stissu
di liberu e giulivu si da vantu.

Puru di tantu in tantu, o quannu ridi
la Primavera tra lussuriggianti
ciuriti praterii, o quann'Autunnu
spinci la testa carrica di frutti
e di racina, chi cuntrasta all'oru
biundu culuritu,
l'omu di la citati a summi sforzi
si allunga o si strascina
purtandusi a li campi la catina.

Sugn'iu, sugn'iu (cussì dicìa Martinu,
tra un lucidu intervallu di sua menti),
lu snaturatu figghiu,
cui l'internu affilatu (unicu avanzu
di la materna ereditati) porta
a la tenera matri, strascinannu
li servili catini di lu vintusu fastu
e di la non mai sazia ambizioni

The man who comes out of the shell
by shaking off the guidance and protection
of Mother Nature's wisdom,
loses his orientation and gets lost;
the more he moves away from her,
the more confused and lost he will become
and (when the clamoring of false ideas
is interrupted for a little while)
he'll hear the call to go back whence he started.

The city with its luxury and pomp
its many shows, its comforts and magnificence
will for a little time deceive him,
but afterward he will begin to feel
his inner passions grow
and these will grow as years go by,
until they'll rule his heart tyrannously.

While all these passions are devouring him,
he will call Nature but in vain.
His habits have so tightened up his chains
that he won't know how to get free.
Meanwhile in his delusions
he boasts that he is happy and unbound.

Nevertheless, from time to time,
when Spring smiles with its splendid fields
all blossoming or when the Autumn lifts
its head all filled with fruit and grapes,
which with their wondrous hue compete
with the blond-colored gold,
with great exertion man
moves from the city to the fields,
dragging his chains along.

"I am the one, I'm the degenerate son,
(that's what Martinu would say when he
a lucid moment in his mind enjoyed)
to whom the inner longing (the last thing
remaining of his mother's heritage)
brings to his tender mother, carrying
the servile chains of winded pomp
and of the never satisfied ambition

chi mi rudinu l'alma di continu:
oh! matri, all'occhi toi chi sù mischinu!
   Trovu attornu a sti aratri,
tra rocchi e tra virdura,
la mia diletta matri,
la provida natura;
   chi cu li vrazza aperti
mi tira ad idda e chiama,
e in affilati certi
mi mustra la sua brama;
   chi cu sinceri affetti
parr'a lu cori e dici:
"Un essiri ti detti
pri fariti felici;
   un cori pri godiri.
duvi veraci istinti
spusanu a li doviri
piaciri ben distinti:
   liggi ci trovi impressa
unica e singulari,
sculputa da mia stessa
di amari e farti amari.
   Chista ti stendi e accrisci
l'essiri d' ogni latu,
chista ti attacca e unisci
a tuttu lu creatu;
   senz'idda su la terra
straniu diventi a tutti
tra na perpetua guerra,
chi t'isula o ti agghiutti.
   La menti e l'intellettu
ti detti a rilevari
chi chiddu è giustu e rettu
chi a tutti pò giuvari:
   li sensi a custodiri
la propria tua esistenza,
e a fariti sentiri
la grata compiacenza;
   l'occhi pri contemplari
l'oggetti varii e tanti,
chi tutti vennu a fari
un ordini costanti;
   l' oricchi nova scena
ti aprinu grata ancora;

that gnaw my soul continuously:
How wretched I appear in your eyes, Mother!
   I find around these plows
through rocks and vegetation
my own beloved mother,
the nature that provides,
   who with her open arms
beckons me to her side,
and with some earnest signs
shows me her eagerness;
   who with sincere affection
speaks to the heart and says:
"I gave a life to you
so you'd know happiness;
   a heart so you'd enjoy;
where instincts that are true
wed distinct pleasures to
responsibilities;
   printed therein you'll find
a law, one of a kind,
I carved there with my hands:
love and make all love you.
   This lays down and increases
your being from all sides;
this law binds and unites
your life with all creation;
   without it, here on earth,
a stranger to all men
you will be, fighting wars
that isolate or kill you.
   A mind and intellect
I gave to you to see
that something is correct
when it will help all men;
   the senses so you can
preserve your own existence
and so that you can feel
a sense of gratitude,
   the eyes to contemplate
how many varied objects
contribute to construct
an order that is constant;
   the ears a scene that's new
and pleasing offer you

tenera Filomena
li alletta e li ristora;
    tra sulitaria rocca
d'un passaru la vuci
li cori e l' almi tocca
cu lu so cantu duci.

    Li canni armuniusi
di li mei pastureddi
fann'ecu a graziusi
canti di varii oceddi.

    Lu to odoratu anch'avi
tributu consolanti
di effluvii suavi
tra tanti ciuri, e tanti.

    Li frutti faju datu
suavi e dilicati.
chi all'occhiu, all'odoratu,
e su a lu gustu grati.

    Veni, dilettu, veni,
la matri tua ti chiama
tra li vuschitti ameni,
sutta na virdi rama.

    La paci, in cui mi fidu,
trovi cu mia sulidda,
e Amuri, chi lu nidu
conz'a na turturidda.

    La fidiltà di attornu
mi trovi tra li cani,
attenti notti e jornu,
amici e guardiani.

    Palazzi mei priggiati
sunnu sti eccelsi munti,
sedi la maistati
tra la sublimi frunti:

    vera magnificenza,
vera grandizza è in iddi;
umana arti e potenza,
quantu sù picciriddi!

    Osserva comu spiccanu
dda supra querci e ruvuli,
chi li soi testi ficcanu
in menzu di li nuvuli!

    Quanti sti rocchi alpestri
cuntennu in macchi e in grutti

the tender Philomel[1]
appeals, delighting them.
    Upon a solitary bluff
a sparrow's lovely voice
touches your heart and soul
with its melodious song.

    The harmony of flutes
my little shepherds play
provides a pleasing echo
to songs of many birds.

    Also your sense of smell
receives a soothing homage
from the perfume that comes
from many different flowers.

    I gave you many fruits,
so delicate and sweet
that are such welcome sights
for eyes and sense of smell.

    Come, my beloved, come,
your mother beckons you,
here in these sheltered woods
under a verdant branch.

    You will find peace, in whom
I trust, alone with me.
And love, who makes a nest
for a sweet turtledove.

    Fidelity you' ll find
among the dogs around
who are attentive friends
and guardians day and night.

    My cherished palaces
are these high mountain peaks
on whose sublime foreheads
sits majesty supreme.

    The true magnificence,
real greatness lies in them,
all human art and power,
how puny in comparison!

    Observe how they stand out
those oaks and durmasts there
whose highest branches stick
their heads inside the clouds.

    In all these alpine cliffs,
what throng of living species,

di alati e di pedestri
razzi viventi tutti!
   In aria suspisi
attornu a chiddi alturi
filìanu ad ali stisi
l'aquili e li vuturi;
   di chiàppari li troffi,
li macchi a cunfaluni
di arèddara, sù stoffi,
sù adorni a ddi ruccuni.
   Ammira di ddà susu
comu un perenni ciumi
ruina maestusu
l'unni mutannu in scumi!
   Dintra l'occulti vii
di sti gran munti in funnu,
li sali e gallerii
li mei ricchizzi sunnu.
   Chiddi chi umanu ingegnu
metti a lu primu rangu,
l'oru e li gemmi, eu tegnu
tra rocchi, crita e fangu.
   L'àgati, li graniti,
li marmi chiù vistusi,
sù a terri e petri uniti
senz' ordini confusi.
   Fannu di li mei grutti
li basi e li pilastri,
uniti a rocchi brutti,
porfidi ed alabastri.
   Vidi com'iu disprezzu
st'inezii, a cui vui dati
tantu valuri e prezzu,
chi pr'iddi vi scannati!
   Ma lassa sti caverni,
nesci a l'apertu e godi
li mei biddizzi esterni,
diffusi in varii modi.
   Oh! quanti specii, oh quanti
aspetti variati
presentanu li pianti
all'occhi mei purgati!
   Quanti famigghi interi
nutricanu d'insetti,

winged and land based, inhabit
caves and the undergrowth!
   Suspended in midair,
around those altitudes,
eagles and vultures circle
on their wings widely spread;
   bunches of wild capers,
thickets of ivy shaped
like flags adorn and clothe
the face of the great cliffs.
   Admire from up there how
a permanent, great river
majestically runs,
turning its waves to foam!
   Through hidden paths and tracks
deep down in these great mountains,
in halls and galleries
my treasures you can find.
   Those things the human mind
considers in first place:
the gold and precious gems,
in mud, rocks, clay I keep.
   The agate and the granite,
the most dramatic marbles
are mixed haphazardly
with plain rocks and with dirt.
   Porphyry, alabaster,
which represent the base
and pillars of my caves
are mixed with ugly rocks.
   Observe with what disdain
I treat these things you deem
so prized that you will slaughter
each other to possess them.
   But leave my caves and go
outside and there enjoy
the beauties I array
in various displays.
   How many species, say,
how many varied shapes
the plants present before
my purged and limpid eyes!
   How many families
feed on insects and fly

chi poi volanu a scheri
canciati in farfalletti!

La viti, ch'è di razza
debuli e in vasciu situ,
vidi comu si abbrazza
lu chiuppu pri maritu!

Chistu pri cumpinsari
la sua sterilitati
li rappi fa spiccari
chi d'idda s'à aduttati.

St'ulivu, ch'à sfidatu
lu tempu e li staggiuni,
da un truncu fracassatu
rinova un faidduni.

Li palmi e pini sunnu
piramidi fastusi;
l'epochi di lu munnu
jeu tegnu in iddi chiusi.

Lu gratu murmuriu
di l'acqua, chi ddà scurri,
all'ervi dici: Addiu,
jeu partu, chi vi occurri?

Vuliti nutrimentu?
Versu di mia stinniti
li radichi, e a mumentu
lu nutrimentu avriti.

L'arvuli in ricompenza
li rami ad idda stènninu,
di la sulari ardenza
cu l'umbri la difènninu.

Vidi quantu sù grati,
quantu riconoscenti!
St'essiri inanimati
s'amanu da parenti.

Nè cridiri chist'unni
inabitati: acchiàna
supr'acqua, e mi rispunni
gracchiannu la giurana;

cu squami poi d'argentu
guizzanu muti in funnu
àutri, chi a stu elementu
additti da mia sunnu.

Li susurranti apuzzi
sparsi tra ciuri ammira;

after they change, in swarms,
as little butterflies.

Look how the fragile vine,
which lies low on the ground,
the poplar trees entwines,
hugging it as a husband.

The tree to compensate
for its sterility,
makes the grape bunches grow
that he from her adopted.

This olive tree that has
weather and seasons braved
brings forth a brand new shoot
out of its tattered trunk.

My palms and pine trees are
majestic pyramids:
the eras of the world
inside of them I hid.

The pleasing whispering
of water that there flows
says to the grass: Farewell!
Need anything before I go?

Do you need nourishment?
Your roots my way extend
and in a while I'll send
the nutrients you want.

The trees in recompense
extend their branches over,
providing a cool cover
that shield it from the sun.

Look how obliged they are
and how appreciative!
These beings without soul
as kin each other love.

Nor should you think these waves
are uninhabited.
A frog came to the surface
and croaking thus replied:

with silver scales, some others
dart silently below;
they're in the element
that I to them bestow.

Look how the buzzing bees,
spread out among the flowers,

79

tornanu a li cidduzzi
ricchi di meli e cira:
   l'armonica unioni
si d'iddi scupririssi,
di tua condizioni
tu ti virgugnirissi.
   Ultra di l'indefessi
alati mei vicini,
Febbu, chi gira e tessi,
ni porta pilligrini.
   Presenta ogni staggiuni
li specii soi distinti
a sbardi ed a squatruni
di pinni variopinti.
   Soi nunzii e missaggeri
la Primavera manna
rindini, chi leggeri
scurrinu d'ogni banna;
   poi junci accumpagnata
di quagghi, di sturneddi,
e di na smisurata
fudda di varii oceddi.
   Jeu tutti li cunfidu
all'arvuli e a li prati
pri farisi lu nidu,
nutrirsi li cuvati.
   Multi l'està, vulannu
cu nova reda allatu,
in cerca sinni vannu
di un clima timpiratu.
   Di lòdani in autunnu,
di turdi e calandruni,
di pettirrussi abbunnu,
di pispisi e pinsuni.
   L'invernu li gaddazzi,
li groi, li nivalori,
e in margi e pantanazzi
aju anatri e trizzoli.
   Nè cumpagnia mi manca
di armenti e greggi, e chista,
no, nun mi opprimi e stanca,
ma grata m'è a la vista.
   Mi opprimi e stanca,
oh! quantu tumultu di citati,

to their dear cells return,
richer with wax and honey:
   If you could just discover
their union's coalition,
you would be quite ashamed
on seeing your condition.
   Beside my winged neighbors
who fly untiringly,
Phoebus, who spins and turns,
more pilgrims sends our way.
   And every season offers
its own distinctive species,
in squadrons and in swarms
with multicolored feathers.
   Spring sends the swallows then
as heralds, messengers,
who light upon their wings,
scurry from here to there.
   In its wake, countless swarms
of birds of many species
accompanied by quails.
and starlings then arrive.
   To trees I then entrust them
and to the fields, so they
can make their nests and feed
their offspring as they need.
   Many in summertime,
flying with their new brood,
depart in search of climes
that are more temperate.
   In autumn I am filled
with skylarks and with thrushes
and with red-breasted robins,
titlarks, and other birds.
   In winter time, woodcocks,
lapwings, and cranes arrive,
while in the swamps and stagnant
pools, ducks and teals will thrive.
   Nor do I lack for herds
of cows and sheep, and these
don't tire me at all; indeed,
on seeing them I'm pleased.
   What does oppress me though
a lot, is city noise,

e da vulgari chiantu
fastu di sfacinnati:
  cabbali, intrichi, frodi,
disordini e scompigghi ...
oh! cechi e in strani modi
diggenerati figghi!"
  Cussì a lu cori di Martinu parra
l'ingenua Natura. E la ragiuni,
chi di la verità senti la vuci,
la gusta e trova duci,
l'accogghi, si commovi ... ed eccu già ...
Ma li passioni indomiti e sfrenati,
chi da la prima etati
suggiugata l'avìanu, opponnu ad idda
negghia di van'idei,
chi li veraci ottenebra e cunfunni.
Cussì Martinu, chi gustatu avìa
un lampu di saggizza, è riturnatu
machina, comu prima
da l'àbiti muntata.
E comu navi in timpistusu mari
senza timuni nè pilotu, tali
resta l'afflittu a la discrizioni
ed a l'arbitriu di li passioni;
e senza chi si accurgìa
di l'internu complottu e di l'intricu,
pri lu ristanti di sua vita è trattu
a fari chiddu ch'avìa sempri fattu.

the vulgar tears of folk on whom
the nothing doers thrive.
  Cabal, intrigues, and fraud,
disorders, and confusion...
oh blind, and in strange ways,
degenerate scions!'
  That is how honest Nature spoke
directly to Martinu's heart. And reason,
which heard the voice of truth,
enjoyed a taste of it and found it sweet;
he welcomed it, was moved
and he was almost ready to...
But his untamed and brazen passions
which from an early age
had subjugated it, put up a haze
of vague, illusive thoughts
that the true ones obscured and mixed.
This way Martinu, who'd enjoyed a flash
of wisdom, just returned to being
a robot driven by habit, like before.
And like a ship out in a stormy sea
without a rudder or a pilot, so
the wretch stayed bound to the description
and under the control of passions;
and without ever realizing
the inner plotting and intrigue,
for the rest of his life he was drawn
to do exactly what he'd always done.

---

1. Philomela or Philomena was changed by the gods into a nightingale after she and her sister Procne killed the young son of Tereus and served him as a meal to him. Tereus has attacked Philomela, his wife, cutting her tongue before. Procne was changed into a swallow, Tereus into an owl, and the murdered son into a sandpiper. But Philomel has come to represent the sweetness of the nightingale's song against a background of sadness and pain.

IDILIU VII
POLEMUNI

Supra un ruccuni, chi si specchia in mari,
rusicatu da l'unni e li tempesti,
chi orribili e funesti
sòlinu ntra ddi grutti ribbumbari;
duvi lu solitariu so nidu
l'àipi cu vuci rauchi e molesti,
assurdannu ogni lidu,
sòlinu spissu uniti visitari;
scuntenti, e cu la testa appinnuluni,
sidìa lu sventuratu Polemuni.
    Polemuni, chi saggiu conuscìa
l'aspettu di li stiddi e li pianeti;
e quali d'iddi è ria,
e quali cu benigna luci e pura
prumetti ed assicura paci,
bunazza e tempi assai discreti;
cunusceva l'influssi chiù segreti
di l'Ursa granni, chi nun vivi mai,
di Castori e Polluci
lu beneficu raggiu;
di li Pleadi acquusi
lu nuvulusu aspettu, e d'Oriuni,
chi torbidu riluci,
previdìa li tempesti, e di li venti
l'induli chi cumanna all'elementi;
pirchì supra na spiaggia l'avìa apprisu
da Proteu stissu, chi di la sua grutta,
comu fussi vicinu,
leggi in frunti di Giovi lu distinu.
    Ah! distinu tirannu! E chi ci giuva
a Polemuni lu so gran sapiri,
si tu ci si nnimicu?
Si poveru e mendicu,
disprizzatu da tutti,
nun trova amanti chiù, nun trova amicu?
Guardalu ntra ddu scogghiu,
cu na canna a li manu,
sulu e spirutu in attu di piscari,
chi sfoga lu so affannu cu cantari!

Idyll VII
Polemuni

Upon a ledge that's mirrored by the sea,
worn ragged by the storms and waves,
ill-boding horribly
ever reverberate inside those caves;
where sea gulls often come in pair or more
upon their hidden nests to check,
deafening every shore
with their annoying, raucous shrieks;
the wretched Polemuni sat unhappily,
with his head down between his knees.
    And Polemuni, who was very wise
and knew the mien of planets and of stars
and recognized which brought calamities
and whose beam was benign and pure,
and would peace promise and insure
good weather and some favorable times;
the most occult effects he came to know
of the Great Bear[1] who never dips below
the waves, and the beneficent, bright ray
of Castor and of Pollux[2];
the cloudy look of water bearing Pleiades[3],
and of Orion[4] whose
aspect darkly glows;
he could predict the tempests and the winds,
the disposition that rules over elements;
because he'd learned them on a beach
from Proteus[5] himself, who from his cave,
read destiny on the forehead of Jove
as though he were quite near to him.
    Oh cruel destiny! What good is all
this knowledge to poor Polemuni
if you're his enemy!
If poor and penniless,
disdained by everyone,
he cannot find a lover or a friend?
Just look at him upon that ledge,
holding a fishing pole in hand,
weak and alone, intent on fishing,
as he now vents his sorrows in a song.

Polemuni canta:	*Polemuni sings:*

"Sù a lu munnu, e 'un sacciu comu,
derelittu e in abbandunu!
Ni di mia si sa lu nomu!
Ni pri mia ci pensa alcunu!
  Chi m'importa si lu munnu
sia ben granni e spaziusu,
si li stati mei nun sunnu
chi stu vàusu ruinusu?
  Vàusu, tu sì la mia stanza;
tu, cimedda, mi alimenti;
nun aju àutra spiranza,
siti, vui, li mei parenti.
  Ccà mi trovanu l'alburi,
ccà mi trova la jilata,
ccà chiantatu in tutti l'uri,
paru un'alma cunnannata.
  Si a qualch'àipa chiù vicina
ci raccuntu li mei peni,
già mi pari, chianciulina,
ch'ascutannu si tratteni.
  Na lucerta, amica mia,
di la tana un pocu 'nfora,
piatusa mi talìa,
chi ci ammanca la palora.
  Tra silenzii notturni,
ogni grutta chianci e pena:
di luntanu "ohimè!" rispunni
a l'afflitta Filomena.
  Jeu fratantu all'aria bruna,
di li stiddi a la chiarìa,
cercu in chiddi ad una ad una
la tiranna stidda mia:
  quali viju chiù sanguigna,
quali scopru chiù funesta
già la criju dda maligna
chi mi fulmina e timpesta;
  unni gridu: ria potenza,
chi, abitannu dintra ss'astru,
chiovi in mia la quint'essenza
d'ogni barbaru disastru,
  si tu allura previdisti
ch'avìa ad essirni di mia,

"I'm in the world and don't know how,
wretchedness and abandonment's my fare,
no one here knows my name,
nor is there anyone who cares.
  Does it matter if this world
is so spacious and so wide,
if all things that I possess
on this rocky ledge reside?
  You, rock, are my only room;
and with you, my pole, I feed.
I possess no other hope;
you're my only kin, indeed.
  At the break of dawn I'm here,
when the hoarfrost falls I'm here,
at each hour I'm stuck here:
I am like a soul condemned.
  If my sorrows I relate
to a sea gull standing by,
she appears to linger on
and a tear shines in her eye.
  There's a lizard, friend of mine,
sitting near her lair to look
with compassion in her eyes
who just lacks the words to speak.
  In the silence of the night
every cave feels pain and cries
and from far away, alas,
the poor Philomel[6] replies.
  And meanwhile in the black air,
in the starry glow of night,
I search each and every star
to find which caused my sore plight.
  If I see one that's more bloody,
when I see the meanest star,
I am certain that's the one
that sends me pain and despair.
  I then scream: "Oh wretched Power
who reside inside that aster
and keeps showering on me
the quintessence of disasters.
  If before you could predict
what was to become of me

83

ed un scogghiu 'un mi facisti,
si la stissa tirannia.

Si tu sì cu sennu e menti,
potestà d'àutu intellettu,
pirchì un vili omu di nenti
ài pri to nimicu elettu?

Quali gloria ti nni veni,
numi barbaru e inumanu
di li mei turmenti e peni,
si la forza è a li toi manu?

Jeu li vittimi chiù cari
t'aiu forsi profanati?
Ma nè tempii nè otari
a tia trovu cunsacrati.

Quannu, afflittu e vilipisu,
qualchi vota mi lamentu
culpi tu ca mi ci hai misu
ntra ssu statu violentu.

Quali barbaru tirannu,
mentri brucia, ad un mischinu
c'impedisci ntra dd'affannu
lu gridari di cuntinu?

Sì na tigri, già lu viju,
chi ti pasci di lamenti;
lu to spassu e lu to sbiu
sù li mei peni e turmenti.

Una 'un passa, àutr'è vinuta;
sù spusati peni a peni,
l'una e l'àutra s'assicuta,
comu l'unna chi va e veni.

Ah! meu patri lu predissi,
e trimava ntra li robbi,
ch'eu nascivi ntra l'ecclissi
e chiancìanu li jacobbi.

Si mai vitti umbra di beni,
sulu fu pri tirannia,
acciò fussiru li peni
chiù sensibili pri mia.

Da miu patri a mia lassati
foru varca, nassi e riti;
tannu tutti èramu frati,
tutti amici e tutti uniti.

Si vineva da la pisca,
currìa menzu vicinatu;

and you did not make me rock,
you are truly tyranny.

If you have a mind and sense,
the high gift of intellect,
why did you, as enemy,
a poor worthless man select?

Oh what glory can you gain,
you inhuman, cruel god,
from my torments and my pain
if the power's in your hands?

Your most cherished sacrifices
somehow I tried to defame?
But no temples have I found,
nor an altar in your name.

When afflicted and reviled
I complain somewhat irate,
I blame you for placing me
in so violent a state.

Say, what cruel tyrant could
stop a man who's in despair,
and deny to him the right
with the world his woes to share?

You're a tiger, I can see
who in woes finds nourishment.
All my suffering and pain
are your pastime, merriment.

One's not gone, another comes.
Woe is joined to other woes.
And they one another chase
like the wave that comes and goes.

Oh my father, who was shaking
in his boots, had prophesied,
I was born in an eclipse
while the somber owls cried.

If I saw a glimpse of good
it was only tyranny,
so the suffering would be
more unbearable to me.

From my father I received
fishing nettings and a boat.
We were all like brothers then
and true friendship we were taught.

When from fishing we returned,
half the neighbors soon arrived.

facìa Nici festa e trisca,
stannu sempri a lu miu latu;
   si tardava ad arrivari,
la mia varca pr'un momentu,
la vidìa ntra un scogghiu a mari,
chi parrava cu lu ventu,
   e in succursu miu chiamava
quanti Dei ntra li sals'unni
l'ampiu Oceanu nutricava
pri ddi soi strati profunni.
   Quannu, ahimè, poi si canciàu
la mia sorti 'ngannatrici,
ntra un momentu mi livau
varca, riti, amanti, amici.
   Quannu pensu a dda nuttata,
pri l'affannu chianciu e sudu:
na timpesta spiatata
mi ridussi nudu e crudu.
   Canciau tuttu ntra un istanti;
la miseria mi circunna,
e lu iornu chiù brillanti
pari a mia notti profunna.

   Cussì l'afflittu si lagnava, e in tantu
l'unni, li venti e tutta la marina
fermi ed attenti ascutanu; e li figghi
di Nereu ntra li lucidi cunchigghi
versanu perni ntra singhiuzzi e chiantu.
Nun c'è cui fazza strepitu; anzi tutti
cu silenziu profunnu
s'impegnanu, acciocchì li soi lamenti,
ripercossi da l'Ecu ntra li grutti,
putissiru a lu celu iri vicinu,
pri placari lu barbaru Distinu.
   Ma chi! l'aspru, inflessibili tirannu,
ntra lu comuni affannu
timennu chi pietà nun lu vincissi,
s'arma lu pettu duru e azzariatu
di setti scogghi e setti vàusi alpini,
e all'oricchi vicini
accenni trona, fulmina e timpesti
pri 'un sintiri ddi vuci aspri e funesti.
   A tanta crudeltà freminu l'unni,
li venti e la marina ampia famigghia

Nici hopped with renewed joy,
staying always by my side.
   If my boat did not come back
with the others, I could see
Nici standing on a rock
as she spoke to wind and sea.
   And she would, to help me, summon
all the gods on salty waves
that the mighty ample Ocean
nurtured in its deepest caves.
   My deceiving destiny,
alas, changed in a dash.
And I lost this way boat, nets,
lover, friends, in just a flash.
   When I think upon that night
out of breath I sweat and cry.
A most cruel storm at sea
left me naked, high and dry.
   In an instant all did change;
utter poverty surrounds me;
the most blazing, sunlit day
as dark night just seems to be."

   This afflicted man complained this way,
while the waves, the winds and beach
listened carefully to him; the offspring
of Nereus[7], in their vibrant shiny shells,
pour out pearls with tears and sighs.
No one dares to make a sound:
their deep silence is, in fact,
their way to make his lamentations,
that Echo amplified throughout the caves,
rise high up to the heavens
and try to placate unbending Fate.
   But no! That harsh, inflexible tyrant,
who saw the common suffering,
fearing that pity could win over him,
shielded his steely chest with seven rocks,
and added seven alpine cliffs to boot,
and summoned thunder, lightning, storms
so those who were nearby could never hear
those woeful and ill-omened cries.
   Before such cruelty the waves rebelled,
the winds and the whole family on shore

85

si turba e si scumpigghia;
e intorbidati poi li vii profunni,
criscinu, comu munti supra munti;
disprezzannu li limiti e sotannu
supra lu scogghiu unn'era Polemuni,
l'agghiuttinu e lu levanu d'affannu:
ed in menzu a li vortici chiù cupi,
vuci s'alzau, chi flebili e dulenti
squarciau li negghi e dintra li sdirrupi
'ntunannu, ripiteva amaramenti:
"Pri l'infelici e li disgraziati
qualchi vota è pietà si l'ammazzati".

was troubled and upset;
and once the ocean depths were stirred,
they rose up like a mountain over mountains,
disdaining limits and they crashed on top
of the rock ledge where Polemuni was,
swallowing him and freeing him from pain,
and in the midst of those deep vortices,
a feeble and most woeful voice was heard,
tearing through fog and deep in the ravines,
repeating bitterly this sore refrain:
"For the unhappy and ill-omened men,
sometime it's merciful to murder them."

---

1. The Great Bear: The poet is referring to the *Ursa Major* Constellation which is always visible.

2. Castor and Pollux, the Divine Twins, were sons of Jove who seduced Leda by transforming himself into a beautiful swan. When they died, they were placed in the sky as the Gemini Constellation and they were believed to help in navigation.

3. The Pleiades, a group of seven stars. Before being transformed into stars by the gods, they were the seven daughters of Atlas.

4. Orion was known as the hunter before he was transformed into a constellation.

5. Proteus was a sea god, son of Neptune, who had the power to foretell the future, but to avoid providing such prophecies he assumed different shapes and forms.

6. Philomel: the nightingale, Cfr. "Martinu."

INVERNU
IDILIU VIII

Era già la staggiuni in cui lu suli,
guardannucci a traversu e a la sfuggita,
lassa li nostri campi abbandunati
a li chiù lunghi notti e a li riguri
di nivi e di jilati,
mentri in rigidu aspettu e minacciusu
l'aria, lu celu e li superbi venti
dichiaranu la guerra a li viventi.

Omini e bruti, feri, oceddi, insetti,
timidi e rannicchiati, o in mura, o in tani,
in cavi trunchi d'arvuli robbusti,
tra li vini di la matri terra,
in caverni, o tra grutti, o tra capanni
ni timinu li danni, e di rinforzi
e di ripari chiù tinaci e spissi
armanu li ricoveri e se stissi.

Cussì, mentri cui vivi e cui respira,
pri cautilarsi da lu denti acutu
di lu friddu nnimicu e di la fami,
spiega in propriu vantaggiu industria ed arti,
Muntànu, vecchiu saggiu e vigilanti,
sidutu in menzu di la sua capanna
tra li figghi, li nori e li garzuni,
s'appoja ad un vastuni, e alzannu un pocu
la facci veneranna: "Ottanta, dissi,
inverni, ugnali a chistu, annu concursu
a fari ch'in bianchizza la mia testa
cuntrasti cu li fardi di la nivi,
stisi supra sti munti a nui d'intornu;
mastru d'esperienza a la mia menti,
ogn'unu di sti inverni m'à insignatu
li mezzi a providiri a li fururi
di li soi successuri, acciocchì quannu
la terra, oppressa sutta nivi e jazzi,
nni nega tuttu, sterili e diserta,
binidicennu allura li ben sparsi
suduri e li passati mei travagghi,
mi riposu a lu focu, facenn'usu
di l' ammassati a li felici jorna
provisioni, chiù di gemmi e d' oru
utili e necessarii a la vita.

Winter
Idyll VIII

It was the season when the sun already
looking at us obliquely and for a short time,
leaves our meadows, and abandons them
to the much longer nights and to the rigors
of snow and freezing rains.
While looking ominous and threatening,
the air, the sky and the most awesome winds,
against all human beings war declare.

Men, animals, birds, wild beasts, and insects
timidly crouching in their walls or lairs
or in trunk cavities of mighty trees
or down inside the veins of mother earth,
or in some cave, a grotto or some huts
are fearful of the harm; all reinforce
with stronger, more resistant, thicker boards
and clothing their abodes and their own bodies.

This way, while all the folk who live and breathe,
make use of their own industry and art
to their gain so as to protect themselves
from the sharp tooth of the unfriendly cold
and hunger, a wise, vigilant, old man,
Muntànu, sitting in the middle of his hut,
together with his sons, their wives, and help,
leaning against a rod, and lifting up
his august face a bit, speaks thus: "Eighty winters,
the same as this, contributed to make
my head compete in whiteness with the drifts
and banks of snow upon these mountains peaks
surrounding us. A master of experience,
every winter has imparted to my mind
the necessary means with which to guard
against its fury and of those to come,
so when the land, oppressed by snow and ice,
denies us everything, all barren and
deserted, blessing the well-spent energy
and all the labor I performed before,
I can rest here beside the fire, and use
all the provisions that I, in happy days,
accumulated here, which are
more necessary and more useful to our lives
than precious gems or gold.

Chistu è lu tempu in cui, pròvidu e saggiu,
Giovi, chi tuttu regula e guverna,
la larga di l' està profusioni
cu li bisogni equilibrannu, esattu
riduci tuttu ntra lu so liveddu.

Putiti ora vidiri a quali oggettu
lu vecchiu (a cui lu tempu già passatu
è specchiu chi rifletti lu futuru),
cumula e sarva ... Grazii, dunqui, a Giovi
(chi a mia la menti, a vui reggi li forzi,
e li fatii di l' omu tra la terra
di beni abbunda). Già tuttu è provistu,
e a sustiniri lu crudili assaltu
di lu friddu e la fami, ànnu lu fenu
a zibbeffu li voi dintra li staddi;
li vacchi e li viteddi tra li grutti
ànnu la parti sua; pecuri e crapi
sunn'anchi a lu cuvertu, e pri ristoru,
ultra di la frascami e la ramagghia,
abbundanu di pampini e di pagghia;
a lu riddossu, sutta li pinnati,
scaccianu favi ed oriu li jumenti,
e lu sceccu, agnunatu in un cantiddu,
si rusica suliddu
di li putati vigni li sarmenti;
si cci à datu lu scagghiu a li palummi;
l'indieddi, lu gaddu e li gaddini
'mmenzu di lu vinazzu e lu fumeri,
ponnu a piaciri so scavuliari;
l'anatri e l'ochi l'ànnu a vidir'iddi:
ci scialanu tra l'acqui e li ciumari.

Ora pinsamu a nui: prima di tuttu
mittemu ligna sutta lu quadaru;
si fazzi allegra vampa, a riscaldari
l'acqua ch'è dintra, nui chi sem'attornu,
e la capanna tutta. Ora è lu tempu
ch'unu di li domestici animali
mora pri nui. Ma mi dirriti: Quali?
Lu voi, la vacca, l'asinu, la crapa
sù stati sempri a parti tuttu l' annu
di li nostri travagghi, e na gran parti
duvemu ad iddi di li nostri beni:
vi pari chi sarrìa riconoscenza
digna di nui na tali ricompenza?

This is the time when Jove[1,] who's provident
and wise, and regulates and rules all things,
the summer's large profusion balances
with what our needs require, reaching thus
a level that's appropriate and just.

You can now see what the real purpose was
for the old man (for whom the time gone by
is like a mirror that reflects the future)
to save and put away...Thanks thus to Jove
(who drives my mind and gives your strength to you
and who repays men's work upon the earth
with ample goods). Now all has been prepared;
we're ready to sustain the harsh assault
of winter and of hunger too: inside
the stables oxen have hay in abundance,
the cows and calves have theirs inside the caves;
while sheep and goats are sheltered underneath
a roof and feed on leaves and hay, as well
as other foliage and brushwood in quantity;
and underneath a roof the mares are well
protected and can munch at leisure on barley
and on fava beans; meanwhile, the donkey
sheltered in a corner by himself
chews upon the sarments from
the freshly pruned vineyards;
the doves have all been given seeds galore;
the turkeys with the rooster and the hens
are free to rummage through leftover mare
and through manure at will; the ducks
and geese can forage for themselves as they
splash joyfully in rivers and in ponds.

Let us now think about ourselves: and first
of all, let's put wood underneath the pot;
and light a cheerful flame so it will heat
the water in the pot, and us around it,
as well as the whole hut. The time has now
arrived for one of our domestic animals
to die for us. But, you will ask, which one?
The ox, the cow, the donkey and the sheep
have always been a part of our hard work
throughout the year and we all owe to them
a large part of the goods we have amassed.
Do you believe we would show gratitude
worthy of us with such a recompense?

Ma lu porcu? Lu porcu è statu chiddu
chi a li travagghi d'àutri ed a li nostri
è statu un ozziusu spettaturi;
anzi, abbusannu di li nostri curi,
mai s'è dignatu scotiri lu ciancu
da lu fangusu lettu, a proprii pedi
aspittannu lu cibbu, e cu arroganza.
nni sgrida di l'insolita tardanza.
Chistu, chi nun conusci di la vita
chi li suli vantaggi, e all'àutri lassa.
li vuccuni chiù amari, comu tutti
fussimu nati pri li soi piaciri;
chi immersu tra la vili sua pigrizzia,
stirannusi da l'unu e l'autru latu,
di li suduri d'autru s'è ingrassatu;
Sì, chistu mora e ingrassi a nui: lu porcu
lu vili, lu putruni …
sì, l'ingrassatu a costu d'àutru, mora".

Lettu già lu prucessu, e proferuta,
fra lu comuni applausu e la gioia,
la fatali sintenza, attapanciatu,
strascinatu, attaccatu, stramazzatu
fu lu porcu all'istanti; un gran cuteddu,
sprofundannusi dintra di la gula,
ci ricerca lu cori e ci disciogghi
lu gruppu di la vita; orrendi grida,
gemiti stripitusi, aria ed oricchi sfàrdanu,
e a li vicini e a li luntani,
ed anchi fannu sentiri a li stiddi
la grata nova di lu gran maceddu.
Saziu già di la straggi, lu cuteddu
apri, niscennu, spaziusa strata
a lu sangu ed a l'anima purcina:
l'unu, cadennu dintra lu tineddu,
prumetti sangunazzi; e l'àutra scappa
e si disperdi in aria tra li venti,
o, com'è fama, passa ad abitari
dintra lu corpu di un riccuni avaru
giacchì nun potti in terra ritruvari
chiù vili e schifiusu munnizzaru.

A li strepiti intantu, ed a li vuci,
e multu chiù a lu ciàuru di lu grassu,
l'abitanti di tutta dda cumarca,
e chiddi supra tutti, a cui lu sangu

What of the pig? The pig has been the one
who has been quite an indolent spectator
to the others' daily work, as well as to our own.
In fact, taking advantage of our concern
and care, the pig has never evene bothered
to lift his side off of the muddy bed on which
it spends its day, expecting us to bring
its food before its feet, chastising us
with arrogance for being late sometimes.
This beast who knows advantages alone
in life and leaves to others the most bitter
mouthfuls, as though we all were born
to serve his pleasures, who immersed in sloth,
just stretches from one side to the other,
getting fat on other folk's sweat;
yes, let the pig die and fatten us instead:
the pig, the foul and lazy beast…
Yes, let it die, the fat on others' sweat."

Having the trial read annnouncing the fatal
verdict, to universal praise and joy,
the pig was grabbed immediately, tied up
with ropes, dragged in and stunned.
An awesome knife was sunk into its throat,
to seek its heart, and sever its life knot;
the horrid screams and noisy shrieks of pain
resounded in the air and in the ears of those
who lived in the vicinity and far
away, even to the stars above, announcing
the welcome news about the awesome slaughter.
The knife, already sated with the massacre,
opened, as it emerged, an avenue
for the pig's blood and for its porcine soul.
The former was collected in a pail,
and promised some black pudding, while the latter
escaped and was dispersed by wind in air,
or, as the legend says, it went to dwell
inside the body of an avaricious,
wealthy man, as it could not discover
a filthier and more disgusting garbage
dump here on earth.

At all the rowdiness and the loud yelling,
but more for the aroma of the fat,
all the inhabitants in the vicinity
and those especially in whom the blood

rivugghi ntra li vini (o per età virdi,
o pri focu d'amuri, chi li jeli
renni tepidi e grati), allegri tutti
concurrinu: giacchì costumi anticu
fu sempri, e comu sagru conservatu,
chi, quannu un porcu celebri si scanna,
si fa festa comuni a la capanna.

Veni ammugghiata ntra na saja russa
la biunna Clori, e da li stritti pieghi
l'occhiu azzurru traluci, com'un raggiu
di luna 'mmenzu a nuvula sfardata.
Melibeu l'accumpagna; e ntra la facci
sicci leggi la gioia, in parti figghia
di chidda chi a li cori di l'astanti
Clori purtatu avìa cu la sua vista.

Veni la vrunittedda inzuccarata
Joli, chi ad ogni passu, ad ogni gestu
pinci na grazia nova. Un virdi pannu
ci gira pri la testa, ed abbassannu
s'unisci cu lu blù di la fodedda,
chi, spinta pri li fanghi, e sustinuta
da lu vrazzu sinistru, si raccogghi
tutta ad un latu in morbidu volumi.
Dameta c'è vicinu; lu so cori
penni da l'occhi d'idda, e si nutrisci
di puri affetti, comu la gentili
irvuzza nata supra di li rocchi,
chi s'apri a la ruggiada matutina.

Veni di l'occhiu nivuru e brillanti
Licori, la grassotta; allegra in facci
ci ridi primavera, ad onta ancora
di l'invernu chi regna ntra li campi.
Pannu nun soffri la rusciana testa,
nè saja, nè autru impacciu, eccettu un raru
suttilissimu velu, ch'è chiuttostu
trastullu di lu ventu chi riparu.
Tirsi c'è appressu, comu un agnidduzzu
a cui la pasturedda ammustra e proi
tennira irvuzza cota frisca frisca
cu li proprii soi manu gentili.

Filli ed Ergastu, sutta un palandranu,
chi fa tettu e pinnata a tutti duj,
juncinu, e li pasturi tutti intornu
pri cuntintizza battinu li manu.

was boiling in their veins (because of youth
or flames of love, which take the bite from frost
and make it mild) all in good cheer joined in;
for that has been an ancient custom that
we have preserved as sacred through all time,
that when an awesome pig we aim to slaughter,
a common feast is held inside the hut.

The blond haired Clori came, whose head was covered
with a red shawl and through its narrow folds,
her blues eye shone just like a Moon beam
when it appears through broken clouds.
Melibeus was with her and on his face
you could read the joy that is in part a kin
of the same joy brought to the hearts of all
when Clori first appeared before the group.

Jole, the young, adorable brunette,
was there, who with each gesture and each step
she took a novel charm displayed. She wore
a green cloth all around her head and when
she lowered it, it blended with the azure tint
of her skirt, which held by the hem with her l
eft arm, was pushed and gathered on one side
to form a soft and fluffy volume.
Dameta was near her and his heart pinned
upon her eyes and nourishes itself
with pure affection, like the tender grass
that is born on a cliff amog the rocks
that opens up to welcome morning dew.

Licori, the plump one, with black and dazzling,
eyes came. All full of cheer, upon her face
spring was all smiles to spite the winter time
that still was ruling in the countryside.
Her reddish head did not make use of scarves
or shawls, or other bothersome accessory,
except a rare and very thin veil which
gave pleasure to the wind more than protection.
Tirsi was next to her, just like a little lamb,
to whom the little shepherdess hands out
some sweet and tender grass she has just plucked
with her own gentle hands.

Under a mantle which acted as a roof
and cover for the two of them, Ergàstu
and Filli then arrived and all around
the shepherds started clapping hands with joy.

Filli pr'affruntu cala l'occhi, e in facci
senti na vampa, e fora ci scannìa
'mmenzu a lu biancu, comu in orienti
la 'nsunnacchiata spusa di Tituni,
Cussì di tempu in tempu a la capanna
autri e poi autri ninfi cu pasturi
vannu supravinennu, comu appuntu
quannu metti a spirari maistrali,
chi si vidinu in funnu a l'orizzonti
ad una, a dui, a tri iri assummannu
nuvuli, e dipoi nuvuli, e dipoi
nuvuli arreri, e nuvuli d'appressu.

    Già s'accordanu bifari e sampugni,
e flauti e ciarameddi; 'mmenzu a tutti
sbulazza l' alligria; da cori in cori
si rifletti e ripigghia, e si tramanna,
sempri multiplicannusi e criscennu.

    Mutti, induvini, scherzi, jochi e danzi
scurrinu supra l'uri destinati
a preparari e a cociri li cibi;
già la tavula è lesta; ni dà signu
Muntànu cu lu scòtiri, ridennu,
na campana di voi: battinu tutti
li manu; e poi cu sauti e strambotti
vannu a sediri e mettinu a manciari.

    Da principiu lu briu cedi a la fami,
primu istintu fra tutti, e nun si senti
chi un rumuri di piatti e di cannati,
e certu surdu traficu di denti;
a pocu a pocu, sulitaria e bassa,
gira qualchi parola, accumpagnata
di quasi un menzu scàccanu o d'un sgrignu.
Comu ntra lu spaccari di l'alburi,
'mmenzu di li silenzii ruggiadusi,
si fa sintiri qualchi rauca nota
chi una lòdana azzarda sutta vuci;
ma quannu poi si vesti l'orizzonti
di purpura, e poi d'oru, allegri tutti
turdi, merri, riiddi e calandruni,
e passari e cardiddi e capifuschi
rumpinu a tutta lena, e cu li canti
vannu assurdannu l' aria e li chianuri;
tali dintra li ninfi e li pasturi,
sudisfatta la fami, l' alligria

Filli cast down her eyes and, blushing, felt
a flame that glowed against the whiteness
of her face, like the sleepy bride of Tithonous[2]
when dawn arrives to light the eastern sky.
So then, from time to time, inside the hut,
some other nymphs and shepherds kept arriving,
as happens when in fact the Northwest Wind
begins to blow and one can start to see
on the horizon some little clouds amassing,
one at a time, at first, then two, then three,
and then more clouds start to accumulate,
and after that, some other clouds appear.

    'Twas time to tune the fifes and the reed pipes,
the flutes and the bagpipes. Good cheer was buzzing
all around the room, it went from heart to heart,
it was transmitted and passed on to all,
ever increasing, multiplying steadily.

    Witty remarks, jokes, riddles, games and dances
filled the few hours that they spent
in preparation and in cooking of the food;
the table was already set, Muntànu gave
the sign by shaking with a smile a cow's
bell, which evoked a general applause,
as everyone with leaps and funny jokes
went to sit down and then began to eat.

    At the beginning the good cheer gave way
to appetite, which our first instinct is,
and all that you could hear was a loud noise
of clashing dishes, moving of carafes,
combined with a dull trafficking of teeth.
In time, a few soft voices were perceived
accompanied by some restrained guffaw and sneer.
As when the dawn is breaking in the midst
of silences imbued with dews, you hear
a few half-hearted raucous cries, emitted
softly by some skylark, and when the sky
is dressed with purple first and then with gold
all joyfully the thrushes, ravens, larks,
kinglets, and sparrows, finches and blackcaps,
break silence with great energy and deafen
the air and valleys with their cheerful song;
that's how among the shepherds and the nymphs,
once they had satisfied their hunger, cheer
took the first place and sat upon the throne;

pigghia lu primu locu e sedi in tronu;
e pirchì fora 'nforzanu li nivi,
e chiù di chiù lu tempu va 'ncalzannu,
pri nun pinsari a guai, peni ed affanni,
si duna manu a un vinu di quattr'anni.

Già la chiacchiara 'ngrana; a tutta lena
'ntisu o nun 'ntisu, ogn'unu parracia;
si rumpi pr'accidenti qualchi piattu,
pr'accidenti si 'mmestinu cannati,
e giranu d'intornu allegramenti
specii, muttetti, brinnisi e risati.

Già li cani s'azzuffanu pri l'ossa:
unu arrizza lu pilu, autru lu schinu
si torci com'un arcu, àutru abbassatu
sgrigna li denti e cu l'occhi di bracia
mmurmura amminazzannu. Eccu la guerra:
tavula, piatti, tiàni, carrabbi
minaccianu disordini e ruina.
Passiddà! Passiddà! gridanu tutti;
e fratantu, guardannusi li gammi,
cu li spinci o ritira ammanu ammanu
e l'àutri poi, mittennusi a lu largu,
si vidinu li visti di luntanu.

Sciota accussì la tavula, s'intriccia
grata armunia di flauti e sampugni;
s'invitanu li Musi, e l'occhi intantu
di tutti sù ad Uraniu, a cui, durmennu,
l'api chiù voti supra di lu labbru
ci fabbricaru vrischi di ducizza.
Iddu fratantu, teneru, amurusu,
guarda Nici chi, zarca e 'ncripidduta,
si strinci tra li panni e si cci agguccia,
comu la viiuledda tra li campi,
chi scanzannu la barbara jilata,
'mmenzu pampina e pampina s'ammuccia.
Milli affetti ad un puntu lu pasturi
scòtinu, e nun putennu tra lu cori
tiniri a frenu l'amurusu affannu,
in tali accenti prorumpìu cantannu.

Uraniu canta:

Vidi, Amuri, ch'è 'ngridduta,
comu trema la mia Nici!

and as outside the snow was falling heavier,
and weather was then worsening some more;
in order not to think of all their woes,
their struggling and their suffering,
they broke out wine that was four years of age.

Already conversation's going strong; they are
all chattering with zest, heard or unheard;
some dishes shatter accidentally,
and accidentally carafes are bumped,
while witty sayings, toasts, cajoling, laughs,
go all around the room most cheerfully.

The dogs now start to fight for the bones.
One's hair is standing, another has it back
arched like a bow, another crouching snarls,
showing its fangs, with eyes like burning embers,
and menacing with growls. The fight begins.
The table and the dishes, pots and carafes
are all in danger of destruction.
"Get out of here! Get out!" They yell as one.
Looking out for their legs, meanwhile, some lift
them out, while others quickly pull them in,
and others still remove themselves from harm
watching the goings on from far away.

Having they cleared the table, they begin
a pleasing harmony of flutes and reed pipes.
The Muses they invite and eyes converge
meanwhile upon Uranus, whom the bees
more than one time, as he was sound asleep,
placed on his lips of sweetness a good measure.
Meanwhile with tenderness and love, he looks
at Nici, who quite pale and shivering,
now wrapped herself and huddled in her clothes,
just like the violet that in the field,
in order to avoid the cruel frost
seeks out a hiding place between the leaves.
A thousand feelings stir inside the shepherd
and at a certain moment, when he felt
unable to restrain his heart, he starts
of his anxieties of love to sing:

Uraniu Sings:

"Love, you see, how my Nici
is all cold and shivering!

Ah! succurri l'infelici,
lu to focu porta ccà.

    Vidi comu di li manu
ni fa un pugnu e poi lu ciata,
pri cacciari la jilata,
ch'ostinata si sta ddà.

    Senti comu tramuntana
ciuscia, grida ed amminazza!
Lu so friddu, chi n'agghiazza,
veni, Amuri, e calma tu.

    Senti, oh diu! comu li grandini
li canali strantulìanu!
Li dui poli, ohimè! trunìanu,
la timpesta strinci chiù.

    Oh! lu lampu!... 'Un ti scantari,
Nici mia, nun c'è paura,
contr'un'alma bedda e pura
trona e fulmini 'un ci nn'è.

    E si un tempu cu Semeli
Giovi fici stu delittu,
fu ingannatu, fu costrittu,
ni chiancìu turnatu in se.

    Si l'invernu 'un ti rispetta,
nun sì sula, o Nici amata;
sutta l'orrida jilata
la natura oppressa sta.

    Oh! si vidi la muntagna,
tutta è bianca di un culuri,
à canciatu cu l'orruri
la sua prima maistà.

    Scapiddati e senza frundi
li grand'arvuli ramuti,
ntra li trunchi arripudduti
ci ànnu nivi a tinghi-tè.

    La vaddata e la scoscisa
risa è sterili e infelici;
chiù 'un ci canta la pirnici,
'n'ocidduzzu chiù nun c'è.

    Dda funtana, unni l'estati
rinfriscavamu l'arduri,
l'unni soi gnilati e duri
scarzarari chiù nun pò.

    Cu li radichi a lu celu,
lu gran pignu è in terra stisu,

Ah! please succor her and bring
your own fire over here!

    You can see how she has made
of her hand a closed, tight fist
and she breathes to chase the frost
that remains there stubbornly.

    Listen how the north wind blows,
how it threatens us and howls!
Its cold air is freezing us.
Please, Love, find us some relief!

    Listen, God, how the hail shakes
the roof tiles upon the roof.
The poles' thunder offer proof
that the storm is more intense.

    Oh the lightning ! Don't you worry,
my dear Nici, have no fear.
For a soul so true, sincere,
thunder, lightning pose no threat.

    And if once with Semele[3],
Jove committed this offense,
he was fooled and forced, but once
he regained himself, he wept.

    If the winter won't respect you,
Nature, too, lies quite oppressed
underneath the horrid frost.
Nici dear, you're not alone.

    Oh, if you the mountain see
that displays one color, white,
its majestic and true sight
has become a horrid place!

    The great trees with many limbs
wear no cover and no leaves.
On their twisted limbs they have
a thick coverlet of snow.

    All the valleys and the cliffs
have been made all sterile, bare.
There's no partridge singing there.
No more sweet birds can be found.

    And the fountain where in summer
we found solace from the heat,
cannot free its hardened waves
from the prison of the ice.

    With its roots to face the sky,
on the ground lays the great pine,

duvi un tempu ci avìa incisu,
Nici mia, lu nomu to.

Urvicati ntra la nivi
li capanni a lu straventu,
si distinguinu a gran stentu
pri lu fumu chi c'è ddà.

Ddà vicinu ad un tizzuni
l'anzianu pastureddu
stimpunìa cu dd'aliteddu
la cadenti fridda età.

La cumpagna a lu so latu,
cu li gigghia affumicati,
di li tempi trasannati
vanta sempri la virtù.

La lanuta rocca, intantu,
va smagrennu e scinni jusu,
e li cianchi di lu fusu
vannu unciànnu sempri chiù.

Ma la figghia spintulidda
sta affacciata a la campagna;
e l'amanti, chi si vagna,
ricunforta comu pò.

L'aspru invernu rigurusu
pr'iddi è placidu e clementi:
granni Amuri onnipotenti
stu purtentu è tuttu to.

Nici mia, chi pensi forsi
di passari l'invirnata,
sula, fridda e scumpagnata,
ntra sti jeli chi ci sù?

Nè t'incrisci di te stissa?
Nè di mia ti pari forti?
E lu soffri? E lu cumporti?
Tantu cruda sarai tu?

Ntra l'angusta mia capanna,
no, nun trovi meli e raschi,
si purtaru li burraschi
li spiranzi di l'està,

Puru ddà ci truvirai,
a tia sula cunsagrati,
li crapetti appena nati,
e una stipa ch'è a mità.

Lu tributu poi chiù granni,
lu rigalu finu e veru,

on which I your name and mine,
my dear Nici, once had carved.

Buried underneath the snow,
though protected from the gusts,
all the huts could be seen just
from the smoke that rose from them.

Seated by a burning log,
the old shepherd barely could,
on that meager burning wood,
bear his faltering old age.

His companion by his side
with her brows with smoke all stained,
her old virtues still maintained
of the years that have gone by.

And meanwhile, the woolly spool
has grown thinner, moving down
while the spindle sides have grown
and get thicker ever more.

But her daughter nearly grown,
looks out to the countryside
toward her lover who's outside
and she helps him as she can.

The severe and noxious winter
for them is mild and serene.
O omnipotent, great love,
this portent is wrought by you.

My sweet Nici, do you think
you can spend, cold and alone,
and without companion
these harsh, freezing winter days?

For yourself you've no regrets
and for my sake you don't care,
and its burdens you will bear?
Are you then so harsh and mean?

In my little, narrow hut
no, you won't find milk and honey.
The hopes of the summertime
have been swept away by storms.

Nonetheless, you will find there
young kids born just days before,
which I held for you in store
and a cupboard half way full.

But the greatest of my tributes
the most fine, the gift most true

è d'un cori assai sinceru,
tuttu amuri e tuttu to.

    Deh! gradiscilu, e ti juru
pri li summi Dei felici,
ch'ogni grutta dirrà: Nici!
Nici sempri eu cantirò.

is the heart I offer you,
all in love and yours alone.

    Please accept it. I now swear
on the happy, supreme Gods
each cave will sing Nici's name
and I'll ever do the same."

----

1. Jove: The Roman name for Zeus. He is the father of the Greek gods.
2. Tithonous: This is a reference to Aurora, the goddess of dawn, who fell in love with Tithonous, a mortal, and married him granting him immortality. He did not ask for the gift of youth as well and he grew old and decrepit. He begged Aurora to change his fate but as he was already immortal she changed him into a grasshopper.
3. Semele: The daughter of Cadmus, Semele was loved by Jove who promised to grant her any wish she wanted. She expressed the desire to see him in all his glory and unable to go back on his word, Jove appeared to her brighter than the sun incinerating her.

Selezioni di *La Lirica*

Selections from the Lyrical Poems

I
LU VIAGGIU RETROGRADU

I
The Retrograde Journey

L'innatu Geniu,
chi mi strascina,
dissi acchiappànnumi:
"Orsù, camina".

  Ed ingulfannusi
tra li sfunnati
abbissi e vortici
di età passati,

  in parti rampica,
in parti affunna
tra na voragini
di obliu profunna.

  Ddà spissu incontrasi
(oh incontri grati!)
cu li gran Genii
di chiddi etati,

  chi quasi ciàcculi
brillanti e chiari,
vennu ddi tenebri
a rischiarari.

  In aria Pindaru
vidi e stupisci,
cerca ragghiuncirlu,
ma ci spirisci.

  Scopri la tenera
Saffu, chi spira
ciammi, ch'infocanu
anchi la lira.

  Scontra tra un sequitu
di grazii pronti
lu lepidissimu
Anacreonti;

  di allegri giuvini,
di Ninfi allatu
'ntricciannu brinnisi
menzu 'ngriciatu:

  "Nostra delizia,
(miu Geniu dici)
salvi, e in ogni epoca
regna felici;

The innate Genius
who's dragging me
said, "Come, let's walk!"
as he grabbed me,

  And made his way
into the vast
chasms and depths
of epochs past.

  He climbed in part,
in part descending,
into the heart
of deep oblivion.

  There one encounters
(o joyful meetings)
the greatest geniuses
of those epochs,

  who like real beacons
that brightly shine
those dark abodes
illuminate.

  He saw surprised
Pindar[1] in air,
he reached for him
but he just vanished.

  He saw the tender
Sappho[2], whose flames
even the lyre
will set on fire.

  He met some graces
who came behind him,
the most amusing
Anacreon[3],

  Sharing some toasts,
halfway tanked-up
with cheering youths
and nymphs by him.

  "Our own delight,
(my Genius said)
greetings, in every era,
rule happily.

no, non t'invidiu
trastulli e danzi;
ma lu to seculu,
li circustanzi".

    Dici, e poi seguita
lu so viaggiu
duvi risplendiri
vidi un gran raggiu.

    Eccu Teocritu,
chi di Geruni
A la grand'epoca
'ntriccia curuni.

    O Cignu amabili,
pri cui fastusa
scurri la sicula
fonti Aretusa!

    Li trummi cedanu;
cui d'idd'incugna
a lu gran meritu
di tua sampugna?

    Chiddi decantanu
straggi e bravura,
chista la simplici
bella natura.

    Oh pazzi! E cridinu
li menti umani
felicitarisi
d'idda luntani!

    Dici, e incaminasi
pri oscuri vii
di Dafni all'epoca,
cara a li Dii;

    lu trova in placida
silva tranquilla,
unn'acqua un vausu
limpida stilla;

    ci pendi tacita
sampugn'allatu
lu cani all'alitu
ci sta curcatu;

    di attornu pascinu
vacchi infiniti,
l'echi ribumbanu
di li muggiti;

No, I don't envy
your games, your dances;
but circumstances
of your great age."

    He said resuming
his journey where
he saw a shiny
and wondrous ray.

    Behold Theocritus[4]
who's weaving crowns
to the great era
of king Geron[5].

    O loving Swan
for whom in Sicily
the famous fountain flows
of Arethusa![6]

    Let trumpets cease;
which one of them
can we compare
to your reed pipe?

    Those sing of carnage
and of great skills,
but this one sings
of simple nature.

    Oh insane ones!
Do human minds
think they can be
glad far from it?

    He spoke and walked
along dark ways
to Daphne's [7]days,
dear to the Gods.

    He found him in
a peaceful wood
where from a cliff
clear water fell.

    His reed pipe hung
by his side mute;
his dog stretched out
next to his breath;

    around him cows
grazed in great numbers,
their bellowing
reverberating far;

li prati ridinu	the fields were smiling
sutta li curi	under the care
e lu bon' ordini	and ministry
di li pasturi;	of some sheepherders;
e intantu sedinu	and in the meantime
ddà spinsirati	Justice and Peace
Paci e Giustizia	sat without worry
stritti abbrazzati.	in tight embrace.
Ccà juntu fermasi	Once in this place,
miu Geniu, e dici:	My genius said,
"o grata imagini	"O pleasing image
di età felici	of happy days!
S'in mia t'insinui	If you're inside me
cu tali ciarmi	with so much charm,
com'è possihili	how can I ever
da tia staccarmi?"	let go of you?"

---

1. Pindar: Greek poet (520-442 BC) who celebrated the victories of athletes in the Olympic Games.
2. Sappho: Greek poetess from Lesbos who lived between the VII and VI century BC.
3. Anacreon: Greek lyrical poet (VII Century BC) from Ionia. Meli was called the new Anacreon.
4. Theocritus: Cfr. Sonnet II of Buccolica
5. Geron: One of the tyrants of Siracusa.
6. Arethusa: Aretusa was a nymph loved by the river god Alpheus. To escape the god she begged her father to change her into a stream and she flowed under the Ionian sea from Greece to Siracusa. Alpheus, however, crossed the sea and their waters were mixed in Siracusa.
7. Daphne: A nymph pursued by Apollo. The gods changed her into a laurel and Apollo adopted the tree as this symbol.

ll
LA NASCITA DI AMURI

Da la vaga Citeria,
non tra stentu e tra duluri,
ma tra risu ed alligria
a lu munnu nacqui Amuri.

Quantu nicu, tantu beddu,
e si ben proporzionatu,
chi parìa cameu di aneddu
di un valuri smisuratu.

Li Dei tutti a stu portentu
inarcavanu li gigghia,
cuntimplannu ad occhiu attentu
sta stupenda meravigghia.

Lu stupuri nun li lassa,
anzi chiù si avanza e crisci,
pirchì chiù chi tempu passa
lu bambinu sminuisci.

Era inutili lu tantu
latti ad iddu; di lu velu
scurrìa fora tuttu quantu,
e lassau na striscia in celu.

La Dia mesta e scunsulata
chi lu figghiu ia mancannu,
a lu Fatu s'è indrizzata,
sta prighera presentannu:

"A chi darmi un beddu figghiu
si mi manca natu appena?
Suggeriscimi un cunsigghiu.
pri nutrirlu e darci lena?"

Rispus'iddu: "Si a la luci
n'àutru partu purtirai,
quannu chistu darà vuci
l'àutru crisciri vidrai".

Sta ricetta, mi crid'iu,
non fu pr'idda amara tantu ...
Basta, l'ordini eseguiu,
e l'affari iu d'incantu.

Eccu in fini fu avvirata
di lu Fatu la sintenza,
di una figghia s'è sgravata,
chi chiamau: Corrispondenza.

A lu nasciri di chista

II
The Birth of Love

From the shores of fair Cythera,[1]
not from struggling or from woe,
but in cheerfulness and laughter
love was born unto the world.

He was small as he was handsome
and so well proportioned too,
that he seemed to be a cameo
on a priceless golden jewel.

All the gods at such a sight
raised their eyebrows in dismay,
contemplating all absorbed
this astonishing display.

Their amazement did not end,
and indeed in time increased,
all because as months went by
the child's size instead decreased.

All the milk they gave to him
seemed in vain; for all would leak
from his velum in the sky,
leaving there a milky streak.[2]

The poor goddess was distraught
as she saw her child get smaller.
To the Fates she turned her thought
and addressed them with this prayer:

"Why give me a handsome boy
just to let him fade away?
Please advise me on the way
I can give him strength to grow."

"If another child you'll bear,
you will see with your own eyes,"
they replied, "this one will grow
when the other one first cries."

To my thinking, such advice
was not difficult to heed.
So the order she obeyed
and succeeded in her deed.

So the sentence of the fates
in the end was all fulfilled.
She gave birth to a sweet daughter
and she called her Correspondence.

At her birth the little cupid

pigghiau ciatu lu puttinu,
e quant'idda forza acquista,
l'àutru crisci e fa caminu.

   Già ci spuntanu l'aluzzi,
chi s'impinnanu a momenti,
poi, niscennu li manuzzi,
vola in aria e fa portenti.

started growing normally
and, as she acquired more strength,
he made progress equally.

   Little wings began to sprout,
which grew feathers bye and bye.
Grabbing courage with his hands,
he made marvels in the sky.

---

1. Cythera: Venus, the goddess of Love, was venerated in this island.
2. Milky streak: An allusion to the formation of the Milky Way.

III
LI CAPIDDI

Chi tirribiliu!
chi serra-serra!
deh curri, o Veneri,
sparti sta guerra!
   Quindici milia
cechi Amurini,
tutti si 'ngrignanu,
fannu ruini.
   Cui punci e muzzica,
cu' abbrucia ed ardi,
cui tira ciacculi,
cu' abbiia dardi.
   Ntra lu spartirisi
li cori prisi,
vinniru a nasciri
sti gran cuntisi.
   A sta notizia
la Dia di Gnidu
curri, precipita,
ittannu un gridu:
   "Ed è pussibili.
chi 'un c'è momentu
di stari 'nzemmula
tanticchia abbentu!
   Giacchì nun giuvanu
menzi e riguardi,
vi farrò a vidiri,
muli bastardi ..."
   Dissi, e 'un truvànnucci
megghiu riparu,
l'afferra e carcera
tutti di paru;
   poi cu finissimi
fila indorati
l'ali chi sbattinu,
teni 'nchiaccati ...
   Deh! ferma, a Veneri,
vidi ca sbagghi,
pirchì voi crisciri
li mei travagghi?
   Lu miu martiriu

III
The Hair

Oh what turmoil!
Quite an uproar!
Please, Venus come,
to end this war.
   Fifteen thousand
blind Cupids are
causing mayhem,
heard from afar.
   Some burn and seethe,
some prick, some sting,
some arrows throw,
some torches fling.
   When they fought over
the captured hearts,
the harsh dispute
had its sad start.
   When Cnidus' Goddess[1]
heard of the news,
she quickly ran
not so amused.
   "But is it possible
that we can't share
a moment's peace
when you're all there?
   Since kindly ways
can't be the rule,
now I'll show you,
you bastard mules..."
   she spoke. Not knowing
how she'd prevail,
she locked them all
inside a jail.
   Then she proceeded
their wings to hold
with very thin
threads made of gold.
   Please Venus, stop!
You are not right.
Why do you want
to grow my plight?
   Was my travail

Giovanni Meli

ti parìa pocu,	so slight and tame,
vulisti agghiunciri	you put more wood
ligna a lu focu?	upon the flame?
Chisti chi liganu	These threads you used
l'aluzzi ad iddi,	their wings to block
di Nici amabili	are the most lovable,
su li capiddi.	sweet Nici's locks.
Dintra li bucculi	Those little cherubs,
(ohimè, chi arduri!)	look how they swing
comu svulazzanu	inside the ringlets
li nichi Amuri!	(oh how love stings!)
Parti s'aggiranu,	Without a pause
privi di paci,	some quickly run
di la sua scufia	into her net,
ntra lu 'ntilàci,	out of her bun.
cui di li Zefiri	Some from the zephyrs
cerca ristoru,	wanting surcease,
sauta e fa smoviri	the golden threads
li fila d'oru.	move through with ease.
Parti si curcanu	Others recline
supra lu coddu,	upon her neck
ch'è un finu avoliu	that's like a fine,
pulitu e moddu;	soft ivory.
e di ddà mannanu	And they hurl lightnings
saitti e lampi;	and darts from there.
ahi! cui pò reggiri	Who can resist
ntra tanti vampi!	such fierce warfare?
Ah! vinni a chioviri	Ah this harsh war
in mia sta guerra!	rained in my heart.
Stu tirribiliu!	Oh what uproar!
Stu serra-serra!	Oh what mayhem!

----

1. Cnidus' Goddess: Cnidus was an ancient city in Asia Minor which had a famous temple dedicated to Venus.

IV
LV GIGGHIU

La benna lacera,
spinnatu tuttu,
chiancìa Cupidini
a chiantu ruttu;
  rucculiàvasi
pallidu e zarcu:
"Me matri Veneri
mi rumpiu l'arcu!"

  "Oh! beni stìjati
(ci dissi allura)
tu sì diavulu,
non criatura;
  'ncrepati, ruditi;
sì, ci aju gustu,
almenu termina,
speddi stu sustu."

  A st'improperii
s'ingatta e taci;
ma dintra è torbidu,
nun trova paci.
  Posa lu guvitu
supra di un ciuri,
finci di dormiri,
ma 'un dormi Amuri.

  Poi tuttu 'nzemmula,
pigghiannu ciatu,
grida: "Vittoria,
l'arcu è truvatu;
  l'arcu infallibili,
chi va pri milli,
e l'adorabili
gigghiu di Filli".

  Dissi, e di un subitu
scuccau un dardu,
si 'ntisi un murmuru:
Ahi! ahi! com'ardu!

IV
The Brow

The little Cupid
to tears gave way,
with torn blindfold,
and feathers frayed.
  He kept on wailing,
distraught and gray:
"My mother Venus
my bow destroyed!"

  "It serves you right
(she scolded him).
You are a devil,
not cherubim.
  So seethe and fret,
I say with joy,
so this upset
will end at last."

  At these reproaches,
he was not pleased;
he sat there brooding
and without peace.
  He placed his elbow
upon a flower
and feigned to sleep,
but Love can't sleep.

  Then all at once,
catching his breath,
he yelled: "I won!"
I found my bow:
  the flawless bow
that's good as gold
is the adorable
eyebrow of Filli."

  He spoke and quickly
let a dart fly.
There was a whisper:
"Ahi, how I sigh!"

Many of these odes were written or inspired by ladies of the Palermo aristocracy. This one was written in 1777 for Maria Sigismonda Sieripepoli, widow of Carlo Ventimiglia, marquis of Regiovanni.

V
L'OCCHI

Ucchiuzzi niuri
si taliati
facti cadiri
casi e citati;
  jeu, muru debuli
di petri e taiu,
cunsidiratilu
si allura caju!
  Sia arti maggica,
sia naturali,
in vui risplendinu
biddizzi tali,
  chi tutti 'nzimmula
cumponnu un ciarmu
capaci a smoviri
lu stissu marmu.
  À tanta grazia
ssa vavaredda,
quannu si situa
menza a vanedda,
  chi, veru martiri
di lu disiu,
cadi in deliquiu
lu cori miu!
  Si siti languidi,
ucchiuzzi cari,
cui ci pò reggiri?
cui ci pò stari?
  Mi veni un piulu,
chi m'assutterra,
l'alma si spiccica,
lu senziu sferra.
  Poi cui pò esprimiri
lu vostru risu,
ucchiuzzi amabili,
s'è un paradisu?
  Lu pettu s'aggita,
lu sangu vugghi,
sù tuttu spinguli,
sù tuttu agugghi.
  Ma quantu lagrimi,

V
The Eyes

Black loving eyes,
if you look coy,
houses and cities
you will destroy.
  I'm but a wall
of stone and sand;
if I should crumble,
please understand.
  It may be magic
or nature's way,
but many beauties
you do array,
  and all together
they form a charm
that my defenses
all but disarm.
  Such winning graces
have your bright eyes
when they conspire
in playful guise
  that a true martyr
from its desire
my heart so wretched
may soon expire.
  If you are languid,
dear, gentle eyes,
who can continue,
who can just gaze?
  Such woe I suffer
it makes me groan,
gone is my reason,
my soul's undone.
  Who can express,
enchanting eyes,
to show your laughter?
It's paradise.
  My pressure rises
and my head spins.
I am all needles,
I am all pins.
  How many tears,

106

ucchiuzzi amati,
ma quantu spasimi
chi mi custati!
  Ajàti làstima
di lu miu statu:
vaja, riditimi,
ca sù sanatu!

beloved eyes,
must I still weep?
How many sighs?
  For my sad state
to pity yield.
Come now, start smiling,
and I'll be healed!

This ode was probably inspired by Lucia Migliaccio, duchess of Floridia, who became king Ferdinand's morganatic wife. The first eight lines were translated by Goethe who visited Palermo around the time when the ode became famous.

VI
LU LABBRU

Dimmi, dimmi, apuzza nica:
unni vai cussì matinu?
Nun c'è cima chi arrussica
di lu munti a nui vicinu;

Trema ancora, ancora luci
la ruggiada ntra li prati:
duna accura nun ti arruci
l'ali d'oru dilicati!

Li ciuriddi durmigghiusi
ntra li virdi soi buttuni
stannu ancora stritti e chiusi
cu li testi a pinnuluni.

Ma l'aluzza s'affatica!
Ma tu voli e fai caminu!
Dimmi, dimmi, apuzza nica,
unni vai cussì matinu?

Cerchi meli? E s'iddu è chissu,
chiudi l'ali e 'un ti straccari;
ti lu 'nzignu un locu fissu,
unni ài sempri chi sucari:

lu conusci lu miu amuri,
Nici mia di l'occhi beddi?
Ntra ddi labbri c'è un sapuri
na ducizza chi mai speddi;

ntra lu labbru culuritu
di lu caru amatu beni
c'è lu meli chiù squisitu:
suca, sucalu, ca veni.

Ddà ci misi lu Piaciri
lu so nidu ncilippatu,
pi adiscari, pi rapiri
ogni cori dilicatu.

A lu munnu 'un ci pò dari
una sorti chiù filici
chi vasari, chi sucari
li labbruzza a la mia Nici.

VI
The Lips

Tell me, tell me buzzing bee,
what so early do you seek?
There's no redness yet appearing
on the nearby mountain peak.

And along the field the dew
is aglow, still quivering.
Oh, take care you do not wet
your most dainty golden wing.

Pretty flowers, sleepy-eyed,
are still snug and tightly closed
in their verdant buds abiding,
all with heads that droop and doze.

But your gentle wing is weary;
yet you soar, in air you streak.
Tell me, tell me, buzzing bee,
what so early do you seek?

If it's honey you desire
fold your wings, strive no more.
I will show you one sure realm
where you'll find enough to store.

Don't you know my love,
my Nici with the lovely eyes?
On her lips such flavor rests;
it's of sweetness a great prize.

On the lips incarnadine
of my own beloved joy,
there is honey most divine:
kiss them sweetly and enjoy.

For it is right there that pleasure
hid its honey-covered nest
as to capture with this treasure
every heart of love possessed.

In the world there cannot be
a more joyful destiny
than to kiss and suck upon
the sweet lips of my own Nici.

This ode was translated into German by J. Herder, and it has the curious distinction, according to Giorgio Santangelo, of being the only Italian poem translated into Finnish. The motif of honey residing on the beloved's lips goes back to Theocritus and is used by many poets, but none with Meli's gracefulness.

VII
LA VUCCA

Ssi capiddi e biundi trizzi
sù jardini di biddizzi,
cussì vaghi, cussì rari,
chi li pari nun ci sù.
    Ma la vucca cu li fini
soi dintuzzi alabastrini,
trizzi d'oru, chi abbagghiati,
perdonati, è bedda chiù:

Nun lu negu, amati gigghia,
siti beddi a meravigghia;
siti beddi a signu tali
chi l'uguali nun ci sù.
    Ma la vucca 'nzuccarata
quannu parra, quannu ciata,
gigghia beddi, gigghia amati,
perdonati, è bedda chiù.

Occhi, in vui fa pompa Amuri
di l'immensu so valuri,
vostri moti, vostri sguardi
ciammi e dardi d'iddu sù.
    Ma la vucca, quannu duci
s apri, e modula la vuci,
occhi... Ah vui mi taliati!...
Pirdunati, 'un parru chiù.

VII
The Mouth

Oh, those braids of golden hair
are a garden sweet and fair;
they're so beauteous and rare
none comparison will dare.
    But the mouth with eburnine,
pearly teeth so neat, so fine,
Golden Braids that all outshine,
please don't mind, 'tis more divine.

My dear brows, I can't deny
you're as lovely as the sky,
you're so lovely to the eye,
all who see you simply sigh.
    But the mouth's a sugar beet
when she opens it to greet,
lovely brows that love entreat,
please forgive me, 'tis more sweet.

Love has chosen you, dear eyes,
just to flaunt his greatest prize.
All your actions, all your sighs
represent his flames, his guise.
    But the mouth I so adore
when her words begin to pour.
Lovely eyes, why do you stare?
Please forbear ... I'll say no more.

VIII
La vuci

Vola in aria na vucidda
cussi grata, cussi linna
chi lu cori già ni spinna,
duci-duci si nni va.
L'Amurini supra l'ali
l' equilibranu suspisa;
ora cala ed ora jisa,
ora immobili si sta.

D'ogni pettu e d'ogni cori
com'avissi già la chiavi,
duci, tenera e suavi,
l'apri e chiudi a gustu so.
Trasi dintra sinu all'alma,
la sulleva, l'accarizza,
cu na grazia, na ducizza,
chi spiegari nun si pò.

Quannu flebili e dulenti
duna corpu a li duluri,
l'arpa stissa di l'Amuri
nun è tenera accussì.
Quannu poi scappànnu
vola, quannu poi si ferma
e trilla, pari a nui chi l' aria brilla,
tuttu e allegru, tuttu è insì.

S'idda rumpi qualchi nota,
di li Grazii persuasa,
già lu stomacu nni scasa,
nun si ciata affattu chiù.
Quannu sempri sminuennu,
quasi manca, quasi mori,
si fa straggi di li cori,
dillu, Amuri, dillu tu!

VIII
The Voice

A sweet voice flies in the air
that's so lovely and so fair,
that my heart already swoons
and it sweetly disappears.
The cute Cupids on their wings
hold it balanced in midair,
now it rises, then it wanes,
now it does not move from there.

It can open up and close
every heart and every breast
as if it the key possessed
in a sweet, soft, tender way.
Deep inside the soul it goes,
lifts it up with its embrace
with such sweetness and such grace,
no one can explain or say.

When it voices some distress
with a weak and woeful plaint
even love's own lyre can't
emulate its tenderness.
When it runs away in flight,
when it stops and starts to trill,
we think air is shining bright,
all is cheerful, all says yes.

If a note by chance should break
by persuasion of the Graces[1]
the poor stomach then takes flight,
there's no breathing taking place.
When it starts to fade away,
nearly dying, in dismay,
tell me, Love, if any heart
can withstand such harsh array.

----

1. Graces: According to Hesiod the Graces were daughters of Zeus and Eurinome. Their names were Aglaia, Euphrosyyne and Thalia and they were constant attendants to Venus. They personifiy gracefulness.

IX
L'ALITU

Profumeddu gratu e finu,
di cui l'aria s'impanna,
d'unni veni? Cui ti manna?
Quantu va ca l'induvinu?

    Qualchi spratticu dirrìa
ca sì figghiu di li ciuri,
e li spiriti chiù puri
tutti sunnu uniti in tia;

    di li ciuri, è veru, n'ài
la fragranza la chiù pura;
ma però si senti allura,
ca li superi d'assai.

    Dirrìa nàutru: Un zefirettu
di l'arabici cuntrati,
tanti effluvii prelibati
còsi, e vinni ccà direttu;

    si li voscura Sabbei,
si d'Arabia li virduri
avirrìanu tali oduri,
ci starrevanu li Dei.

    Profumeddu, chi nni dici?
Ridi a tanti dicirii!
Però a mia nun mi trizzìi,
tu sì l'alitu di Nici.

IX
The Breath

Pleasing, fine, delightful scent
that the air all permeates,
where are you from? By whom sent?
I can guess, you want to bet?

    Some naïve man might opine
that you are the flowers' son
and within you do combine
the best essences in one.

    You possess, that is for sure,
of the flowers the sweet smell,
but one can discern full well
you surpass them all by far.

    Other people would suggest
that a little zephyr went
to Arabia for the best
and brought back the greatest scents.

    If the forest of Sabha[1]
and the green lands of Arabia
had these awesome scents in store,
all the Gods would go live there.

    What say you, my sweet bouquet?
You're amused at such hearsay!
You can't fool me, no, no way!
You are Nici's fragrant breath.

----

1. Sabha: Sabha is a city and region in Arabia.

X
LU PETTU

Ntra ssu pittuzzu amabili,
ortu di rosi e ciuri,
dui mazzuneddi Amuri
cu li soi manu fa.

Ci spruzza poi cu l'ali
li fiocchi di la nivi,
'ntriccia li vini e scrivi:
lu paradisu è ccà.

Ma un' importuna nuvula
m'ottenebra lu celu:
appena ntra lu velu
na spiragghiedda c'è.

Armata d'una spingula,
chi pari na laparda,
modestia si lu guarda:
ch'è rigurusa, ohimè!

Un Amurinu affabili
l'ammutta a jiri a mia,
ma l'àutru, oh tirannia!
turnari poi lu fa;

Pietusu a li mei lagrimi,
chiddu lu spinci arrèri,
ma torna poi 'nnarrèri,
e sempri veni e va.

Li sguardi si sammuzzanu
ntra dda spiragghia nica,
ed idda li nutrica,
li pasci quantu pò;

idda la menti guida
a li biddizzi arcani,
nni teni vivi e sani
lu sulu aiutu so.

Si mai sintisti affettu,
Zefiru amurusu,
lu velu suspittusu
allarga un pocu chiù;

e si lu to nun basta
alitu dilicatu,
pigghiati lu miu ciatu,
e servitinni tu.

X
The Bosom

In your delightful bosom,
an orchard filled with roses
and buds, love's hand composes
two lovely little bunches.

Then with his wings he sprayed
of snow flakes a thin coat
and crossing the veins he wrote:
our paradise is here.

A cloud most importune
my heaven did obscure,
a tiny crack was bare
between the veil and her.

Armed with a little pin,
a halberd fierce and hard,
modesty stands on guard
how rigidly, my Lord!

A kindly little Cupid
the veil pushed toward me,
but then, oh tyranny!
the other made him turn;

with pity for my tears
he fought off the attack
but then he went right back
continuing back and forth.

My glances dive headlong
into the tiny crack
which lets them have a snack
that feeds them for a bit;

it guides the mind to where
the secret beauties dwell;
we are alive and well
thanks only to its help.

If ever you felt love,
my Zephyr, sweet and kind,
that cruel veil unbind
and lift it a bit more;

and if yours won't suffice,
o delicate sweet breeze,
then take my own breath, please,
and use it as your own.

XI
LU NEU

Tu felici, tu beatu,
nzoccu si, purrettu o neu!
Ntra ssu pettu dilicatu,
oh! putissi staricc'eu!

   Ntra ssi nivi ancora intatti
comu sedi! comu spicchi!
Ah! Lu cori già mi sbatti,
fa la gula nnicchi-nnicchi.

   Di lu coddu a li confini
sì na guardia vigilanti,
pri li vaghi dui furtini
di la piazza chiù impurtanti.

   Ah! si mai pigghiannu a scanciu,
o pri audacia singulari,
qualchi manu fa lu granciu,
facci tu terra trimari;

   ma quann'eu poi m'ammaraggiu,
e l'arbitriu mi manca,
fammi qualchi bon passaggiu:
cu l'amici vaja franca.

XI
The Beauty Mark

Beauty mark, you are so blessed!
(or are you a little mole?),
who dwell on so sweet a breast!
if I too could share your role!

   And in such untrammeled snow
how you glisten, how you fit.
This poor heart is beating so,
how my gullet longs for it!

   At the endline of the neck,
ever vigilant, apprized
the two fortresses you check
that contain the noblest prize.

   Oh, if ever by mistake,
or with sheer audacity,
someone's hand should slip your brake,
chase him off immediately!

   But if I should then get lost,
my resistance being poor,
please allow me to get past.
Let it be! What are friends for?

For the two poems, "The Bosom" and "The Beauty Mark," Meli claimed that they were translations of two little Oriental songs for which he tried to "preserve the spirit of the texts as well as to moderate the licence of the expressions." This was a ruse to silence the censors who could object to the sensuality contained in the poems. How things have changed! The odes were inspired, according to Giorgio Santangelo, by Lady Mela Cutelli and Lady Marianna Mantegna respectively.

XII
LU NON-SO-CHI

In riguri, viiuledda,
bedda bedda nun ci sì;
   ma in tia regna, in tia privali
certu tali non-so-chi,
   pri cui misa a beddi accantu,
d'iddi, oh! quantu, spicchi chiù.
   Si sù chisti vaghi stiddi,
suli in iddi splendi tu.
   È la rosa un arricrìu
pri lu briu, la maistà;
   sta vaghizza l'occhi abbagghia,
la plibbagghia curri ddà;
   ma in un cori dilicatu
lu to ciatu, oh quantu pò!
   Quali ciamma, quali affettu
svigghia in pettu un guardu to!
   È simpaticu, è gentili,
nè virili cori c'è,
   chi 'un si senta risbigghiari
li chiù cari e duci ohimè.

XII
The Don't Know What

To be frank, my violet
a true beauty you are not,
   but in you prevails and reigns,
a most certain don't know what,
   so when standing next to beauties,
you outshine them all by far.
   If they are resplendent stars,
like the sun more bright you are.
   For their might and majesty
roses are a great delight
   and their brightness blinds the eye
whereto flies the vulgar throng,
   but on men with gentle hearts
your breath starts a greater song.
   Oh what flame, what jubilance
can one glance from you engender!
   It is charming, it is tender,
you will find no manly heart
   that will fail to feel the rise
of soft moaning and sweet sighs.

XIII
LA SIMPATIA

A la bella Dia di Gnidu
lu gran cintu portentusu
fu rubbatu da Cupidu,
Diu potenti e capricciusu;
  ed a Fillidi sua cara
ci lu cinsi e dissi poi:
"La natura ben prepara,
eu compisciu l'opri soi:
  grazia, spiritu, biddizza
tinn'à datu senza cuntu;
e si vidi cu chiarizza,
ch'era in gana tra ddu puntu.

  Jeu stuputu a sta eleganza,
pri nun darimi pri vintu,
la magnetica pussanza
ti presentu tra stu cintu;
  di cui n'aju vistu provi
in mia matri ed in Giununi,
pri cui chista tirau Giovi,
comu fussi un picuruni.

  La sua forza è singulari,
tuttu cedi a lu so imperu,
da putiri conquistari,
si tu voi, lu munnu interu".

XIII
Charm

One day Cupid, that capricious,
mighty God, bent on a heist
stole the awesome, magic belt
from the beautiful goddess
born in Cnidus[1] and he knelt
  to place it on Filli's waist,
his beloved, adding this:
"Nature makes good preparation
I her work bring to completion;
  She has given you wit, grace,
and great beauty in profusion;
you can tell that in that phase
she was feeling generous.

  At such elegance I cower,
but not wanting to resign
the magnetic awesome power
of this belt I will define.
  I have often seen its use
from my mother and from Juno[2]
who was able to lead Jove[3]
like a he-goat on a leash.

  The belt's power is unique;
in its way no one can stand
and you can, if you so wish,
have the world at your command."

---

1. Cnidus: The goddess born in Cnidus was Venus.
2. Juno: Juno is the Roman name for Hera, the wife of Zeus.
3. Jove: Jove is the Roman name for Zeus, the father of the gods. He was also called Jupiter.

XIV
LI GRAZII

Doppu chi l'Asia,
già quasi tutta
cadiu per Elena
arsa e distrutta,
   in tonu seriu
li Dei pinsaru
a sti disordini
dari riparu.
   E pirchì vittiru
chi la Biddizza
junt'a li Grazii
gran focu attizza,
   perciò decretanu
chi mai chiù visti
fussiru 'nzemmula
chidda cu chisti.
   Dunca spartendusi
da Citerìa
li Grazii pigghianu
pri n'autra via.
   Ci va Cupidini
manu cu manu,
stanti lu geniu
so juculanu.
   Trovanu in Fillidi
grata accugghienza,
e in idda fissanu
la permanenza.
   intantu Veneri,
scuntenti e mesta,
gira sbattendusi
sula la testa;
   pri terra ed aria,
città e chianuri
scurri spiannucci:
"Chi nn'è di Amuri?"
   Ma poi truvannulu
letu e cuntenti,
dissi sgridannulu:
"Ah! sconuscenti!
   Cussì dimentichi,

XIV
The Graces

After all Asia
in Helen's[1] wake
suffered destruction
and much heartbreak,
   with somber looks
the gods did intend
to these disorders
to put an end.
   And realizing
that beauty joined
with the Graces[2] sparks
prodigious fires,
   they stipulated
that the two virtues
would never be
together found.
   Therefore, parting
with Cytherea,[3]
Grace just went
another way.
   Owing to Cupid's
playful nature,
he went along,
holding their hands.
   They found in Filli
a grateful welcome
and chose to stay
permanently.
   Venus, meanwhile,
gloomy and sad,
wandered alone,
beating her head.
   Through land and air,
through towns and dales,
she roamed and asked:
"What news of Love?"
   But when she found
him joyful, glad,
she scolded him,
saying "Ingrate!
   Thus you forsake,

barbaru, ingratu,
la matri propria,
chi fa addivatu?"
   "Matri, pirdunami,
dissi Cupidu,
mi parsi a vidiri
ccà lu miu nidu:
   l'anni mi scursiru
cussì suavi,
chi 'un potti accorgirmi
chi tu mancavi."

ungrateful pup,
your loving mother
who brought you up?
   "Forgive me, Mother, "
Cupid replied,
"I thought I saw
my nest right here.
   The years went by
with so much joy
I did not notice
you were not here."

---

1. Helen: A reference to Helen of Troy whose abduction by Paris caused the Trojan war.
2. Graces: Cfr. "The Voice," VIII.
3. Cytherea: Another name for Venus.

XV
LU GESUMINU

Gesuminu, tu m' ammaschi,
e nun viju lu pirchì!
Stari in menzu di sti raschi,
nun lu negu, ch'è un gran chi.

Ma li rosi e l'amaranti
ci aju vistu unni sì tu:
un onuri datu a tanti,
è finitu, 'un vali chiù.

Cu ssa boria e ssa livata,
tu ti cridi quasi un re?
Ma nun passa ssa iurnata,
ca finisci cu l'olè.

Supra donni lu so fastu
nuddu mai fundari pò;
forsi v'amanu, ma a tastu,
oggi sì, dumani no.

Vidi 'nterra spampinatu
ddu galofaru ch'è ddà?
Chistu ajeri fu aduratu
comu nàutra deità.

Ora 'un tocca chiù cantusciu,
si ci spii, dici: Ohimè!
pirchì sugnu afflittu e musciu,
pietà pri mia 'un ci nn'è!

Benchì elettu ntra li ciuri,
gesuminu, ora sì tu,
forsi avrai pri successuri
li chiù tinti chi ci sù.

Chi unni regna l'incostanza,
è cuccagna: e sai pirchì?
Pirchì ogn'unu avi spiranza,
oggi no, dumani sì.

XV
The Jasmine

Jasmine, why such arrogance
with me? I do not see why.
Being 'round such elegance
is a treat, I can't deny.

But some roses there I see,
amaranths, as well. An honor
granted to all cannot be
worth a lot. It's useless, done.

With such airs and such conceit
you believe you're royalty?
But before this day is gone,
all will end in mockery.

No man can boast of success
when a woman is concerned.
Testing them, they love you, yes,
for today, tomorrow no.

That carnation on the floor
with its petals strewn about
was adored one day before
by the people as a god.

No silk gown will it adorn
and when asked, this it will say:
"Ah, because I'm limp, forlorn,
no compassion comes my way.

Although now among all flowers,
jasmine, you're the top, maybe
you will have as your successors
the worst flowers that we see.

For where fickleness commands,
it's a free for all: a mess.
Why? Because all men can hope:
no today, tomorrow yes.

XVI
L'ARUTA

Malannata chi vi vegna,
rosi, gigghi e gesuminu;
nudda Ninfa chiù vi tegna
ntra lu so pittuzzu finu;

Nici pallida e trimanti,
anelanti e strangusciuta,
sarria morta ntra un istanti,
si nun era pri l'aruta.

Sia decretu di l'Amuri,
sia destinu sconuscenti,
li chiù beddi ntra cert'uri
su suggetti a st'accidenti:

a lu cori si cci abbiia
una negghia, un nuvuluni,
chi li torci, sforasiia!
comu vipari e scursuni;

e ci movi tanta guerra,
chi lu velu palpitanti,
laceratu cadi a terra,
e ni tremanu l'amanti.

Ciuri, vui superbi assai
pri tant'abiti pumpusi,
ntra st'oceanu di guai
stati friddi ed uzziusi!

A chi tantu esaggerati
la fraganza chiù esquisita,
si ci accrisci, o ciuri ingrati,
lu disordini a la vita?

Ma l'aruta, ch'è pudica,
benchì pocu sociali,
e la chiù fidili amica
di li spiriti vitali.

Non ostenta lu so fastu
cu li varii culuri;
e nun duna nuddu rastu
di l'intrinsecu valuri.

Chi virtù, benchì privata,
benchì povera e dimissa,
vivi simplici e beata,
e s'appaga di se stissa.

XVI
The Rue

A big curse upon you, roses,
and on lilies, jasmine, too;
in her fine and lovely breast
let no nymph now harbor you.

That poor Nici, pale and trembling,
out of breath and in despair,
would have perished in a flash
if the rue had not been there.

Whether by decree of Love
or ungrateful destinies,
but at times those who are fair
are prone to catastrophes.

A great cloud, a mighty fog,
their hearts enters like a quake,
God forbid, and makes them writhe,
like a viper or black snake.

And it causes them such war
that their heaving veils it tears,
which then lands upon the floor,
making lovers fret in fear.

You proud flowers that provide
pomp and grandeur to a dress,
look on coldly and aloof
in the midst of such distress.

Why do you exaggerate
your exquisite fragrance so,
haughty flowers, if in life
it will make disorders grow?

But the rue, who's very modest,
though its social skills are few,
is the most trustworthy friend
that the zest of life renews.

It won't boast about its pomp
with a multitude of hues,
and of its intrinsic worth
it won't give you any clues.

For great virtue, although private,
although humble and sedate,
lives quite simply and in bliss,
in herself her needs she sates.

Giovanni Meli

XVII
LA COLICA

Na dogghia colica
già ni rapia
lu megghiu mobili
di Citeria.

La Parca orribili,
di dardu armata,
dintra li visceri
s'era appustata.

"Addiu (gridavanu
tutti l'amanti)
addiu, va chiuditi
regnu galanti".

Tutti sti lagrimi
junceru in celu;
ed eccu Veneri
s'arma di zelu:

"Giovi, proteggimi,
(dissi cu impegnu)
vacilla l'àncora
di lu miu regnu.

Rendi sta giuvina,
rendila a mia;
poi crepi invidia
e gilusia".

Dissi: (oh prodigiu!)
Giovi balena;
e in terra canciasi
tutta la scena:

cessa lu spasimu,
Nici è brillanti,
rivali crepanu,
ridinu amanti.

XVII
The Colic

A colic pain
almost did rob
the best heartthrob
in all Cythera.[1]

The horrid Parcae,[2]
armed with a spear
took a position
in her viscera.

All lovers yelled,
"O gallant state,
farewell, you may
shut down your gate."

All of these tears
went up to heaven.
Behold then Venus
by her zeal driven:

"Protect me, Jove,"
she said steadfast.
"The realm of love
is crumbling fast.

Give back this youth.
Give her to me.
Let envy burst
and jealousy."

She spoke (oh wonder!),
his lightning flash
earth's scene transformed
in just a dash.

The spasms ceased.
Now Nici is gay,
her rivals burst,
her lovers play.

---

1. Cythera: The ancient name of Cerrigo island in the Peloponnese where Venus was particularly venerated.
2. Parcae: Death. Also known as Morae or Fates, they were three sisters named Atropos, Clotho and Lachesis who controlled birth, life, and death of mankind.

120

XVIII
LU SISTEMA SESSUALI DI LI CIURI DI LU CELEBRI LINNEU

XVIII
The Sexual System of Flowers by the Famous Linnaeus[1]

Nici, sai pirchì stu ciuri,
chi sta sutta la tua gorgia,
tanta pompa e lussu sforgia
di fraganzi e di culuri?
  Pirchì è un lettu nuziali,
chi natura à preparatu
a na zita ch'avi allatu
deci spusi in fiocchi e in gali.
  Vidi quantu sù galanti
l'apparati, li curtini!
Quantu vaghi, quantu fini
sù li rasi di li canti!
  Tra na conca chi c'è 'mmenzu
sta la spusa, e ogni maritu,
aspittannu lu so invitu,
a l' abbrazzi è già propenzu.
  Tra li palpiti amurusi
si distilla la ducizza,
chi si cogghi a stizza a stizza
poi da l' api industriusi ...
  Ma tu canci, ohimè, d'aspettu!
Tu ti copri di russuri!
Nun è chistu, ah no, lu ciuri,
chi conveni a lu to pettu!
  Eccu ccà chist'àutru: osserva,
cca c'è sula na spusina,
chi na pura ciamma fina
per un Zefiru cunserva.
  Iddu parti all' alba avanti,
e radennu prati e lidi,
tra li ciuri si providi
di l' essenzi fecundanti.
  Senza pausa scurri, e in fretta
movi l'una e l'autr'aluzza,
e amurusu poi li spruzza
su la spusa chi l'aspetta.
  Vidi comu a lu so ciatu,
idda s'allima e ravviva?
Nici, apprendi a quantu arriva

Nici, do you know the reason
why this bloom above your breast
flaunts in color and in zest
so much pomp and luxury?
  That's because a nuptial bed
Mother Nature has prepared
for a bride who next to her
ten young grooms in tails and bows.
  Notice how gallant and chic
are the curtains in design!
And how elegant, how fine
are the silks along the corners!
  In a basin in the middle
stands the bride and every mate,
waiting there for her invite,
who is ready to embrace her.
  Through the amorous heartthrobs
sweetness is distilled at last,
which will then be soon amassed
by the bees with industry…
  But your looks alas are changing.
you are blushing through and through!
No, this bloom is not for you,
It's not proper for your breast!
  Here's another one. Observe!
Here there's only one young bride
that a fine, pure flame will hide
for a Zephyr yet to come.
  He leaves early, before dawn
and goes razing dale and shore
to collect from each bud core
the right fecundating spore.
  Without pausing, in a hurry,
with both wings he moves in air
and sprays them with loving care
on the bride that's waiting there.
  See how she revives and glows
when his breath she feels above?
Nici, learn what a fine love

121

Giovanni Meli

un amuri dilicatu!
   Ed ammira, o cori miu,
jetta l'occhiu a tutti banni:
quant'estisu, quantu granni
è l'imperiu di stu Diu!

can accomplish with its might.
   And esteem it, my dear heart,
look around in every place;
and see how vast is the space
that lies in this God's domain.

---

1. Linnaeus: Charles de Linnaeus (1707-1778) was a famous Swedish physician and naturalist who had written a classification of plants and animals.

XIX
LA MUNITA FAUSA

È persu, è persu, o Amuri,
è persu lu negoziu;
nun c'è chiù dicituri,
tutta la genti è in oziu;
e sai chi nn'è la causa?
Curri munita fàusa.

Li beddi duppii antichi,
di *Cori meu, eu t' amu,*
ora, si tu li strichi,
su pannidduni e ramu;
lu chiantu, chi cumpagnu
fu a la cuppella, è stagnu.

L'unzini, chi currìanu
di vintidui carati,
chi per impronta avìanu
Li sguardi appassionati,
ora si ni fai prova,
chi sù? Testi di chiova!

Li ginuini e scuti
di li *Suspiri ardenti,*
di li Discursi muti,
Paroli rutti in denti ...
L'intressu, ohimè! la briga
falsificau la liga.

Currìa ntra li striguni
un tempu sta munita;
la fici poi comuni
qualchi caiorda ardita;
ora cui junci campa,
teni lu cugnu e stampa.

Dimm'ora: Cui è dd'armali,
chi arrisicari vogghi
lu propriu capitali
a frunti di sti 'mbrogghi?
Amuri, s'è pri mia,
poi chiudiri putìa.

XIX
Fake Money

It's lost, it's lost, o love
the business is lost;
there are no donors left,
the folks are just bereft
and do you know its cause?
Fake money's the because.

The handsome old doubloon:
My heart, for you I swoon,
if you rub hard, is made
of copper and gold-plate;
weeping, a good comrade
to the cupel, is now tin.

What of the little ounces
worth carats twenty-two once
on which was carved the phrase
The passion-filled love glance ?
Putting them to the test,
they're heads of nails at best.

The Genoese. the crowns
of *Burning sighs* and of
the silent, weeping frowns,
the dying words of love...
Trouble, and interest, my boy,
have falsified the alloy.

This coin was used before
among the sorcerers.
Some daring, lowdown whore
made it familiar then.
So now all will survive,
having the mold, they'll thrive.

Now tell me, who's the ass
who wants to take a chance,
in such a tangled mess,
investing on romance?
Say, Love, if it were up
to me, you can close shop!

123

XX
LI BACCANTI

Li testi fumanu,
già semu cotti,
buttigghi e gotti
vegnanu ccà.
    Vajanu a cancaru
sennu e giudiziu,
oggi sia viziu
la gravità.
    Ntra la mestizia
li guai s'avanzanu,
sulu si scanzanu
stannu accussì:
    la ciospa 'nzemmula
lu calasciuni,
vini abbuluni,
e amici 'nsì.
    Fumu è la gloria,
l'amuri focu,
è un scherzu un jocu
la gioventù.
    Prima chi tremula
vicchiaia arriva,
si sciali e viva
a cui pò chiù.
    Proi ssa ciotula,
bedda Picciotta,
ch'iu ntra na botta
l'asciuchirò!
    Comu rivugghinu
sti bianchi scumi,
vugghia ed addumi
lu cori to!
    Tasta stu balsamu!
tastalu chissu,
l'amuri stissu
ccà dintra c'è.
    Comu arrussicanu
ssi mascidduzzi!
Oh li labbruzzi!
Talè talè!

XX
The Bacchantes

We are well soused,
our heads are sore,
bring cups galore,
brings bottles here!
    To hell with wisdom
and common sense.
Let's all dispense
with seriousness.
    When sadness reigns,
our woes increase.
To find surcease,
this is the way!
    Give us a flute,
a concubine,
plenty of wine,
friends who say yes.
    Love is a fire,
but glory's smoke;
a play, a joke,
our youthfulness.
    Before our shaky
old age arrives,
let us contrive
to drink at will.
    My pretty maid,
hand me your bowl,
and I'll say skoal
and gulp it down.
    See how the nectar
is foaming bright!
May it excite
your heart as well.
    Taste this sweet nectar,
eat a bit more,
for at the core
there's love itself.
    Oh how your cheeks
are blushing so!
Oh how they glow
those lips of yours!

Scurra l'oceanu
l'Inglisi audaci,
ch'eu² ²vogghiu in paci
starimi ccà.

Si poi lu pelagu
vinu sarria,
jeu scurriria
forsi chiù ddà.

Sinu a lu Messicu
vaja l'avaru,
cerchi ogni scaru
di lu Perù.

Ntra ciaschi e bimmali
sù li ricchizzi,
li cuntintizzi
ddà dintra sù.

Morti nun curasi
d'oru o di ramu;
dunca tummamu!
buttigghi, olè!

Spittarla serii
è cosa grevia,
li jorna abbrevia,
sicchi ci fa.

Fora li trivuli;
allargu vaja
grunna e vicchiaia.
resti l'olè.

Gridi: Trinch-vaine;
fraula curtisa,
maetres francisa;
alons touchè!

Tavuli e brinnisi,
amanti, amici,
fannu felici
l'umanità!

Viva lu viviri!
Viva lu jocu,
viva lu focu,
chi in pettu sta!

And let the British
roam the wide sea.
I want to be
at home in peace.

But if the ocean
were really wine,
I'd cross that line.
Of this I'm certain.

Let greedy men
roam far from here!
Search every pier
of far Perù.

Wine flasks and kegs
contain all joy:
there you'll enjoy
all happiness.

We do not care
when we are dead
for gold or lead.
So let's drink now.

Sober is grey,
live not that way;
shortens our days
and makes us thin.

So out with troubles,
chase woes away,
let the "olè"
keep us in cheer.

Yell trinken wein,
my sweet fraulein!
My wondrous wench,
who just speaks French.

Lovers and friends,
banquets and toasts,
make life a feast
for all mankind.

So cheers for living,
hurrah for games!
Cheers for the flames
inside our breasts!

XXI
D. CHISCIOTTI

Sutta un'antica quercia,
chi attraversu spurgìa da un vàusu alpestri,
cu na manu a la frunti, D. Chisciotti
mestissimu sidìa: na rocca allatu
di chiàppari cuverta, e la pinnenti
arèddara d'attornu a la sua cima,
facìanu pavigghiuni a la sua testa;
ripusava oziusa la gran spata
tra la purvuli e l'erva: a un virdi ramu
stava appujata l'asta di la guerra,
sutta un vrazzu lu scutu, e l'elmu a terra.

Comu nuvuli densi di molesti
minutissimi insetti, a scheri a scheri
l'amurusi pinseri
s'affuddavanu tutti a la sua menti;
tra li suspiri ardenti,
quasi accisu Vulcanu, lu so pettu
fumu e ciammi esalava:
e mentri intornu intornu
li valli e li furesti
taciti, attenti e mesti
si stannu spittaturi a la gran scena,
cussì cantannu, sfoga la sua pena:

"Munti e vàusi, menu duri
di lu cori di dd'ingrata;
petri, trunchi, erbetti e ciuri,
chi adurnati sta vallata,
deh! salvatimi d'Amuri,
chi mi à l'alma trapanata;
o parrati vui pri mia
a la cara Dulcinia.

Ciumiceddu lentu lentu,
chi di l'unni cristallini
vai spargennu lu lamentu
a li voscura vicini,
di stu cori lu turmentu
dimmi tu si avirrà fini?
Ah! dumannaci pri mia

XXI
Don Chisciotti

Underneath an ancient oak
suspended sideways from an alpine cliff,
poor Don Chisciotti[1] sat extremely sad,
a hand upon his forehead. The rock face
next to him, overgrown with capers, formed,
together with the ivy hanging from the top,
a dome above his head. His awesome sword
was idle, resting on the dust and grass;
his lance of battle was reclining on
a green branch, his shield underneath his arm,
while his headgear was lying on the ground.

Like some dense clouds of noxious, tiny insects,
coming in endless waves,
thoughts of love
crowded in his mind at once.
For all his burning sighs
his chest, as a volcano in eruption,
exhaled both smoke and flames;
and meanwhile all around,
the valleys and the forests
stood as spectators to the awe-inspiring scene,
and listened silently, engrossed and sad,
as he his sorrow vented, singing thus:

"Mountains, cliffs, that are less hard
than the heart of that ingrate,
rocks, trunks, flowers, tender grass
that adorn this lovely dale,
please, do save me from this love
that has pierced right through my soul
or do speak in my behalf
to my dearest Dulcinea[2].

Tender stream that slowly flow
and disperse my sore lament
through your crystalline, clear waters
to the forests all around,
can you tell me if the torment
of my heart will ever end?
Please do ask in my behalf

a la cara Dulcinia.

to my dearest Dulcinea.

Zefiretti, chi lascivi
cu lu ciatu innamuratu
li mei ciammi ardenti e vivi
chiù m'aviti, ohimè! sbampatu,
ah! squagghiati, vui, la nivi
di ddu cari, ch'è 'gnilatu,
acciò bruci, comu mia,
la mia cara Dulcinia.

Little naughty zephyrs who
with your hot, enamored breaths
have blown on my burning flames
and alas have made them worse,
please, go now to melt the snow
that has frozen up her heart,
so my dearest Dulcinea
can burn also as I do.

Ocidduzzi, chi cuntenti
tra li rami e tra li ciuri
a lu suli già nascenti
intricciati inni d' amuri,
deh! pristatimi l'accenti,
cusì grati e cusì puri,
acciò gratu e accettu sia
a la cara Dulcinia.

O sweet birds that twixt the branches
and the flowers weave and sing
cheerful canticles of love
to the rising sun above,
your sweet voice please lend to me,
that's so pleasing and so pure,
so my song can be accepted
by my dearest Dulcinea.

Da sti vàusi, unn'eu m'aggiru,
miu tirannu amatu beni,
l'aria stissa, ch'eu respiru,
missaggera a tia già veni;
porta acchiusi ntra un suspiru
li mei crudi acerbi peni:
D. Chisciotti è chi l'invia
a la cara Dulcinia".

From the cliffs on which I roam,
my tyrannous cherished love,
the same air that I now breathe
takes my message to your ears
and it brings inside a sigh
my harsh suffering and pain:
Don Chisciotti is the sender
to his dearest Dulcinea."

---

1. Don Chisciotti: The same character from Miguel de Cervantes' novel *Don Quijote de la Mancha* is the protagonsit of Meli's own *Don Chisciotti e Sanciu Panza* a long mock epic poem. This anthology contains one full canto (V) from the epic translated into English. The full work, *Don Chisciotti and Sanciu Panza* is available in a bilingual edition published by Legas in 1997-2005.
2. Dulcinea: Dulcinea del Toboso. She is the woman Don Chisciotti loves in Cervantes' work.

XXII
LA MORTI DI SAFFU

Duna un tonu pateticu la lira!
Ch'infaustu auguriu, ohimè!
La musa mia Polinnia suspira!
oh celu! chi cos'è?

Musa ... ma tu nun senti,
e guardi attenta un'eminenti rocca,
comu cui vidi cosa chi spaventa,
chi l'affliggi e tocca! ...

Cala da l'occhi mei la benna: ahi vista!
La Lesbia donna è in àutu!
Comu a gran passi l'eminenza acquista
di lu fatali sàutu!

Li trizzi scioti, in aria li vrazza!
Anelanti lu pettu!
Lu palluri di morti ci sbulazza
tra lu smarritu aspettu!

Scintillanti lu sguardu e furiusu
or'a lu celu spinci,
ora l'abbascia e lu sprofunna jusu:
inorridisci e 'mpinci.

Ma nova furia eccu la scoti e smovi
con impetu maggiuri,
suspira, ed ogni vàusu si commovi;
sta sulu firmu amuri.

Fèrmati, scunsigghiata, e 'un tinni adduni
ch'è cecu cui ti guida?
L'arbitriu to ci ài datu! Lu picciuni
cui ad un corvu affida?

Quant'è crudu nun sai? Chi ni accanzasti
da supplichi divoti?
Lu cori ch'in deliquiu squagghiasti
tra l'amurusi noti!

Cu la sua lira Orfeu risi placatu
di Plutu lu fururi;
ma quantu di Plutuni chiù spietatu,
Saffu, tu provi Amuri!...

Ma li paroli mei spargìu a lu ventu:
già junta è all'orlu!... Oh Diu!
L'occhiu 'un resisti ... Ohimè! lu bottu eu sentu;
già l'unna l'agghiuttìu!....

L'unna, chi fora gurgugghiannu manna

XXII
The Death of Sappho

O what a mournful sound my poor lyre plays.
What an ill-boding omen, wretched me!
My own muse Polyhymnia[1] also sighs.
Oh god! What can it be?

O Muse...but you don't hear,
and toward a cliff you stare attentively,
as one who sees a worrisome mischief
or something causing him distress or sigh!

Lower the blindfold from my eyes: what sight!
The woman who's from Lesbos[2] stands quite high!
How quickly does she climb up to the heights
for her long, fatal leap!

Her tresses are undone, her arms in air!
Her breathing's hard and deep!
Death's pallor is now buzzing
around her stressed, wild stare.

Her flashing and uneasy eyes are raised
first towards the sky and then
they turn to the abyss below.
She stumbles; she is horrified.

But then behold a novel anger shakes
and moves her with a greater energy.
She sighs, and every cliff now quakes
with pity; Only love stands quietly.

You, ill-advised one, Stop! Can you not see
that he who's guiding you is blind?
You handed him control of your own destiny!
Who hands doves to a hawk in her right mind?

Do you not know how punishing he is?
What did you gain
with all your fervent prayers?
The heart you wasted in your ardent pleas?

Orpheus[3] with his lyre
soothed Pluto's[4] ires,
but how much more hard-hearted was the way
you loved, o Sappho, than his hellish rage!

But by the wind my words are whisked away;
Oh, God! She has already reached the edge!
My eyes can't bear to watch! The splash I hear;
the wave has swallowed her, oh my!...

The wave that through its gurgling sounds

l'ultimu so assaccuni,
chi mentri l'aria 'ngramagghiannu appanna,
risona: Ohimè, Fauni!
    Chiancinu li Nereadi tutti in luttu:
e intenti a li vinditti
Veneri l' arcu ci à ad Amuri ruttu,
li Grazii li saitti.
    Jettanu a terra in Pindu ed arpi e liri
Apollu e li Cameni,
e si disfannu in lagrimi e suspiri
a mari li Sireni.
    La benda torna all'occhi mei.
Mia lira nun duna sonu chiui!
Saffu d'Amuri nun placau mai l'ira:
chi ni spiramu nui?
    Chi ti lusinghi cu sta canzunedda,
poeta miserabili?
Mmatula preghi e incensi la tua bedda:
Amuri è inesorabili!

made clear her final gasping cry,
which, as the air with mourning grew quite dull,
called out: Fauni[5], please!
    The Nereids bereaved wept one and all;
bent on avenging her demise,
Venus then shattered Cupid's bow,
the Graces with his arrows did likewise.
    Apollo[6] and the Camenies[7] did throw
on Pindus[8] harps and lyres in the dust
and Sirens out at sea by tears and sighs
were nearly all dumbstruck.
    The blindfold is returning to my eyes.
My lyre cannot play any more.
Sappho the wrath of love could not appease,
so what can we hope for?
    With such a puny song why are you pleased,
you worthless poetaster?
No matter how you praise and blow incense
to your belle, love's inexorable, hell.

---

1. Polyhymnia: The Muse of high and sacred lyric poetry.
2. Lesbos: The Greek island where Sappho was born.
3. Orpheus: Orpheus, the Thracian singer who could move stones with his song, went down to Hades to try to save Eurydice, who had died after she was bitten by a poisonous snake. The sweetness of his playing convinced Pluto to let his wife return to earth on condition that he not look back at her. He turned around and she was drawn back into Hades. He was later torn apart by the Bacchantes.
4. Pluto: The god presiding over Hades.
5. Fauni: The man Sappho loved unrequitedly. He has come to represent the inexorability of love.
6. Apollo: The god of music and poetry.
7. The Camenies: In Roman mythology they were nymphs specializing in in the art of singing and divination.
8. Pindus: A mountain in Greece sacred to Apollo and to the Muses.

XXIII
LU RUSIGNOLU

La tranquilla notti imponi
paci e calma a tutti quanti,
mentri tu graditu intoni,
rusignolu, li toi canti.

Tu cumpagnu so dilettu,
tu delizia di sta Dia,
tu sì l'organu perfettu
di la vera miludia.

La soavi tenerizza,
chi la vuci tua diffunni,
tutti aspergi di ducizza
celu, campi, vaddi ed unni.

Tra ssa gorgia tua canora
Grazii e Amuri un nidu ci ànnu,
d'unni scuvanu poi fora
tra li noti sbulazzannu;

ch'ora scurrinu affrittati,
ora mustranu, languenti,
chi sù in lingui 'nzuccarati
duci puru li lamenti.

Di l'oricchi a li confini
la tua vuci no, nun mori;
ma li Grazii, l'Amurini
la trasfundinu a lu cori.

Ddà s'insinua, ddà risbigghia
tra li puri e novi affetti,
la patetica famigghia
di l'incogniti diletti.

La tua scena è la foresta,
e li griddi cu ottavini
fannu armonica un'orchesta
a li noti toi divini.

Chi da munti in vaddi e in chiani,
d'ecu ad ecu ribumbannu,
si ripetinu luntani
l'umbri stupidi avvivannu.

Cori fini e non corrutti,
la natura ccà v'invita,
li delizii puri tutti
ccà cunserva di la vita.

Quannu l'omini li spaddi

XXIII
The Nightingale

The serene night can impose
peace and calm to everyone;
meanwhile you, my nightingale
your most welcome songs compose.

You're her favorite companion,
you're this goddess' delight,
you the perfect organ are
of a melody that's right.

The sweet sounding tenderness
that your voice spreads everywhere
permeates with harmony
fields and valleys, waves and air.

Love and Graces have a nest
in your tuneful little throat
from which they then will emerge
buzzing through between each note,

which at times flow hurriedly
or they show with languid tweets
how on sugarcoated tongues
even moans can sound quite sweet.

No, your voice does not die out
at the borders of the ears,
'cause the Graces and love gods
to the heart will bring it near.

There it enters and arouses
in affections pure and new
the emotional ensemble
of some pleasures we don't know.

Your environment's the forest
and the crickets with their flutes
form a tuneful orchestra
to convoy your divine notes.

From the mountains, dales, and plains,
their notes echo and repeat,
in the distance far away
and stunned shadows animate.

Gentle hearts who're not corrupted,
Nature bids you to come here,
which preserves all of the pleasures
that in life we hold most dear.

When men turned their backs against

ci vutaru a sta gran Matri,
si fic'idda in munti e in vaddi
li sublimi soi teatri.
   "Sì" ... , poi dissi, "ingrati figghi,
sì... goditivi di l'arti
tanti commodi e 'mmizzigghi,
ch'idda chiusi vi cumparti,
ch'eu vi lasciu a li rancuri
d'inquieta ambizioni
e a li tristi dissapuri
di buggiarda illusioni".

this great Mother, who's immense,
in the mountains and the dales
she showed her magnificence.
   "Yes," she said, "ungrateful children,
yes, the comfort and caress
of my art enjoy that hidden,
she apportions in largesse.
I now leave you to the rancor
of uneasy, sore ambitions
and the sad dissatisfactions
of deceitful, mad illusions."

XXIV
LU BRIU

Sugnai di vidiri
'ncostu di un fonti
lu saggiu e lepidu
Anacreonti,
   chi a lu so solitu
supra un'arpetta
ja ripassandusi
sta canzunetta:
   "Mentri mi tillica
'mpettu lu briu,
chiù non desideru,
lu munnu è miu.
   Tant'è lu giubilu,
chi all'alma chiovi,
chi non invidiu
nettari a Giovi.

Di onuri e carichi,
d'oru a catasta
ni fazzu un brinnisi,
lu briu mi basta.
   In iddu l'anima
trovu e l'oggettu
d'ogni delizia,
di ogni dilettu.
   Idd'è la sausa,
chi da sapuri
anchi a l'inezii
di un criaturi.
   Li varvasapii
cu gravità
tutti m'intimanu
serietà,
   dicennu: Sciddica
l'etati e scappa,
li moddi cedinu,
la peddi arrappa.
   Su belli chiacchiari:
lu briu distingui
vecchi da giuvini...
Taciti, o lingui.

XXIV
Joy of life

I dreamed I saw
next to a spring
the wise and witty
Anacreon,
   who on his harp,
as was his habit,
was practicing
this little song:
   "While in my heart
there's joy of life
I wish for nothing;
the world is mine.
   The cheer it sows
inside my soul
so overflows
I do not envy
Jove's own sweet nectar.

I have no use
for titles, praise,
for piles of gold.
Life's joy suffices.
   In it I find
the soul and object
of all sweet things,
and all delights.
   It is the sauce
that gives great spice
even to trifles
of a small child.
   The know-it-alls
with gravitas
all recommend
more seriousness,
   saying: age slides
and slips away,
the nerves go limp,
the skin just wrinkles.
   That's worthless chatter:
life's joy distinguishes
young men from old...
Be quiet, tongues.

Eccu viditilu:
mentr'aju ad iddu,
tornu a rinasciri
da picciriddu.
   Mi si rinovanu
tutti l'umuri,
scinni a li musculi
novu viguri ...
   Serii cu savii
vui cunfunditi?
Sciucchizza o invidia
briu nun ni aviti.
   Vecchi misantropi,
da cui fuìu,
forz'è nell'intimu
diri ch'è un Diu.
   Forz'è concediri,
chi senza d'iddu
lu munnu è lugubri,
la vita è un siddu.
   E chi a so arbitriu
si manifesta
Natura all'omini
ridenti o mesta.
   Ricchi solliciti,
ambiziusi,
ah, miserabili,
campati illusi!
   Posti, dominii,
ricchizzi, onuri,
tani di vipari
sù tra li ciuri.
   Lu briu nun calcula
potenza ed oru,
ma in corpi vegeti
paci e ristoru.
   Da oggetti simplici,
da un gestu, un dittu,
stu Diu beneficu
tira profittu ..."
   Ddocu ni spersimu;
era jinnaru,
li gatti, oh l'errami!
mi risbigghiaru.

look there, behold:
while I enjoy it.
I'm born anew
as a young boy.
   All of my humors
are born anew,
the muscles get
vim that is new…
   Do you confuse
serious with wise?
Folly or envy,
you've no life joy.
   Old misanthropes
from whom it fled;
strength is inside
to say it's God.
   Strength's conceding
that without him
the world is dim;
life is a bore.
   And it's his pleasure
if men are given
a cheerful nature
or a sad streak.
   Anxious rich men,
ambitious folk,
o wretched ones,
you live deluded.
   Positions, honors,
riches and power,
hold vipers' nests
among the flowers.
   Life's joy wants not
power and wealth,
but peace and comfort
and strong good health.
   From simple objects,
a gesture, mot,
this helpful god
will gain a lot..."
   There we lost touch.
'twas January,
those cats in heat
awakened me!

XXV
LA PACI

È la Paci la mia amica,
la mia cara vicinedda,
oh chi Diu la benedica!
quant'è saggia, quant'è bedda!

D'idda accantu 'un sentu guai,
campu spicciu, giru tunnu,
e cu pocu, pocu assai,
nent'invidiu tra stu munnu.

Si mi manciu un tozzu duru,
mi l'approva e dici: Sedi;
e stu tozzu vi assicuru,
mi va all'ugnu di lu pedi.

Quannu posu testa a lettu
dormu saziu, com'un ghiru,
grati sonni e di dilettu
di la menti vannu in giru.

Ora volu, com'un cignu,
ora sulcu undusi vii,
e durmennu disimpignu
li capricci e li disii;

e st'imagini sugnati
l'indumani sunn'uguali
a l'imagini ristati
da li giubili reali.

Si lu sagru Munti acchianu,
a lu latu miu s'incugna,
cu li proprii soi manu
poi mi accorda la sampugna.

Di dda supra mentri eu cantu,
viju sutta li mei pedi
terra, mari e tuttu quantu
l'omu ambisci e nun possedi;

e Furtuna tra na rota,
chi currennu a rumpi-coddu
auta e vascia gira e sbota
or'a siccu ed or' a moddu.

Na gran turba appressu d'idda,
chi ci grida supplicanti:
"Oh Dia, ferma na scardidda,
guard'a mia tra tanti e tanti!"

Cumpiangendu sti mischini,

XXV
Peace

Peace is really my true friend.
She is my devoted neighbor.
May the Lord his blessings send!
Oh how fair she is, how wise!

When she stands right next to me,
I don't feel woes, I live free
with the little that I own
I don't envy anyone.

If I eat a piece of bread,
she approves and says: "Sit down!"
And I guarantee, that bread,
reaches down to my toenails.

When I lay my head in bed,
I sleep soundly like a log.
Pleasant and delightful dreams
roam around inside my head.

Like a swan sometimes I fly
and I cross the wavy trails
and in sleep I satisfy
all my yearnings and my whims.

And the images I dream
the next day are just the same
as the images remaining
of past kingly feasts and games.

If I climb the Sacred Mountain[1],
she comes closer, next to me,
and tunes with her own two hands
the sound made by my reed-pipe.

While I sing from way up there,
I observe beneath my feet
earth and sea and all the wares
men yearn for and cannot get;

I see Fortune[2] on a wheel,
turning round at breakneck speed.
High and low, it turns and reels:
one time grass, another weed.

There's a multitude behind
who scream loudly and who plead
"Oh my Goddess, be so kind,
stop a while and look at me!"

Feeling bad for these poor souls,

jeu l'amica strinciu e abbrazzu,
chi li lochi sularini
fa chiù grati di un palazzu;
   chi a guardari si compiaci
la chiù simplici capanna,
lu gran fastu ci dispiaci,
e si vota di dda banna.

   Non perciò la societati
la disgusta: ama l'amici,
e sù pr'idda li citati
ricchi, floridi e felici.

   Ama l'arti ad una ad una,
lu commerciu, li scienzi,
odia sulu di Fortuna
li capricci e prepotenzi.

   Ma poi trema e impallidisci
cu na sincopi murtali
quann'alcunu proferisci:
guerra, liti o tribunali.

   Pirchì accordasi in compensu
da lu celu a un cori drittu,
acciò l'oru, nè l'incensu
non invidii a lu delittu.

   Ma vidennula negletta,
cu maneri assai modesti,
l'omu in idda nun suspetta
na progenii celesti.

   Deh tu fa, Bontati Eterna,
di stu beni imparagiabili
chi l'Europa ni discerna
lu gran prezzu inestimabili!

I embrace and hug my friend
who can make a simple place
much more welcome than a palace,
   who is satisfied to gaze
on a humble, little shed;
she dislikes garish displays
and she turns the other way.

   But she does not feel disdain
for society; she loves friends
and the cities can all gain
wealth, growth, bliss because of her.

   She is fond of all the arts:
all the sciences and commerce,
and of Luck she only hates
her abuses and her whims.

   But she trembles and grows pale,
nearly fainting to the floor,
when someone proposes war,
litigation in the courts.

   That's why heaven in return
handed it to a straight heart
so that neither gold nor praise
he won't envy to a crime.

   But on seeing her neglected,
with her very humble ways,
man in her does not suspect
her celestial progeny.

   Please, Eternal Goodness,
make our Europe[3] realize
the immeasurable prize
of this rare, unequaled good.

----

1. The sacred Mountain: A reference to Parnassus, sacred to Apollo and the Muses.
2. Fortune: Here Fortune is represented as a goddess.
3. Europe: A reference to Europe that at the time was in the throes of the Napoleonic wars.

XXVI
LA FORTUNA

Ah ca passa! allerta, allerta!
La fortuna veni a tia!
Vacc'incontru pri la via,
facci asciari porta aperta ...

　A sti vuci, affacciu, e viju
donn'altera e risplendenti!
Prevenutu da li genti
jeu la porta sbarrachìu.

　Allittata da st'omaggiu
s'avvicina e dici: "Oh bravu!
jeu ti accettu pri miu schiavu,
trasirai tra l'equipaggiu.

　Ven'appressu, e a li toi passi
vidrai nasciri a l'istanti
li rubini e li diomanti,
e tutt'àutru chi bramassi.

　Si voi posti e dignitati
basta sulu chi lu dici ... ".
"Ma dipoi sarò felici?
Spiega, dì la veritati!"

　"Sì, rispusi, ti lu juru
pri sta rota chi susteni
tutti quanti li mei beni,
ed unn'eu mi appoggiu puru."

　"Basta, basta, ben capisciu,
ci diss'iu, stu giuramentu;
lu to grandi appidamentu
già lu viju e ni stupisciu.

　Ma m'è licitu purtari
la mia paci, sta vicina,
chi la sira e la matina
cu mia sempri soli stari?"

　"No, rispusi, avverti a tia,
pri decretu di lu fatu
sta marmotta, chi t'è allatu,
nun pò veniri cu mia."

　"Dunca va', diss'iu, m'addugnu
chi sì instabili e fallaci;
purchì resti in mia la paci,
staju bonu ccà unni sugnu."

　Ristau fridda, comu nivi;

XXVI
Lady Luck

　Ah she's passing! Quick, stand by!
Lady Luck comes now your way,
Go encounter her midway,
let her find your door wide open.

　Hearing this, I looked and saw
a resplendent, haughty woman.
As I was forewarned before,
I threw open my front door.

　So enticed by my respect
she approached and said "Bravu,
You as slave I will accept.
You will be part of my crew.
If you follow after me,
rubies, diamonds instantly
will appear as you proceed
and whatever else you need.

　If you want fame and high places,
all you need to do is speak…"
"But will I be happy then?
Please, explain, tell me the truth!"

　"Yes," she answered, "I do swear
by this wheel on which depends
every one of my gift wares
and on which I too rely."

　"That's enough, I comprehend
your oath's meaning," I replied.
"I can see your true foundation
and I find it quite amazing.
But am I allowed to take
my good neighbor, peace, along
who stays with me from day break
till the sun goes down at night?"

　"No," she answered, "be forewarned
that by destiny's decree
this woodchuck[1] who's next to you
cannot come along with me!"

　"In that case," I answered "Shoo!
you're unstable, false, I see.
I'll remain just where I am
so that peace can stay with me."

　She turned icy, like the snow

poi pretisi fari scasciu;
m'eu mi misi tantu vasciu,
ca di l'occhi ci spirivi.

and she made an awful noise,
but I bent down oh so low
that I vanished from her eyes.

----

1. Woodchuck: Meli himself clarified that if you want to insult someone's intelligence, you call him or her a "marmotta," (a woodchuck).

XXVII
LU GENIU DI ANACREONTI

Struggendu l'Attica
Discordia e Marti,
raminghi scursiru
Musi e bell' arti.

Sbraccaru seculi
timidi, ansanti,
a la barbarii
fuennu avanti.

Doppu tri milia
vicenni e chiui
già quasi scheretri,
vinniru a nui.

Però lu Geniu
di Anacreonti
tutt'ora bazzica
sull'orizzonti;

chi nun truvandusi
ben dignu alloggiu
va trastullandusi
da poggiu in poggiu.

Bell'a vidirisi!
Pari a la cera
lu risu amabili
di Primavera!

Li rai chiù vividi
di lu matinu
tutti accarizzanu
st'estru divinu!

Li Grazii liberi
di ogni ligami
l'allapitianu
a sciami a sciami:

scherzi ed imagini
fini ed ameni
brillanu, abbagghianu
comu baleni.

L'Amuri spreminu,
in iddu immersi,
meli ed ambrosia
da li soi versi.

Sua, benchì simplici,

XXVII
The Genius of Anacreon

With Attica destroyed
by Discord and by Mars[1],
the Muses and Fine Arts
went drifting aimlessly.

For many centuries
unsure and breathlessly
they fled before
barbarity.

After three thousand
events and more
they reached our shore
near skeletons.
The genius, though,
of Anacreon[2]
can still be seen
on the horizon.

As he can't find
a worthy place to stay,
he spends his time in play
from one hill to the other.

He's fair as he can be
and looking at his face
you think that you can see
the loving smile of Spring!

The morning's rays
that most bright shine
all eagerly caress
a talent so divine.

The Graces who are free
from all their ties
like swarms of bees
around him fly.

Images and jests
amusing, fine
dazzle and shine,
like lightning flashes.

And from his verses,
in him immersed,
little Cupids squeeze
honey, and nectar.

His pleasing harmony,

grata armunia
scaccia li trivuli,
l'almi arricrìa.
    Ccà e ddà sbulazzanu
cu gratu intricciu
li jochi a geniu
di lu capricciu.
    Lu briu, chi domina
sta schiera eletta,
tillica e stuzzica,
rallegra, alletta ...
    Mentr'eu cu palpiti
di godimenti
sintìa rapirimi
da sti portenti,
    lu Geniu guardami
gratu e curtisi,
attu a slanciarisi
ad ali tisi.
    Poi tuttu 'nzemmula
si adumbra e fui.
Ahi! pisi e càncari,
culpati vui!

though simple be,
our troubles chases,
pleasing our souls.
    The games abound
here, there around
with charm combined
by whim and mind.
    Life's joy that dominates
this elite crowd,
tickles and stimulates,
cheers and delights…
    While I felt dazzled
by these portents
and felt like swooning
from sheer enjoyment,
    Genius looked at me,
all pleased and kind,
ready to plunge
with outspread wings.
    Then growing troubled
at once he bolted.
Ah, weights and curses,
it's all your fault!

----

1. Mars: The God of war.
2. Anacreon: Cfr. "The Retrograde Journey" (I).

XXVIII	XXVIII
INNU A BACCU	**Hymn to Bacchus**

Quali, o lira, quali mai
Diu beneficu a li genti
risunari tu farai
tra li cordi toi 'ntinnenti?

Forsi Veneri ed Amuri,
primi fonti di la vita?
M'a li miseri è favuri
di li guai sta calamita?

A tia, Baccu, allegru Diu,
spicca st'innu li soi voli,
da tia scinni in nui lu briu
tu sì chiddu chi consoli.

Doppu chi sbuccaru fora
abbuluni pesti e mali
da lu vasu di Pandora,
jennu addossu a li murtali,

scacciau Giovi da li celi
la pietà; ma poi si risi,
pri la morti di Semeli,
a l'impulsi soi curtisi.

D'idda scossu e insinuatu
vosi a' miseri viventi
chi un compensu fussi datu
pri li tanti patimenti.

A st'oggettu estrassi in vita
da la ventri fulminata
lu bambinu, e poi lu 'nzita
tra na coscia sua biata.

Ddà cumpìu li novi luni
di lu patri in compagnia;
natu, poi vinni abbuluni
di iddu attornu l' alligria.

La sua facci spira grazii,
è una flora di delizii,
li Nisei Ninfi mai sazii,
sù di faricci carizii.

Cui jucannu lu scummetti,
nautra cantacci la ninna,
cui sunannu scattagnetti
sàuta e abballa linna linna.

Va Silenu e l' accarizza,

Of what god who's beneficial
to the people, will you sing,
o my lyre, and resonate
through your skilled and knowing strings?

Maybe Venus or else love
who of life is the first spring?
But this magnet of all grief
does it favor those who suffer?

Thus this hymn I raise to you,
o my Bacchus[1], cheerful god.
Life's joy is derived from you.
You're the one who gives relief.

After pestilence and troubles
were let out Pandora's box,[2]
and they landed in abundance
upon wretched mortals' backs,

Jove chased pity from its station,
but thereafter he backtracked
to his noble inclination
for the death of Semele.[3]

Shaken, he reached the conclusion
that all wretched human beings
should receive some compensation
for their countless sufferings.

For this purpose he extracted
from his lightning-stricken womb
a child whom he later grafted
on one of his blessed thighs.

There he spent the first nine moons
in his father's company.
At his birth, around him soon
cheerfulness galore appeared.

His sweet face inspires graces,
it's a garden of delights;
Thracian nymphs can't satisfy
their desire to fondle him.

Some arouse him with a game,
others sing a lullaby,
others, playing castanets,
dance and jump delightfully.

And Silenus[4] goes caress him,

si l' abbrazza e strinci in pettu,
e li guai di sua vicchizza
si cci cancianu in dilettu.

Vucazzialu quannu dormi
tra li gambi adaciu adaciu,
quannu vigghia ci fa 'nnormi
cu la varva sua d'abraciu.

Di ciuriddi adorna e cinci
la facciuzza sua virmigghia,
poi tra l'aria lu suspinci,
e di latu lu gattigghia.

Lu bambinu spiritusu
li manicchi stenni e infila
tra lu so pettu silvusu,
e acchiappannu tira e spila.

Di l'arèddara cucciuta
poi chiù spintu orna la testa,
la barbi-pida-curnuta
capri-razza ci fa festa.

Tra st'allegra cumpagnia
crisci, avanza, spica, ingrassa;
versu l'India poi s'invia,
e rallegra unn'è chi passa.

Doma tuttu l'Orienti,
e cu trenu assai bizzarru
fa di tigri ubbidienti
strascinari lu so carru.

Gloriusu a la turnata
supra un scogghiu rampicanti
di Arianna abbandunata
muta in giubilu li chianti.

Summu eroi, ma non divinu
ti mustrasti a tanti provi,
ma lu donu di lu vinu
ti scuprìu figghiu di Giovi.

Quannu in celu richiamari
già to patri ti vulìa,
ti dignasti a nui lassari
sta memoria di tia.

"Sù, dicisti a la chiurmagghia
di li Satiri bicchigni,
cogghi cogghi, tagghia tagghia
la racina di li vigni".

Tutti allegri a stu cumannu

holding him close to his chest,
and the woes of his old age
are transformed to ecstasy.

Then he rocks him as he sleeps
very softly twixt his legs.
When he wakes up he plays cutesy
with his long and woolly beard.

His sweet face, vermillion red,
he adorns with little buds.
Then he lifts him in the air
and he tickles his right side.

Full of liveliness, the child
his small hands extends and sticks
in his thick and woolly chest
and starts pulling on his hair.

Then when he has grown some more
he adorns his head with ivy.
The horned, cloven footed goats
make him welcome with their cheer.

With this mirthful company,
he grew big and tall and fat.
Then to India he set out,
bringing glee wherein he trod.

Thus he tamed the Orient,
and with a peculiar train,
he had some obedient
tigers pull his cart along.

When in glory he returned,
on a steep and rocky cliff,
for Ariadne[5], who'd been spurned,
he changed tears to jubilation.

As a hero, not divine,
you gave proof in many deeds,
but alone the gift of wine
showed you were a son to Jove.

When your father wanted you
to return up to the sky,
you decided to bestow
this good memory to us.

"Come," you said to your big crew
of he-goatish Satyrs, "come!
Go and gather, cut and store
of the vineyard all the grapes."

Full of joy at this command,

eccu curriri e satari,
pri ddi chiani vennu e vannu
cu carteddi e cu panari.

    Vennu e vannu li ridiculi
Satiretti allegri e sbarii,
comu listi di furmiculi
di frumentu attornu all'arii.

    Cui panara chini attappi
port'appisi tra li corna,
cui ci appenni stocchi e rappi,
e trippannu all'àutri scorna.

    Pri chiù accrisciri la festa
di li toi giulivi riti,
puru adorni la tua testa
di la chiù superba viti.

    Poi cu menti singulari
fai tra un largu e vastu tinu
la racina sdivacari
sin'a tantu ch'è già chinu.

    "Via, dicisti a tutti quanti,
via pistati, dalla-dalla!":
e ogni Satiru a l'istanti
sàuta dintra e pista e balla.

    Già lu mustu acchiana 'nzusu,
già incumincia a riscaldari,
e lu spiritu diffusu
fa li testi sbariari.

    Doppu chi da supra e sutta
vidi e tocchi cu li manu
ch'è pistata tutta tutta,
nè ni resta un cocciu sanu;

    "Basta ccà, cumanni allura,
basta ccà, si copri e scopra:
da se stissa la natura
ben saprà compiri l'opra".

    Eccu in fatti già si avanza
lu rivugghiu, e sàuta e fuma:
va criscennu la fraganza,
va assummannu già la scuma.

    Tuttu è motu ed azioni,
quasi ogn'atomu avi vita,
si scatina, si scumponi,
poi di novu si marita.

    Quann'ai vistu già distrutti

they began to jump and run,
coming, going through the land
with their baskets and their pails.

    Little satyrs come and go
with great cheer, all having fun
and they seem a line of ants
all around the threshing floor.

    Some now carry brimming baskets
dangling from their horns;, some hang
vines and grapes on them, and strike
with horns as they hop away.

To increase the revelry
of your joyful rituals,
you adorn your head as well
with the most superb of vines.

    Then with singular discerning
you make them dump out the grapes
in a vast and spacious vat,
which is filled up to the brim.

    Then you say to everyone,
"Go and squash the grapes with vim!"
And each Satyr right away
jumps inside and stomps and sways.

    Now the must is rising high;
it's beginning to warm up,
and the fumes begin to spread
bringing lightness to each head.

    After you can see and touch
with your hand above, below,
that the grapes have all been smashed
with no single grape left whole,

    "That's enough," you then command,
"let us cover and uncover it,
and then nature by herself
will know how to end her work."

    And in fact, behold, the bubbles
have begun, they plop and fume;
the bouquet is now increasing
and the foam is rising too.

    Every thing is set in motion,
every atom is alive,
it works free, it breaks apart,
then again it weds anew.

    When you see the warring powers

li potenzi guirriggianti
di lu mustu, e chi ridutti
sù in un fluidu pizzicanti,
    gridi: "Orsù, lesti li manu,
chi si passi in vutti e stipi;
ma s'un è placatu e sanu
lu stuppagghiu nun s'intipi".

    Eccu già la chiurma vola
di li Satiri e Silvani,
or'appuzzanu bugghiola,
ora fannu da giurani.

    Cui cu sicchiu, cui cu ciotula
veni, appuzza, vivi e sbaria,
sinn' arrucia e sinni scotula,
gira e sbota a gamm'all'aria.

    Autri 'mmestinu e burdìanu,
autri ammuttanu e si affuddanu,
tutti scialanu e trippìanu,
e a lu tinu poi si abbuddanu.

    Di ccà e ddà cu ciaschi e bummali
sempri tessinu e sbulazzanu,
fannu gran cazzicatummuli,
pri lu briu già quasi impazzanu.

    "Viva Bromiu! Viva!" intonanu
li Baccanti, e comu animuli
vannu in giru, e allegri sonanu
tammureddi cu cirimuli.

    E a Silenu atturniannusi
supra un sceccu lu cunducinu,
va li labbr'iddu liccannusi,
chi di mustu ancora lucinu.

    La sua testa è juta in gloria,
puru l'occhi ancora ridinu;
già lu briu, la murritoria
da lu sceccu lu dividinu;

    ma parannulu tra l'aria
novamenti lu rimettinu;
iddu ridi e in parti sbaria;
chiddi l'asinu scummettinu.

    Di alligrizza tutti addumanu,
spersi su li curi serii,
lu briu sulu regna, e sfumanu
di la vita li miserii.

    Cui lasciannu aratru e vommara,

of the must are all destroyed
and that they have been reduced
to a liquid with a sting,
    you yell out: "Quickly now,
pour it all in casks and barrels,
but if not placated, whole,
do not press the cork on them."

    Now behold the crew of fauns
and of Satyrs fly around,
some are busy filling pails,
others jumping in as frogs.

    Some with buckets, some with bowls
come and bend, drink and get soused,
get all wet, then shake it off.
Then turn, fall legs in the air.

    Others trip and go around,
some now push and form a crowd,
all enjoy and jump about
and dive into the big vat.

    Here and there with flasks and kegs
they all spin and hop about
they make awesome somersaults,
they are almost mad from joy.

    "Long live Bromiu[6], hurray!"
the Bacchantes[7] scream and shout
and like spindles go around,
gladly playing drums with bells.

    And Silenus they surround,
leading him upon a donkey,
while he's licking his lips clean
from the must that makes them gleam.

    His head is in glory now
and his eyes are all aglow;
but life joy, the rowdiness
made him fall down from the ass.

    But they caught him in midair
and put him back on the chair.
He is laughing, partly mad;
they in turn the donkey tease.

    Everyone is joyful, glad,
all grave matters disappear,
life's joy only rules the day,
woes of life all fade away.

    Some the plowshare and the plow

tra lu pratu in ervi e ziddari,
tra l'ardiculi si agghiommara
cu na Ninfa chi fa sguiddari.

    Nun curannu fanghi e zàccani
l'àutri currinu e talianu,
e ridennu a forti scaccani
poi li mani sbattulianu.

    "Gran Dionisiu, a tia si divinu
li gran giubili (altu gridanu
li Bassaridi, chi vivinu,
e chi a brindisi si sfidanu;

    tu Lieu, tu scacci e abomini
l'aspri curi, e tu ti studii
di abbassari insinu all'omini
li piaciri e li tripudii:

    dunc'apprendanu li vausi
a far ecu a lu to encomiu,
e a ripetiri sti applausi:
Viva Baccu! viva Bromiu!"

leave on grass, turds in the fields
and on ivy intertwine
with a nymph who moans and squeals.

    Not concerned with all the mud
all the others, watching, run,
and with guffaws, laughing hard,
they clap hands when they are done.

    "O Dionysius[8], we owe you
our great joys (scream the Bacchantes
very loudly, as they drink
and compete for the best toast),

    You, o Lieu[9], drive away
and abhor the harsh concerns
and to men you always try
to hand down excitement, joy.

    Let the cliffs therefore repeat
this encomium that we mete
and just echo our applause,
long live Bromiu, long live Bacchus!"

---

1. Bacchus: Bacchus, the son of Jove and Semele, was the god of wine and of the grape harvest, as well as the exhaltation of the senses. He is usually portrayed with a bunch of grapes in his hands slightly drunk, followed by a retinue of inebriated women known as Bacchantes, and by satyrs.

2. Pandora's box: Pandora was the woman endowed by the gods with all the feminine graces. To take revenge on Prometheus for the theft of fire, Jove sent her to the world with a box containing all the evils and when she opened the box, evil spread throughout, leaving only hope inside the box.

3. Semele: Cfr. *Buccolica,* "Winter".

4. Silenus: Son of Pan and Gaea, Silenus was a follower of Bacchus, usually represented as a jolly old man riding a donkey.

5. Ariadne: Daughter of Minos, the King of Crete. She helped Theseus defeat the Minotaur in the labyrinth. Theseus eventually married Ariadne, but then abandoned her in Naxos where she was helped by Bacchus.

6. Bromiu: Another name for Bacchus.

7. The Bacchantes: A group of women who followed Bacchus and took part in the festivities known as Bacchanales.

8. Dionysius: Another name for Bacchus.

9. Lieu: Another name of Bacchus.

XXIX	XXIX
LA CICALA	**The Cicada**

Cicaledda tu ti assetti
supra un ramu la matina,
una pampina ti metti
a la testa pri curtina,
e dda passi la jurnata
a cantari sfacindata.

Te felici! Oh quantu à datu
a tia prodiga Natura!
Dintr'a l'umili to statu
d'ogn'insidia sì sicura,
nè a la paci tua si opponi
lu disiu, l'ambizioni.

Benchì picciula sì tantu,
ti fai granni e quasi immenza
propagannu cu lu cantu
la tua fragili esistenza,
e, o si allarghi, o si rannicchi,
ti avi ogn'unu tra l'oricchi.

A tia cedinu l'oceddi
di l'està li forti vampi,
e li grati vinticeddi
pri riggina di li campi
ti salutanu giulivi,
pirchì tu li campi avvivi.

Quannu è Febbu a lu mirìu,
li toi noti sù a lu stancu
passaggeri di arricrìu:
posa all'umbri lu so ciancu,
e a lu sonu di tua vuci
si addurmisci duci duci.

Tra li Musi fusti ascritta,
è notizia avuta in fonti:
induvina cui l'à ditta?
Cui? Lu stissu Anacreonti,
chi fra tanti a tia si ammira
pri suggettu di sua lira.

Dissi ancora ch'ài d'argentu
l'ali, e testa di rubbinu,
ch'ài ruggiada in nutrimentu
di gentili corpu e finu,
senza carni e senza sangu

Sweet cicada, you are perched
on a branch as morning comes
and a leaf shaped like an arch
forms a curtain for your head
and you spend the whole day there,
singing songs without a care.

Happy you! Our Mother Nature
was most generous with you!
In that humble state of yours
from all dangers you're secure,
nor ambitions or wants pose
any threat against your peace.

Though you are indeed quite small,
you grow larger, nay immense,
propagating with your song
your existence that' so frail.
If it wanes or grows intense,
your voice rings in people's ears.

All the birds the scorching blazes
of the summer cede to you
and the welcome little breezes
all salute you as the queen
of the fields in which you thrive
for you make them come alive.

So when Phoebus[1] reaches noon,
your sweet notes provide great aid
to the weary travelers
who will sit down in the shade
and serenely on the ground
sleep at your sweet voice's sound.

You were listed with the Muses,
a good source gave us this news:
can you guess who wrote it first?
Who? Anacreon[2] it was,
who among so many chose
you as subject for his lyre!

He related that you have
silver wings, a ruby head;
your slim body is then fed
not with meat and not with blood
but with dew, which makes your rank

di li Dei quasi a lu rangu;
  e chi spissu all'umbra grata
di li toi vuschitti chiusi,
pri sintiri na cantata
scinni Apollu cu li Musi,
e chi all'arsu mitituri
la stanchizza tu minuri.

  Sì lu geniu di stu Saggiu,
chi li grazii e lu briu
appi in propriu ritaggiu,
tanti preggi in tia scuprìu,
chi t'importa si ridicula
poi ti sparra la furmicula?

  Sì, lu sacciu, e mi fa bili
lu sintiri susurrari
chi stu insettu pricchiu e vili,
chi s'ammazza a cumulari,
ti rimprovera e ti accusa
e di sciocca e di lagnusa,

  Cui nun sa chi un cori avaru
sempri è chiusu a li piaciri?
"Canta, dici, ch'eu preparu
pri lu tempu da viniri,
na risposta tra l'internu ...
ti la cantu tra l'invernu.

  Quann'allura da lu celu
cadirannu muschi vranchi,
pri la fami e pri lu jelu
"sclamirai: Moru li cianchi,
lu miu stomacu è a lanterna!"
va', dirrò, ccà 'un è taverna.

  Giacchì tu ti sì spassata
tra l'estati cu cantari,
spassat'ora l'invirnata
tra lu friddu cu ballari:
a dijunu tra sti valli
sì chiù leggia e megghiu balli!"

  A st'avara sconuscenti
ci poi diri: "Si la vita
si misura da li stenti
tenitilla, e sia infinita,
né crid'iu si possa dari
cui ti l'àja a invidiari.

  Si però la vita è un donu,

almost equal to a god.
  And that often in the shade
of your little bounded woods
comes Apollo with the Muses[3]
just to hear one of your songs,
that relieves the weariness
of the thirsty harvester.

  If the wisdom of this man
who possessed great charm and vim
as his proper legacy
praised in you such qualities,
do not mind the ridicule
when the ant claims you're a fool.

  Yes, I know. It vexes me
hearing insects who're so vile
avaricious, cowardly,
who their lives spend making piles,
who accuse you and admonish
as someone who's lazy, foolish.

  Who doesn't know a greedy heart
is to pleasures always barred?
"Go on, sing, while I prepare
for the future," she declares,
"a good answer I'll provide
when the winter will arrive.

  At that time, when the white flies
will drop down out of the skies
from the cold and from the ice,
you'll complain, "O my poor sides,
I will die! My stomach's bare!
I'll say, go! This is no bar.

  Since you had such a good time
singing through the summertime,
now enjoy this wintry clime:
singing, dancing in the cold.
In these valleys, on a diet,
you'll dance better being light."

  To this hog you can declare:
"If our life's to be assessed
by the burdens we must bear,
you can keep it, may it last
for all time, nor as I judge,
anyone would hold a grudge.

  If, however, life's a favor

146

chi a godirlu datu sia,	that was meant to be enjoyed,
jeu gustannu lu so bonu	the best part of it I savored
di li Musi in cumpagnia,	in the company of Muses;
ho campatu, e ardisciu diri:	I've lived well and I dare say
Tutta mai purrò muriri!"	I can never wholly die."

This ode celebrates Meli's hedonistic idea of life. It corresponds to his vision that life shoulld be enjoyed to the fullest in the bosom of a provident nature.

1. Phoebus: Another name for Apollo, here signifying the Sun.
2. Anacreon: Cfr. "The Retrograde Journey" (1).
3. The Muses: The nine Muses, representing the various arts, lived on Mount Parnassus.

XXX	XXX
IN LODI DI LU VINU	**In Praise of Wine**

Giratu lu girabili
lu briu d'insusu e 'gnusu,
nun potti mai truvarisi
né tana né pirtusu.

Dintra na vigna capita,
già stancu e senza lena,
e sti paroli flebili
pò proferiri appena:

"Pri carità' salvatimi
vui teneri magghioli,
tuttu lu munnu è lastimi,
nessunu chiù mi voli.

Li mali e guai mi oppriminu
in terra dominanti,
l'omini mi discaccianu
da peni oppressi e chianti.

Nuddu mi voli accogghiri:
vui, si pietà sintiti ..."
Dici, e già vidi sciogghiri
li fibri di la viti!

Cci offrinu tantu spaziu
quant'iddu s'introduci,
dicennu: "Vi ringraziu",
e avvivau chiù la vuci,

"pri stu benignu ospiziu,
viti, chi tu mi dai,
stupendu benefiziu
da Baccu n'avirai.

Virrà pri compensariti
Baccu, ch'è patri miu,
in nettari a cangiariti
stu sucu unni sugn'iu.

Chistu sarà delizia,
ristoru a li murtali,
rimediu a la mestizia,
balsamu di li mali.

Purtirà l'equilibriu,
ad onta di lu Fatu,
tra ricca genti e povera,
tra un grandi ed un privatu.

In iddu a rinovarisi

After traveling around,
north, south and everywhere,
life joy could find no lair,
nor a hole in the ground.

He chanced upon a vineyard,
already spent, depressed,
and there these few sad words
he breathlessly expressed:

"Please, save me, tender shoots,
for the whole world is sore
with troubles and with woes:
No one wants me anymore.

The troubles and the evils
that rule the earth do weigh
on me and men oppressed
by woes chase me away.

Nobody welcomes me.
If pity's in your heart…"
He spoke and soon he saw
the hardened fibers thaw.

They offered him a space
where he could fit and stay.
"Thank you," and with a stronger
voice he then spoke this way:

"For this most gracious welcome,
vines, that you've given me,
by Bacchus[1] you will be
rewarded handsomely.

Bacchus, who is my father
as recompense to you,
will change into a nectar
the juice in which I stew.

Delicious it will be,
a solace to all mortals,
for sadness remedy,
a balm for every ill.

It will bring greater balance
in spite of destiny
between the rich and poor,
a private and Grandee[2].

My realm will then return

miu regnu turnirà,
e insemi a consolarisi
l'afflitta umanità".

    Dissi, e li leti augurii
confirmau Giovi. Un lampu
di gioia e di tripudiu
scursi di campu in campu.

renewed through him, and grief
afflicting all humanity,
will find some quick relief."

    He spoke and his glad wish
was soon confirmed by Jove
who sent a joyful flash
that spread throughout the fields.

----

1. Bacchus: Cfr. "In Praise of Bacchus" (XXVIII).
2. Grandee: A Spanish nobleman. Here it simply means, powerful and wealthy. Sicily was dominated by Spain for many centuries.

XXXI
DAFNI

A la forma ed a lu ciauru
sugnu un arvulu di addauru;
puru, ohimè! sti virdi cimi
a li primi tempi foru
fila d'oru a fiocchi o a munti
supra vaga e bella frunti!

Sti mei rami stisi, aperti,
da li pampini cuverti,
foru vrazza bianchi e fini
cu li vini trasparenti;
lu parenti e patri meu
fu lu fluidu Peneu.

Stu miu pedi nun è statu
sempr'in terra sprofundatu,
nè si ruvidu e pisanti;
fu galanti, e sì speditu,
chi l'arditu Apollu istessu
cursi indarnu ad iddu appressu.

Pri salvarimi illibata
fici, ohimè! dda gran scappata,
pri cui chiamami crudili
lu gentili e biundu Iddiu.
Ahi! pers'iu l'anticu aspettu,
e aju figghi a miu dispettu!

Sti razzini, sti jittuni,
ch'in mia formanu un macchiuni,
su li mei figghi e niputi,
cunciputi da mia sunnu
a lu munnu tanti eredi
tra li vini di lu pedi.

Da li mei paterni spiaggi
cca tra prosperi presaggi
da li Musi fui purtata
pri na data profizia:
chi duvìa sta macchia tutta
divintari stanza e grutta,

XXXI
Daphne

I'm a laurel,[1] you'd presume,
by my shape and my perfume,
but, alas, these verdant branches
here on top were once gold threads,
shaped as curls or as a bunch
high upon a fair forehead.

All these branches long and open,
that the leaves now cover up
were my white and slender arms
with transparent and fine veins.
My own father and my kin
was the flowing Peneus.[2]

This my foot not always was
deeply sunken in the ground,
nor so heavy and so coarse,
but quite gallant and so fast
that the bold Apollo chased
after it without success.

To preserve my chastity,
the mad dash I made, alas,
for which "cruel" was the name
the blond god assigned to me.
For my looks I lost the fight
and have children here in spite.

All these grafts and these wild shoots
that form this vast shrubbery
are the children and offspring,
that were all conceived by me.
In this world, I now sustain
many heirs from my foot's veins.

From my own paternal shores,
through auspicious expectations,
I by Muses was brought here
for a specified prediction,
which foresaw that this location
would become a resting station,

acciò quannu Febbu scagghia
rai cucenti e l'occhi abbagghia,
jeu d'Apollu ad un dilettu
umbra e tettu ci pristassi,
e ccà stassi assemi chiusa
la sua paci e la sua Musa.

so that when its burning rays
Phoebus[3] shoots that blind the eyes,
I provide a shade and roof
to one whom Apollo favors,
so that both his peace and Muse
can stay here together close.

----

1. Laurel: Daphne was the daughter of Peneus, a river god. In order to escape the amorous intentions of Apollo, Daphne asked the gods to change her into a laurel tree. They granted her wish. Usually Daphne is represented as a beautiful nymph whose extremities are turning into tree branches as the god is trying to embrace her. The laurel tree came to symbolize Apollo and a crown of laurel is the symbol of poetic excellence.
2. Peneus: The river Peneus flows in the region of Thessaly in Greece.
3. Phoebus: Another name for Apollo as the Sun.

XXXII
LA FILOSOFIA D'ANACREONTI
Dedicatu a Antoniu Forcelli

Saggiu è cui disiu nun stenni
fora mai di la sua sfera,
e nun cura li vicenni
di la sorti lusinghera;
    chi sa cogghiri l'istanti
menu amari di la vita,
l'àutri annega tutti quanti
tra na malaga squisita,
    o tra un siculu licuri,
chi la facci avvia in russu,
e li càncari e li curi
manna tutti in emmaussu.
    S'inflessibil'è lu fatu
cosa mai sperarni d'iddu?
Sia benignu, sia sdignatu
manciu caudu e vivu friddu.
    E di chistu oppognu all'onti
scutu ben timpratu e finu,
armi assai sicuri e pronti
di buttigghi, gotti e vinu.
    È lu suli di jinnaru
lu piaciri a li murtali,
nun si affaccia chi di raru
tra li negghi di li mali.
    Giacchì uman'arti o scienza
a domari nun arriva
di li stiddi l'inclemenza,
l'alm' almenu sia giuliva.
    Sin chi megghiu panacia
nun si trovi a fari smaccu
di ogni scura e trista idia,
jeu mi tegnu forti a Baccu.
    E a vui sfidu, o saggi e dotti,
si scummetta oggi fra nui,
vui cu libbra, ed eu cu gotti,
cu' è chiù allegru e saggiu chiui.

XXXII
The Philosophy of Anacreon
Dedicated to Antoniu Forcelli

A wise man will not allow
aspirations to extend
past his sphere and will not care
for whatever Fate will send.
    He knows how to catch the least
bitter moments in his life
and he drowns then all the rest
in exquisite Malaga
    or Sicilian wine that's best,
that enlivens up his face,
and the troubles of his house
will send to the far Emmàus.[1]
    If inflexible is fate
what can we expect from it?
If benign it's or irate,
it is none of my concern.
    And I face humiliation
with a sturdy, tempered shield:
a secure, strong battle station:
made of bottles, kegs and wine.
    The sunlight in January
is a pleasure for all mortals.
It is not a common sight
midst the fogs of all our woes.
    Since our science, human art
the inclemency of stars
cannot tame, allow in part
that the soul live joyfully.
    Till we find a panacea
that can better lead the fight
against dark and sad ideas,
I will hold my Bacchus[2] tight.
    You I challenge, learned minds,
let us make a bet this day:
you with books and I with steins,
who is wiser, who's more gay?

----
1. Emmaus: The city where the resurrected Christ met two of his disciples who recognized him by the way he broke the bread. Here it means a place far away, because the real location of Emmaus was not clear.
2. Bacchus: The god of wine.

XXXIII
SU LU STISSU SISTEMA

Jeu sù vecchiu, e chiù di mia
fu già vecchiu Anacreonti,
di l'allegra poesia,
di li grazii lu fonti;
    dunca via dammi la lira,
si sù vecchiu, e chi ci fa?
Quann'Apollu e Baccu spira,
tutti semu di un'età.
    È lu briu chi fa l'essenza
di l'amata gioventù,
a cui Baccu ni dispenza,
s'era vecchiu, nun c'è chiù.
    Vecchiu allegru è quasi un ciuri
tra lu riggidu frivaru,
chi si ammira cu stupuri,
chi si apprezza pirch'è raru.
    Jeu sù chistu, o donni cari,
Baccu tuttu mi rinova,
su, sfidatimi a scialari,
ch'eu mi dugnu ad ogni prova.

XXXIII
On the Same System

Though I'm old, Anacreon
was much older before me
who of graces was the fount
and of cheerful poetry.
    So please let me have the lyre,
if I'm old, what does it matter?
When Apollo, Bacchus inspire
we are all of the same age.
    It's the spirit that's the essence
of beloved adolescence.
He whom Bacchus will dispense,
if he was old, he's no more.
    Cheerful old men are a floret
in the cold of February.
With amazement you admire them
for indeed they are quite rare.
    Loving women, so am I,
and by Bacchus I'm renewed.
So dare me to come and play,
I am game in every way.

153

XXXIV
L'ILLUSIONI

Tra un'altura inaccessibili
di la terra a li viventi
lu gran Ben'incomprensibili
situau l'Onnipotenti.

In distanza, a latu oppostu,
la buggiarda illusioni
tra li testi umani à un postu,
e un gran specchiu ad iddu opponi,

chi l'imagini ni accogghi
in abbozzu, e la rifletti
poi cca 'nterra su li spogghi
di caduchi e vani oggetti;

e st'imagini vacanti,
senza nenti di riali,
teni in motu tutti quanti
l'individui mortali.

Ora splendiri si vidi
supra imperii e dignitati;
da luntanu ogn'unu cridi
chi ddà sia felicitati;

e si affretta, si turmenta,
si affatiga ansanti e lassu,
nè c'è cosa chi nun tenta
pri avanzari almenu un passu.

Tra la fudda, ch'è infinita,
lu gran numeru scuntentu
passa in pàsimi la vita,
cu nutririsi di ventu.

Chiddi pochi a cui succedi
di arrivari a ddi confini,
misu apena dintra un pedi,
nun ci trovanu chi spini:

chi l'imagini brillanti,
chi ddà vistu avìanu allura,
è passata multu avanti,
e l'invita a nova altura.

Dunca senza ripusari,
sù da capu, e li soi stenti
s'incumincianu a cuntari
da li novi avanzamenti.

XXXIV
Illusions

On a high peak of the earth,
inaccessible to humans
God located the Great Good
that cannot be understood.

Far away, right opposite,
fraudulent illusion has
an abode in human heads
and a mirror facing it

that the images reflects,
which to earth it then projects
on the bodies of futile
and ephemeral objects.

And these empty images
that have nothing that is real
maintain in relentless motion
every mortal in the nation.

Now you see it shining bright
on empires and lofty chairs:
and from far they all believe
that their happiness lives there.

So they hurry and they fret,
out of breath, they struggle hard.
There's no challenge they won't meet
to advance at least one step.

In that crowd that never ends
the majority of them
live their lives of discontent
nourishing themselves on wind.

The few people who succeed
in arriving at the border,
as they put a foot inside
only find it full of thorns,

for the dazzling images
they had seen up there before,
have moved onto higher ground
and invite them to climb more.

Thus without a day of rest,
they begin anew, and each
new advancement that they make,
marks the start of new travail.

Li doviri ad iddi additti
sù li spini non previsti,
pri cui spissu sù custritti
fari un ponti supra chisti:
    e di stùrdirsi la menti
'mbriacandula di lussu
e di fumi prepotenti,
chi a lu cori 'un ànnu influssu.

    Tra lu fastu, unni scialacqua,
lu so cori è siccu e spinna,
com'un'anatra ntra l'acqua,
chi nun bagnasi na pinna.

    Accussì l'illusioni
si trastulla e si fa jocu
di l'umana ambizioni,
chi mai trova situ a locu.

    Di lu specchiu lu riflessu
mai pri l'omu cadi in fallu;
anchi fa l'effettu istessu
supra un pallidu metallu.

    Nè suduri, nè delitti
mai sparagna un cori avaru,
chi l'imagini ni vitti
supra l'oru e lu dinaru.

    Li periculi chiù astrusi
pr'iddu affrunta a middi a middi,
passa mari timpistusi,
sfida a Scilla ed a Cariddi.

    Quali eccessu 'un persuadi
scelerata fami d'oru?
A toi pedi virtù cadi!
Neghi all'organi un ristoru?

    Tu li visceri a la terra
sin'a funnu ài laceratu!
Unn'accosti sbampa guerra,
ogni drittu è vijulatu!

    Turri a Danaè, e forti muru
su assai debuli pri tia!
La valanza abbucchi puru
tra li manu anchi di Astria!

    Lu gran Messicu distruttu,
morti populi ed lncassi,
menzu munnu ancora in luttu

All the duties these entail
are the thorns they could not see,
which constrains them oftentimes
to build bridges over them,
    and to deaden their poor minds
getting drunk on luxuries
and on fumes of arrogance
that won't influence the heart.

    In that pomp in which they wallow
their heart's barren and they covet
like a duck inside the water
who won't wet a single feather.

    That's exactly how illusion
has a good time poking fun
at the humans' mad ambition
that can't ever find a home.

    The reflection from the glass
for mankind is never false.
It will give the same result
from a metal that is wan.

    There's no hardship and no crime
that the greedy hearts will spare
in whose image there appeared
hints of money and of gold.

    They will face the weirdest perils
for its sake a thousand times;
They will sail through stormy seas,
Scylla and Charybdis[1] dare.

    What excess will not induce
that most wicked thirst for gold?
Virtue falls down at your feet!
You'll deny your limbs repose?

    You have torn out of their depths
the intestines of the earth.
War explodes where you approach;
every right of man is breached!

    Danaè's[2] strong wall and tower
against you, just have no power!
The scales in Astraea's[3] hands
you succeeded to unbalance.

    Mighty Mexico's destroyed,
many folks, the Incas, dead;
Half a world is still in mourning,

155

trema e fremi a li toi passi.
 Da tua rabbia st'innocenti
a salvari 'un è bastatu
lu divisu continenti
da un oceanu esterminatu?
 Cui produci tanti mali
cridiremu chi in se stissu
sia ddu beni originali
a cui l' omu fussi ammissu?
 No, lu specchiu è chi ni 'nganna;
giacchì all'omu la ricchizza
è un castigu, na cunnanna,
chi a bramari chiù l'attizza,
 e perciò a multiplicari
e l'usuri e l' angarii,
li delitti e li ripari,
li timuri e firnicii;
 e st'angustii all'alma impressi,
chi ci rudinu anchi l'ossa,
sempri criscinu, e indefessi
l'accumpagnanu a la fossa.
 Saggiu è cui l'oru a prezzari
cupidiggia non incita,
ma l'idia di sodisfari
li bisogni di la vita;
 e a li curti ed a li sali
va accusì di mala-vogghia,
comu infirmu a lu spitali
strascinatu da la dogghia.
 L'oru è pr'iddu uguali all'unna,
chi scurrennu pri li prati,
li 'nvirdica e li fecunna
di li frutti chiù preggiati:
 si però in un locu resta
tutta in massa ristagnata,
l' erba esterna è sicca e mesta,
dintra è fradicia, ammargiata.
 Cussì avaru sceleratu manna
l'oru tra un subbissu
a lu publicu, a lu Statu gravi,
e inutili a se stissu.
 Avirà da genti accorta

shakes and frets at your footsteps.
 Being a great continent,
set apart by a vast sea,
could not keep those innocents
safe from your ferocity?
 Should we now believe that one
who produces such excesses
is himself that primal good
to which man should have access?
 No, the mirror's the deceiver
since great wealth is for a man
a real a scourge, a penalty
which stirs him to crave for more
 and to multiply, therefore,
the abuse and usury,
the misconducts and amends,
the distresses, and concerns,
 and the woes carved on his soul
that gnaw him down to his bones,
which grow ever without pause
that escort him to his grave.
 Wise is he who values gold
without urging avarice,
but the wish to satisfy
the necessities of life,
 and who goes to Courts and Halls
as reluctantly as does,
carried there by painful woes,
a sick man to hospitals.
 Gold is like a wave for him
that by flowing over fields
makes them green, inducing them
their exquisite fruits to yield.
 But stagnating in one place
the outside grass will grow dry
and wilt while the one inside
will get soggy and decay.
 Thus the wicked greedy man
through gold lust will cause grave harm
to the public and the state,
while for him there'll no gain.
 Some respect and bows he'll get

qualchi omaggio o qualch'inchinu,
pirch'è l'asinu chi porta
li reliquii tra lu schinu.

Vagu giuvini, a tia ridinu
la furtuna e l'elementi,
te felici tutti cridinu ...
tu suspiri e ti lamenti!

Chi ti manca, salvi a tia?
Ma tu guardi fissu e attentu
lu riflessu chi spicchia
dintra dd'occhi ... ah! già ti sentu:

dintra dd'occhi, tra ddu aspettu,
tra ddi labbri, tra ddu risu
tu ci vidi chiaru e nettu
lu gran Beni, un Paradisu.

Chi sia chistu lu riflessu,
e non già l'originali,
lu pacificu possessu
ni è la prova essenziali.

Spissu ad autri lusingheru
lu riflessu sicci appresta
da una spata e da un cimeru,
chi fa partirci la testa;

è l'istintu di natura,
chi fa l'omu sociali,
a ddu lampu si sfigura,
cedi all'impetu brutali.

Già fatt'emulu di Achilli,
sogna e imagina conquisti,
e Deidamii a milli e milli
spasimanti pr'iddu e tristi.

Un gran campu di battagghia
si presenta in fantasia:
idd'è avanti, chi si scagghia
e la Fama lu talia.

Sì, la Fama in chiù di un tomu
(ti l'accordu tua parenti)
farà imprimiri lu nomu;
ma tu mortu chi ni senti?

Si tu campi, a la furtuna
n'è lu meritu dovutu;
cedi ad idda la curuna
ed appenditi pri butu.

by some folk who're circumspect,
for it's donkeys who bear packs
full of relics on their backs...

Handsome youth, the elements
and good luck do smile on you.
Everyone thinks you're content
but you sigh and voice complaints!

What is missing, can you say?
but you're watching with great care
the reflections from those eyes
in the mirror, ah I hear:

in that aspect, in those eyes,
in that smile and in that mouth,
you can see without a doubt,
the great Goodness, paradise.

That this is just a reflection
and not the original
its non-violent possession
is the final, vital proof.

Often flattering to some
the reflection will approach
through a sword or through a crest
which makes them just lose their heads

and man's innate tendencies
that make him a social creature
are so changed at such a sight
he won't fight his brutal urge.

He's a new Achilles[4] now,
dreaming conquests in his head
Deidamias[5] by the thousands
each in love with him and sad.

A great field of battle shows,
conjured by his fantasy,
him up front, with ready blows
while Fame stands there watching him.

Yes, in more than one tome, Fame
(I concede her as your kin)
will then make them print your name:
but what will you hear once gone?

If you manage to survive,
you will owe it all to luck.
So give her the laurel crown
and as vow your life go pluck.

Quannu poi la Patria
grida chi vol'essiri difisa,
curri, o novu Leonida,
va', tua gioria è già decisa.

Autru poi lu lampu osserva
sù la gioria di li littiri,
si sagrifica a Minerva,
ma 'un c'è menzu a farlu zittiri.

Vigghia, suda e si affatìa
su li libri e li scienzi,
ma Virtù, Filosofia,
nun sù dati a vui st'incenzi.

Nun è omaggiu chi dispenza
a la bella Verità,
ma un trofeu chi alzari penza
a la propria vanità.

Sulu cerca ammobbigghiari
lu so spiritu di ciuri
e cu chisti cummigghiari
di lu cori li lurduri.

La raggiuni, lu bon sensu
nun consulta, e sulu in menti
ci à d'oturi un boscu immenzu
per imponiri a li genti.

Ogni massima chi dici
nasci in menti e in bucca mori,
chiù ni ostenta e chiù infelici,
nudda scinni a lu so cori.

E quant'iddu chiù la vana
gloria cerca e bram'e ambisci,
chista tantu si alluntana,
chiù ci sfui e ci spirisci.

'Nzumma ogn'unu lu riflessu
vidi in cosa chi ci manca,
e ci curri sempri appressu,
e si affanna, suda e stanca.

Oh! infelici razza umana
nata a jiri assicutannu
di li beni l'umbra vana,
chi ccà 'nterra nun ci stannu!

Si non fariti felici,
la virtù putrìa a lu menu
di l'interni toi nimici

When the Motherland then cries
that she wants to be defended
hurry, new Leonidas.[6]
Run, your glory's all decided.

For another the flash falls
on the glory drawn from Letters.
To Minerva[7] he gives all,
but no one can shut him up.

He sweats, struggles, stays awake,
over sciences and books,
but philosophy and virtue,
his tribute's not for your sake.

These are not the honest praises
to inspiring Verity,
but a trophy that he raises
to his private vanity.

He just tries to decorate
his own spirit with the flowers
and with these he will then cover
the sore lewdness in his heart.

He will not make use of reason
nor of simple common sense;
he on folks wants to impose
the immense list of his authors.

Each new maxim that he tries,
born in head, on his lips dies.
Trying more, creates more gloom.
None will satisfy his heart.

And the more that he pursues,
craves and yearns for futile glory,
it will move far in a hurry,
fly away and disappear.

In conclusion, we all see
in the reflection things we lack,
And we run right after them
sweating, struggling tiredly.

O unhappy human race
who are born to always chase
of great wealth the hollow shades
that on earth do not reside!

If it cannot make you happy,
virtue can at least provide
in your hands a way to guide

dar'in manu a tia lu frenu;
   tu fratantu l'abbanduni
pri acchiappari l'umbri vani!
Sì (ed oh! ceca 'un tinni adduni)
di la favula lu cani!

and control your inner foes.
   In the meantime you let go
to run after empty shades!
Of the fable you're the dog[8]
(oh, but you're too blind to know!)

----

1. Scylla and Charybdis: A reference to the Strait of Messina, which had two monsters, oen on each shore threatening sailors. Scylla was supposed to be on the Calabrian coast and Charybdis on the opposite side in Sicily.

2. Danae: Danae was the mother of Perseus who was ravaged by Jove, who transformed himself into a shower of gold and penetrated the tower where her father had locked her to keep her safe from the god.

3. Astraea: During the reign of Saturn, Astraea was the goddess of Justice, who was driven away by man's iniquities, ending the Golden Age.

4. Achilles: The greatest Greek warrior, son of Peleus and the sea goddess Thetys, who participated in the Trojan war. He was slain by Paris, who shot an arrow in the only part of his body that was vulnerable: his heel.

5. Deidamia: She was the daughter of Lycomedes, who married Achilles while he was at her father's court. Achilles had been hiding there dressed as a woman to avoid going to the Trojan war.

6. Leonidas: He was the leader of the 300 Spartans who stopped the Persians at Thermopilae in 480 BC.

7. Minerva: The Roman name for Athena, the goddess of wisdom and the arts. She was born fully grown from Jove's brain.

8. Dog: Meli is referring to the Aesop fable about the dog that dropped the meat from its mouth to grab hold of its own image reflected in the water of the river it was about to cross.

XLV
LV DIVORZIU

Stanca di viviri
vita pinusa
fici divorziu
da mia la Musa,
    dicennu: «È angustia
pri tutti dui
lu stari 'nzemmula
uniti chiui.

    Pri nui stu seculu,
ch'è sedicenti
luminusissimu,
nun luci nenti.

    Di voli altissimi
sarrà capaci;
ma unn'è Giustizia?
Unn'è la Paci?

    Unni si trovanu
virtù e costumi?
Dunca a chi servinu
sti tanti lumi?

    Cu l'oru sbuccanu
da un novu munnu
li guai, chi abbundanu
chiù chi nun sunnu.

    La genti a st'ldolu
stendi la manu,
e anchi offri vittimi
di sangui umanu.

    Virtuti e meriti
sagrificati
sunnu a sta barbara
divinitati.

    Si tra stu pelagu
profundu e cupu
cercu ajutariti
chiù ti sdirrupu;

    ma giacchì libera,
e Dia sugn'iu,
un megghiu seculu
mi cercu. Addiu ...»

XLV
The Divorce

Tired of living
a life of woes
my worried Muse
asked for divorce,
    saying: "A bother
this is for us
to stay together
as in the past.

    This century
that is so bright
and so seductive,
provides no light.

    It may be capable
of soaring flights,
but where is Justice?
and where is Peace?

    Where can we find
manners and virtue?
So what's the use
of all these lights?

    With all the gold
from the new world
woes multiplied
a thousand fold.

    Toward this idol
folk stretch their hands
and offer victims
with human blood.

    Virtue and merit
they sacrifice
to this barbaric
divinity.

    If in this lake
so dark and deep
to help I try
I'll sink you more.

    But as I'm free,
a goddess, too,
a better century
I'll seek. Goodbye..."

IV
Di li Canzunetti

IV
from Song Lyrics

Allurtimata	So, finally
jeu chi ti fici,	What did I do?
E vaja, Nici?	Come now, my Nici,
Vaja, chi fu?	what's wrong with you?
E vaja, via	Come now, come on,
vaja, biddicchia,	my pretty one,
ridi tanticchia	come smile at me.
vaja 'un sia chiù!	Let's end this row!
No, nun ci vaju	No, I won't go there
chiù ddà, unni chidda,	to where she lives.
no picciridda,	No, my sweet child,
no, figghia, no	No, my sweet love.
Nun ti scantari,	Don't be afraid!
no, gioia mia,	No, my one joy,
àutra chi tia,	other than you
nun amirò.	there's no one else.
Tu puru aeri,	You too did play
(mi nn'addunavi)	just yesterday
puru jucavi	with that new guy,
cu chiddu ddà.	as I well saw.
Poi si joch'eu,	But if I play,
fai lu cucchiaru,	you start to cry
ed eu, l'amaru	and I, poor guy,
nun dissi un'"a".	said not a "hey".
Mi nni fai tanti,	You've been so mean;
mi rispittiu,	my love grows lean
pirchì lu viu	'cause I can see
ca 'un m'ami chiù.	you don't love me.
Tu mi voi mortu,	You want me dead,
t'aju stuffatu,	you've had enough,
cu stu filatu	and I do dread
mi dici sciù.	you'll shoo me off.
Sì, ca spirisciu,	I'll disappear
mi chiancirai,	yes, but you'll cry
si sintirai:	if you will hear
Iddu nun c'è...	he is not here...
Ma tu chi chianci!	But, you are crying!
No, gioia mia,	No, my dear joy,
nun dicu a tia,	I meant not you,
via spagna-rè.	forget about it.

V
Di li Canzunetti

Forsi pirchì nun m'ami,
aju a cripari in peddi?
Ad àutri, assai chiù beddi,
ci dissi: Sciù-nna-ddà.
    E tu, ti cridi, forsi,
o pezza di sumera,
chi àutr'asina a la fera
di tia nun ci sarrà?

    'Mmatula ti ni veni
cu l'aria e lu sfrazzu,
e via chi sugnu pazzu!
o qualchi ghignalì!
    Jeu chiù stimari a tia?
Jeu fariti chiù 'nnormi?
Va' curcati, va' dormi,
cosa pri mia nun sì.

    Bon'è chi t'aju ad occhiu;
cridimi, ch''un mi pischi;
sti modi picciuttischi
cu mia 'un fannu chiù.
    Si 'un vai di francu a francu,
si nun stai a li patti,
chi t'aju a diri? Statti:
però ci perdi tu.

    Ch'a mia, chi sù tinutu
pri onestu e facci bianca,
na crocchiula nun manca,
certu la truvirò.
    Sarrà carni di vacca,
non jencu, comu tia,
almenu è tutta mia,
ma in tia 'un c'è meu nè to.

    E comu la sai tutta!
Davanzi billi-balli,
darreri pri tri calli
tu canci anchi a lu Re.

V
From the Canzunetti

Perhaps 'cause you don't love me
I have to drop down dead?
To other girls much prettier
than you, "Get lost!" I've said.
    And maybe you believe,
my silly donkey-poo,
there's not another donkey
down at the fair but you?

    It's useless to parade
with pomp and arrogance.
You think that I am a mad,
born yesterday, by chance?
    I, show respect for you?
I, show you courtesy?
Go on to bed and sleep.
You're not my cup of tea.

    I'll keep my eyes on you,
these childish ways of yours
have all but run their course.
Know, I won't fall for them.
    If you can't be sincere,
if you can't honor pacts,
it's fine. You're free to act.
You'll be the loser here.

    For I, who have a reputation
as an authentic gentleman,
without any trouble can
easily find myself a lass.
    She may not be so fine,
and not as fair, of course,
but at least she'll be mine:
with you no mine or yours.

    You know all kinds of tricks;
before me, preen and dance,
behind me, for three pence
a King you will exchange.

Cunta cu mia ssa robba?
Chi cridi chi sugn'orvu?
Tra picciunastra e corvu
gran differenza c'è.

Tu cridi ca sù chiacchiari
sù ditti pri un'inciuria?
e chi sta prima furia
fra picca passirà?
  E sti palori a sganga,
ti cridi tu, gramagghia,
chi sù fumu di pagghia,
chi allura si ni va?

T'inganni, puviredda!
Ver'è chi l'àutri voti
ti fici sti rivoti,
chi po' 'un duraru chiù;
  ma l'arcu poi si rumpi
s'assai lu tiri e smovi,
e truniannu chiovi,
ora sta allerta tu.

Jeu po' ch'aju a 'nfuddiri
cu tia, curuzz'amatu?
Nun mi l'aju sunnatu,
nè mi lu 'nzunnirò.
  Agghiuttu, agghiutu, agghiuttu!
Ch'è stomacu di ferru?
Ma guarda si poi sferru,
lu peju idd'è lu to.

Sì foddi, sì 'nfirnicchia,
sì fausa, e sì ciràula,
oh pesta! chi diavula!
Nàutra 'un si truvirà!
  Finèmula sta vernia!
jeu mancu cu vossia,
vossia mancu cu mia;
bonciornu... scucchia-ccà.

You think that I don't know?
You think that I am blind?
Big difference you'll find,
twixt fledglings and a crow!

You think this conversation
was meant just to harass?
And that my irritation
would quickly fade and pass?
  And that my words of scorn
you think, o foolish one,
are flashes in the pan
that fade once they're born?

Oh no my dear! You're wrong,
It's true that in times past
my censures did not last
in time for very long,
  But when the bow you bend
too tautly, it will snap.
Then rains with thunderclap!
Beware, you understand?

Am I to go insane
with you, heart of my heart?
I did not dream that part
nor will I dream it again.
  I swallow swallow, swallow!
Is my gut made of steel?
Beware, the brunt you'll feel
if I my top will blow.

You're crazy, you're a bother,
you're fake and you're dishonest,
a devil and a pest,
like you there is no other.
  Let's end this sad affair:
Your ladyship one way,
And I another. Good day!
Let's cut the rope right there!

LU GIARDINU D'AMURI	The Garden of Love

Nici, si nun sì barbara
ed ami a mia mischinu,
fammi na vota trasiri
dintra ssu to jardinu.

Ntra ss'urticeddu amabili,
vasu di rosi e sciuri,
c'è acqua chi assaggiannula
astuta lu miu arduri.

La nsalatedda tennira
davanzi la tua porta,
lu ciauru mi stuzzica,
li peni mi conforta.

Chiù dintra poi si vidinu
violi e sempriviva
unni si fa la zagara,
filici cui ci arriva!

Cci su li minnulicchi,
chi smovinu la gula;
mi liviria l'angustia
na minnulicchia sula.

C'è un pedi di lumia,
fa un ciauru stupennu,
cci acchianiria tra st'arvulu
e ci staria in eternu.

Si vidinu chiantati
cu regula e misuri
li priziusi fraguli
accantu sti toi mura.

Nici, si nun sì barbara
e m'ami veramenti,
fammi na vota trasiri
ca nun ti toccu nenti.

L'acqui sù na delizia,
si ddocu dintra trasu
non stuzzicu, nun pizzicu,
ciauru, toccu e vasu.

Nici, if you're not cruel
and for this wretch you care,
let me, let me once at least
come inside your garden fair.

In your lovely little orchard
that with roses is replete
flows such water whose sweet taste
soothes the burning thirst and heat.

And the tender tasty salad
that is growing at your gate
my keen sense of smell excites
and my buds will surely sate.

And as I gaze farther in
violets and evergreen,
orange blossoms I see inside:
blessed he who this has seen!

There are almonds green and tender
that my gullet so excite.
Every woe and every plight
one sweet almond would destroy!

And there is a lemon tree
on which I would surely climb
for its fragrance's heavenly.
I would stay there for all time.

Precious strawberries are there
all around next to your walls
which were planted with great care
and observance of the rules.

Nici, if you're not cruel
and for me you truly care,
let me come inside one time!
I won't touch a thing in there!

Oh, the waters there are bliss!
if you let me come inside,
I won't tease, I will not sting
I'll just smell, and touch and kiss.

VI
ORIGINI DI LA PUISIA

Quannu nuda azzardau la Viritati
mustrarisi ccà 'nterra a li murtali,
fu sfazzunata, e cu l'anchi stuccati
a li Licei ricursi pi spitali.

Sula Filosofia n'appi pietati,
l'accugghìu, la curau di li soi mali.
Ma comu chù appariri pri li strati,
stanti l'odiu di l'omini fatali?

Ccà fu, chi tutti dui si stracanciaru
cu mascari, bautti e dominò,
chi da la Finzioni s'impristaru.

La favula è stata, dunca, ed è lu so
salvu-cundutta; e tutti tri di paru
cumponnu, o Poesia, l'essiri to.

VI
Origins of Poetry

When Truth attempted here on earth to show
herself to mortals brazenly all nude,
she was mistreated and with broken legs,
Liceums as her hospital pursued.

Philosophy alone some mercy showed,
welcoming her, and caring for her ills.
But how could she appear in public view
if hearts of men such awesome hatred filled?

At that, to camouflage themselves both chose,
borrowing all from Make-Believe, and wore
carnival masks, long cloaks with hoods, and clothes.

Fable has been and still remains, therefore,
their own safe-conduct; and all three compose
your essence, Poetry, your inner core.

VIII
A L'ACCADEMIA PATRIOTICA IN OCCASIO-
NI DI UN DISCURSU RICITATUSI A FAVURI
DI L'IDIOMA SICILIANU

Vivi la matri vostra, Iddiu la guardi,
amatila, e 'un circati na matrigna:
sia cura e triddu di muli-bastardi
lu zappari di l'esteri la vigna.

L'istintu di natura anchi a li pardi,
anchi a li tigri stu dovir'insigna;
urla lu lupu quann'à fami, o s'ardi,
nè s'impresta lu gergu di la signa.

Lu sulu pappagaddu 'nfurgicata
s'avi na lingua pri parrari a matti,
facennu d'ocedd'omu capriata.

Multi accademii eu sacciu accussì fatti
grec'itali-latini. Allurtimata
ch'aviti 'ntisu? Na sciarra di gatti.

VIII
To the Patriotic Academy. On the Occasion
of a Speech Recited in Favor of the
Sicilian Idiom.

Your mother is alive, may God save her,
love her and do not look for a stepmother;
let hoeing vineyards of a foreigner
of bastard mules should be the care and bother.
Natural instincts teach that all must meet
this duty, leopards with tigers along.
Wolves howl when they are hungry or in heat,
nor will they borrow from a monkey's tongue.

Only the parrot has created a muddlesome
tongue to converse with people who're insane,
creating a mixed man-bird, weird idiom.

Many academies I know are made like that:
Italian-Greek-and Latin. In the end,
what did you hear? A bunch of fighting cats.

Giovanni Meli

XVI

Umbri, figghi a la notti, chi abbitannu
stati ntra grutti ed orridi furesti,
deh! chi l'estremu miu spiritu resti
a chianciri cu vui lu propriu dannu.

Si mai ccà junci, accasu caminannu
chidda, chi l'alma di riguri vesti,
in flebbili lamenti e vuci mesti
diciticci: Murìu, murìu d'affannu.

D'un inutili lagrima si forsi
bagna la fridda cinniri, 'un spirati
chi sia cumpassioni di cui morsi;

è strania ntra ddu cori la pietati;
e si chianci, n'è causa chi si accorsi
che mortu iu, nun c'è chiù cui pr'idda pati.

XVI

O shadows, children of the night, who abide
inside dark caverns and horrendous woods,
permit my dying spirit to reside
and weep together with you its own hurt.

If ever, walking here and not by choice,
the one who clothes her soul with ice and rock,
with weak laments and a most plaintive voice
tell her, "He died, he died from sheer heart break."

And if she's moved a useless tear to shed
on the cold ashes, do not hope it flows
from feelings of compassion for the dead.

Compassion is most alien to her heart,
and if she weeps, it is because she knows
that with me gone, no one for her will smart.

Favuli morali

Moral Fables

Illustrations by
William Ronalds

PREFAZIONI	PREFACE

Mentr'era tra un macchiuni,	While I was in a grove,
cu un libru tra li manu,	with a book in my hands,
un saviu Vicchiuni	a wise old man approached
si accosta chianu chianu,	and moving very slowly,
e dici a lu miu latu: 5	came standing next to me, 5
"Cos'ài ca sì turbatu?"	and asked: "What's troubling ye?"
"Ch'aju ad aviri? Guarda,	"What else? Just look at this!
un bonu libru adocchiu,	I ogled this good book,
viju ch' 'un teni scarda,	I saw it was in shreds,
lu trovu un crivu d'occhiu! 10	a veritable sieve. 10
Sta camula è un 'orrenda	These moths are a great plight.
pesti, chi tuttu smenna!	They chew all things in sight!"
Lu midagghiuni anticu	That ancient Patriarch
l'osserva e lu rividi,	examined it with care
poi dici: "S'eu ti dicu, 15	and cried: "Would you believe me, 15
ch'è sorti, nun mi cridi;	if I said it's your luck?
pri mia, s'è misu all'asta,	This book, to my advice,
prezzu nun c'è chi basta".	if sold, would have no price."
Jeu dissi tra di mia:	I mumbled to myself:
"O chistu è tuttu pazzu, 20	"He's either quite insane, 20
o puru mi trizzìa".	or else he's teasing me."
Vitti lu miu 'mbarazzu	The old man read my thoughts
lu Vecchiu, e, un pocu cursu,	and though with some disdain
ripigghia lu discursu:	began to speak again:
"Mi pari ammaraggiatu; 25	"You seem to be surprised. 25
tu cridi ch'eu scaminu?	You think I lost my senses?
Eu parru da sennatu,	I speak as a sane man,
e a diriti anchi inclinu	and I'm inclined to tell you
l'arcani mei chiù granni,	secrets I've held in store
chiusi da centu ed anni. 30	a hundred years or more. 30
Sacci ch'eu scinnu drittu	Know then that I descend,
ri linia masculina	in a straight line of males
da Esopu, ch'in Eggittu	from Aesop who in Egypt
fu un mari di duttrina,	was a vast sea of knowledge
chi apprisi in maggiur parti 35	that in great part he took 35
non già da libri e carti,	not from some learned book,
ma d'armali e insetti,	but from insects and beasts,
chi sù pri l'omu muti;	who to all men are mute.
iddu cu li perfetti	Through keen and perfect senses,
sensi e sua gran virtuti, 40	through worthiness supreme, 40
ddi gerghi avennu in pratica	and knowledge of their tongues,
composi na grammatica,	a grammar he composed.

chi cu fidecommissu
la stissa d'iddu scritta
dipoi ni l'à trasmissu 45
in linia sempri dritta,
e in primogenitura
mentri sua razza dura.
　Dunca eu, misi ad esami
sti fogghi camuluti, 50
trovu chi sti riccami
sù littiri sculpiti,
sù cifri ed asterischi
di codici armalischi.
Pr'istintu di natura, 55
di l'animali a gloria,
la camul'avi cura
d'incidirni l'istoria,
li mutti, li sentenzi,
e l'arti e li scienzi. 60
　Scurri li libri tutti,
non superficiali,
li mastica, l'agghiutti,
ni fa sucu vitali;
poi tra l'intagghi scrivi 65
li fatti chiù istruttivi".
　"Chi fatti, intagghi ed arti,
jeu ripigghiai, chi mutti?
Lu senziu mi parti!...
Eh via! comu si agghiutti 70
sta pinnula? 'Un sia mai,
vidi ch'è gross'assai".
　Lu Vecchiu nun desisti;
ma, mortu di li risi,
mi dici: "Capiristi 75
un turcu ed un cinisi?
Puru sù tutti dui
omini comu nui".
　"Va beni, eu ci rispusi,
ti vogghiu anchi accurdari, 80
li gerghi li chiù astrusi
chi sianu pri tia chiari;
ma di': Poi tra sta prova
chi sucu sicci trova?
Na cosa ben ridicula 85
sarrìa st'acquistu a nui;

That very manuscript
has been passed on to us
who have been the trustees 45
from first born to first born,
in a straight line of males
until the bloodline fails.
　So having analyzed
these moth-consumed old pages, 50
all this embroidery
I see as sculpted letters,
as asterisks and codes
transcribed in beastly modes.
Instinctively endowed 55
to praise the animals,
the moths have been entrusted
to carve their histories,
their words and sentences
their arts and sciences. 60
　Moths run through every book,
not superficially;
they chew and they digest it,
and make a vital lymph
from it. Then they proceed 65
to carve noteworthy deeds."
　"What deeds, what art, what carvings,
what sayings?" I replied.
"You're driving me insane.
Come on! How can I swallow 70
this pill? It could not be!
It seems too big to me!"
　The old man did not stop,
and, laughing all the way,
said: "Can you understand 75
a Turk or a Chinese?
And yet they're similar;
they're men just like we are."
　"All right," I answered him.
"I even grant you that 80
you clearly understand
the most abstruse of idioms.
But, tell me, what's the gain
from all your care and strain?
For us the gain would be 85
ridiculous indeed!

169

si parra, si matricula	For if a moth could speak,
na bestia sempri chiui:	a beast he'd prove to be;
nun giuva, nè instruisci,	he's useless, vain. It's good
bon'è ca 'un si capisci". 90	he can't be understood!" 90
Ripigghia lu Vicchiuni:	The old man then replied:
"Tu decidisti allura	"You would decide like that,
a colpu, ed a tantuni!	by groping in the dark?
La causa 'un è matura;	Your reasoning's unsound.
ni teni scritti e carti? 95	Have you some parchments, books? 95
Ai 'ntisu mai li parti?	And have you heard their side?
Si nun capisci un jota	If you don't understand
di li brutali accenti,	but one single iota
la sua raggiun'è ignota;	of all the beastly accents,
si dunca a lu presenti 100	their reasoning's unknown. 100
ti mancanu sti guidi,	So lacking such a guide,
cu' è bestia? Cui decidi?	who's dumb? Who can decide?
Tant'è, chi nun sù muti,	Besides, they are not mute!
la vuci la sintemu;	Their voices can be heard.
ànnu li senzi acuti, 105	Their senses are quite sharp, 105
e chistu lu videmu;	that's something we can see.
conuscinu li priculi,	They know where dangers lurk;
notanu l'amminiculi.	they notice every quirk.
Pirchì pri aviri un rastu	To sniff a quail or pheasant
di quagghi o di faciani, 110	why does a man rely 110
l'omu, chi à un nasu vastu,	upon a dog's sharp nose,
ricurri e indinga un cani?	when his own is quite large?
Signu ch'è persuasu	A sure sign that he knows
chi un cani à megghiu nasu.	dogs have a better nose.
L'aquila in vista avanza 115	The eagle's sight is far 115
di assai la specii umana;	superior to man's;
da l'àutu e in gran distanza	from far high in the air
scuprisci tra la tana	an eagle can pin point
na picciula sirpuzza,	a snake's protruding head
chi affaccia la tistuzza. 120	emerging from its bed. 120
Lu gaddu! E si pò dari	The rooster! Is there better
barometru chiù certu?	barometer around?
Anzi si pò chiamari	In fact, it can be called
un'almanaccu apertu,	an open almanac
e insemi un bon curdinu 125	and also a good charm 125
cu lu risbigghiarinu.	with a built-in alarm.
Chi cura e viggilanza	What care, what vigilance
à pri lu so puddaru!	does he show for his coop!
Contra di cui si avanza	Against those who advance
scudu si fa e riparu; 130	he makes himself a shield; 130

lu pettu esponi, azzarda,
periculi nun guarda.
  Manteni l'armunia
tra tutti, e quannu alcuna
gaddina s'inghirria,   135
curri, e cu pizzuluna,
cu gridi e colpi d'ali
la rendi sociali.
  Si coccia in terra à vistu
d'oriu o di frumentu,   140
nun pensa farni acquistu
pri propriu nutrimentu,
ma fermu, e a pedi 'ncutti,
chiama, e li sparti a tutti.
Chi meravigghia poi   145
si tantu ossequiatu
ven'iddu da li soi?
E l'omu, chi vantatu
si è di raggiuni tempiu,
non imita st'esempiu?   150
  Chi mai dirrò di l'api?
chi munarchii ben saggi!
Rispettanu li capi,
e chisti a li vantaggi
di la societati   155
sù tutti dedicati.
  Si avissi lena e ciatu
dirrìa di li furmiculi.
Ma basta: Aju pruvatu
li bruti non ridiculi,   160
e chi anchi li chiù tenniri
ni dunanu di apprendiri.
  Lu tessiri e filari,
cu pedi e cu manuzzi
ni l'àppiru a 'nzignari   165
tarantuli e virmuzzi,
chiddi chi assai pulita
ni tessinu la sita.
  Li nostri primi nanni
a li castor'intenti,   170
di casi e di capanni
forsi li rudimenti
apprisiru e imitaru,
chi poi perfezionaru.

he'll bare his chest, he'll dare,
for dangers he won't care.
  The harmony he keeps
among all; when a hen
is feisty and rebels,   135
he'll run and with some shrieks,
with blows from wings and beak,
he'll teach her to be meek.
  And if he spots some grains
of barley or of wheat,   140
he does not run to take it
for his own nourishment,
but standing firmly there,
he beckons all to share.
It is no wonder then   145
to see him so revered
inside his chicken coop.
And does not man, who boasts
of being reason's temple,
just copy his example?   150
  What shall I say of bees?
What monarchies most wise!
They honor all their chiefs
and these devote themselves
to the felicity   155
of their society.
If I had strength and breath,
I'd speak about the ants.
But that's enough! I've proved
beasts are not comical   160
and even the most tender
advice can surely render.
  We all had to be taught
the art of spinning, weaving
by tiny hands and feet   165
of spiders and small worms,
those tiny worms who spin
silk that's as fine as skin.
  Our most remote ancestors,
by watching beavers work,   170
the rudiments of huts
and houses must have learned
and building on their skill,
they made them better still.

Apprènniri ni fici	175	The fish known as kingfisher	175
l'arti di lu piscari		taught us the art of fishing.	
lu pisci Piscatrici,		He has two fishing poles	
chi dui cimeddi in mari		protruding from its head.	
sporgi d'intesta, e adisca		He casts them out to fish	
pisci cun iddi, e pisca.	180	to snare and catch his fish.	180
S'in oggi pratticamu		If bleeding is an art	
nuiàutri la sagnìa,		we practice in our day,	
o grossu ippopotàmu,		o hippopotamus,	
l'apprisimu da tia,		we learned it all from you,	
chi s'ài li vasi chini	185	for when your veins grow thick,	185
ti l'apri cu li spini.		with thorns you'll bleed them quick.	
Forsi a ddi menti virgini,		Perhaps it was the moth	
in chidd'età di allura,		who gave those virgin minds	
la camula l'origini		in times long gone and past	
detti di l'incisura,	190	the model for engraving,	190
ed anchi, si nun sbagghiu,		and wrong though I may be,	
di l'arraccàmu e intagghiu.		for carving and embroidery.	
Si divi a la cicogna		The use of enemas	
l'usu di lu clisteri:		we owe to the good stork,	
chista, quannu abbisogna,	195	for when he feels the need,	195
si adatta a lu darreri		he puts in his behind	
lu beccu d'acqua chinu,		of water a full beak,	
chi caccia all'intestinu.		and pumps it up his creek.	
Si cridi ch'un'apuzza		Some think that when a bee,	
pusata tra na frunna,	200	sitting upon on a leaf,	200
a modu di varcuzza		was carried by a wave,	
purtata via da l'unna,		as though it'd been a boat,	
all'omini appi a dari		was what gave man the key	
l'idia di navigari		to navigate the sea.	
Dirriti: Ma lu sceccu	205	You say, 'What of the ass?	205
si vidi ch'è turduni,		You see he is quite stubborn	
nun senti virga e leccu;		and heeds no whips or calls.	
c'è chiù? Cu lu vastuni		Moreover, if you hit him	
si torci gruppa e schina,		he twists his rump and balks	
e a forza vi camina!	210	and then he hardly walks.'	210
Vui chistu interpretati,		Do you interpret this	
vera turdunaria?		as asininity?	
Ma comu lu pruvati?		But how can you prove that?	
Pò darsi chi disia		It may be that he needs	
pri lu so sangu tardu	215	a stronger sharper blow	215
un stimulu gagghiardu.		because his blood is slow.	
Pò darsi di una razza		Perhaps he's of a race	
di Stoici e di Zenuni		of Stoics and of Zenos	

chi soffrinu la mazza,		who choose to suffer clubs	
li càuci e l'ammuttuni,	220	with kicking, shoving, too,	220
pri farisi li senzi		to make their senses used	
avvezzi a l'inclemenzi.		to be more harshly bruised.	
Pò darsi chi pri oprari,		It may be that to work	
vol'essiri infurmatu		he wants to be informed	
di chiddu ch'avi a fari,	225	about what he must do,	225
pri farlu regolatu:		so he can do it well.	
truvandusi a lu scuru		And if he's in the dark	
nun opera sicuru.		he lacks the proper spark.	
Lu servu, chi discurri,		When his own master says	
quannu lu so patruni	230	to him, 'Run quickly, run!'	230
ci dici: Prestu, curri!		without explaining why,	
nè spiega la cagiuni,		or where he is to go,	
nè duvi lu destina,		a servant who's no fop	
s'imbrogghia e nun camina.		will get confused and stop.	
Ora, chi ni vuliti	235	So what do you expect	235
da un sceccu, chi muntati		from a poor ass you ride	
senza d'avirni uniti		without your having joined	
li lingui e voluntati?		your idioms and wills?	
Data sta verità,		Given these facts as true,	
è assai chiddu chi fa.	240	he does much more than he should do.	240
E poi vi sia accurdatu		And should I grant you that,	
tra tanti e tanti armali,		among so many beasts,	
lu sceccu pr'insensatu,		the ass is dumb and silly,	
pri stupidu e minnali,		and lacks good sense, so what?	
ch'importa? Tra nui stissi	245	Among our human kind	245
quantu ci nn'è di chissi		many an ass you'll find.	
Sarrà forsi infamata		Shall we perhaps defame	
perciò la specii umana		our human species then,	
pirchì in ogni nidata		because in every brood	
dui terzi pri zuzzana	250	if you take out the best,	250
toltu lu frontispiziu,		two thirds or even more	
sù scecchi pri giudiziu?		are donkeys to the core?	
Agghiunciu anchi dicchiui:		But I am not yet through!	
sta stissa asinitati		Their asininity	
chi disprizzati vui,	255	that you despise so much,	255
li rendi cari e grati		is what makes them beloved	
a chiù di un pirsunaggiu,		to many men who lack	
ch'è scarsu di curaggiu.		a strong or valiant back.	
Ma poi, d'iddi in compenza,		But to make up for them	
sù armali scaltri, oh quanti!	260	there are smart beasts aplenty.	260
Esalta la prudenza		The elephant's great prudence	
Pliniu di l'elefanti;		by Pliny was exalted.	

ed àutri ànnu abbastanza	Some other beasts possess
scaltrizza e vigilanza.	awareness, craftiness.
La vulpi eh! chi vi pari? 265	What say you of the fox! 265
Lu lupu!...Oh ch'è scaltruni!	The wolf's so very smart!
E cui lu pò gabbari?	Who can deceive that beast?
Lu corvu! E' maraguni!	The raven? Oh how stealthy!
Nui, d'iddi a li malizii,	Each of us is a novice,
nun semu chi novizii. 270	compared to all their malice. 270
Pirchì natura vosi	Nature distributed
spàrtiri tra viventi	to every living being,
a ogn'unu la sua dosi	of instincts and of talent,
d'istinti e di talenti	a dosage that was proper
quantu putìa bastari 275	which would have guaranteed 275
sua specii a cunsirvari.	survival of each breed.
Juncennu all'omu, vitti	When nature came to man
chi consumati avìa	it saw it had used up
l'istinti supraditti;	those instincts I have mentioned.
perciò ni arrisiddia 280	So from the animals 280
di bestii na gran parti,	it gathered some, in part,
e all'omini li sparti.	and put them in man's heart.
Perciò spissu tra omaggi	That's why we often see
videmu l'omu-vulpi,	the Fox-Man flattering
chi ossequia li malvaggi, 285	and courting evil people. 285
ch'è iniqu e li soi culpi	His wickedness and guilt
li scàrrica e deponi	he will unload and place
supra li genti boni.	on a more honest race.
Videmu l'omu-lupu,	We see the Lion-Men
chi pari un midagghiuni, 290	resembling an old coin, 290
seriu, devotu e cupu:	solemn, devout, and somber,
ostenta la raggiuni,	whose reasoning with honey
'mpastata cu lu meli,	seems blended, but, meanwhile,
ma ntra lu cori à feli.	in his heart, there is bile.
L'omu-liuni à un funnu 295	The Lion-Man at heart 295
intrepidu e custanti;	is daring and quite constant.
precipiti lu munnu,	The world may fall apart,
sta firmu ddà davanti,	but he will stand right there,
ed a la sua ruina	and face his own downfall
opponi pettu e schina. 300	with chest high, standing tall. 300
C'è l'omu-signu intentu	There are then Monkey-Men
a li gran modi e l'usi,	who follow fashion's ways,
bandera ad ogni ventu	—flags blowing in the wind—
muta, riforma e scusi	who change, reform, and rip
abiti, vrachi e insigni, 305	their clothes, their pants and banners, 305
guardannu l'autri signi.	to ape all changing manners.

E' l'omu-talpa chiddu
chi campa innamuratu
di cui non cura d'iddu,
e tantu n'è accicatu,   310
chi chiù nun cridi all'occhi,
m'à chiàcchiari e 'mpapocchi.
    Cussì c'è l'omu-cani,
chi abbaia di tutt'uri
poveri, a viddani,   315
a latri, a traditura,
ma dànnucci lu tozzu
proi lu cannarozzu.
    Avemu l'omu-gattu,
chi metti a diri: *meu*,   320
appena vidi un piattu:
avidu, comu Ebreu,
a tuttu stenni l'ugna,
pigghia, e dicchiù sgranfugna.
Tralasciu li becchi-omini   325
pri tema a li Satirici;
jeu citu li fenomini,
a modu di l'Empirici,
e passu e mi cunfunnu
di jiri troppu affunnu.   330
    Avanti, ca c'è chiui...
Ci sunn'omini tali,
(ma dittu sia tra nui)
chi sù sutta l'armali,
quant'è sutta di un signu   335
na cascia, o pur'un sgrignu.
    Tal'è lu riccu avaru,
na specia d'omu-cascia:
si sarva lu dinaru,
lu chiudi, si l'incascia,   340
si sicca e infradicisci
sempri guardandu l'isci.
    Ci sù, senza ch'iu nomini,
l'omini-pupi veri,
o sia l'automat-omini: 345
l'amica, o la mugghieri,
o servu un lazzu movi,
e ci fa fari provi.
    Tu cridi, fors'iu sia
cursu, o di mala gana,   350

The Mole-men are the ones
who spend their lives in love
with those who love them not.
They are so blinded that   310
they won't believe their eyes,
but empty, silly lies.
    There are then Dog-Men, too,
who bark continuously
at thieves, and at betrayers,   315
at peasants, and the poor,
but throwing them a bone,
they quickly change their tune.
    Cat-Men there are as well
who start by saying "Miau,"   320
but when they see a plate,
as greedy as a Jew,
with their long-reaching paws,
they grab and show their claws.
I leave the He-goat-Men   325
as themes for satirists;
I cite phenomena
as would empiricists.
But I will let this pass,
lest I get lost, alas.   330
    Let us proceed, there's more...
There are some men who are
—let's keep it to ourselves!—
much lower than the beasts,
much like a safety box   335
is lower than a fox.
    Such is the greedy rich,
a sort of Strong-box-man.
He saves all of his money,
he locks it in a box,   340
he withers and grows mold,
with eyes glued to the gold.
    There are then Puppet-Men,
without my naming them,
that is Automat-Men.   345
Their mistresses or wives
or servants move a string,
and make them do their thing.
    Perhaps you think I'm hasty,
or that I bear ill-will   350

contra la specii mia?
Ah! la natura umana,
(e cui nun sinn'adduna?)
cadìu in vascia fortuna!
È lu gran Culiseu,   355
chi di l'anticu fastu
nun serba pri trofeu,
chi qualchi oscuru rastu,
chi appena si discerni
tra li ruini eterni!   360
    E' la raggiuni addunca
l'occhiu di grassu in nui?
Ma quantu sia piiunca,
già lu viditi vui,
risona lu so titulu,   365
ma, 'un à vuci in capitulu.
    Capitulu, eu sentu,
quannu li passioni
focusi e in movimentu,
a la riflessioni,   370
chi timida si affaccia,
chiudinu porta in faccia.
    In quali specii, o razza
di bruti o d'animali,
si trova una sì pazza,   375
chi tanti oltraggi e mali
s'impegna a speculari
contra di li soi pari?
    Privari tra na vampa
di vita centu e middi,   380
fatti a la stissa stampa
cu carni e cu capiddi,
è un'arti di cui l'omu
ni à scrittu chiù d'un tomu.
Ogn'unu vanta in sè,   385
pri guida la raggiuni.
Chistu è lu peju, ohimè!
Raggiuni a miliuni,
quant'omini sù in munnu!
Va pisca tra stu funnu!   390
    Chisti mantennu in guerra
li regni cu li regni,
fomentanu ccà 'nterra
causi, liti e impegni;

against humanity.
Alas, but human nature
(who cannot see that's so?)
has fallen very low.
It's the great Coliseum   355
that of its ancient pomp
preserves as a last trophy
but some obscure faint sign
you hardly can discern
in ruins sempitern.   360
    Is reason then the one
advantage left to us?
How powerless it is,
you can see for yourself:
its title sounds affective,   365
its voice is not effective.
    Effectiveness I call
when fiery emotions
hold sway within the heart,
and slam the door with force   370
upon reflection's plea
which knocks but timidly.
    What species, say, what breed
of brutes or animals
knows someone who's so mad   375
that he works hard to bring
abuse and woeful tears
upon those who're his peers?
    Depriving in a flash
a thousand of their lives   380
who're made from the same mold,
with the same hair and flesh,
an art is on which men
more than one book can pen.
Every man boasts that he   385
is guided by his reason.
That's the worst of it!
We've reasons by the millions
as many as men are.
Who's right? Go count each star!   390
    And reasons are what keep
one realm at war with others,
fomenting here on earth
suits, quarrelling, and pledges;

la genti anchi maligna	395	and even wicked folk	395
la sua raggiuni assigna.		their reasons will invoke.	
L'avvisi e manifesti,		The posters and the banners	
chi sù tra li nimici		which are between two foes	
preludii di funesti		lamentable preludes	
guerri desolatrici,	400	of devastating wars	400
tutti, da capu a fini,		all will, from first to last,	
sù di raggiuni chini.		their reasoning broadcast.	
Li scartafazii immenzi,		"The endless dossiers	
ch'ingrassanu lu Foru,		which make Court Houses bulge	
chi estorcinu sentenzi,	405	extorting sentences	405
e da li vursi l'oru,		and gold out of one's purse,	
ch'imbrogghianu lu munnu,		entangling every life,	
tutti raggiuni sunnu.		are with good reasons rife.	
Raggiuni, chi derivanu		They're reasons that derive	
d'àutri, e chist'àutri ancora	410	from others, which in turn,	410
di àutri, ch'in fini arrivanu		from other reasons come,	
a scarruzzari fora		and which at last derail	
di li raggiuni, ed ànnu		from reason's track and meet	
radica tra l'ingannu.		their roots in sheer deceit.	
Ch'in nui li passioni	415	For passions in our hearts	415
si affaccianu a lu spissu		appear quite often masked	
cu mascari assai boni,		with truly good intentions;	
e poi fann'un'aggrissu:		they then lay things to waste.	
la mascara comuni		The common mask they wear,	
è pr'iddi la raggiuni.	420	is reason that is clear.	420
Però tra l'animali		But for the animals,	
lu sulu e nudu istintu		alone and without rivals,	
regna senza rivali		instinct will reign supreme	
dintra lu so recintu,		within its boundaries;	
e li soi visti fissa	425	it sets its sights upon	425
su la sua specii istissa.		the species that's his own.	
Addunca cui procura		So then whoever tries	
li bruti studiari		to study animals,	
studia la natura,		is studying our nature,	
unico e singulari	430	a book that's singular,	430
libru di arcani senzi		unique, whose hidden clues	
chi acchiudi li scienzi".		all science can disclose."	
"Benissimu, diss'iu,		"That's fine," said I. "Perhaps,	
tu forsi pischi a funnu;		you are on the right track.	
però lu senziu miu	435	But my poor brain appears	435
mi pari a nàutru munnu:		to be in other worlds.	
sì beni ài peroratu,		You pleaded with such art	
ch'eu sù menzu ammazatu.		that I'm convinced, in part.	

Micci ài saputu induciri
cu li maneri e l'arti: 440
via, mèttiti a traduciri
sti camuluti carti...".
Dissi, e lu Vecchiu esponi
li soi traduzioni.
Jeu agghiuncirò pri restu   445
qualchi moralità,
chi scinni da lu testu,
(sibbeni 'un ci sia ddà)
pr''un dirimi li genti
chi 'un ci aju misu nenti.   450

With manners and with style,
you have persuaded me.   440
So then, begin translating
these moth-consumed old papers..."
I said and the old man
his versions then began.
However, I will add   445
a moral to the tales
derived right from the text,
(although it is not there)
so people won't complain
there's nothing here that's mine.   450

I
LI SURCI

Un surciteddu di testa sbintata
avìa pigghiatu la via di l'acìtu,
e faceva na vita scialacquata
cu l'amiciuni di lu so partitu.

Lu ziu circau tirarlu a bona strata,
ma zappau all'acqua, pirchì'era attrivitu,
e dicchiù la saìmi avìa liccata,
di taverni e zàgati peritu.

Finalmenti mucidda fici luca;
iddu grida: Ziu ziu, cu dogghia interna;
so ziu pri lu rammaricu si suca;

poi dici: "Lu to casu mi costerna;
ma ora mi cerchi? chiaccu chi t'affuca!
Scutta pri quannu jisti a la taverna".
*****

I
The Mice

A little mouse who was lightheaded, brash,
had gone the way of wine to vinegar,
living in sheer debauchery with dash,
along with bosom pals who were his par.

His uncle tried to show him the right way,
but dug in water, for he'd grown too sure.
The taste of lard had made him a gourmet,
expert on taverns, pubs: an epicure!

He finally was caught in Kitty's claw.
"Uncle, oh, uncle!" in great pain he cried.
His uncle was distressed by what he saw,

and then he said: "I'm really mortified,
but, may you hang, just now you see my way?
The price for going to the taverns pay!"
*****

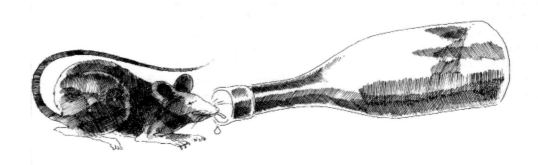

179

II
LI GRANCI

Un granciu si picava
di educari li figghi,
e l'insosizzunava
di massimi e cunsigghi,
'nsistennu: "V'aju dittu
di caminari drittu".

Chiddi, ch'intenti avìanu
l'occhi in iddu, e li miri,
cumprendiri 'un putìanu
drittu chi vulìa diri:
sta idia tra la sua cera
d'unni pigghiarla 'un c'era.

Iddu amminazza, sbruffa,
l'arriva a castiari,
ma sempri fici buffa:
mittennulu a guardari,
vidinu cosci e gammi
storti, mancini e strammi.

Alza l'ingegnu un pocu
lu chiù grannuzzu, e dici:
"Papà, lu primu locu
si divi a cui ni fici,
vaìti avanti vui,
ca poi vinemu nui".

"'Nzolenti, scostumati,
grida lu patri, oh bella!
A tantu vi assaiati?
L'esempiu miu si appella?
Jeu pozzu fari e sfari,
cuntu nun n'aju a dari.

Si aviti chiù l'ardiri,
birbi, di riplicari..."
Seguitau iddu a diri
seguitar'iddi a fari...
Tortu lu patri, e torti
li figghi sinu a morti.

*****

II
The Crabs

A crab had as a goal
to educate his brood;
wise maxims he'd extol,
as he this aim pursued,
repeating always: "Straight!
I told you to go straight!"

His youngsters were quite clever;
their interest was keen,
but they could not discover
what going straight could mean.
There was no way to glean
"straight" concepts from his mien.

He threatened them with ire,
he even punished them,
his plans, though, did misfire,
for when they looked at him
they saw just crooked stems
and weird, left-leaning gams.

The crab's maturest son
was struck by a fine thought:
"As maker you're the one,
by you we should be taught!
So show us how to walk,
there is no need to talk!"

"You, insolent upstart!
You certainly have nerve!
You think you are so smart!
As model I should serve?
I'm freer than the breeze.
I do not have to please.

And if you dare, you lice,
to answer one more time..."
He kept up his advice,
and they their pantomime.
Wrong father, crooked young
till death will come along.

*****

180

III
LI BABBALUCI

Purtandusi la casa su la schina
dui babbaluci all'umbra di una ferra,
cu la vucca di scuma sempri china
si ìanu strascinannu terra terra.

Diss'unu: "Sta mia vita ch'è mischina!
Chiù chi ci pensu lu miu senziu sferra!
Una frasca sdisèrrama e scintina
vidi comu va in aria linna e sgherra!"

L'àutru, niscenn'un cornu da la tasca,
si arma lu cannocchiali so maniscu,
guarda, e poi dici: "Un ti pigghiari basca;

chistu è un jocu di sorti buffuniscu;
pri tantu vola in àutu sta frasca
pirchì è vacanti, ed avi ventu friscu".
*****

III
The Snails

Under the shade of a cane brake, two snails
who bore their homes about like refugees
were dragging their slow bodies on their trails
and foaming at the mouth continuously.

"My life is really wretched!" said one snail.
"The more I think, the more it bothers me.
Look how that stubble, so inept and frail,
flies in the air with elegance and glee."

The other pushed a horn out of its pouch,
prepared to aim its handy telescope,
looked up and said: "You have no cause to grouch!

It's part of destiny's ironic scope.
The stubble flies so high into the air
because it's empty and the breeze is fair."
*****

182

IV
L'AQUILA E LU RIIDDU

Ci fu un tempu (secunnu certa cronica
truvata tra l'arcivu di Parnassu),
chi l'oceddi facìanu vita armonica
in bona cumpagnia, tra jocu e spassu:
avìanu liggi santi, e cuvirnati
eranu da eccelenti maggistrati.

Duvìanu un jornu eligirsi un Regnanti,
perciò si radunaru supra un munti:
mitteva ogn'unu li soi preggi avanti
facennu, senza l'osti, li soi cunti:
l'aquila, supra tutti, e lu vuturu
cridìanu avìri lu votu sicuru.

Ma li saggi l'esclusiru, dicennu:
"La forza e robustizza sù gran preggi
tra lu statu salvaggiu, ma duvennu
star 'n società, li privileggi
maggiuri sù l'ingegnu e la prudenza;
meritanu perciò la preferenza.

Chi si chista a li forti si cuncedi
ni mittemu a periculu evidenti
di tristi abbusi e la primaria sedi
centru di la tirannidi addiventi;
pertantu lu talentu sia la prova
di elezioni, e in chiddu unni si trova".

Decisu lu cunsigghiu in sensi tali,
si applicaru a pinsari un sperimentu
pri scopriri in cui chiù l'ingegnu vali,
ed in cui spicca prudenza e talentu;
ma l'aquili, adoprandu forza e dolu,
li tiraru a fissarisi a lu volu.

Stabileru pri tantu, chi cui chiui
vulava in àutu fussi Re assolutu.
Vinniru a prova; ma però ci fui
n'oceddu leggerissimu e minutu,
chi pigghiau tra la testa di nascostu
di l'aquila chiù forti lu so postu.

Chist'aquila a li stiddi sinni va,
e 'un videndusi oceddi a lu so latu,
ritorna gloriusa, e dici: "Olà,
sù Re, pirchì chiù in àutu aju vulatu";
m'addunannusi l'àutri di chiddu

IV
The Eagle and the Kinglet

According to a certain history,
discovered in Parnassus' archive,
birds long ago lived in good company,
enjoying fun and games, and simply thrived.
They had good, saintly laws, a government
by magistrates most wise and excellent.

One day, they needed to elect a king
and gathered high upon a mountain peak,
and every bird began, not reckoning
with his own host, of his great skills to speak.
The eagle, most of all, thought he would be
(the vulture, too) assured of victory.

The wise birds, though, excluded them with this:
"Both strength and sturdiness are a great prize
among the savages, but not for us
who live in a society. The wise
intelligence and prudence value more,
and they deserve our preference, therefore.

For if it's given to those who are strong,
we place ourselves in dire jeopardy
of certain, vile abuse, before too long,
making our Seat a den of tyranny.
Let talent thus determine the selection,
and let the one with more win the election."

The Council thus agreed to stand behind
this plan and sought a way of testing it
which would reveal the sharpest, finest mind,
the one who had more prudence and more wit.
The eagles, though, by using fraud and might,
convinced them to rely alone on flight.

Thus they established that the bird who flew
highest would be proclaimed King Absolute.
The trials came, at last, but there was, too,
a bird that was quite tiny, nay, minute,
who stowed away, unseen, do you know where?
in the head feathers of the strongest eagle there.

This eagle flew so high he reached the stars,
but when he saw there was no one abreast,
with pride he flew back saying: "There you are,
I'm now your King-Elect! I am the best!"
The others, noticing the bird-vedette,

ch'aveva 'ntesta, gridanu: Re iddu.
    L'aquila esclama, e dici: "Vinni smentu,
lu sforzu di vular'eu l'aju fattu".
Ripigghian'iddi: "Però lu talentu
a li toi sforzi à datu scaccu-mattu;
impara quant'importa avir'ingegnu,
e multu chiù pri governari un Regnu".
    Soggiunciu ccà na nota: Nun si osserva
stu termini reiddu in nudda lingua,
ma tra la nostra sula si conserva;
vogghiu chi ogn'unu, perciò, la distingua
pri la chiù antica lingua originali
sin da quannu parravanu l'armali.
*****

just pointed straight at him cried out: King-let![1]
The eagle then retorted: "You are wrong!
    It was my strength that made me climb that height."
But they replied: "Although you are quite strong,
his talent has checkmated your great might.
Learn the importance, thus, of a sharp wit,
especially when realms depend on it!"
    And here this note I'll add: "Reiddu"
is a term not found in any other tongue,
except our own. And so, because of this,
I'd like all men to know it is not wrong
to claim our tongue's the oldest and goes back
to when all beasts for talking had the knack.
*****

----

1. Though I tried to convey Meli's playfulness here, by using "king-elect" and "kinglet," I am afraid I was not entirely successful. Meli is playing with the name of the bird "riiddu," which means means "kinglet," but by separating the word as "re iddu" it means "he king" that is, "he is the king, not you!"

V
LU SURCI E LU RIZZU

Facìa friddu, ed un surci 'ngriddutizzu
mentri sta tra la tana 'ncrafucchiatu,
senti a la porta lamintari un rizzu
chi ci dumanna alloggiu, umiliatu:

"Jeu, dici, 'un vogghiu lettu, nè capizzu;
mi cuntentu di un'angulu, o di un latu,
o mi mettu a li pedi 'mpizzu 'mpizzu,
basta chi sia da l'aria riparatu".

Lu surci era bon cori, e spissu tocca
a li bon cori agghiùttiri cutugna;
sù assai l'ingrati, chi scuva la ciocca!
Trasi lu rizzu, e tantu sicc'incugna

chi pri li spini lu surci tarocca,
e dispiratu da la tana scugna:
e dicchiù lu rampugna
l'usurpaturi, e jia gridannu ancora:
"Cui punciri si senti nèscia fora".
*****

V
The Mouse and the Hedgehog

Curling upon himself on a cold day,
a mouse was burrowed deep inside his hole
when from outside he heard a hedgehog say
"Please, share your cubby with this wretched soul!

I want no pillows and no bed, "he cried.
"A tiny corner will do fine. I pledge,
if I am sheltered from the cold outside,
to sleep here at your feet, right at the edge."

The mouse had a good heart and it's his kind
who're forced to swallow the most bitter gall,
for earth spawned many men who're thankless, blind.
The hedgehog, once inside, began to sprawl.

Stuck by the other's spines, the wretched mouse,
cursed and gave up his home in desperation,
But the usurper hurled more provocation,
by screaming loudly with intent to chide:
"If you don't like the needling, go outside!"
*****

VI
SEGUITA LU STISSU SUGGETTU

Ma lu rizzu pagau la penitenza,
pirchì lu Celu teni la valanza,
e boni e mali azioni cumpenza
cu l'estrema esattizza e vigilanza.

N'omu, ch'avìa ddà 'ncostu la dispenza,
s'era addunatu di qualchi mancanza
di lardu e caciu, e misu in avirtenza
vitti lu surci fùiri in distanza.

L'aveva assicutatu, ma nun potti
jùncirlu, chi pigghiatu avìa la tana,
d'unni lu rizzu lu spustau la notti;

m'appena l'alba in orienti acchiana,
va cu petri e quacina, e a quattru botti
(cridennu dari a lu surci 'mmattana)

attuppa, mura e 'nchiana
lu pirtusu chi ad iddu era nocivu,
e fu lu rizzu sippilutu vivu.

Cirnennu ora lu crivu:
Paga d'ingratitudini la detta
l'ingratu, e cui fa beni, beni aspetta.
*****

VI
On the Same Subject

The hedgehog though did pay the penitence
for Heaven which maintains a proper scale,
gives good and evil their just recompense
with great exactitude and without fail.

Nearby, inside the pantry of his house,
a man had noticed that his cheese and lard
were disappearing fast. The fleeing mouse
one day he spied while he was standing guard.

He chased him, but in vain, to the same hole
from which the night before that spiny beast
had forced him to go out into the cold.

As soon as dawn had risen in the east,
the man went back with mortar and with rocks,
and thinking he was murdering the mouse,

with just a few but masterful quick strokes,
he sealed the hedgehog in with little blocks,
and buried him alive in his new house.

Essentially this tale this truth unlocks:
debts of ingratitude ingrates will always pay;
those who do good, expect good deeds to come
[their way.
*****

VII
LU CANI E LA SIGNA

Un gentil'omu avìa na signa e un cani,
chi tinìa 'ncatinati tra un perterra:
vitti la signa un jornu chi lu pani
di lu cumpagnu era rimastu a terra;
ci spia: "A tia la fami 'un manca mai,
pirchì ora 'un manci? Dimmi, chi cosa ài?"

Rispunn'iddu: "Malatu 'un micci criju;
ma ci aju tra lu cori na gramagghia:
lu patruni avi assai chi nun lu viju;
cui sa?..." Ma lu parrari idda ci stagghia:
"Poh! Nun c'è àutru? E di': Senza di tia
lu patruni, chi forsi 'un mancirìa?"

Replica: "Nun lu sacciu; ma mi costa
ch'una vota eu mi spersi, e mi circau".
Ripigghia l'autra: "Nàutra vota apposta
vinni cu un lignu e ti vastuniau,
e tu, da veru saccu di vastuni,
ci liccasti li manu e li garruni".

"Chistu, dici lu cani, voli diri
aviri gratitudini, ed un cori
chi la cunserva a costu di muriri".
Ma dici l'autra: "Tu tantu ti accori
per iddu, ed iddu (si tu spii a mia)
mancu pinseri e trivulu à di tia".

Grida lu cani: "Menti pri la gula,
tu, chi sì tutta pazza ed incustanti
cerchi cumpagni pri nun stari sula.
Lu patruni mi stima, e non ostanti
ch'iddu nun mi stimassi, eu sempri esattu
ci sarrò pri ddu beni chi mi à fattu.

Un cori a la mia specii vosi dari
gratu e riconoscenti la Natura,
pirchì duvìa sirviri pri esemplari
all'omu stissu e ad ogni criatura,
acciò profitti di nostra allianza,
e apprenda gratitudini e custanza".
*****

VII
The Dog and the Monkey

A man possessed a monkey and a hound
and he would keep them on a terrace chained.
One day, right on the floor, the monkey found
his comrade's bread uneaten had remained
and asked: "You never lacked good appetite
before. Why don't you eat? Are you all right?"

The dog replied: "There's nothing really wrong,
but I feel such forebodings in my heart.
I have not seen the master for so long...
Who knows..." The monkey quickly cut him short.
"Pshaw! Is that all? You think, perhaps, the boss
would not eat any more to mourn your loss?"

"I do not know," he said, "but I recall
once I was lost and he came after me."
"And once," replied The other animal,
"he came armed with a rod quite purposely
to beat you, and you, spineless sack of bones,
went up to lick his hands and anklebones!"

The dog replied, "My gratitude is real!
That means I have a heart that will stay true,
though I may lose my life." "Why do you feel
such love for him, when he has none for you?
If you ask me, "the monkey said to boot,
"for you he really does not give a hoot!"

"You're lying through your teeth," with angry tone
the dog replied. "You're fickle and insane.
You seek companions not to be alone.
The master cares for me, and then again,
if he had no esteem, I still would be
as diligent for all he's done for me!

A grateful and a thankful disposition
bestowed upon my species Mother Nature
because it meant it as an exhibition
for man himself and every living creature,
so he could profit from our brotherhood
and learn fidelity and gratitude."
*****

VIII
LU GATTU, LU FRUSTERI E L'ABATI

Trasìu tra un rifittoriu di frati,
(o forsi era di monaci) un frusteri,
e cu lu Guardianu, o puru Abati,
osservava li vanchi, li spadderi,
e di lu locu la capacità,
com'è l'usu di cui girannu va.

Vidi chi passiava cu gran sfrazzu
un grossu gattu di culuri 'mmiscu:
ci luceva lu pilu, e a lu mustazzu
parìa un suldatu svizzaru o tudiscu;
lu guarda, e dici: "Per Bacco, che un gatto
non v'è in Soria sì grosso e sì ben fatto!"

Lu reverennu ci rispunni: "E puru
vossia nun vidi chi li preggi esterni,
o sia fisici, ch'iu nenti li curu;
ma li preggi morali, o sia l'interni,
chisti lu fannu raru e singulari,
e ci farrò vìdiri e tuccari".

Cussì dittu, cumann'a un fratacchiuni:
"Mettici un piattu di pisci davanti".
Chistu ubbidisci e porta un gran piattuni
chinu di vopi e trigghi, ed a l'istanti
chi lu posa, ci dici: "Guarda ccà";
e immobili lu gattu si sta ddà.

Vinniru àutri dui gatti (o chi tirati
di li pisci a l'oduri, o puru apposta
ci foru da lu laicu avviati)
e ogn'una d'iddi a lu piattu si accosta;
ma lu gattu robbustu, in un balenu
c'è supra, li rincùla e teni a frenu.

Ammira cu stupuri lu frusteri
l'onuratizza d'iddu e la pusssanza,
quannu, duvennu entrari, un cucineri
grapi na porta, e a fudda si sbalanza
una truppa di gatti, e tutti a un trattu,
tiranu pri avvintàrisi a lu piattu.

Tintau lu grossu gattu argini fari,
dànnucci supra; ma mentri cummatti
cu quattru o tri, vidi àutri sfirrari:
ddocu si perdi e nun sta chiù a li patti;
torna, si afferra la chiù grossa trigghia,

VIII
The Cat, the Foreigner, and the Abbot

In a monks' dining hall (or was it friars'?)
walked in a visitor, exchanging views
with the good Abbot (or was he a Prior?).
The stranger showed keen interest in pews,
their backs, the dining hall's capacity:
in short a tourist's curiosity.

There was a cat whose colors were all jumbled
who walked as though for none he had regard.
His coat was shiny bright and he resembled
—with his mustache— a Swiss or German guard.
The stranger said: "By Jove, what a fine cat!
In Persia you won't find one that's so fat!"

As a reply, the glowing Abbot said:
"And yet you've only seen what is outside
his body, which I prize the least; instead,
what makes him rare, and gives me much more pride,
are all his moral values, what's inside.
The proof will leave you certain and wide-eyed."

Thus having spoken, he called on a monk:
"Lay out before him a plate filled with fish."
The monk obeyed and as he came to plunk
— full of sardines and mullets — a large dish,
he said to the strong cat: "Guard this, beware!"
and the cat simply did not budge from there.

Drawn by the smell, two other cats arrived,
(or let in by the layman for this end),
and to get near the plate each one then strived,
but the tough cat was ready to defend
the plate of fish and made them beat retreat,
holding them back in impotent defeat.

The stranger had a puzzled and stunned look
on seeing the cat's honesty and might,
but when a door was opened by a cook,
a slew of cats was let into the site,
and they immediately went toward the dish,
attempting to get by and grab the fish.

The mighty cat did try to stem the tide,
and fought with them but as he clashed with three,
he noticed others sneaking past his side.
Facing defeat, he gave up custody
he turned around to grab the largest fish

sfiletta, e l'autri poi cui pigghia pigghia.

Dici lu Reverennu: "Lu miu gattu
avi giudiziu o no ? Forza e coraggiu
tentau... Poi pinsau ad iddu. E beni à fattu:
fari megghiu putìa l'omu chiù saggiu?"
L'àutru tistìa, e dici: "Padre mio,
ben vi spiegate, vi ho capito, addio".

*****

and fled. The others fought to get their wish.

The Abbot asked: "My cat is wise, isn't he?
He tried at first with courage and with might,
then thought about himself. That's strategy!
The wisest man could not have been more right!"
The other shook his head, and with a sigh:
"How well I see your point of view! Good-bye."

*****

IX
LA RINDINA E LU PARPAGGHIUNI

Na rindina pusatasi vicinu
a un parpagghiuni, ch'era supra un ciuri,
guardannulu ammirava, in ali e schinu,
l'inargintati e varii soi culuri;
ma supra tuttu poi c'invidiava
li quattr'ali, chi all'aria spiegava,

e dicìa tra se stissa: "E' veru ch'iu
c'un paru d'ali giru pri lu munnu,
ma quantu, ohimè! mi affannu e mi fatìu,
e tra li vasti mari mi cunfunnu!
Cu quattru, senza incommodi e disaggi,
chiù prestu mi farrìa li mei viaggi".

Fratantu vidi a chiddu, chi vulannu
quattr'ali appena in aria lu sustennu:
pocu s'inalza, e va sempri pusannu!
Si compiaci in se stissa: "Ed ora apprennu,
dici, chi tra l'oggetti chiù brillanti
assai c'è di superfluu e di vacanti".

Non tutti li vantaggi di apparenza
sù tali valutannusi in sustanza;
vi dunanu di arrassu compiacenza,
ma vana poi truvati l'eleganza,
e chiddu, chi apparisci a nui vantaggiu,
tanti voti è molestia o disaggiu.
*****

IX
The Swallow and the Butterfly

A swallow, having stopped his wanderings,
came down to rest upon a flowered bough,
next to a butterfly whose silver wings
and many-colored back evoked a wow.
He envied her four wings especially
which she displayed in air with majesty.

He said within himself: "Ah, wretched me!
It's true I roam the world with just one pair,
but how bewildered I become at sea!
Its vastness how my wings and courage wear!
If I had four of them, how trouble-free,
how quick and easy would my travels be!"

Meanwhile, he saw that when the butterfly
flew off, her four wings barely could sustain
short bursts of flight that weren't all that high.
Thus he rejoiced and said: "This truth is plain
to me. In objects that are shiny, bright,
there's much that is superfluous and trite!

Many advantages that seem apparent,
when checked for substance very simply aren't!
They give you pleasure when they're far away,
but all their elegance is vapid play,
and what appears to us to be a gain,
is oftentimes a bother and a pain."
*****

X
LU CRASTU E LU GADDU-D'INDIA

Mentri pasceva un crastu
sutta di na carrubba,
in tuttu lu so fastu
si affaccia, e cu gran tubba,
un gaddu-d'India, e acutu
ci scàrica un stranutu.

Surprisu a l'impensata
lu crastu retrocedi;
l'àutru a dda sbravazzata,
vidennulu chi cedi,
si cridi ch'àja chiddu
soggezioni d'iddu.

E sicci para avanti
in tutta la sua gala,
superbu e minaccianti,
la 'nnocca allonga e cala,
stenni lu coddu e sbruffa,
sfidannulu a la zuffa.

Lu crastu rinculannu
lu so vantaggiu adotta,
gran campu guadagnannu;
poi torna e dà la botta
chi lu stinnicchia a terra,
e termina la guerra.

Nun apprittati troppu
cui soffri e sta cuetu;
truvati qualch'intoppu
chi vi arrinesci a fetu:
Pinsati a lu cuntrastu
di gaddu-d'India e crastu.
*****

X
The He-Goat and the Turkey

While a he-goat was grazing
beneath a carob tree,
a turkey came up lazing
in all his majesty,
and looking straight at him,
a sneeze let out with vim.

Caught by surprise, the goat
instinctively moved back;
but the vain turkey thought
it had been his attack
that made the goat retreat
for fear of sure defeat.

The turkey faced the goat
with proud and puffed up chest,
threats gurgling from his throat.
He dipped and raised his crest,
then snorting, stretched his neck
as though about to peck.

But in his brief retreat,
the goat had gained more ground
to make his charging fleet.
He laid, on the rebound,
the turkey in the dust,
thus ending that brief joust.

Do not tease folks too much
who suffer and stay still;
you may find one who's such
to make you pay the bill.
This fight between he-goat
and turkey's food for thought.
*****

191

XI
L'ORTULANU E LU SCECCU

Sei tùmmina di terra, metà ad ortu,
metà a jardinu, un povir'omu avìa;
e li zappava dànnusi cunfortu
pri lu fruttatu chi ci prumittìa;
m'appena chi li frutti maturaru,
li parpacini l'aggramignaru,

sibbeni arvuli e frutti non maturi
ristaru intatti, e l'ervi di l'ortaggiu;
pirtantu appoja a profitti futuri
li soi spiranzi, e si duna coraggiu.
Ma pri sua sditta na notti surtiu
chi lu capristu l'asinu rumpiu.

E sdetti in mezzu all'ortu e a lu jardinu,
manciannu e scarpisannu l'insalati,
facennu d'ogni cosa un'assassinu,
rusicannu li frutti anchi ammazati,
rumpennu rami cu jittuni e 'nziti,
e insumma fici fracassi infiniti.

Lu patruni, in sbigghiarsi la matina,
chiù chi scurri, chiù chi metti a 'mpallidiri,
vidi lu dannu so, la sua ruina:
"Li latri, dici, dannu dispiaciri,
ma lu sceccu però liberu e sciotu
unni pò fari guastu è un tirrimotu".

*****

XI
The Orchardman and the Donkey

A poor man had six little plots of land,
half growing greens, half planted with fruit trees;
he hoed and tilled the ground because he planned
to sell his fruits and make some gains from these.
As soon as fruits, though, started to mature
some thieves came and they made a thorough tour.

Nevertheless, the fruit that was not ripe,
as well as all the greens, were left intact.
So he on future profits set his hopes,
accepting his great losses as a fact.
To his bad luck, however, one sad night
the donkey broke its halter and took flight.

And in the orchard ended its wild flight
where it began to trample and to munch
the salads, ruining all things in sight,
sinking its teeth on fruits with a sharp crunch,
destroying branches which had buds on them
and grafts: in short, the donkey caused mayhem.

The gardener, when he awoke, alas,
the more he saw the whiter he became
on witnessing the damage and his loss:
"A thief can cause distress, "he then exclaimed,
"but when a donkey's loose, with a free rein
where he can cause harm, he's a hurricane!"

*****

Giovanni Meli

XII
LU LIUNI, LU SCECCU ED AUTRI ANIMALI

Un liuni un sceccu vitti,
chi pascìa tra la gramigna;
lu squatrau, ma nun lu critti
una preda d'iddu digna.

Nonostanti sicci accosta
pri truvarsi un'ammucciagghia,
stanti chi facìa la posta
ad un ursu di gran vagghia.

Trema l'asinu, e si annicchia
in vidirlu avvicinari;
iddu pàrracci a l'oricchia,
e ci dici: "'Un ti scantari;

statti firmu avanti a mia,
ch'eu ti guardu d'ogni tortu".
Ddu animali si cantìa,
pri lu scantu è menzu mortu;

puru fa quantu ci dici
pirchì sbàtttiri 'un pò chiui;
cussì stannu comu amici,
stritti e 'ncutti tutti dui.

Lu liuni già in distanza
scopri l'ursu, chi si affaccia,
e ad un sàutu si sbalanza,
curri a dàricci la caccia.

L' animali, sin di allura
chi lu Re tra ddi cuntrati
era apparsu, pri paura
tutti si eranu 'ntanati,

ed avennu cu esattizza
da l'ingagghi taliatu
l'amicizia e la 'ncuttizza
ch'a lu sceccu avìa accurdatu,

incomincianu a guardarlu
per un grossu personaggiu,
onorarlu, ossequiarlu,
ed a fàrici anchi omaggiu.

a lu signu chi dd'armali
pri li tanti vampaciusci
si è scurdatu quantu vali,
chiù se stissu nun cunusci.

XII
The Lion, the Donkey, and Other Animals

Once a lion saw a donkey
who was feeding on some grass,
sized him up and he concluded
he was just a worthless ass!

Nonetheless, he drew much closer
just to find a place from where
he could watch and lay in ambush
for a valiant and great bear.

When he saw the beast approach,
the ass shook and was dismayed,
but the lion spoke quite softly,
saying: "No, don't be afraid!

Just keep still in front of me!
I will guard you from all foes."
The poor donkey was quite wary;
from the fear he nearly froze.

Still he did what he was told,
since he could no longer flee.
Thus they stayed together there,
tight and close as they could be.

But already in the distance
the great bear had shown his face,
and the lion in a bounce
started out in his swift chase.

All the animals around,
since the King had come so near
to the places where they dwelled,
in their holes had hid in fear.

But observing from their hiding,
they all saw with interest
the close friendship that the lion
had accorded to that beast.

So the animals regarded
the poor ass a VIP
who was worthy of great honor,
obsequies, and flattery.

So much so that he forgot,
on account of all that fuss,
what in essence he was worth,
that he was a poor jackass.

S'ingannaru, ed iddu ed iddi,
chi applicaru a lu liuni
ddi viduti picciriddi,
chi a lu vulgu sù comuni.
   Cu' è politicu, li miri
chiusi l'à cu chiavi e toppi,
e pri 'un farli travidiri
batti oremi, e joca coppi.
                         *****

They were wrong and so was he
for applying to a King
some nearsighted, common goals
which are shared by underlings.
   Politicians' true objectives
are concealed with care and art
and to keep them out of sight,
they say club and then play heart.
                         *****

Giovanni Meli

XII
LI CANI E LA STATUA

Dui cani seguitannu lu patruni,
d'Apollu tra lu tempiu si ficcaru;
ddà vidinu li genti a munzidduni
inginucchiati avanti di l'otaru,
duv'era na gran statua colossali,
chi un Diu raffigurava naturali.

    Un cani dici all'àutru: "Oh fortunatu
marmu, chi à cultu ed adorazioni!"
Rispunni lu cumpagnu: "S'è insenzatu,
nun senti gusti e consolazioni;
s'avi menti, avi in idda anchi ripostu
quantu ci custa junciri a ddu postu.

    Tu nun sai quantu colpi di mannari,
di pali e mazzi in barbara manera
fu custrittu in principiu a suppurtari
pri esseri smossu da la sua pirrera;
e poi quanti àutri colpi di scarpeddu
pri assimigghiari a un Diu ridenti e beddu?

    Li summi posti, li gradi eminenti
nun sù facili tantu a conseguirsi,
custanu serii e lunghi patimenti,
e chisti nun purrìanu mai suffrirsi
s'in parti la frenata ambizioni
nun ci sturdissi la sensazioni."

XIII
The Dogs and the Statue

By following their master, once two dogs
inside Apollo's temple poked their nose
and saw a multitude of demagogues
upon their knees before a shrine, where rose
a statue that was truly tall and broad
which had the features of a living god.

    One dog said to the other: "Lucky stone,
that's object of a cult and adoration!"
"If he is senseless, feelings are unknown,"
the other said, "as well as consolation.
If he possesses brains, he can retrace
the costly journey made to reach this place.

    You cannot know how many wicked blows
with axes and sledgehammers and with mace
he was made to endure, how many woes,
as men dislodged him from the quarry face,
how many times the chisel had to prod
to shape him like a handsome, smiling god.

    High rank and the most eminent positions
are never very easily attained;
they're bought with long and heavy tribulations,
which could not even have been entertained
if partially at least men's great ambition
had not reduced their feelings and sensations."

XIV
LU GATTU E LU FIRRARU

Aveva un gattu disculu un firraru,
chi la notti facìa lu malviventi,
e multu chiù in decembru ed in jinnaru;
lu jornu poi durmìa tranquillamenti,
ed unni vi criditi chi durmìa?
Tra la strepitusissima putìa.

Ma quannu poi cissava lu fracassu,
pirchì già si mittevanu a manciari,
si arrisbigghiava e vinìa passu passu.
Lu patruni lu sgrida in accustari:
"Bestia, dormi tra strepiti e bisbigghi,
e a la scrùsciu di labbri ti arrisbigghi?"

Si ponnu a tutto l'omini avvizzari,
comu anchi l'animali: ma l'istintu
nun si fa mai da l'abiti smuntari,
pirchì a la guardia di la vita è 'mpintu;
perciò lu scrusciu di li labbri e di piatti
basta pri arrisbigghiari omini e gatti.

*****

XIV
The Blacksmith's Cat

A blacksmith had a rascal of a cat
who often spent his nights in fun and play
— and in the winter oftener than that! —
but he would sleep profoundly through the day,
and where do you suppose he slept? In the shop
which was extremely noisy as a rule.

But when at dinner time the noise would stop,
the cat awoke — he surely was no fool! —
and sauntered to the kitchen in slow strides.
"You sleep through whispering and shouts, you rake!"
on seeing him approach his owner cried,
"but at the sound of lips you soon awake!"

Man can become accustomed to all things,
and beasts can too. But our instinctive drives
can't be ignored, despite conditioning,
for they are charged to keep watch on our lives.
Therefore, the noise that lips and dishes make
is strong enough both men and cats to wake.

*****

197

XV
LA VULPI E L'ASINU

Una vulpi fuìa scantata tutta,
e si guardava davanti e darreri,
circannu pri ammucciarisi na grutta.
"Cui ti assicuta? ci spia un sumeri".
"Nuddu". "Ai fattu delittu, impertinenza?"
"Di nenti mi rimordi la cuscenza".
"Addunca pirchì fui, di chi ti scanti?".
"Ti dicu: Mi fu dittu chi è nisciutu
ordini di la Curti fulminanti
di catturari un tauru curnutu;
nun sacciu chi delittu c'è 'mputatu:
basta, si criri reu di un'attintatu".

  "E tu ch'ài di comuni a tauru e vacca?"
"Beatu, asinu, tu, chi nun sai nenti!
Tra sti affari a jittarivi na tacca
cridi chi ci sta assai lu malviventi?
L'invidiusu? L'occultu 'nnimicu?
Basta chi ti denunzia per amicu,
  o chi dica d'aviri ritruvatu
qualchi vestigiu di li toi pidati
tra ddi lochi chi chiddu à frequentatu,
o con àutri pretesti mendicati,
lu judici, o zelanti o ambiziusu,
ti fa sudditu so dintra un dammusu,
  ed incuminci a pàtiri stritturi,
ad esseri subùtu, esaminatu:
nuddu azzarda parrari in to favuri,
cuntu d'iddu da tia ni vonnu datu:
fussi anchi d'innoccenza un tabbirnaculu,
si tu ni nesci vivu è un gran miraculu".
  Dissi, e si la sbignau. Lu sceccu intantu
(benchì sceccu qual'era) tra sè dissi:
"Cuscenza lesa genera lu scantu:
piccati vecchi criju chi ni avissi:
jeu chi a lu munnu non cacciu nè minu,
vaju sicuru pri lu miu caminu".
                        *****

XV
A Fox and a Donkey

    A fox was on the run, quite terrified,
and kept on looking to his back and front
while searching for a cave wherein to hide.
A donkey asked: "Are you the object of a hunt?"
"Oh, no!" "Brashness or crime did you commit?"
"My conscience does not bother me a bit."
"So then why run so fast, why so afraid?"
"Let me explain. The Court, I've been advised,
a warrant for a horned bull has displayed.
His crimes have not as yet been itemized,
but that is not important. They believe
that some crime he'd attempted to conceive."

    "And what have you to do with cows and bull?"
"O blessed ass who live in ignorance!
In times like these, a felon or a fool,
an envious or secret foe, his chance
won't miss to slander you with some big lie.
You're the bull's friend: that's all he needs to say,
    or mention that someone discerned a trace
of your footprints near where the bull was seen,
or through some other false or trumped-up case
induce a judge who's zealous, over keen,
to make you his trustee inside his jail;
and there you'll be exposed to harsh travail,
    questioned, subjected to the third degree.
Nobody will dare speak in your defense,
they'll want you to explain his knavery.
Though you may be a shrine of innocence,
the most sincere of animals alive,
it 'd be a miracle if you survive!"
    Once he said this, the fox just disappeared.
Though a dumb ass, he thought in the meantime,
"A guilty conscience generates our fear.
I think he may have had a few old crimes.
Since I am one who minds his own affairs,
I can go on my way without a care."
                        *****

XVI
LI FURMICULI

Misi l'ali na furmicula,
e sollevasi a momenti
su li troffi di l'ardicula,
e di l'ervi chiù eminenti.

L'àutri a terra rampicannu
si stuperu a sta vulata;
l'ammiravanu, esclamannu:
"Oh chi sorti! oh fortunata!"

E da bravi adulaturi,
chi unni vidinu appuggiari
la fortuna, ddà li curi
vannu tutti ad impiegari,

cussì chisti, anchi di arrassu,
cu li ossequii e riverenzi,
affrittavanu lu passu
pri ottenirinn'incumbenzi.

Ma ristaru trizziati,
chi prescrittu avìa la sorti
l'ali d'idda e li vulati,
pri preludii di la morti.

Si mai cadi, si sfazzuna
cui sta in cima di la scala:
li favuri di fortuna
sù carizzi cu la pala.
*****

XVI
The Ants

On sprouting wings, an ant
flew quickly higher than
a poison ivy plant,
beyond where ants could scan.

The others who were grounded
all marveled at his flight
and they exclaimed astounded:
"What luck! What great delight!"

And like good sycophants,
who flattery will pile,
as well as blandishments,
on men to whom luck smiles,

these ants did not disdain
to run in his direction
some benefits to gain
through praise and genuflection.

Indeed, a foolish sight,
for fate had once decreed
that the ant's wings and flight
to his sure death would lead.

All those atop the stairs
of falling should beware:
the favors fate bestows
are thorny like a rose.
*****

XVII
ESOPU E L'OCEDDU LINGUA-LONGA

Vidi Esopu in terra stisu
un'oceddu; ma si accorgi
chi per arti ci sta misu;
una lunga lingua sporgi
da lu beccu, chi la lassa
a l'arbitriu di cui passa.

Ed infatti china tutta
di furmiculi già era;
licca ogn'una, ma poi scutta
la sua detta tutta intera,
chi la lingua in ritirarisi
veni tutti ad ammuccàrisi.

Ridi Esopu, e dici: "Or iu
differenza nè divariu
nuddu affattu ci nni viu
tra st'oceddu e l'usuraiu:
'Mpresta, e poi cu usuri e frutti,
tuttu agghiommara ed agghiutti".

*****

XVII
Aesop and the Woodpecker

One day wise Aesop saw a bird
who was stretched out upon the dirt.
A trick from this he soon inferred
because its long tongue was inert,
protruding far out of its bill,
inviting all to get their fill.

In fact, a colony of ants,
descending on the tongue, soon set
to draw from it its sustenance
but then in full repaid its debt,
for when the bird drew back its tongue,
it swallowed the entire throng.

Wise Aesop laughed and then averred:
"I really see no difference
between this cunning little bird
and usurers' routine offense:
They lend, but through their usury,
they gobble all your treasury."

*****

200

XVIII
LI CUCUCCIUTI

Si avìa pisatu un'aria di frumentu,
cu li voi cuncirtati a varii stracqui;
ma nun si spagghiau beni, chi lu ventu
spirau cuntrariu, e poi vinniru l'acqui;
perciò la pagghia ristau supra tutta
comu chiù leggia, e lu frumentu sutta.

Dui cucucciuti o tri di primu volu
ci foru supra pri pizzuliari;
ma trascurrennu lu supremu solu
àutru chi pagghia 'un pottiru truvari,
e ni ristaru cursi e nichiati
malidicennu tutti ddi cuntrati.

Dicianu: "Lochi fatti pri li staddi,
non siti degni d'essiri abitati
chi da li suli scecchi e li cavaddi".
Ma l'àutri oceddi chiù scaltri e addistrati
di l'aria scavulìanu lu funnu,
e trovanu frumentu grossu e biunnu.

Quannu in un Statu ci sù fazzioni
e partiti, e politicu scuncertu,
li suggetti prudenti, saggi e boni
si stannu sutta, misi a lu cuvertu,
e lassanu a li pagghi li chiù leggi
godirisi l'onuri e privileggi.
*****

XVIII
The Skylarks

With oxen all in files of three's arrayed
some peasants had begun to thresh some grain,
but they'd not separated wheat from hay
because the wind had changed. Then had come rain
and chaff because it's lighter had remained
on top, while wheat had to the bottom drained.

Two or three skylarks, out for their first flight,
came *to the threshing-floor and started pecking,
but searching only on the topmost site
they found just worthless chaff for all their trekking.
So feeling vexed and quite dissatisfied,
they started cursing the whole countryside.

They kept complaining: "Place fit for a stable!
— good only as a donkey's residence! —
To live here surely no one would be able!"
But other birds with more experience
searched at the bottom of the threshing-floor
and found large grains of golden wheat galore.

When there are many factions in a land
and great political disharmony,
wise, good, and prudent subjects will withstand
by staying under cover, out of jeopardy,
letting the lightest straw stay at the top edge
to reap the honors and the privilege.
*****

XIX
LI SCECCHI ED ESOPU

Dui scecchi cu li coddi 'uncrucicchiati
l'unu raspava all'àutru. Nun ci leggi
lu vulgu nenti chiù chi asinitati.
Li guarda Esopu, e grida: "Oh testi leggi!
    Gran lezioni è chista; profittati:
Lu bisognu reciprocu, iddu reggi
tutti li societati, e li bilancia,
l'unu raspannu all'àutru unni ci mancia".
*****

XIX
The Donkeys and Aesop

There were two donkeys whose necks formed a cross,
scratching each other. Common people read
a proof of asininity in this,
but Aesop looked and said: "O empty heads!
    This is a lesson mankind should not miss.
Interdependence is in fact the thread
that holds society in balanced pitch
by letting people scratch each other's itch."
*****

202

XX
LA CUCUCCIUTA E LU PISPISUNI

Mi si permetta stu piccciulu prologu,
l'applicu a li D. 'Ninnari stu apologu.
  Na cucucciuta vidìa passiari
un pispisuni linnu ed attillatu,
chi appena in terra si vidìa pusari,
sbriciu, galanti, e di coddu alliggiatu.
Dissi tra d'idda: "Ci vurrìa spiari
chi pretenni accussì 'mpipiriddatu?
Cu st'eleganza, dimmi, chi ci abbuschi?..."
Ci accosta, e vidi chi ammuccava muschi.
                    *****

XX
The Skylark and the Wagtail

This little prologue let me now recount.
To foppish men I link this brief account.
  A skylark often saw a wagtail pass
who looked most trim and wore tight-fitting clothes;
his feet seemed barely treading on the grass,
so chic was he, high-necked and decked with bows.
The skylark said within herself: "Who does
he think he is with such a haughty pose?
His elegance, what does he think it buys?"
Then she approached and saw him eating flies!
                    *****

XXI
LU RUSIGNOLU E L'ASINU

Tra murtiddi di addàuri curunati
un rusignolu armonicu aggiuncatu,
'ngurgiava sinu a perdita di ciatu
li suavi soi noti, e varii e grati.

Tenniri cori ed almi dilicati
stavanu attenti di un macchiuni allatu;
pri lu piaciri avevanu scurdatu
li guai, da cui vinìanu molestati,

quannu improvisu un sceccu cu la pagghia
jetta un arragghiu, e subitu 'mpannedda;
sclàmanu chiddi: "Oh pesta a stu gramagghia!"

Grida un viddanu: "St'armunia 'ncasedda,
jeu sulu apprezzu l'asinu chi arrragghia,
pirchì mi servi pri varda e pri sedda".

La Musa è bona e bedda,
(dici lu vulgu a lu guadagnu intentu)
ma soni e canti sù cosi di ventu.

Nè vuci, nè strumentu,
nè tuttu Pindu basta a sodisfari
lu tavirnaru chi voli dinari".

*****

XXI
The Nightingale and the Donkey

Amidst some myrtles crowned by laurel leaves
was perched a pleasant-sounding nightingale
who warbled his diverse recitatives
of sweet and pleasing notes throughout the dale.

Behind some bushes, listening with care,
there were some delicate and tender hearts
whose pleasure was so great that they could bear
the troubling sorrows tearing them apart.

When suddenly, his mouth still full of hay,
a donkey started to hee-haw and run.
Those folks complained: "Oh, what a useless pest!"

"There's nothing sweeter than my donkey's bray,"
a peasant yelled. "I am the only one
who values his hee-haws. He serves me best!"

The Muse is beautiful and fair,
say folks intent on profit and on gain,
but melodies and songs are things of air.

No instrument and no refrain,
nor all of Helicon have ever satisfied
the tavern keeper who wants to be paid.

*****

XXII
LA CAMULA E LU TAURU
A Nici

Nun lu negu, sì l'estrattu
di l'onuri e la custanza,
ed ài datu anchi lu sfrattu
a suggetti d'impurtanza;

e cunfessu chi stu tali,
chi ti mustra affezzioni,
nun è oggettu chi prevali,
nè di dari apprensioni.

M'aju a menti... Orsù cuntàmula,
certa istoria strepitusa
di un'insettu dittu camula,
di natura pittimusa.

Dunca c'era a sti cuntorna
un gran tauru grassu e grossu
chi manciannucci li corna
dav'a un vecchiu truncu addossu.

A sti botti affaccia un pocu
un virmuzzu la sua testa,
e poi grida: "Olà, cu'è ddocu?
Cui lu truncu mi molesta?"

Nun si digna di rispundiri
di l'armenti lu bascià,
e cridendulu confundiri
a lu truncu forti dà.

Lu virmuzzu sinni ridi,
dipoi dici: "Ci scummettu,
chi la forza, in cui tu fidi,
ccà si perdi, senza effettu.

Ieu mi fidu di pruvarti,
cu evidenza e cu cirtizza,
chi pò chiù la flemma e l'arti
chi la forza e robbustizza".

Sia lu tauru diggià stancu,
pri li sforzi fatti avìa,
sia diggià vinuta mancu
la sua boria e bizzarria,

pigghia pausa, e dici: "Orsù
ieu ti accordu sicuranza;
dimmi prima cui sì tu?
D'unni nasci sta baldanza?

XXII
The Weevil and the Bull
To Nici

I cannot deny you are
the quintessence of esteem
and you've shunned and driven far
many lovers of importance.

This new beau, I must confess,
who is showing you affection
is no man to win success
or to cause me apprehension.

I've in mind this brief narration,
so allow me to relate it,
on the source of much vexation
that's the insect known as weevil.

Once in the vicinity
lived a big and strong old bull
who in daily drudgery
an old tree would strike and butt.

When a worm heard all those blows,
stuck its little head outside
and yelled out: "I say, what goes?
who's molesting my old tree?"

The great Sultan of the herd
did not bother to reply
and continued hitting hard,
thinking he could scare the weevil.

But the little worm replied
with a smile: "I'll wager that
the great might that is your pride
will be lost against this trunk.

I am certain I can show,
with no doubts or hesitation,
patience and the skills one knows
are more powerful than might."

And the bull, because perchance
had expended all his strength,
or because his arrogance
and eccentric thoughts had waned,

paused a moment and then said:
"I am willing to believe you.
But first tell me who you are!
And what makes you so self-sure?"

"Ieu sù un'essiri, rispundi,
di misuri pocu esatti,
lu miu corpu 'un currispundi
cu lu grandi di li fatti:
   chistu truncu, chi a lu cozzu
azzannau li corna toi,
mi lu arrùsicu pri tozzu,
pozz'eu farlu e tu nun poi".
   "Va'...sì pazzu", dici, e parti
lu gran tauru; ma l'insettu
da lu truncu nun si sparti,
nè abbanduna lu progettu;
   a lu signu, chi passatu
chiù di un lustru, oh meravigghia!
lu gran truncu sbacantatu
cadiu in pulviri e canigghia!
   Chi ni dici tu, curuzzu,
cu lu beddu to talentu?
Nun è statu chi un virmuzzu
chi produssi stu portentu!

     *****

"I'm a being, I concede,
who cannot be measured rightly.
For the greatness of my deed
does not match my puny body.
   And this trunk that dulled your horns,
as you struck it, is to me
like a piece of bread or corn.
I can eat it, but you can't."
   "Sure, you're crazy!" the bull said,
and departed. But the insect
did not leave the trunk. Instead,
he continued his long project.
   Then in time, five years or more,
O great wonder! The great trunk
emptied out down to its core,
crumbled into piles of dust.
   So what do you say, dear heart,
with your talent and your beauty?
This great portent had its start
from a puny little worm!

     *****

XXIII
LU CAGNOLU E LA CANI

Un cagnolu na strùmmula si vidi
scurriri attornu sula, e firriari;
pri spratichizza un'armali la cridi,
chi avìa, com'iddu, vogghia di jucari;
perciò ci accosta calatu calatu,
ma fu cu na spaddata ribbuttatu.

  Ci struppiàu lu mussu a signu tali,
chi rucculannu cursi tra na 'gnuni.
Cridennu chi so figghiu avissi mali,
nesci la matri e mustra li scagghiuni,
e in viderlu trimanti e stupefattu,
ci dumanna: "Cui fu? chi ti ànnu fattu?"

  Iddu rispunni: "C'era un'armaluzzu,
chi sulu sulu girava e currìa;
mi accostu pri ciorarlu, e appena struzzu,
mi duna un'ammuttuni, e mi struppia..."
"Talè, talè, vidi ca torn'arreri!"
dissi, e scantatu si jittau 'nnarreri.

  La matri ridi, e poi dici: "Oh babbanu!
Chistu è un pezzu di lignu. La sua forza,
lu so motu è vinutu da la manu
di lu picciottu chi la scagghia e sforza;
tutta la sua putenza e tuttu chiddu
spiritu, chi dimustra, nun è d'iddu".

  Sai com'è pressu a pocu: lu patruni
ammett'in casa pri spassu e piaciri,
(comu tu sai) Ruffìniu e Corbelluni:
pari ad un scioccu in chisti di vidiri
di lu patruni cu la grazia in frunti
un superbu Gradassu e un Rodomumti.

  Si mai la grazia da iddi alluntanati,
nun avrannu chiù fumi nè valìa;
divintirannu strùmmuli scacati,
scuprennu ogn'unu l'essenza ch'avìa,
chi tolta in iddi l'indoli maligna,
in sustanza nun sù chi trunchi e ligna.

*****

XXIII
The Puppy and Its Mother

A little puppy saw a whirling top
that by itself was turning round and round.
Because he lacked experience, the pup
believed it was a beast on playing bound
just like himself. So he tried to get close.
But as he did, he was struck on the nose.

  His nose and mouth were hurt in such a way
that he ran quickly to his hiding place.
Thinking her pup had met with some foul play,
the mother came outside with snarling face,
and when she saw him trembling and afraid,
she asked: "What happened? Why are you dismayed?"

  "A little beast there was," he answered her
who kept on running and on turning round;
When I got close enough to hear its whir,
it struck me hard and knocked to the ground.
Look out, look out, it's coming back again!"
he said and quickly to retreat began.

  But as he hid, the mother simply smiled:
"That's just a piece of wood. Its might's a gift.
All of its spinning motion, silly child,
comes from the lad who made it spin so swift.
All of the confidence and all the vim
that he displays do not belong to him."

  This more or less is how these stories go:
a mighty Lord allows into his home
Sir Ruffian and Con Man, as you know,
for pleasure and for fun. But then to some,
with their Lord's power written on their face,
they're like Gradassus or some other ace.

  But if they're kept away from their lord's might,
their haughtiness and power are no more;
they will become like tops who've lost their flight,
aand they'll revert to what they were before.
And if you take away their evil bent,
in substance twigs and wood they represent.

*****

207

XXIV
LU RIZZU, LA TARTUCA E LU CANI

A la tartuca sutta un scornabbeccu
dissi lu rizzu: "Oh pazza! fa sciloccu,
e tu vai cu visera e cu cileccu,
e dicchiù porti supra lu marroccu!"
    Rispunn'idda: "Tu all'àutri metti peccu!
E pirchì armatu di dardi e di stoccu
'ntempu di paci vai, facci di sceccu,
comu duvissi sustiniri un bloccu?"
    Mentri àutri inciurii sù pronti a lu sbuccu,
rumpi sta quistioni un canibraccu,
chi l'immesti e li sbatti a trucc-e-ammuccu;
    poi dici: "Ogn'unu stia tra lu so scaccu;
sapi chiù 'ncasa propria un pazzu o un cuccu,
ch'in casa d'àutri un saviu ed un vicchiaccu".
*****

XXIV
A Hedgehog, a Turtle, and a Hound

Beneath a terebinth, a turtle heard
a hedgehog say: "It's hot and yet you roam
with visor and a vest, you crazy bird!
and carry on your back a heated dome!"
    "In others," she replied, "why look for fault?
In time of peace, it's utterly absurd
to walk about expecting an assault,
armed with a sword and darts, you ugly turd!"
    To this debate a foxhound put a halt,
as more offensive words were yet apace;
He struck at them and hurled them in the air,
    saying: "Let each remain in his home base!
A fool or dolt inside his house is more aware,
than wise old men in other people's place."
*****

XXV
LU SCECCU-OMU E L'OMU-SCECCU

Un bon'omu avìa un sceccu assai turduni.
La sorti, ch'è bizzarra e stravaganti,
cancia lu sceccu in omu, e lu patruni
lu cancia in sceccu; ma com'er'avanti
ristau la menti in iddi: pirchì 'un vali
la sorti a trasmutari lu morali.

Cunsidirati chi peni ed affanni
diva suffriri un'omu, chi raggiuna,
assuggittatu a un sceccu grossu e granni,
fatt'omu da un capricciu di furtuna!
Puru arriventa cu coraggiu eroicu,
e la nicissitati lu fa stoicu.

Vinni lu casu chi duvennu fari
lungu viaggiu lu sceccu patruni,
metti lu sceccu servu a carricari
di bagagghi e di robba a munsidduni,
senza considerari chi 'un putìa
reggiri a lu gran pisu e la fatia.

L'afflittu carricatu a summu stentu
tir'avanti pri un migghiu, ed arriventa;
all'àutru migghiu lu passu è chiù lentu,
e a spinciri li pedi suda e stenta;
ogni pitrudda ci duna cuntrastu;
ma l'àutru dà mazzati a tuttu pastu.

Finalmenti vicinu a na lavanca
trùppica, cadi, e supra di na rocca
s'apri la testa e si struppedda un'anca;
lu patruni pri rabbia tarocca;
ma lu so taruccari nun apporta
vit'a lu sceccu, nè la robba porta.

L'espedienti sulu, chi ci resta,
è lu pisu addussarisi di chiddu,
e parti su la schina, e parti in testa
jirisillu adattannu supra d'iddu,
chi ci rinesci tantu chiù gravusu,
quantu menu a li pisi ci avìa l'usu

XXV
The Man-Donkey and the Donkey-Man

A worthy man had a dumb-witted ass.
But Fate, which is extravagant and weird,
turned donkey into man, and man, alas,
into a donkey. But, as it appeared,
their brains remained what they had been before,
for Fate can't change morality's true core.

Imagine what vexation and what stress
the fellow who could think must have felt then,
subjected to a big and dumb jackass
whom fortune's whim had changed into a man!
Yet he endured with courage quite heroic,
and sheer necessity made him a stoic.

When for the donkey-master came the need
to make a journey to a distant land,
the donkey-servant he did load with speed
with burdens that were mountainous and grand,
without consideration and restrain
for the poor ass who could not stand the strain.

The hapless donkey, loaded to the hilt,
went forward for about a mile and tried his best,
but for the next his legs just seemed to wilt.
Each step was of his stamina a test,
and little stones were a great source of woes.
His master though continued to rain blows.

Approaching a ravine then finally
he tripped, and as he fell upon a rock,
he split his head and even sprained his knee!
The master angrily began to stalk,
but all his cursing just could not restore
the donkey's life, nor carry all he bore.

There was but one thing left for him to do:
that is, to try to load upon his back,
and on his head as well, without ado,
all of the items in the donkey's pack:
a thing that he did not appreciate
because he was not used to bear such weight!

Stenta, suda, si affanna, spinci forti,
cadi, si susi, si sconquassa, ed eccu
comu st'armali, ad onta di la sorti,
torna com'era, ed è dui voti sceccu;
e comu tali cu lu pisu addossu
finisci allavancandusi tra un fossu.

La sorti è un ventu chi alza li sumeri
e ci fa fari voli sorprendenti;
ma da se stissi poi cadinu arreri.
Cadissiru iddi suli sarrìa nenti,
ma tanti voti sù perniciusi
all'omini onorati e virtuusi.

*****

Sweating, he strove and pushed with all his might,
he fell, got up, he wrecked himself and then,
just like the animal he was, in spite
of Fate, returned to be himself again,
and was thus twice a donkey, and as such,
with his great load, he fell into a ditch.

Fate is a wind that raises donkeys high
and causes them to do surprising things,
but they fall back alone 'cause they can't fly.
I would not mind if on their downward swings
they fell alone. But often they prove ruinous
to people who are honest, virtuous.

*****

XXVI
LA RINDINA E LA PATEDDA

Stanca da li viaggi, supra un scogghiu
chiusi l'ali e pusau na rindinedda;
un pocu sutta c'era na patedda,
chi pri tettu ci offriu lu so cummogghiu.

"Ti ringraziu, ci dissi, nun lu vogghiu"
"Ma tu sempri stai ddocu? Oh puviredda!
Jeu giru mari, paisi, castedda,
osservu tuttu, e doppu mi la cogghiu".

"Dimmi, l'àutra spiau, li lochi visti
sù d'acqua e petri?" "Sì". "C'è armali?" "Oh
quanti!
L'omini sù a dui pedi?" "Comu chisti".

"Periculi cinn'è di vita vostra?"
"Cui li pò diri?" "Basta; 'un jiri avanti:
tuttu lu munnu è comu casa nostra".
*****

XXVI
The Swallow and the Limpet

Exhausted by her traveling, a swallow
folded her wings and landed on a rock
on which a limpet dwelled in waves quite shallow.
Her shell the mollusk offered as sun block.

"I thank you, "said the swallow, "but, no, thanks."
"Are you stuck here, forever in one place?
Poor thing! I roam through oceans, river banks,
castles and towns. Then to more sights I race."

"Tell me," the limpet said. "In these new views,
do you see water, rocks?" "Yes." "Animals?"
"Many!" "And men walk on two feet?" "Like these!"

"Are there things to your lives inimical?"
"Who can know that for sure?" "Stop! Say no
more!
The world is really like the house next door!"
*****

211

XXVII
LA FURMICULA E LA CUCUCCIUTA

Veru chiù ch''un si dici: Li disigni
di lu poveru mai, mai vennu a fini:
suda, travagghia, fa cunti e rassigni,
pri un granu dà la facci tra li spini,
sparagna, si allammica, si assuttigghia,
lu diavulu veni e ci li pigghia.

Aveva la furmicula a gran stentu,
tissennu sempri campagni e chianuri,
risiddiatu un pocu di furmentu,
chi avìa sarvatu in suttirranii scuri,
spirannu, cu sta picciula dispensa,
reggiri l'invernu a l'inclemenza.

Ven'intantu l'autunnu e na timpesta
c'insuppa tutta la provisioni,
chi si tali, qual'è, sarvata resta,
sicci ammuffisci e va in corruzioni;
pri tantu aspetta 'nchiaruta l'aurora,
e pri asciucarla si la nesci fora.

Aveva appena nisciutu di sutta
l'ultimu cocciu, chi cala affamata
na cucucciuta, e ci la mancia tutta,
dicennu: "Ccà la tavul'è cunsata;
veramenti Natura appi giudiziu,
la furmicula à fattu in miu serviziu".

Da l'àutru latu, amarraggiata, afflitta
cunsidirati quantu l'àutra resti!
"Jeu, dici, travagghiai, la maliditta
si l'à manciatu, chi ci fazza pesti.
Oh celu! E tu chi sai quantu mi custa
pirchì mi rendi sta cumpenza ingiusta?"

Mentri l'afflitta sfugava l'affannu
contra lu Celu, vid'in aria un nigghiu,
chi va la cucucciuta assicutannu,
e già la strinci tra lu crudu artigghiu.
La furmicula osserva tuttu, e dici:
"Bonu ci stia; ma intantu eu sù infelici

XXVII
The Ant and the Skylark

How true it is, indeed! A poor man's plans
a happy end can never truly gain.
He works, he sweats, he weighs each circumstance,
scratching his face on thorns for bits of grain;
he saves, he racks his brain, and he grows thin:
the devil takes it all to his chagrin!

An ant, who at great sacrifice had combed
continuously through countryside and plains,
had gathered in a subterranean dome
a bit of wheat, and hoped that his few grains
would be sufficient to sustain his life
during the winter months, in the cold strife.

In the meantime, the autumn came and rain
soaked through the ground and flooded all he'd saved,
and had he left it soaking wet, the grain,
would just have rotted in the humid cave.
He waited for the dawn to light the sky,
and dragged each grain of wheat outside to dry.

He had brought out the last of the saved wheat,
when suddenly a skylark did appear,
swooped down and hungrily devoured it,
saying, "The table has been set right here!
Great Mother Nature showed sagacity
when she created ants to work for me!"

Imagine on the contrary how sad
and how afflicted must the ant have been:
"I worked," he cried, "then came along that cad
and ate it all, a curse upon her kin!
Oh, Heaven! You who know how much it cost,
why give a recompense that's so unjust?"

While venting all his anguish against God,
the wretched ant observed high in the air
the skylark being chased by a sharp-clawed,
ferocious kite who caught her in his snare.
The ant saw the whole thing and had this thought:
"It serves her right! But I am still distraught.

212

La cruda morti d'idda e lu so mali,
sibbeni in apparenza sia vinditta,
m'a mia nun mi suffraga, e nenti vali
a cumpinsari in parti la mia sditta;
soffru travagghi, sfuma lu profittu,
e intantu mi assicuta lu pitittu!

Ma è mali assai maggiuri, si nun sbagghiu,
l'essiri assicutata da lu nigghiu;
giacchì, sibbeni è pena lu travagghiu,
puru diri si pò salamurigghiu;
chi ultra chi vi procaccia lu manciari,
ci dà sapuri e vi lu fa gustari".
*****

Her cruel death and all her suffering
a rightful vengeance may appear to be,
but it won't satisfy my needs or bring
a compensation for my misery.
I work hard and my profits simply flee,
and now starvation is pursuing me!

But if I am not wrong, a greater woe
by far is to be chased by those fierce kites!
For working means fatigue, as well I know,
but, it's like sauce, it perks our appetites,
because not only does it give us food,
it gives it flavor, making it taste good.
*****

Giovanni Meli

XXVIII
LI CANI

Si fannu stu dialogu dui cani:
"Tu 'ncatinatu! E pri quali delittu?"
"Nun è castigu, sù carigni umani;
lu patruni di mia nn'avi profittu:

mi à vistu cacciari pri li chiani,
mi apprezza, e timi chi ci vegna dittu:
Lu rubbàru, o si spersi; perciò un pani
mi duna, ed ossa, è ccà mi teni strittu..."

"Fratannu in premiu di l'abilitati
lu bon patruni to riconoscenti
ti à fattu privu di la libirtati?

Si a stu modu li meriti e talenti
sù da l'omini in terra premiati,
è gran fortuna nun avirni nenti".
*****

XXVIII
The Dogs

These views and attitudes two dogs were sharing:
"You...here, in chains? And for what kind of crimes?"
"It is not punishment. It's human caring.
My master profits from my skills, sometimes.

He saw me hunting in the open plain,
and values me, but he's afraid to hear
'They stole him,' or 'he's lost!' That's why the chain!
He feeds me bread and bones, but keeps me here!"

"So as reward for your ability,
your master with exquisite gratitude
has turned your freedom into slavery.

If worth and talent are by man thus viewed
down here on earth, far better it would be
neither to hear, to smell, nor even see."
*****

XXIX
LU RUSIGNOLU E LU JACOBBU

A lu jacobbu dissi un rusignolu:
"Di', sta pittim'amara è cantu o picchiu?"
Rispus'iddu: "Gnuranti fraschittolu,
chi canti ad aria misu in cacaticchiu,
si 'un sai di contrapuntu, ergo citrolu!
Sai spàrtiri lu tempu a spicchiu a spicchiu?"
'Nterrumpi l'àutru: "Sarai bon pedanti,
ma non pri chistu sì un bravu cantanti".
*****

XXIX
The Nightingale and the Owl

"I say," asked of an owl a nightingale,
"this boring tune of yours, is it a wail
or singing?" "O truly ignorant upstart!"
the owl cried. "You're so smug about your art!
Not knowing counterpoint means you're not smart.
Do you know how to split time in all its parts?"
The other said: "A scholar you may be,
but to sing well that's not a guarantee!"
*****

XXX
LU MERLU E LI PETTIRUSSI

Un merlu vitti cu l'ali caduti
alcuni pettirussi, e ci à spiatu:
"Chi vi avvinni ca siti arripudduti?
Tu pirchì zoppu? E tu pirchì spinnatu?"
Rispusiru: "Ni semu divirtuti
cu na cucca, e 'ncappammu tra un viscatu".
Diss'iddu: "Ohimè! cu smorfii e jucareddi
st'èrrami cucchi smennanu l'oceddi!"

*****

XXX
The Blackbird and the Robins

Having observed some robins who seemed down,
a blackbird went to ask why they looked sad:
"What happened that you seem so pale and drawn?
Why are you lame? And who plucked you, my lad?"
They answered him: "While having a good time
with this cute owl, we all got stuck in lime."
"These playful owls with their seductive way,"
the blackbird cried, "on guileless birds do prey!"

*****

XXXI
LA SIGNA E LA VULPI

Vi scrivu e vi presentu tali e quali
lu dialogu, comu era distisu
dintra lu camulutu originali,
traduttu da lu Vecchiu. È assai concisu
pirch'è traduzioni litterali;
di lu miu nent'affattu ci aju misu;
tali, com'era, da mia si cunsigna:
Vi prevengu chi primu parra signa.
   "Cummàri cumu stati?""Ih! tinta assai!"
"Dativi cura"."E chi? st'infirmitati
è d'una specii ch'un si cura mai".
"E pirchì?""Pirch'è mali di l'etati»
"Pribbìru! Pocu fa minni addunai,
chi avivu tutti li cianchi spilati".
"E chist'è nenti, ci sunn'àutri guai".
"Quali sù?""Sugnu modda pri mitati".
"Mischina! chianciu sta vostra muddura!"
"Vogghiu a l'oricchia pri stu bonu offiziu,
darti un rigordu. Accostati addrittura".
"Ah tu muzzichi! ahi! ahi!" "Metti giudiziu:
vulpi e lupi nun cancianu natura,
lu pilu pirdirannu e no lu viziu".
     *****

XXXI
The Monkey and The Fox

Allow me to rewrite and to present
this dialogue exactly as inscribed
in the moth-eaten, ancient document
that the Old Man translated and transcribed.
Because it is a literal translation
it is concise. I've added no critique
and pass it on without an explanation.
I'll simply say the monkey's first to speak:
   "How are you, neighbor?" "Not so good, for sure!"
"Take care!" "Oh my disease has reached a stage
no worldly medicine can ever cure."
"How come?" "It's a disease that comes with age."
"How true! In fact, I saw a little while ago
that round your waist you'd lost your hair." "There's
       more.
I am afraid I've got much greater woe!"
"What else?" "My body feels half soft and sore."
"Oh wretched fox! Your soreness I regret."
"For your concern, I'll whisper in your ear
something that you won't easily forget!"
"Ah, but you're biting me!" "Reflect, my dear!
Foxes and wolves all of their hair may lose,
but they won't change their nature and their vice!"
     *****

XXXII
L'URSU E LU RAGNU

Saziu di meli sinu tra li naschi,
un'ursu ripusava tra la tana.
Un ragnu, appisu a li soi riti laschi,
sicci fa avanti, e dici: "La Suvrana
Altizza Vostra comu soffri in paci
l'insetti molestissimi ed audaci?

Ver'è ch'è un gran discapitu lu so
mittirisi cun iddi a tu pri tu;
ma affidarni l'incaricu a mia pò:
l'attaccu e ‹mburdu a tutti quantu sù.
Fissu e chiantatu a la porta davanti
sarò na sintinedda viggilanti."

L'ursu accetta l'offerta, ed eccu un velu
vidi distisu avanti di l'entrata.
Ma poi s'accorgi chi ‹un è tuttu zelu;
giacchì ogni musca chi resta 'ncappata,
è preda di lu ragnu chi la suca,
e la testa e li vini ci l'asciuca.

E puru chistu l'avirrìa suffertu;
ma quannu vidi poi chi vespi ed api
tràsinu franchi, comu fussi apertu,
dici: "Sta riti d'ingiustizia sapi;
teni a frenu li picciuli, nè vali
pri li grossi, chi fannu maggiur mali.

Conchiudu: "O tutti o nuddu. A disonuri
jeu tegnu, ed a viltà, lu dominari
li deboli e li vili. Tu procuri
lu sulu to vantaggiu, e voi lasciari
la taccia a mia di vili e di tirannu?
Sfunna e vattìnni pri lu to malannu".
*****

XXXII
The Bear and the Spider

His belly gorged with honey, a great bear
is resting in his lair most peacefully.
A spider, swinging on her wide-spaced snare,
approaches him: "Your Royal Majesty,
how can you tolerate without much caring
such insects who're so bothersome and daring?

It is demeaning to yourself, it's true,
to take them on directly one by one,
so why not let me do that task for you?
I'll charge and bind them in the web I've spun.
Before your cave unmoving I will dwell;
I'll be a most attentive sentinel."

The bear approves the spider's proposition
and sees a net spread out before his lair,
but soon he learns it has been a delusion,
for every fly that falls into the snare
becomes the spider's prey which he then drains
of life by sucking on its head and veins.

The bear might have been able to endure
such deeds, but when the wasps and bees
fly in unchecked as through an open door,
he says: "This net smells of inequities.
It does control the small, but can't disarm
the larger ones who cause much greater harm."

So I conclude: "All or no one! I say
it's a dishonor and a cowardice
upon the weak and lowly to hold sway.
You're seeking only your own benefice,
blotting me as tyrannical and base.
Clear out and catch your death some other place!"
*****

XXXIII
LU LEBBRU E LU CAMALEONTI

Dissi lu lebbru a lu camaleonti:
"Tu mi pari un complessu di portenti;
quanti voti ti guardu, tu ti appronti
di aspettu e di culuri differenti;
ed ultra poi di chistu, ancora sentu
chi ti alimenti d'aria e di ventu".
Rispusi: "Pri castigu fui da Giovi
canciatu da lu primu aspettu umanu,
pirchì pri ambizioni tali provi
cu l'impiegu facìa di corteggianu".
Ripigghia l'àutru: "Cercati l'eguali
dunca tra l'anticàmmari e li sali".
*****

XXXIII
The Hare and the Chameleon

The hare once said to the chameleon:
"You seem of portents a real monument,
for when I look at you, you just put on
colors and aspects that are different.
And in addition, I have heard it said
that wind and air are all that you are fed."
The other said: "It was a punishment
from Jove who changed me from my human form
because upon such changes I was bent
by my ambition and the courtiers' norm."
The hare replied: "So then to find your peer
in waiting rooms and halls you must appear."
*****

219

"XXXIV
LI VIRMUZZI

L'intressu propriu pinci a nui l'oggetti
ora boni ora pessimi, a secunna
di unni a guardarli qualcunu si metti.
L'esperienza di sti fatti abbunna:
tra li tanti lu Vecchiu vi cunsigna
dui virmuzzi tra un filu di gramigna.

L'unu spia: "Cullega, chi si dici?"
Rispunni l'àutru: "Guai! C'è mali novi!
Liberu è già lu campu a li nimici
pri fari supra nui crudili provi:
vennu li feri agneddi a devorari
st'ervi, e nui chi ci semu ad abitari".

Ripigghia chiddu: "E li benefatturi
lupi, benigni lupi, ni lassaru?
Sù stati di l'agneddi lu terruri,
vigghiannu sempri pri nostru riparu:
per iddi ancora intatta si conserva
la nostra vita, ch'è affidata a st'erva".

"Ahimè! l'àutru esclamau, ahimè! li cani
e li pasturi armati ed a munseddu
l'assautaru anchi dintra di li tani,
e ni ficiru orribili maceddu.
Li barbari tripudiu ni fannu,
chiancemu in iddi nui lu propriu dannu".

*****

XXXIV
The Little Worms

At times things are portrayed as bad or good
according to our own self-interest,
and to perspectives wherefrom they are viewed.
Experience makes such facts manifest.
The Old Man out of many tales will plead
this of two worms who shared a blade of weed.

The first worm asked: "How is it going, Friend?"
The other cried: "There's bad, bad news ahead!
Our enemies are free now to descend
on us and tear us cruelly to shreds.
Those fearsome lambs are coming to consume
these grasses and will make themselves our tomb."

The other added then: "And what about
the wolves, our benefactors who're so kind?
Have they abandoned us? They've been, throughout
the lambs' great scourge, and always well-inclined
toward us. And since upon this grass we thrive,
we owe it all to them if we're alive."

"Ah, wretched us!" the other worm exclaimed.
"Many armed shepherds with their dogs pursued
the wolves into their lairs, by hate inflamed,
and butchered them, in ways both harsh and crude.
Now those barbarians hold joyful feasts,
while we our troubles mourn and those poor beasts."

*****

XXXV
LA VULPI E LU LUPU

Standu na vulpi supra na finestra
di un casalinu vecchiu inabitatu,
guardava a bassu in macchi di jinestra;
un lupu, chi vidennusi guardatu,
ci spia: "T'aju a dari?" Idda surrisi
dicennu: "Aju squatratu quantu pisi".

"Tu nun sì tantu leggia, iddu rispusi;
ma puru si tra nui ci fussi lega,
tintiriamu l'imprisi chiù azzardusi.
‹Ntavulamu un trattatu; pensa, spiega,
ditta li leggi tu, ch'eu tutti quanti
juru osservarli comu saggi e santi".

"Benissimu, diss'idda, pri cuscenza
sacciu quantu pò avìrinni lu lupu,
onuri ni poi vìnniri a cridenza:
'nzumma si Giovi 'un è pri tia chi un pupu,
si fidi in tia, nè probità ci trasi,
stu trattatu unni posa e metti basi?"

"Lu vantaggiu reciprocu", ripigghia
lu lupu. Ma la vulpi: "Ccà ti vogghiu.
L'amur propriu nun dormi, sempri vigghia,
e si ci torna commodu un'imbrogghiu,
posponi, scarpisannu ogni trattatu,
all'utili comuni lu privatu".

"Dunca, ripigghia l'àutru, già si vidi,
chi cu la tua manera di pinsari
la guerra sula è chidda chi decidi..."
E idda: "Chi àutru da tia si pò spirari?
Unni c'è radicata la malizia
allignari ‹un ci pò mai l'amicizia".
*****

XXXV
The Fox and the Wolf

A fox was looking down out of a room
of a deserted, broken down, old hut
at this lone wolf who moved in growths of broom
who when he felt himself observed, yelled "What?
Do I owe anything to you?" She smiled
as she exclaimed: "I cannot be beguiled!"

I've got your number, too!" the wolf replied.
"But if the two of us had an agreement,
the greatest enterprises could be tried.
Let's make a deal!" Reflect, explain, present
your case, dictate your terms, and I'll abide
by them, as true laws, sacred, bona fide."

"That's really nice!" she said. "I know quite well
how keen a sense of conscience wolves can have!"
Your honor is a virtue you can sell
on credit!" So, if you consider Jove
a puppet, and if honesty and trust
mean naught, on what will our agreement rest?"

"Reciprocal advantage," said the rake.
the fox replied, "That's where the problem lies."
"Self interest is always quite awake.
It never sleeps. If it should realize
that cheating's easier, it will postpone
the common good in favor of its own,

stepping on all agreements." "And, therefore,"
the other said, "according to this view,
the only way to settle things is war?"
"What else can one expect from one like you?
When malice is so rooted in the heart,"
she said, "no friendships there can ever start."
*****

221

XXXVI
L'INGRATITUDINI O SIA LA VECCHIA E LU PORCU

Na vecchia chi tiratu
si avìa da un puzzu l'acqua,
ni sdivacau lu catu
tra un lemmu, e poi si sciacqua.

Un porcu arsu di siti,
vidennu l'acqua, scappa,
e senza offerti, o inviti,
arriva e si l'appappa.

Nun pensa farci mali
la vicchiaredda pia,
e godi ca dd'armali
si sazia e si arricria.

Vivennu quantu pò,
lu porcu poi nun lassa
fari da paru so:
lu lemmu ci fracassa.

La vecchia a sta vinditta
si pila e si contorci,
dicennu mesta e afflitta:
"Faciti beni a porci!"

*****

XXXVI
Of Ingratitude, that is,
the Old Woman and the Hog

An aged woman drew
some water from a well
and poured the pail into
a bowl to wash herself.

A hog, parched from great thirst,
approached and saw the water,
and though unasked, immersed
his snout into the bowl.

The woman did not think
of hurting him. In fact,
it pleased her he could drink
to his own heart's content.

But as he drank a slew,
the hog did what a hog
will usually do:
he broke the woman's bowl.

So at that awful deed,
she tore her hair and cried:
"To bite the hand that feeds
is what a hog knows best!"

*****

222

XXXVII
ANIMALI NOTTURNI E GIOVI

Lupi, vulpi e àutri bestii di rapina,
uniti a li jacobbi e a varvajanni,
facìanu istanza a Giovi ogni matina
contra Febbu, pirchì in terra spanni
tanta luci, pri cui vennu obligati
stàrisi in grutti e tani ‹ncrafucchiati;

e chi l'està ci robba li megghiu uri
di scurriri li campi, e di circari
da cavaleri erranti l'avventuri:
conchiudevanu in fini chi cui fari
vosi la luci putìa farni a menu,
bastannu di la notti lu serenu.

Giovi primu usau flemma, finalmenti
stancu da tanti instanzi bestiali
ci dici: "Virgugnativi, insolenti,
chi siti sutta assai di l'àutri armali;
pirchì la luci a vui nun torna a versu,
ni vuliti privatu l'universu?

Comu si vidirìanu senza luci
l'operi mei magnifici ed esatti?
Cui li viventi avviva? Cui produci,
cui fecunda li campi? O siti matti,
o furbi, chi timiti a chiaru lumi
esponiri li vostri rei costumi".

Quannu mi si accurdassi la licenza,
dirrìa chi si la luci è na sustanza
chi rischiara li corpi, la scienza
rischiara l'almi, e ottenebra ignoranza.
Cui da saggiu si regula e conduci,
scurri francu tra l'una e l'àutra luci.
*****

XXXVII
Nocturnal Animals and Jove

Wolves, foxes with some other beasts of prey,
together with owls and nocturnal birds,
each morning went to Jove just to inveigh
against the sun, for Phoebus — they concurred —
spread too much light on earth, and forced them all
to hide inside their caves and lairs and crawl.

And they complained as well that summer's light
the hours takes away in which it's best
to raid a field or, like an errant knight,
to seek one's fortune. He who was obsessed
to make the light, might well have done without,
for the night's glow sufficed to go about.

At first Jove listened calmly. Finally,
weary of such irrational requests,
exclaimed: "Ill-mannered boors, great shame on ye!
You are inferior to other beasts.
So then, because to light you are averse,
you'd like me to deprive the universe?

How could one ever see without sunlight
my perfect and most admirable works?
Who gives life to the living? Who the might
to make things grow? You must have gone berserk,
or you are sly and fear that the sun's glow
your wicked ways to everyone may show."

If I were given license to conclude,
I'd say that if light is a circumstance
that brightens bodies, science must be viewed
as what enlightens souls and ignorance.
He who conducts himself as a wise man,
this and the other light can freely span.
*****

XXXVIII
LA SORTI O SIA LI SIMINSEDDI E LI VENTI

Dui troffi di cardedda,
l'una si trova nata
supra na finistredda
di casa sdirrupata,
e l'àutra tra li cimi
di turri àuta e sublimi.

Sti dui cu lu favuri
di tutti l'elementi
spicanu, e fannu ciuri;
sti ciuri finalmenti
fannu li siminseddi
chini di sfiluccheddi.

Già sicchi e maturati,
sti siminseddi vannu,
da venti traspurtati,
pri l'aria vagannu,
sirvenducci di vila
li sfiluccheddi e pila.

Perciò succedi spissu
chi chidda nata bassa
s'alza, e lu ventu stissu
in cima poi la lassa
di gran turri, e crisci,
prospera ddà, e ciurisci.

L'àutra a l'incontru nata
ch'era tra tanta altizza,
doppu ch'in aria nata,
cadi tra la munnizza
in lochi vili e vasci,
unni germogghia, e nasci.

Pò insuperbirsi chidda,
e disprizzari a chista?
Forsi si divi ad idda
l'essiri ben provvista
di un locu àutu, eminenti?
Fu l'opra di li venti!

*****

XXXVIII
Destiny, that is, the Little Seeds and the Wind

Two tufts of chicory
just happened to go sprout
one on the window sill
of an old ruined hut,
the other grew to glower
on top of a tall tower.

These two tufts, favored by
the elements and weather,
matured and grew quite high,
and flowering together
produced their little seeds
with filaments replete.

The tiny flower seeds
by then mature and dry,
were carried by the breeze
which blew very high.
Their filaments and hair
were sails for them in air.

Therefore, we often find
the seed grown up below
is raised high by the wind,
and dropped so it can grow
on top of the high tower,
there to mature and flower.

The other, "au contraire,"
who'd sprouted at great heights
by swimming through the air
on garbage heaps alights,
in humble dirt below
where it will sprout and grow.

Now can the former spore
the latter one despise?
Can it claim credit for
his place in a high-rise,
which makes him such a prince?
Give credit to the winds!

*****

224

XXXIX
LI CRASTI

Na quantità di crasti in un sticcatu,
mentri chi si scurnavanu tra d'iddi,
ni fu da un strifizzaru unu acchiappatu,
chi un ferru ci ficcau tra li gariddi,
e in presenza di tutti l'ammazzau,
l'unciau, lu battiu beni, e lu scurciau.

L'àutri eranu mossi a vindicari
lu so mortu cumpagnu, e allura certu
eranu in statu di putirlu fari;
ma nun fu di durata lu cuncertu,
pirchì testi di crasti, e testi assai:
pignata di comuni 'un vugghi mai.

Da multi si dicìa chi l'ammazzatu
era superbu e chinu di arroganza:
"Na mala spina ni avemu livatu,
quali sconsu ni fa la sua mancanza?
Menu consumu d'erva, e la sua parti
crisci la nostra, pirchì a nui si sparti".

Si eranu cuitati a stu cunfortu,
quannu lu strifizzaru trasi arreri,
ed eccu cadi nàutru crastu mortu.
Tornanu l'àutri a mettirsi in pinseri,
freminu; ma poi trovan'anchi in chistu
li soi difetti, ch'era fàusu e tristu.

Vidinu poi chi la processioni
seguita a longu, nè la straggi speddi;
vannu trasennu in costernazioni
ed in timuri pri la propria peddi:
perciò tennu consigghiu espressamenti
pri risolviri un giustu espedienti.

Ma mentri si consulta e si riscontra
da una parti all'àutra ogni progettu,
e si matura cu lu pro e lu contra,
menzu sticcatu è già sbrigatu e nettu,
pirchì, scannannu a drittu ed a traversu,
lu strifizzaru tempu nun ni ha persu.

XXXIX
The He-Goats

A herd of he-goats in a wide corral,
each other butted with their horns and fought.
A butcher came and took one animal
and quickly plunged a knife into his throat,
killing him dead before the other goats.
Then puffed and beat him to remove his coat.

The other beasts had moved to make him pay
for slaughtering their comrade, and right then,
there was no doubt they could have won the day.
Short-lived, however, was their common plan,
for many he-goats' heads can't think, though joined:
a common pot won't reach the boiling point.

The slaughtered beast they started to deride.
Some thought he'd been a snob, an egoist:
"They've taken a sharp thorn out of our side.
Is there a reason why he should be missed?
There's less demand upon our grass. Indeed,
there is more grass on which we all can feed."

This thought had eased their nervousness a bit,
when into the corral the man returned,
and in a flash another goat was hit.
The other beasts grew even more concerned,
but afterwards they found that this one, too,
had faults, and that he was mean and untrue.

But seeing the procession's long duration,
seeing the massacre go on and on,
the he-goats soon fell prey to consternation,
afraid they'd lose the hides they called their own.
Therefore, they called a council purposely
to come up with the proper remedy.

But while among themselves they talked at length,
weighing all propositions from each quarter,
debating every weak point, every strength,
half the corral fell victim to the slaughter,
because the man, who'd wasted no daylight,
had kept on killing he-goats left and right.

L'ultimi, ah tardi! apprisiru, e a so costu,
chi duvìa farsi a privati odii un ponti,
lu nimicu comuni avennu 'ncostu!
E chi tra gran piriculi, li pronti
e li chiù arditi risoluzioni
sunnu a salvarci unici menzi boni.

*****

The last ones learned too late, at their expense,
that when a common foe threatens a war,
with private hatreds we should all dispense.
For when great dangers knock upon our door,
the swiftest and most daring resolution,
the only good means is to save the nation.

*****

XL
LU LUPU RUMITU E LU CANI

Un lupu vecchiu chi nun putìa chiui
scurriri e assassinari li campagni,
fàttusi un rumitoriu, sicc'inchiui;
li zocculi si adatta a li calcagni,
na corda tra lu cintu, e in schina e testa
na menza peddi d'asinu pri ‹mmesta.

Cu li pedi davanti ‹ncrucicchiati,
l'occhi modesti, stisu tra la porta,
a cui passa di ddà la caritati
dumanna umiliatu, e poi l'esorta
a fùiri ogni viziu e pompa vana,
e supra tuttu la carni munnana.

Tra tanti bestii chi sù a lu munnu,
ni trova alcuni sciocchi a signu tali,
chi cridinu stu lupu di bon funnu,
simplici, e senza nudda umbra di mali;
chisti, a cui putìa chiù, facianu a prova
dànnucci carni, e pani, e caci, ed ova.

Lu vidi un cani, e dici: "Eh via! si sapi
chi tra li lupi la divuzioni
è stratagemma vecchiu e chiù nun capi,
nè trova locu tra li testi boni.
Vinisti a mali tempi; st'etati
chiù nun si cridi a lupi mascherati".

"Almenu, ripigghiau lu lupu astutu,
mi divi esseri gratu pirchì vivu
da saggiu, nè chiù fazzu lu sbannutu,
nè sugnu chiù a li pecuri nocivu".
L'interrumpiu lu cani: "Ma stu beni,
chi tu vanti, da tia certu nun veni:

veni da li toi forzi già mancanti,
pri cui fari nun poi maggiuri dannu
ch'otteniri pri pura caritati
chiddu chi a forza carpivi rubbannu:
nzumma qualunqui pirsunaggiu fai,
lupu nascisti e lupu murirai".

*****

XL
The Hermit-Wolf and the Dog

An agèd wolf who could no longer scour
and murder through the countryside, had built
a hermitage, in which to spend his final hour.
Thus he began to wear a rope as belt,
put wooden shoes below his heels, and spread
a piece of donkey hide on back and head.

Lying before his door with his feet crossed,
with downcast eyes, and with a humbled mien,
he meekly begged some alms of those who passed.
He then exhorted everyone to shun
all vices and vain pomp, but most of all,
against bad, worldly flesh he made a call.

Among the many beasts who live on earth,
the wolf found some so dumb and credulous
that they believed he was good-hearted, worth
his words, and totally ingenuous.
And these among themselves tried to compete
in giving him more bread, cheese, eggs and meat.

On seeing this, a dog exclaimed: "Come, come!
With wolves devotion is an ancient ruse!
We know it well and it won't work, old chum,
on anyone who has a brain to use!
You came along at a bad time. Today
no one believes wolves wearing false array."

"You ought to be more grateful for, at least
I live more wisely, and don't roam or sweep
the countryside," replied the cunning beast,
"and I'm not harmful to your precious sheep."
The dog just cut him short: "This goodly deed
you're boasting of, from you does not proceed!

It is derived from your depleted might
whereby you cannot cause a greater harm
than to obtain from alms and with no fight
what once you used to steal through force of arms.
In sum, whatever character you play,
wolf you were born and wolf you'll surely die!"

*****

XLI
LU CUNVITU DI LI SURCI

Un surci di àutu rangu, pirchì natu
supra di un campanaru, essennu un jornu
scinnutu a terra, vidi in un fussatu
tanti àutri surci a un munnizzaru attornu.
Li compianci dicennu: "Oh miserabili!"
Dipoi ci parra cu maneri affabili:

"Ci pinsiriti a ripulirvi! E quannu?
Pirchì abitari in lochi sporchi e bassi,
l'aria chiù impura sempri respirannu?
Sollevativi. E ogn'unu si spicchiassi
in mia, chi staju unni ogni ventu batti,
sicuru anchi da trappuli e da gatti.

E pri farvi vidiri ch'è lu veru
quantu dicu, v'invitu pri dumani,
quannu lu suli è sutta st'emisferu,
a cenari cu mia tra li mei tani,
si avriti lu curaggiu appiccicari
dda turri o agugghia chi a menz'aria pari".

Li surci ci accunsentinu, e cuntentu
si parti ogn'unu, e a disiari attenni
l'ura prefissa di l'appuntamentu
pr'interveniri a stu invitu solenni.
Multi però, di umuri chiù baggianu,
nun ci vonn'iri cu li manu in manu:

Ma cui ci porta crusti di furmaggiu,
cui tozza duri, cui castagni e nuci,
cui ficu sicchi pri lu cumpanaggiu,
e cui di turti muddicheddi duci.
Cussì tutti a lu tempu stabilitu
si ficiru truvari a lu cunvitu.

Lu Baruneddu di lu campanaru
muntatu in cirimonia li ricivi;
l'introduci a traversu di un sularu
supra di un curniciuni, unni giulivi
vidinu stisi comu in un tirrazzu
pani, lardu, prisuttu, acci e tumazzu

Li cunvitati stupefatti ammiranu
lu situ, la viduta, la eminenza,
mettinu a passiaricci e respiranu.
Finalmenti a lu tàffiu poi si penza;
si alliffanu li mussi, e dannu saccu

XLI
The Banquet of the Mice

A high-born mouse — for he was born and raised
in a high steeple — coming to the ground,
at a small band of mice one morning gazed
who in a ditch ran through a garbage mound.
"Oh, wretched lot!" he cried with great compassion.
Then he continued speaking in this fashion:

"How can you ever cleanse yourselves? And when?
Why live in such a foul and filthy place?
Why breathe air so impure in this pigpen?
Rise up! Why not reflect upon my case?
I live where the wind blows, in the fresh air,
secure from cats and every kind of snare.

To show the truth of everything I say,
I now invite you all to come and dine
tomorrow in my home, when the sun's ray
has sunk below our far horizon's line;
that is, if you are brave enough to dare
to climb that tower looming in midair."

The mice accepted all, and merrily
departed to await with trepidation
the hour of the date set previously
to honor that most solemn invitation.
Many of them who were naive and candid
did not want to go in just empty-handed.

So some of them brought him a crust of cheese,
a few brought walnuts, chestnuts and stale bread;
some brought dried figs to eat along with these,
others sweet crumbs of cakes contributed.
Thus all of them, at the appointed hour,
converged as they'd agreed on the bell tower.

The little Baron of the airy spire
received them all quite ceremoniously
and going through an attic led them higher
upon a ledge where they observed with glee
bacon and bread, ham, celery, and cheese
displayed as a mosaic sure to please.

With some astonishment the guests admired
the setting for its eminence and site;
they paced right by the food and they respired.
At last they licked their chops with great delight,
as they prepared to mount a wild attack

pri fari allegri di dda robba smaccu.
   Mentri sù tra lu megghiu di lu spassu,
lu sagristanu li campani sona;
li surci, non avvezzi a ddu fracassu,
nun sannu si sù fulmini o su trona;
ci pari chi lu munnu si sprofunni,
e lu spaventu li sturdi e cunfunni.
   Lu Baruni à vogghia di gridari:
"Nun vi scantati ch'è cosa di nenti!"
Si sgargia indarnu, nun li pò frinari,
lu ribumbu è lu sulu chi si senti;
chiddi attirruti currinu a tantuni
pricipitannu da lu curniciuni.
   Lu surci di lu locu si dispiaci
pri'un aviri previstu sta frittata:
"Ma eu nun ci culpu", dici, e si dà paci;
mancia e si godi la campaniata.
Lu tradutturi è terminatu ccà,
ed eu ci aggiunciu sta moralità:
   L'esperienza ni fa dotti, e l'armi
ni sumministra a reggiri custanti
contra li colpi di li fàusi allarmi,
e n'insigna a distinguirli a l'istanti
da li veri periculi; e di fatti
utili è all'omu, a cani, a surci e a gatti.

       *****

meant to fill up their bellies like a sack.
   But as they were enjoying their repast,
the sacristan began to ring the bell.
The mice who were not used to such a blast,
knew not if it were thunder or a shell.
They thought the world was coming to an end.
Confused and scared, they could not comprehend.
   Although the Baron tried so hard to shout,
"Oh, don't be scared! It's nothing...the vibrations..."
his voice was drowned. He could not stop the rout.
All they could hear were the reverberations.
The terror-stricken mice began to flee
and one by one fell off the balcony.
   The mouse who was the host was quite displeased
that he had not foreseen this accident.
"It's not my fault!" He said, and thus appeased,
he ate. To him bells were a condiment.
The old Translator ended his tale here,
but I would like this moral to make clear.
   Experience can make us wise. With arms
she can provide us so we can stand fast
against the blows brought on by false alarms,
and teach us to distinguish them at last
from the true dangers that we face. So then,
it's useful to cats, dogs, and mice and men.

       *****

Giovanni Meli

XLII
LA CORVA E LU GROI

Stavasi mesta ed accufurunata
na mugghieri di un corvu. Passa,e spia
un groi: "Dimmi cos'ài? Chi sì malata?"
Rispusi: "Assai, ma di malincunia.

Mentri aspittava ccà la ritirata
di miu maritu, na vulpazza ria,
fingennusi già morta, stinnicchiata
stavasi a panz'all'aria tra la via.

Iddu la scopri, cala, si l'afferra,
luttanu in aria, ma la vulpi ocidi
lu corvu, e tutti dui scòppanu a terra".

Dissi lu groi: "Stu munnu è un gran teatru!
C'è cui chianci e cui ridi! Ma nun ridi
a longu la mugghieri di lu latru".
*****

XLII
The Raven's Wife and the Crane

A raven's wife was sad and looked unwell.
A crane passed by and just to do her part,
"What's wrong?" she asked. "Please, tell me, are you ill?"
She answered: "Yes, but with an aching heart.

While waiting for my husband to come back,
a mean and spiteful fox I saw with dread
stretched out upon the road, and on her back,
making believe she was already dead.

My husband saw, dove, and picked up his prey,
they struggled in the air; and he was killed.
Raven and fox fell on the ground headlong."

The crane exclaimed: "This world is like a play:
some people cry, some laugh. So it was willed,
but laughing by thieves' mates will not last long!"
*****

230

XLIII
LU SURCI E LA TARTUCA

Durmìa sutta na macchia na tartuca;
un surci la tuccau, la vitti dura,
la critti petra o radica di vruca;
pinsau di farni esperimentu allura;
ma mentri supra ci azzicca lu denti
arriminari e smoviri la senti.

Si arrassa, la cuntempla tutta intera,
e vidi ch'avi testa, ed occhi e vucca.
Dici tra d'iddu: "È armali tra la cera!
Ma la casa strascina unni si aggiucca!
Forsi avi assai chi perdiri e di toppi
nun si fida; oggi si aprinu cu sgroppi".

Spia: "Pirchì pigghiariti sta pena
di purtariti la casa unn'è chi vai?"
Rispunni chidda: "Pri stari serena
unni mi piaci, e nun aviri mai
a lu miu latu lu malu vicinu,
chi è preludiu di pessimu matinu".
*****

XLIII
The Mouse and the Turtle

A turtle was asleep beneath a bosk.
A mouse, on touching her, felt her hard shell
and thought it rock or root of tamarisk.
So he began to poke the beast and smell,
but when to sink his teeth in it he tried
he felt the turtle stir and move inside.

The mouse retreated, gazed at the whole beast,
and saw it had two eyes, a mouth, and head.
He thought: "It is an animal, at least!
But takes its house along to make its bed.
Too much to lose, perhaps, and does not trust
door locks which nowadays even twigs can bust."

The mouse asked her: "Why bother to transport
your house wherever you may go?" "To live
in peace just where I please," was the retort,
"away from neighbors who're insensitive
and importune. Such neighbors are, I say,
all harbingers of an ill-omened day."
*****

231

XLIV
LI SCRAVAGGHI

C'era sparsa pri terra certa stuppa,
pirchì li manni avìanu ddà cardati;
un scravagghiu ni arrunza e mett'in gruppa
di la sua schina na gran quantitati,
cridennu farsi maistusu e grossu
cu ddu volumi vavaciusu addossu.

    Mentri camina si senti tirari
li pedi di darreri... Vota, e guarda;
ma sbutannu si senti chiù 'mpacciari,
e prova un non so chi, chi lu ritarda!
Vidi chi tra li gammi c'è un'imbrogghiu;
si dà coraggiu, e dici: "Minni sciogghiu".

    Tenta sbrugghiari un pedi, mentri spinci
l'àutru in aiutu a chistu, chiddu spintu
in autri fila s'impidugghia e 'mpinci...
Torna a sbutarsi, e chiù si trova cintu...
Si cunfunni a la fini, e chiam'aiutu
d'unu ch'aveva assai 'ntisu e vidutu.

    Chistu, senza spustarsi, dici: "Avogghi,
amicu, di gridari quantu poi;
cui si à fattu li 'mbrogghi si li sbrogghi.
L'imbrogghi (gira e sbota quantu voi)
sempri sù 'mbrogghi. Guai pri cui ci trisca,
ed a cui pri sbrugghiarli sicc'immisca".
*****

XLIV
The Black Beetles

There was a lot of tow upon the ground
because some people had been combing flax.
A beetle made with it a little mound
and then arranged it high upon his back,
believing that this airy, bulky load
more majesty and size on him bestowed.

    As he began to walk, he felt some thing
pulling on his hind feet. He turned to look,
but as he did his body seemed to cling
to something thwarting him, some kind of hook.
When round his legs he saw entanglements,
"Now, I'll get free," said he with confidence.

    He tried to free one foot; when he devised
to raise the other one, the first got stuck
in other threads and was immobilized.
He turned again. At last, when panic struck,
he called for help, now utterly distraught,
to someone who had seen and heard a lot.

    "It's useless, Friend!" unmovingly opined
the fellow. "You can scream till doom's day come!
Let him who got himself into a bind,
get out! For troubles are most bothersome.
No matter how you twist and turn, they cause chagrin
to him who's stuck and those who meddle in!"
*****

XLV
LA PATEDDA E LU GRANCIU

Mentri chi na patedda
durmeva cuitedda,
e forsi si sunnava,
un granciu la vigghiava,
appittimatu e duru
‹ncostu di lu so muru;
e tra sta positura
chiù jorna e notti dura.

Surtìu chi assaiand'idda
d'àpriri na 'ngagghidda
pri vìdiri si attornu
erasi fattu jornu,
chiddu, chi sempri 'mpressu
ddà stavasi indefessu,
profitta vigilanti
di l'opportunu istanti,
bastanducci sta 'ngagghia
pri oprari la tinagghia.

Trasènnucci la punta,
fa leva, e tuttu smunta
lu so cuverchiu e tettu;
ed eccu chi l'insettu,
chi pri timuri e scantu
s'era guardatu tantu,
appena chi un minutu
trascurasi, è pirdutu,
e veni devoratu!
Guai, guai pri cu' è vigghiatu!

*****

XLV
The Limpet and the Crab

A limpet was asleep
in waters not so deep
and maybe she was dreaming.
A nearby crab was scheming,
attentive, on the ball,
and hiding near a wall.
The crab stayed on that site
many a day and night.
It happened suddenly:
the limpet tried to see
if morning had arrived,
and to this end she strived
by opening her shell,
but only for a spell.
The crab who was right there,
untiringly aware,
was quick and quite adroit
that moment to exploit.
And since a tiny crack
sufficed for his attack,
he stuck his claw's sharp tip,
and pressed against the lip
unhinging thus the roof,
which brings us to the proof:
the mollusk tried quite hard
against her foes to guard,
by living in great fear,
but failed to persevere,
and was forever doomed,
and by a crab consumed.
Have pity on such folk
who watchful eyes evoke!

*****

233

XLVI
LI CIAULI E LU TURDU

Dui ciàuli scutularu
tra un vàusu li facenni,
e ddocu poi ‹ntunaru
na chiàcchiara sullenni.

Spartutisi li lodi
prima e li cirimonii,
parraru poi di modi,
di ziti e matrimonii.

Sparraru li vicini,
li soggiri, l'amichi,
si cunfidaru infini
li soi galanti intrichi.

Dissiru unni tinìanu
li nidi situati;
quantu ciauliddi avìanu
di già menz'impinnati;

multi ni ripitavanu
scacciati in ova e morti;
'nzumma ciarmuliavanu
e sempri a vuci forti.

Un turdu, chi passannu,
l'intisi, dissi: "Oh sciocchi,
chi jiti abbanniannu!

Timiti anchi ssi rocchi;
nè chiàcchiari, nè picchi,
silenziu ci voli,
li macchi ànnu l'oricchi,
li petri ànnu paroli".

E quasi profetatu
lu turdu avissi, un cuccu
avìanu risbigghiatu,
chi ddà tinìa lu giuccu.

Chistu chi aveva apprisi
li lochi designati,
unni ci avìanu misi
li cuvi e li nidati,

vinuta già la notti
di ddà sbulazza e scappa;
junci, e tra quattru botti
nidi e ciauliddi appappa.

*****

XLVI
The Crows and the Thrush

Two crows perched on a bluff
expressed their every care
by talking off the cuff
and with a loud fanfare.

And having spent some time
on praising their positions,
they talked about the clime,
of weddings and traditions.

They spoke ill of their friends,
their neighbors and in-laws,
confiding, in the end,
their secret love seesaws.

They mourned the multitude
of young who'd died unhatched;
their chatter they pursued
as in a shouting match.

And so they did disclose
where all their nests were laid,
how many little crows
with feathers each one had.

But then a passing thrush,
on hearing them said: "Chumps!
Don't talk so loudly! Hush!

Be wary of tree stumps.
No chatter and no tears.
Be silent! Do not shriek!
for bushes here have ears
and even rocks can speak."

The thrush may well have been
a prophet, for their clatter
an owl they had not seen
alerted to the matter.

This owl, as they conferred,
had heard the place described
where nests and nestlings were,
and when nighttime arrived,

flew off out of that place
in search of the crows' nest.
She found it in good grace
and ate the crows with zest.

*****

XLVII
LU PASTURI E LU SERPI IMPASTURA-VACCHI

Spissu pri riparari a qualchi mali,
o pri dari a un delittu la sua pena,
si commetti la cura a certi tali,
a cui chiù di li rei feti la lena.
Eccu un'esempiu truvatu con arti
tra li tradutti camuluti carti.

Un pasturi avìa vacchi fàusi e barri,
chi jianu spissu pri viola storti,
facennu guastu a li lavuri e all'orti,
appurtannu disturbi, intressi, e sciarri.

Mentr'iddu ci gridava: Avò-irri-arri,
ci accosta un serpi, e parra di sta sorti:
"Pri servìriti, a costu di mia morti,
mi offru d'impasturarli pri li garri".

Accetta lu pasturi lu serviziu,
pirchì di lu sirpazzu tradituri
nun vidi di luntanu l'artifiziu.

Ferma li vacchi, è veru, ma in poc'uri
ci suca latti e sangu a pricipiziu,
e lassa peddi ed ossa, schitti e puri.
*****

XLVII
The Shepherd and the Snake That Hobbles Cows

Quite often just to find a resolution
for problems or to punish a misdeed,
we will entrust its proper execution
to someone worse than those who did the deed.
Here's an example that I've neatly clipped
from the translated worm-gnawed manuscript.

A shepherd had some cows with stubborn quirks
who often trod in narrow, crooked paths,
destroying crops and damaging field works,
creating problems, many claims, and wraths.

While he was shouting vain commands at them,
a snake approached and spoke this way to him:
"I'll help you, though it may cost me my life:
with pasterns hobbled cows can't cause much strife."

The offer was accepted by the man
because the evil serpent's cunning way
was such he did not see through the whole plan.

It's true he stopped the cows without delay,
but he drained all their milk and blood, as well,
leaving them skin and bones: an empty shell.
*****

235

XLVIII
LI SIGNI

Vistu avìanu li signi da luntanu
da l'omini un gran tempiu fabricari;
e mentri ci vugghievanu li manu
pri fari chiddu chi vidìanu fari,
subitu in testa ci sautau lu griddu
di fabricarinni unu uguali a chiddu.
    Pri tantu tutti quanti s'impegnaru
a traspurtari lu materiali
di ligna, petri, e taju; sparagnaru
sulu (in virtù di l'ugna soi) li scali:
mettinu manu all'opra, e pri disastru
ogni signu è 'ngigneri e capu-mastru.
    Ogn'unu fa da capu e d'architettu,
e fabrica a so modu, incominciannu
unu da la suffitta e da lu tettu;
nàutru veni la cubula inalzannu;
c'è cui cumincia da lu campanaru,
c'è puru cui principia da l'otaru.
    Tutti sti pezzi restanu isolati
senza li basi e senza appidamenti,
a li primi, perciò, vintuliati
precipitanu a terra, e ogni scuntenti
signu fabricaturi, chi c'è sutta,
di sua bestialità la pena scutta.
L'operi chiù ammiranni (ni convegnu)
sù da imitarisi; però esaminati
prima si aviti li forzi, l'ingegnu,
li circustanzi, li menzi adattati;
chi oprari senza piani, nè disigni
è l'imitazioni di li signi.
    *****

XLVIII
The Monkeys

Some monkeys had observed from far away
how men were building an enormous temple,
and while their hands were itching for the day
when they could imitate those folk's example,
a fancy thought took shape in every mind:
to build another shrine of the same kind.
    Therefore, they all agreed to work together
to carry the material, — the stones,
the lumber, and the clay —. They did not bother
for ladders: in their claws they had their own.
But as they started working, it was clear
each monkey was head man and engineer.
    Each acted as a boss and architect,
and worked just as he pleased, beginning from
the roof and ceiling, starting to erect
the building's dome, and there were even some
who the bell tower had begun to build;
foundations for an altar one had filled.
    So all the parts they built stood there alone
without connection and without a base,
and after the first winter winds had blown,
they crumbled to the ground upon that race
of monkey builders, sorry and unwise,
who'd won for their stupidity first prize.
Praiseworthy deeds, of course, we all agree,
are to be imitated, but, please see
if you possess the strength, the proper means,
the circumstances, and intelligence:
for working without blueprints or a plan
is something monkeys do, but not a man.
    *****

XLIX
LU CIGNALI E LU CANI CORSU

S'avìa fattu in un voscu na tuccata;
e un cignali ed un corsu mortalmenti
firuti tutti dui tra na vaddata
urlavanu di rabbia e di turmenti:
l'unu dintra lu pettu avìa dui baddi,
l'àutru gran scagghiunati in ventri e spaddi.

Lu porcu, avennu 'ntisu lu lamentu
di lu cani ci dici: "Eu chianciu e penu,
ma tu nun ridi, e nenti sì cuntentu;
ora tra l'uri estremi dimmi almenu
pirchì nimicu a la mia razza? Quali
vantaggiu porta a vui lu nostru mali?"

Rispunni: "Ultra l'istintu, chi nn'incita,
nui semu nati e campamu sirvennu,
cu l'obbligu di esponiri la vita
di lu patruni ad un capricciu, o cennu;
semu comu suldati additti all'usu
di lu conquistaturi ambizziusu".

*****

XLIX
The Boar and the Hound

Within a wood a hunt had taken place
and a wild boar, together with a hound,
both wounded mortally stood face to face
howling with rage and from their painful wounds;
the first had in his chest two shards of lead,
the other had deep gashes in its back and head.

The wild pig, when he heard the hound's lament,
addressed him thus: "I'm crying, in great pain,
but you're not laughing, you are not content!
Now that we are near to the end, what gain
can all our suffering bring to your kind?
Just tell me that! Why is your hate so blind?"

"Aside from what our instincts will command,
we're born and live to serve. And each one strives
to please. From us, our masters can demand,
with just a sign or whim, we risk our lives.
We are just like the many men of war
who fight for an ambitious conqueror."

*****

237

L
CANI MALTISI E CANI DI MANDRA

Sidìa na pasturedda sutta un chiuppu,
e un'agnidduzzu ci pasceva allatu,
mentr'idda si tineva pri lu tuppu
un canuzzu maltisi, chi scappatu
era pr'istintu di libertinaggiu
ad una dama chi facìa viaggiu.

A na certa distanza un forti e grossu
cani di la sua mandra valusuru
stavasi a li talài ed a riddossu;
ma a lu nicu (chi arditu e prosuntusu
pirchì protettu) ci acchianau la verra,
minacciusu di fari all'àutru guerra.

Idda lu teni forti, ed amminazza
lu grossu a jirisinni: "Su spirisci,
ci dici, pani persu, mala razza..."
Eccu fratantu un lupu comparisci,
e parti pri l'agneddu. A lu momentu
la pasturedda cadi in svenimentu.

Lu canuzzu ci scappa, e ancora curri;
ma lu cani di mandra coraggiusu
stagghia lu lupu, e l'agneddu succurri,
e doppu un gran cuntrastu sanguinusu,
lu lupu appi la peju ed è scappatu,
e lu cani turnau 'nsanguniatu.
Lu pasturi sintennu lu successu
dissi a la figghia: "Ài vistu lu periculu?
Si lu cani di mandra 'un t'era appressu
ti puteva salvari ddu ridiculu?"
Quann'utili e piaciri 'un poi componiri,
l'utili a lu piaciri nun posponiri.

*****

L
The Maltese and the Sheepherder's Dog

A shepherdess sat underneath elm trees
and next to her a little lamb was grazing.
She cuddled in her lap a cute Maltese
who from her mistress' arms had started racing,
— a noble lady who was on a trip —
to heed for naughty escapades the whip.

A certain distance off a strong, large hound,
who was the valiant guardian of the herd,
stood watch by going from the low to the high ground.
The little dog by anger was then stirred,
and as he felt protected and secure,
against the other boldly threatened war.

She held her and with threatening, harsh tones
told the large dog to go away from there:
"Beat it, you good for nothing, lazy bones!"
Meanwhile, a wolf appeared and raced to where
the lamb was grazing. The poor shepherdess,
on seeing him, swooned, losing consciousness.

The little dog took off. She simply scrammed,
but the courageous hound did not take flight
and stopped the wolf, to succor the poor lamb.
And following a long and bloody fight,
the wolf, who'd had the worse of it, just fled,
and the sheep dog returned all stained with blood.
The shepherd, having heard what had occurred,
said to his daughter, saying: "The danger did you see?
If the sheep dog had not been near the herd,
could that small, silly dog have set you free?"
When usefulness and pleasure can't be sewn,
the usefulness to pleasure don't postpone!

*****

LI LU SCECCU E L'API	LI The Donkey and the Bees
Viziu molestu e bruttu è chiddu di li scecchi, mettiri mussu a tuttu, ‹ncucciari tra li necchi.	Jackasses have a vice, a mean and ugly trait: they stick their snouts in things and they are obstinate.
Chistu si pò vidiri tra la chiù chiara luci quantu veni a diri lu Vecchiu chi traduci.	This fact can be confirmed, as clear as a bright day, by what the Old Translator is now about to say.
Suspisa a li dui capi da travi na pinnata, multi fasceddi d'api chiudìa tra na murata.	There was a shed which rested on both sides on some beams and which was then closed off by many honeycombs.
Un sceccu, chi livatu si aveva lu capistru, sicc'era avvicinatu cu l'aria di ministru.	An ass who'd freed himself of his restraining rope, approached the honeycombs as though he'd been a pope!
Versu di li fasceddi sporgi lu mussu avanti; ma l'api sintineddi accorti e viggilanti,	He leaned with his snout nearer to where the honey was, but those who were on guard, were vigilant, sharp bees.
appena chi tanticchia lu vidinu accustari, ci dicinu a l'oricchia: "Ccà tu nun ài chi fari;	As soon as he got close, they whispered in his ear: "It's not a place for you, you don't belong in here.
nun è locu pri tia, vota, vattìnni all'erva giacchì idda ti cunserva". Ma predicaru a un'ortu	So turn around! Go feed on grass that's on the ground 't will be more satisfying and keep you safe and sound."
di cavuli e di trunza. Lu sceccu è veru tortu, 'ngnuranti cu la 'nzunza. 'Ncucciusu dici: "Afforza	Their preaching went unheeded, like talking to a wall! Jackasses are quite stubborn; their ignorance is gall!
ccà vogghiu stari; esiggi rispettu la mia forza; da vui nun soffru liggi". Sti sensi sù tra pocu	So stubbornly he said: "I'll stay just where I please! My might demands respect; I won't obey some bees!"
purtati dintr'a chiddi, ed eccu tantu focu, tant'ira sbampa in iddi chi ogn'apa è già un'Achilli, armata d'asta e dardu;	These feelings were announced to all the bees in there in whom they sparked such fire, such ire everywhere, that every bee was armed

nèscinu a milli a milli
con impetu gagghiardu:
  na squatra attacca l'occhi,
e un nuvulu si sparti
tra oricchi e tra crafocchi
d'ogni segreta parti;
  tri squatri sani sani,
chi sù quantu la rina,
tiranu a li custani
ch'av'iddu tra la schina.
  Li gammi 'un sunnu esenti
da lu tremennu attaccu,
ma quattru riggimenti
ci vannu a dari saccu.
  Pri accrisciri li baschi,
chiù squatri e battagghiuni
si avventanu a li naschi
cu dardi e cu spuntuni.
  Uncia com'utri a ventu
lu sceccu tra momenti,
dà cauci, fa lamentu,
si sbatti inutilmenti.
  Si accorgi, benchì tardu,
quantu periculusu
è l'essiri tistardu,
l'essiri prosuntusu.
                    *****

with arrow and with lance.
As fearless as Achilles,
they started to advance.
  A team attacked the eyes;
of bees a large patrol
split up between the ears
and every secret hole;
  And three full-strength platoons
then launched a wild attack,
upon the donkey's sores
that festered on his back.
  The legs were not exempt
from that tremendous raid:
four regiments were sent
to finish the blockade.
  More teams, and more battalions,
to add to his great sorrows,
attacked the nostrils fiercely
with pointed sticks and arrows.
  The jackass soon became
a wineskin that's wind-blown,
and struggling uselessly;
he kicked and loudly moaned.
  He realized, too late,
it's dangerous, alas,
to be presumptuous,
to be a stubborn ass!
                    *****

240

LII
LU CORVU BIANCU E LI CORVI NIURI

Scuppàu da la Lapponia
supra sti spiaggi stancu,
sbattutu da li turbini,
un raru corvu biancu.

Pusau, vinni a calmarisi
l'affannu e ciatatina;
poi cerca di truvarisi
la razza sua curvina.

Ni vidi un sbardu nìvuru,
e all'aria e a lu linguaggiu.
conusci chi sta specii
è di lu so lignaggiu.

Vola, e l'agghiunci all'àstracu
di un turrigghiuni anticu;
ci dici chi desidera
d'essirci sociu e amicu.

Si li culuri spàttanu
tra nui di l'ali e schinu,
nè tonica fa monicu,
nè cricchia fa parrinu.

Li corvi da principiu
scossi a dda novitati,
lu guardanu, l'ammiranu
di supra e da li lati;

ma macchia nun truvannucci,
dicinu: "Chistu in nui
cu sta bianchizza attirasi
l'occhi, e ni oscura chiui".

Pertantu lu sdilliggianu,
dicennu: "Nun è onuri,
nun è decenti e propriu
pri corvi stu culuri.

'Nzamai na corva scùvacci
na tali meravigghia,
sarrìa pri nui gran scandalu,
corvu chi a tia sumigghia".

Lu meritu, ch'è in àutri,
e a nui nun fa riflessu,
o passa pri demeritu,
o restasi depressu.

*****

LII
The White Raven and the Black Ravens

From distant Lapland, driven
by storms, fatigued and sore,
there came a rare, white raven
upon our very shore.

He landed, caught his breath
and gained some peace of mind.
Then he went out to look
for his own raven kind.

He saw many black ravens
all gathered in a throng,
and judged them of his species,
by aspect and by tongue.

Upon an ancient tower
he flew to join them, and
he said he wished to be
their partner and their friend.

"Our wings and back don't match
in color. That's the least,
for habits don't make monks,
nor tonsures make a priest!"

The ravens were quite shaken
and they began to stare.
They looked him over well,
examined him with care.

Not seeing any stains,
"With his white hue," they swore,
"he will attract attention
and show our blackness more."

So they insulted him
by saying: "It's not right,
or decent or quite proper
for ravens to be white!

If raven ever hatched
a marvel of this hue,
what great disgrace for us,
a bird that looked like you!"

The worthiness of others
which does not shine in us
is seen as a demerit
or is put down with fuss.

*****

LIII
LA FURMICULA

C'era tra un chianu un vàusu,
e chistu aveva in cima
na petra, e dipoi nàutra
supra di chista prima.

Circannu na furmicula
di suli qualchi ucchiata
supra la petra appiccica,
ch'era la chiù elevata.

Mentri chi assulicchiavasi,
si vidi pri la testa
strisciari e attornu chioviri
di petri na timpesta.

Eranu alcuni giuvini,
ch'avianu jutu in cerca
di petra misa in àutu
da sèrvici pri merca.

Vidennu sfriciarisi
l'insettu sti rigali,
a terra si precipita,
comu s'avissi l'ali.

Juntu chi fu, la purvuli
un cacciaturi prova,
ed a ddà petra ammirasi
chi supra l'àutri trova.
La povira furmicula
 trema a ddà botta strana,
vidi la petra càdiri,
e subitu s'intana;

 e dici, 'ncrafucchiandusi
dintra ddi lochi chiusi:
"Posti eminenti!...Càncaru!
Chi sù periculusi!"

*****

LIII
The Ant

There was a granite block
that stood high on a ledge
on top of which a rock
was balanced at the edge.

A little ant went climbing,
while looking for some sun,
above the boulder, aiming
to reach the highest one.

While he enjoyed the heat,
he saw a hail of stones
land all around his feet
and nearly smash his bones.

It was a band of boys
who'd sought a rock quite high
as target to employ
as they let pebbles fly.

But when the insect saw
his head buzzed by those things,
he fled from there as though
he'd been endowed with wings.

A hunter then arrived
and just as a test fire
to hit the rock contrived
that of the two was higher.
The ant began to tremble
on hearing that loud whack.
On seeing the rock tumble,
he hid inside a crack.

But as he dug in it
he murmured in dismay,
"High places, holy shit!
They're dangerous, I'd say!"

*****

LIV
LA MUSCA

Na musca si crideva cosa granni
pirchì supra lu re, di la riggina
passiava, e gustava li vivanni
chi li cochi apparicchianu in cucina;
e chi anchi putìa viviri in comuni
cu lu tauru superbu e lu liuni.
  China la testa di sti vani fumi
chiù nun vidi la sua fragilitati,
e tuttu a propriu meritu si assumi
chi nun à l'andamenti limitati.
Nun sapi ch'unni posa, la pirsuna,
chi l'avi supra, d'idda nun si adduna.
  Fratantu si li re, si li riggini
da sta musca sù appena calculati,
figuramu l'insetti chiù mischini
di qual'occhiu ponn'essiri guardati!...
Nò, nun tanta superbia, cala l'ali,
scàntati chù di tutti da sti tali.
  Tardi, e senza profittu apprinnirai
sta verità, ch'eu vegnu ora da diri,
quannu tra na tinagghia sbattirai
d'una tarantulicchia, chi scupriri
mai tu putivi tra li toi fastusi
idei, tutti sublimi e grandiusi.
*****

LIV
The Fly

A fly believed he was the real McCoy
because he could stroll on the king and queen,
and many delicate repasts enjoy
prepared by chefs well-versed in "haute cuisine,"
and also for the fact that he could dwell
with the proud lion and the bull as well.
  His head became so full of heated air,
he could no longer see his feebleness,
and since his actions no one tried to pare,
ascribed it to his merit and success.
He did not know the man on whom he rested
was not at all aware that he existed.
  If such a worthless fly, meanwhile, could deem
great kings and queens not worth a second glance,
consider, if you will, how small must seem
the smallest insects, with such arrogance!
Oh...No...don't be so proud, don't fly so high!
More than the rest, of them you must be shy.
  You'll know too late how true my words have been,
while struggling for your life against the claws
of a small spider you'd not even seen,
because it was too small to give you pause,
compared to the great thoughts inside your brain,
which are sublime and grand, but much too vain.
*****

LV
LU ZAPPAGGHIUNI E L'OMU

Un'omu s'era appena appinnicatu,
chi s'intisi a la facci na lanzetta,
chi àvia sinu a lu vivu penetratu;
l'arduri lu fa scòtiri a l'infretta,
apri l'occhi, smicciannu attentamenti
tuttu a l'intornu, e nun discopri nenti.

S'ingatta cotu cotu, e si tratteni
lu ciatu in pettu, e poi l'oricchi affila
pri sèntiri si c'è cui va, o cu veni,
o peditozzu di cui si la sfila;
ma nun senti chi un rùsicu noiusu
e un non so chi, chi ci sfricìa stizzusu.

"Atomu insolentissimu, ci dici,
dimmi: Sì tu chi punci, e chi fai mali?
Sì tu? Palisa almenu eu chi ti fici
pri cui m'ài datu spuntunati tali?
Pirchì picciulu tantu, tantu infestu,
e tantu noiusissimu e molestu?"

"Giustu, ci rispus'iddu, pirchì nenti
jeu cuntu tra lu munnu, aju pinsatu
stu nuiusu e molestu espedienti;
ti l'avirrissi mai tu imagginatu
sta invisibili mia specii di bestia,
senza pruvarni duluri e molestia?"

*****

LV
The Mosquito and Man

A man had barely drifted into sleep
when on his face he felt a little lance
that had pierced through his skin and sunk in deep.
Rudely awakened by the sting, a glance
he cast about the room with utmost care,
but he discovered there was no one there.

He calmed himself and stilled his heaving chest;
then perked his ears that he might better hear
the footsteps of some uninvited guest
who might be trying to escape from there,
but all he heard was an annoying buzz
and felt some kind of vexing, noxious fuzz.

"Most insolent of atoms," he exclaimed,
"are you the one who stung me to such pain?
Are you the one? Why am I being blamed?
Tell me why I deserve your sharp disdain!
Why is it that you are so very small
and yet you're the most bothersome of all?"

"Exactly right!" he said. "Since here on earth
I count for nothing, I conceived this tool,
this mean expedient, to prove my worth.
Would you have thought of me, a molecule,
a small, invisible, mean kind of beast,
if I did not cause pain and were a pest?"

*****

244

LVI
LU STRUZZU, L'AQUILA ED AUTRI ANIMALI

Nasci in nui l'amur propriu e cu nui mori,
ed è un istintu ch'avemu in comuni
cu l'animali tutti chi ànnu cori.
Lu libru chi traduci lu Vicchiuni
ci lu dimustra tra un dialoguzzu
unni parra cu l'aquila lu struzzu.

Lu struzzu avìa vidutu da luntanu
vinìri, e da un'autizza smisurata,
l'aquila, chi di poi di manu in manu
calannu, 'ncostu ad iddu era pusata.
"D'unni veni?" spiau. "Da Calicutti,
rispunni, e d'àutri regni ignoti a tutti".

"Bellu piaciri! lu struzzu ripigghia,
di aviri un paru d'ali sì robbusti
da sollevarsi in àutu tanti migghia!
Scurrìri un munnu!...Chisti sù li gusti!
Ci avirrìa, ad esser'aquila, un gran preu,
senza però scurdarmi ca sugn'eu".

Lu stissu replicaru unitamenti
na tartuca, un gamiddu e un elefanti,
chi eranu a stu dialogu presenti:
e ci scummettu chi si ddà davanti
tu puru, o miu lettturi, ti truvavi,
lu stissu unitamenti replicavi.

*****

LVI
The Ostrich, the Eagle, and Other Animals

Self-love is born and dies with us. It's part
of instincts Mother Nature has created
in every animal that has a heart.
The volume that the Wise Old Man translated
with this brief tale to show this truth will seek,
wherein an ostrich and an eagle speak.

An ostrich had observed from far away
an eagle at great heights above a cloud,
descending slowly till it came to sway
upon a branch, majestically proud.
"Where are you coming from?" he asked. "Calcutta!
and from some realms unknown to men," he uttered.

"It must be wondrous..." said the ostrich then,
"to be endowed with wings so powerful
that lift you higher than our eyes can scan...
To roam the world...that's really wonderful!
To be an eagle...oh, so pleased I'd be,
without forgetting though that I'm still me!"

The turtle, camel, and the elephant
who stood as witnesses to this exchange
shared all exactly the same sentiment,
and I can bet that if you'd been in range
to hear their words, my readers, you'd have said
precisely what each animal then did.

*****

LVII
L'OMU, LU TRUNCU, E LU PASTURI

Un omu bonu assai
jeva a sfogari spissu
tutti l'amari guai
avanti a un truncu fissu.

Lu vidi un pastureddu,
chi passa pri accidenti,
e dici: "Oh puvureddu!
Partuta è la tua menti!

A un truncu senza oricchi,
duru, chi azzann'accetti,
sti lagrimi e sti picchi
pirchì tu spargi e jetti?

Sùsiti. Chi ni accanzi?
Chi grazia ti pò fari?
Cunta li toi lagnanzi
a cui ti pò giuvari".

"Lu sacciu, ci rispusi,
perdu lu tempu e l'uri:
ma ricchi e facultusi
sù menu surdi e duri?

Almenu na ritagghia
ccà c'è chi mi cunsola:
mi sfogu, e nun mi stagghia
stu truncu la parola".

*****

LVII
A Man, a Tree Trunk, and a Shepherd

A man most excellent
would often go to vent
his bitter misery
to an unswaying tree.

By chance a shepherd boy
who was just passing by,
beheld him and he said:
"Poor man! You've lost your head!

Why pour and waste your tears
on trees that have no ears,
that are ax-dulling hard
and cannot have regard?

Get up! What can you gain?
Your weeping is in vain.
Your troubles tell to those
with means to ease your woes."

"I'm wasting breath and time,
I know," the man exclaimed,
"but are the rich less hard,
or have they more regard?

At least with this old tree,
one thing will comfort me.
I vent my woes at will
and it will keep quite still."

*****

LVIII
LU CERVU, LU CANI E LU TAURU

Un gran cervu inalberava
dui ramuti e longhi corna,
di cui tantu si picava,
ch'impunìa tra ddi cuntorna;
    pirchì nuddu ancora avìa
tra l'armali di ddu locu,
fattu prova si valìa
cu ddi corna o multu o pocu.
    Ma un livreri, peddi ed ossa,
nun curannu l'armatura,
sicci scagghia, e a prima mossa
chiddu fui e sàuta mura;
    e fuennu grida: "Amici,
nuddu veni ad aiutarmi?"
"Corna persi, un tauru dici,
lu coraggiu è chiù di l'armi".
                    *****

LVIII
The Stag, the Greyhound, and the Bull

Once, a large stag who possessed
two branched horns that were quite grand
was with them himself impressed
and cast fear around the land,
    That's because of all the beasts,
no one ever had assessed
if his horns were worth at least
what he deemed them in a test.
    But a mighty skinny hound
for those weapons felt no dread
and attacked him. At the first round,
the poor stag jumped walls and fled,
    and while running, "Friends," he cried,
"none will come to my defense?"
"Worthless horns!" A bull replied,
"Courage's more than armaments!"
                    *****

LIX
LA CIAULA E LU PAPPAGADDU

Vidutu avìa na ciàula
pasciutu e accarizzatu
un pappagaddu in nobili
alloggiu situatu.

Cuntrafacìa li passari,
si li sintìa cantari;
cuntrafaceva l'omini,
si li sintìa parrari.

Un jornu capitannulu
da sula a sulu, accosta,
dicennu: "Fammi grazia,
jeu sù vinuta apposta:

Dimmi, qual'è in origini
lu veru to linguaggiu?
Ca tanti tu ni arròzzuli
ch'eu sturdu e mi ammaraggiu".

Rispusi: "In confidenzia
sù finti sti mei provi;
veru linguaggiu propriu
in mia nun cinni trovi.

Jeu conoscii chi l'omini
vonnu essiri adulati;
replicu zoccu dicinu:
cuntenti sù e gabbati.

Jeu d'iddi li carizzi
guadagnu e li favuri,
ed iddi si confirmanu
chiù tra li proprii erruri".

*****

LIX
The Crow and the Parrot

A crow once saw a parrot
who lived in luxury,
well-nourished and well-cared for
by true nobility.

He imitated sparrows
when he could hear them squawk;
he imitated people
when he could hear them talk.

The crow then saw the parrot
all by himself one day
and went to ask this question:
"This wish please grant, I pray!

What was at the beginning
the tongue that you first used?
You dabble in so many
I am perplexed, confused."

"In confidence," he answered,
"my talking is all fake.
A real and proper language
I really cannot speak.

All men want flattery,
as I learned long ago.
I simply mouth their words;
they're fooled, but they don't know!

And thus all their attention
and favors I receive,
and they find validated
the lies that they believe."

*****

LX
LU CARDUBULU E L'APA

All'apa lu cardùbulu
dissi: "Eu ben discernu
in vui talenti e industria,
ma schiavi di un governu.

Pri l'essiri sensibili
in terra nun si dà
preggiu maggiuri e nobili
chiù di la libertà.

Li liggi di ogni generi
sù cippi, sù catini;
o mura, chi vi chiudinu
tra picculi confini.

Tra l'abbundanza triscanu
pochi chi sù a la testa;
soffrinu tutti l'àutri
travagghi e feria sesta.

L'usu vi fa soffribili
lu jugu chi vi affliggi;
ma eu natu e avvezzu liberu
da nuddu soffru liggi;

nun aju cui mi sindica
li gesti e l'azzioni,
e campu divirtennumi
senza soggezioni".

"Ma chi durata cuntanu
sti preggi toi vantati?
(rispusi l'apa), spèddinu
tra un cursu di un'estati.

Appena chi finiscinu
in terra ciuri e frutti,
all'ultima miseria
vi siti già ridutti.

Circati li ricoveri
contra di li jilati;
ma nenti ci sarvastivu,
e nenti ci truvati.

Vantativi ora liberi!
nun dura la bunazza;
vita perciò precaria
avi la vostra razza."

Intornu a lu discreditu

LX
The Hornet and the Bee

Said to a bee a hornet:
"You clearly demonstrate
great industry and talent,
but you're slaves of the State.

For sensitive, free beings
there is no greater prize,
or one that is more noble,
than living with no ties.

All laws of every fashion,
are yokes and chains that bind,
or barriers that hold you
to a small world confined.

The few who live on topside,
enjoy great affluence;
the others suffer sorrows
and days of abstinence.

Your habit makes the yoke
more bearable for you.
Born free, and used to freedom,
I can endure no law.

My actions and my gestures
no one but me must please.
I live my life with glee
without fear and at ease."

"The prize of which you're boasting,
just how long will it last?"
the bee said. "It will finish
when summer has gone past.

As soon as fruits and flowers
have vanished from the trees,
you'll see yourselves reduced
to utter misery.

You will start seeking shelter
against the freezing wind.
But nothing did you save,
and nothing you will find.

Go on, boast of your freedom!
Fair weather is short-lived.
Your species' life uncertain.
That's why you do not thrive."

And as for the disdain

datu a la società,
provu ch'in idda trovasi
la vera libertà.

La tua è licenza, è un viviri
da latru e da sarvaggiu,
in preda a li disordini
e a lu libertinaggiu.

Ma in essiri chiù nobili,
capaci di cultura,
la societati è un meritu
chi li gran specii onura.

Cui chiù la liggi venera
chist'è liberu chiui;
la liggi è partu propriu,
dunca obbidemu a nui.

Nè pirchì fatta trovasi
nesci da sti confini;
l'avuli, chi la ficiru,
ni àvianu tra li rini.

E si li nostri vizii
ni soffrinu disaggiu,
è pocu sagrifiziu
riguardu a lu vantaggiu.

Di nui si in ogni singula
la forza è poca o nenti,
la liggi, la cuncordia
la rendinu imponenti.

Cu tanti onuri e commodi,
chi vidi a pochi dati,
li gran sollecitudini
sù appena compensati.

Si ossequia l'individuu,
chi sedi da regnanti,
sta di la liggi in guardia,
e n'è rappresentanti.

Chistu a lu beni, all'ordini
vigghia, providi e accurri;
premia lu veru meritu,
e a miseri succurri.

Chist'è di menti savii
la vera libertati,
qualunqu'àutra è deliriu
di testi scavigghiati.

Si di lu beni publicu

for our society,
only within her bosom
exists true liberty.

Yours is a life of license,
for wild beasts, thieves — obscene! —
who are prey to disorders
and ways of libertines.

But for a nobler being
who culture can produce,
society's an honor
that higher species use.

Whoever venerates
the law more, is more free.
The law is our own child;
thus, we ourselves obey.

The fact that it exists
does not make it less true,
The loins of those who wrote
the laws, contained us too.

And if we feel some hardship
because of our own vices,
compared to all the gains
they're puny sacrifices.

Our strength is small or nothing,
if taken one by one,
but it becomes impressive
through laws and union.

The honors and the comforts
we've granted to a few,
can barely compensate them
for all the things they do.

We honor the one being
who leads our government
because he guards our laws.
He's their embodiment.

He watches over order,
provides for our welfare,
rewards real worthiness
and succors all the poor.

That's freedom, to my mind,
for all who're wise and sane.
Anything else's the folly
of a dislocated brain.

If we lose sight of the good

si perdi in nui l'idia,
o casa di diavulu,
o chiamala anarchia".

*****

of the community,
then either devil's home,
or call it anarchy."

*****

LXI
LI PASSAGAGGHI O SIA LI MUSCHI E LA TARANTULA

Du muschi tra na cammara
vidinu a la finestra
passari na tarantula
da la sinistra a destra.

Junta chi fu, di un subitu
la vidinu turnari,
ed in sensu cuntrariu
lu so viaggiu fari.

Quann'è arrivata all'angulu
torna, e di ddà ripassa;
stu zichi-zachi seguita,
e sempri passa e spassa.

Dici na musca all'àutra:
"Sentu pigghiarimi dica,
multu mi scannalianu
sti passagagghi, amica".

L'àutra, chiù timiraria,
ci dici: "Lassa fari;
è ostrutta tra lu ficatu,
e voli passiari".

"Nò, dici l'àutra, trappuli
e inganni minni aspettu;
cui voli stari stìacci,
pri mia mi la sbanchettu".

Dici, e diventa pruvuli.
Ma l'àutra sciocca e tosta
si resta dunniannusi,
pirdennu tempu apposta.

Ma poi vulennu nèsciri
si vidi 'nviluppata,
ed eccu la tarantula
di supra c'è sotata.

Cu vui si parra, o fimmini:
Fuìti sti canagghi,
chi cercanu 'ncapparivi
cu li soi passagagghi.

*****

LXI
The Flies and the Tarantula, that is, Courting

Two flies inside a room
regarded with some caution
out of the window frame
a spider's rightward motion.

When coming to the end,
they saw him turn around,
and start back on his journey
but this time leftward bound.

Then when he reached the corner,
he turned again. Thenceforth,
he kept up his zig-zagging,
and just went back and forth.

One fly said to the other,
"I'm feeling somewhat wary,
This zigging and this zagging,
my friend, seems awful scary!"

The other who was bolder
replied: "Do not think twice!
He's likely constipated
and needs the exercise."

The other said: "Oh, no!
I smell deceit, a trap.
Stay if you like; you're free.
I won't. I am no sap!"
Thus spoke and took a powder.
Quite foolish and unsound,
the other fly remained,
to dilly-dally round.

But when she tried to leave,
she found herself entangled,
and by the spider's jaws
she was entrapped and mangled.

I'm talking to you, Ladies.
Shun those men with no worth
who try entangling you,
by walking back and forth.

*****

LXII
LA TADDARITA E LI SURCI

Na taddarita stavasi
tuttu lu jornu 'nchiusa
tra tani, unni abitavanu
li surci a la rinfusa.

E chisti la suffrevanu
tra la sua cumpagnia:
un surci la cridevanu
siccu pri malatia.

Idda però, in curcarisi
lu suli, si la sbigna,
e l'ali sparpagghiandusi
all'aria si cunsigna;

e in idda sammuzzannusi,
tissennu a tutti banni,
passa li notti a vìdiri
li furti e contrabbanni.

E quannu a casu incontrasi
cu varvajanni o cucchi,
l'adùla cu lodaricci
li belli soi pilucchi.

Li cosi visti sbòmmica;
nè sunnu sparagnati
li surci unn'idda 'nzemmula
ci passa li jurnati.

A chiddi chi si acciurranu
li surci pri lu cozzu,
cala cu sta notizia
meli pri cannarozzu.

Alliscianu, accarizzanu
la taddarita ria,
cun iddi si la portanu,
sirvennucci di spia.

Ed a li tani subitu
juncinu a strata fatta,
s'appostanu e si aggranfanu
li surci a la strasatta.

Genti di aspettu duppiu
(ditti da nui faccioli)
scugnatili, fuitili,
sfrattatili, figghioli.
*****

LXII
The Bat and the Mice

A bat spent her day time
inside a darkened lair
together with some mice
who also lived in there.

And they would tolerate
her company because
they thought she was a mouse,
made skinny by disease.

But when the sun would set,
she'd always disappear,
flapping her wings about
and bobbing in the air.

She dove with wings outspread
and here and there she strayed,
observing in the night
thefts and illegal trade.

And when she met some owls
or other birds of prey,
she'd flatter them by saying
"How well you look today!"

She'd blurb out all she knew.
Nor would the mice she spare
with whom she spent her day,
revealing when and where.

The information tasted
to those who hunt for mice
and grab them by their necks,
like honey — mighty nice! —

They flattered and caressed
the wicked bat. And since
they used her as a spy,
they took her on their hunts.
They quickly reached the lairs,
proceeding straight and true.
And after they laid siege,
the mice they grabbed and slew.

The folks who have two natures,
(we know them as two-faced),
my daughters, must be shunned,
forever shunned and chased.
*****

LXIII
LI LUPI

A tempu chi l'armali discurrevanu,
dui lupi, ntra na grutta 'ncrafucchiati,
'nzemmula sti discursi si facevanu:

"Nui semu veramenti diffamati;
cui ni voli lu sangu e cui la peddi;
'nzumma semu dui testi abbanniati.

Facemu straggi, è veru, di l'agneddi,
ma ch'avemu a muriri di miciaci?
Si 'un manciamu, pri nui lu munnu speddi.

Manciati, nni dirannu, oriu e spinaci;
chisti 'un su nostru pastu, e chi curpamu?
L'à fattu la natura, vi dispiaci?

Dispiacitivi d'idda, nui ch'entramu?
Si ccà c'è culpa, è la sua; lu nostru coriu
nui cu fari li ltri arrisicamu.

Si nni putissi alimintari l'oriu,
e avissimu lu commodu di jiri
a sonu di campana a rifittoriu,

in chistu casu, sì, si putissi diri,
vidennuni ammazzari un'animali,
oh, li mostri chi fannu inorridiri!

Stu casu non in nui, ma tali quali
nellomu si verifica appuntinu,
nell'omu chi si vanta razionali.

Prodighi la natura e lu distinu
l'abbundaru di mezzi pri campari;
ervi, frutti, simenzi, ed ogghiu e vinu;

puru chisti non ponnu sodisfari
l'intemperanza sua: lu sceleratu
àutru non fa chi ocidiri e squartari.

Doppu ca ad una vacca ci à sucatu
tantu tempu lu latti, poi la scanna:
chista è la ricompensa di st'ingratu!

Lu voi chi in so serviziu si affanna,
l'agevola tantu, poi pri paga
da l'omu a lu maceddu si cundanna!

Nè stu crudili e barbaru si appaga
di la simplici morti; nè cuntenti
resta si prima 'un ci fa vozzu o chiaga:

comu sunnu ddi belli complimenti,
privannulu di attivu e di passivu,

LXIII
The Wolves

In times gone by, when animals conversed,
two wolves were hidden well inside a cave,
and in these musings deeply were immersed:
"We are defamed as scoundrels and as knaves.
Some want our blood, and others want our hide.
Like bandits, they complain, we all behave.

That we kill lambs can never be denied,
but what are we supposed to do? Starve, then?
Not eating is like saying we had died.

Eat spinach or some oats, will say some men,
but that is not our food. Are we to blame?
It's nature willed it so. If in your ken

someone's at fault, complain to nature, aim
your blame at her, not us, for when we steal
upon our hides someone may put his claim.

If we could be sustained with a good meal,
of corn, or go to dinner at our leisure
by heeding a refectory's bells' peal,

then in that case they could say with displeasure,
on seeing how we slaughter animals:
'Monsters! In killing they derive much pleasure!'

That does not correspond to us at all,
A perfect portrait though that is of man
who likes to boast that he is rational.

Nature and destiny in their great plan
lavished on him abundant means to live,
giving herbs, fruits, wine, with oil and grain.

But to men's overreaching drive, these did not give
a moment's pause. The wicked racketeers
just kill and tear apart — Insensitive! —

A cow whose milk they've drained for many years
they'll put to death without a second thought;
that's how the ingrates pay for their arrears!

The ox, who in their service, always sought
to make life easier, as recompense,
is to the slaughterhouse by men then brought.

Nor are these cruel and barbaric 'gents'
content to cause his death; they are not pleased
until they pay him further compliments,

giving him sores and blisters and disease,
or cutting off his masculinity,

pri cui resta a la specii indifferenti;
  o chidd'àutru d'esponirlu anchi vivu,
ad essiri di cani laceratu,
chi ci pari un spettaculu giulivu;
  e si lu godi supra d'un sticcatu,
e si cumpiaci di li lamintusi
grida di chidd'armali turmintatu.

  Nè l'oceddi ntra l'aria vennu esclusi
di l'esegranna sua gula; nemmenu
l'abitaturi di li campi undusi:
  'nzumma, quantu viventi lu tirrenu,
l'aria e l'acqua producinu, sù pastu
di l'omu, o sù li soi vittimi almenu.

  E pri nun degradari lu so fastu
cu taccia di barbaru, decidi
chi sù machini, e d'arma 'un ànnu rastu.

  Ma lu puntu 'un sta ddocu; sta, si cridi,
chi nun àjanu sensu; ntra stu casu
a li soi sensi proprii nun dà fidi;
  ed è insensatu, o tavuluni rasu,
iddu lu primu, quannu nun rifletti
chi l'animali ànn'occhi, vucca e nasu,
  e chi chisti sù l'organi perfetti
di lu sensu, e pri propria esperienza
divi pruvari in sè li stissi effetti,
  e si fa qualchi picciula avvertenza
a li convulsioni e a li lamenti
d'un 'armali chi soffri violenza,
  div'essiri convintu internamenti,
chi lu sensu 'un è sua privata doti,
ma ch'è comuni a tutti li viventi.

  Nun bastanu pertantu li rimoti
pretesti pr'ammazzàrinni qual'unu,
ma motivi pressanti e a tutti noti.

  Lu nostru sulu casu è l'opportunu,
chi 'un avennu àutri menzi pri campari
senza straggi muremu di dijunu.

  Lu propriu individuu conservari
è prima liggi; nè avemu àutru mensu
pri putiri la vita sustintari.

  L'omu, chi sempri adùla e duna incensu
sulu a se stissu, vistu chi nun spunta
lu pretestu, chi l'àutri 'un ànnu sensu,
  n'à truvatu unu novu: osserva e cunta

so by his species he cannot be teased;
  or yet displaying him quite openly
— just to provide men with a jolly show —
where dogs will tear its flesh most cruelly,
  while folks enjoy this kind of rodeo,
sitting upon a fence, taking delight
in the poor animal's sad cries and woe.

  The birds in the air, from their huge appetite
are not exempt; nor does the endless list
of creatures of the sea escape their might.

  In sum, all animals that now exist
on earth, in air, and in the sea are food
for man, or are his victims at the least.

  And man decided that — so no one could
reduce his pomp, by calling him a Hun —
beasts are machines and with no likelihood
  to have a soul. The point's not if they have one,
the point's that man believes beasts, as a rule,
are senseless. Here he doesn't trust his own,
  or is insensitive or a plain fool,
because, in the first place, he should reflect
that beasts have eyes, mouth, nose, that is, the tools,
  the perfect organs that our sense affect,
and, drawing on his own experience,
man should know beasts will feel the same effect.

  If he but paid some mind to evidence,
seeing the spasms and the suffering
of beasts who're victims of some violence,
  assuredly he would no longer cling
to the belief that senses are alone
man's gifts, not shared by other living things.

  On such bizarre pretexts one can't condone
or justify the killing of a beast,
the need must be more urgent and well-known!

  Ours is the only one that meets the test,
for we no other means to live possess,
and we would starve to death once killing ceased.

  Self-preservation's law—which we profess—
comes first, nor have we any other ways
that will allow us to live on, alas!

  Failing pretexts that senses hold no sway
in beasts, man, who is always fawning on
and flattering himself, will promptly say
  that he has found a new and truer one:

li denti di l'armali, si sù fatti
a pala, o puru a chiovu cu la punta:
    decidi chi li denti larghi e chiatti
sù destinati a manciar'ervi e frutti,
e li puntuti sù a li carni adatti:
    dipoi conchiudi chi li specii tutti
di denti imaginabili l'av'iddu,
perciò l'onnipossibili s'agghiutti.

    Facènnuci anchi bonu stu so griddu,
pri cui si cridi in drittu di manciari
a crepapanza di chistu e di chiddu,
    nun pò mai l'abusu giustificari
di carni, giacchì ntra tanti denti
quattru suli scagghiuni pò cuntari;

    quattru si ponnu diri o picca o nenti
tra trenta, o trentadui, chi n'avi in vucca,
o chiatti o di figura differenti.

    Cu quali drittu dunca scanna e ammucca
quanti armali ci sù? Sta conseguenza
da li principii soi certu nun sbucca.

    E si mai pò vantari na dispenza
di carni, in forza di li denti a punta,
la quantitati è parca e non immenza.

    Chi quattru a trentadui giustu ci spunta,
com'unu all'ottu, pirchì in trentadui
ottu voti lu quattru si cci cunta;

    perciò la carni nun trasi a lu chiui,
ntra li soi cibi, chi in ottava parti;
pirchì dunqui ni mancia chiù di nui?

    Pirchì arriva a manciarisi li quarti
di la sua propria specii?..." "Passu passu,
l'àutru ripigghia, 'un smuvemu sti carti:
    l'omu è dui voti lupu, e ccà ti lassu".
                    *****

he studies and observes the shape of every tooth.
If they are shovel-like or pointed like a nail
    and he decides that those that are flat, smooth
are destined to eat fruit and grass in dales,
the pointed teeth are meant to savor meat.
    He then concludes that man in all details
can meet the test as he has all kinds of teeth
and thus can swallow everything in sight.

    Even if we allow such fine conceit,
through which he feels entitled to the right
to gobble this and that in vast amounts,
    he cannot justify the other plight
of eating too much flesh, for you can count
inside his mouth but four canines alone.

    Four teeth can't be considered paramount:
they're few, out of the thirty-two he owns,
(or thirty) which are flat or of another form.

    On what authority does he go on
to kill and gulp down every beast? His norm,
his principles, such deeds can't justify.

    Assuming that the rules were uniform,
and sharp teeth could lay claim to a meat supply,
the quantity is meager, not immense.

    Since four to thirty two is but a tie
that equals one to eight, (that's common sense,
because in thirty two, four goes eight times),
    meat should account, in proper consequence,
for just one eighth the food that he consumes.
So then why does he swallow more than us?

    And quarters of his species he presumes
to go on eating...?" "Oh, let's not discuss
that part," the other said. "Don't raise the subject!
    Man's twice the wolf and lots more dangerous!"
                    *****

LXIV
LA SURCIA E LI SURCITEDDI

Dintra un crafocchiu d'una pagghiarola,
ch'era in funnu a na stadda, avia la tana
na surcia cu li figghi nichi ancora.

Lu chiù grannuzzu na jurnata acchiana,
s'affaccia ntra la stadda, e ntra un momentu
torna jittannu na gran vuci strana.

"Mamà, mamà, chi vitti, chi spaventu!
Ivì ca tremu... aiutu!..." E mentri esprimi,
l'afflittu ganguraru 'un avi abbentu.

La matri, chi pri affettu sempri timi,
si scuncerta ed occurri premurusa:
"Chi vidisti? Chi fu? Pirchì ti opprimi?"

"Vitti... ripigghia cu lena affannusa,
vitti... aiutu, figghioli... ancora tremu!...
Vitti na bestia, grossa, spavintusa,

cu na vucca chi, a tutti quantu semu,
pari chi sani sani nni agghiuttissi;
e sbruffa forti, e fa un terruri estremu;

e zappa cu superbia, comu avissi
a fari gran fracassi; e a la sua vuci
tutta la casa pari chi cadissi".

"Nun c'è àutru? rispusi duci duci
la matri; va cuètati, babbanu;
ddocu sù chiù li vuci ca li nuci;

chistu è n'armali bonu, un pocu ofànu:
si chiama lu cavaddu, e quannu zappa,
è un trasportu di focu juculanu;

pari in vista chi l'aria s'appappa,
ma lu so cori è comu carta bianca;
nun ciunna, nun divora, e mancu attrappa;

'nzumma cu chisti armali a manu franca
trattatici sicuri, e 'un dubitati:
l'àutri un vannu d'iddi un pilu d'anca".

Cussì dici la matri, ed ammirati
stavanu tutti a sèntiri li figghi
cu vucca aperta ed oricchi affilati.

Poi ripigghia lu primu: "Meravigghi,
mamà, nni cunti; ma ti vogghiu diri
'nzoccu poi vitti 'mmenzu a certi stigghi.

Un'armalu chi facìa piaciri
sulu a guardarlu: era di pilu griciu,

LXIV
The Mother Mouse and Her Young

Under a hay loft, deep inside a stable
there was a hole in which a mother mouse
had young still immature and not quite able

to know truth. Once, the eldest left his house,
peered in the stable and ran back inside,
squealing so loud dead men he'd have aroused.

"Ma...Ma...You don't know what I saw," he cried.
"What fright! I'm shaking still!" And as he strove
to speak, his chin was quivering in stride.

The mother, always fearful out of love,
was quite distressed and ran to her son's side.
"What did you see? What are you frightened of?"

"I saw..." He started, breathing hard, dismayed,
"I saw...oh, help me, brothers! Oh, what fright!
I saw an animal so large it made

my blood run cold. His mouth in just one bite
could swallow each and everyone of us.
He terrified me, snorting with great might,

and when he proudly stamped his foot, a fuss
he threatened to let loose; and his loud cry,
which shook the house, could have proved ruinous."

"Is that all?" said the mother with a sigh.
"Go on, you need not fear, you silly goose!
With him there's really less than meets the eye!

It's called a horse. A bit vain and obtuse,
but a good animal. He stamps his feet
so as to let his playful spirits loose.

His breathing all the air seems to deplete,
but in his heart he's really very meek.
He will not scratch, devour, nor mistreat.

With animals like him you need not sneak,
but treat them openly and without fears.
Compared to others he's perhaps unique."

Thus spoke the mother and her little dears
were hanging from her lips in admiration,
with mouths wide open and with perked-up ears.

The first mouse then resumed his own narration:
"You're telling wonders, Ma! But let me say
what else I saw there in that same location:

a little beasty whose hair was all gray
who was a veritable joy to see,

e adaciu adaciu si videva jiri;
  li genti ci dicianu: miciu, miciu,
ed iddu, cu mudestia ed occhi bassi,
'ncugnava vasciu vasciu e sbriciu sbriciu,
  e parìa chi la testa si ficcassi
sutta quasi li pedi di li genti,
e chi mancu la terra scarpisassi.

  Avìa na vuci melenza, languenti:
si turceva lu coddu, e si jittava
facci pri terra a tutti li momenti".

  "Basta!..., gridau la matri, chi trimava:
mi arrizzanu li carni, e friddu friddu
sentu un suduri chi tutta mi lava!

  Ah! figghiu, figghiu, tu sì picciriddu!
Giudichi da l'esternu! Oh, si sapissi!...
Scànzanni, o Celu, da li granfi d'iddu!

  E si avversu distinu a nui prescrissi...
(ah! chi a sulu pinsarlu mi cunfunnu!)
fa chi prima la terra ni agghiuttissi!

  Di tutti l'animali chi ci sunnu,
chistu è lu chiù terribili; nun cridi
nè cridiri lu pò cui nun à munnu!

  A sti cudduzzi torti 'un dari fidi;
guàrdati di sti aspetti mansueti;
l'occhiu è calatu, però nun ti sbidi.

  Chisti sù sanguinarii, inquieti,
crudi, avari, manciuni, spietati,
tradituri, latruni, ed indiscreti.

  Impieganu li jorna e li nuttati
ntra na 'gnuni, cuvannu qualchi prisa,
cu l'occhi chiusi e li manu ligati,

  a signu chi cu passa li scarpisa,
pirchì si fannu purvuli e munnizza;
ma, fattu colpu, la sua testa attisa.

  Nèscinu l'ugna e tutta la fierizza,
e mittennusi in cima a li canali,
passanu di lu fangu a chidd'altizza;

  e tantu in iddi crudiltà prevali,
chi 'un s'appaga di morti violenta,
ma pruvari ci fa tutti li mali.

  Prima nni rumpi l'ossa, e poi nni allenta,
nni strascina, nn'ammutta; e morti arriva
tantu crudili chiù, quantu chiù lenta.

  Celu, fammi chiù tostu d'occhi priva,

walking demurely with a gentle sway.
  People kept calling him: `Here, Puss...Pusseee!`
and he with modesty and with eyes low
would rub against their legs most longingly.

  It almost seemed as if he wished to go
beneath the people's feet with his own head;
his paws did touch the ground, but barely so.

  His voice was sweet, melodious, well-bred,
he turned his neck and every little bit
he stretched upon the floor as though in bed."

  "Enough!" the mother cried, seized by a fit,
"you're giving me the shivers. I can feel
cold daggers pointing at my stomach pit.

  My child, my child, you're young and what seems real
may be quite false. Oh...if you only knew!
From his claws Heaven spare us and conceal!

  And if by adverse fate that is our due,
(Ah...just to think of it my mind goes numb!)
let earth then swallow us without ado.

  Among all beasts he's the most troublesome,
the worst on earth. This truth you can't believe
unless you've learned of life a minimum.

  Don't trust such hypocrites! Don't be naive!
Of such tame looks and manners be on guard!
Their eyes seem closed, but all things they perceive.

  They are bloodthirsty, restless, and rock hard,
traitorous, thieving, heartless, indiscreet,
selfish and greedy and without regard.

  They spend whole nights and days just to complete
their sly, prey-catching schemes, with eyes half closed,
and claws well-sheathed, stretched out before men's feet,

  and to their trampling constantly exposed,
becoming dust and garbage as a chore,
but once they've done the deed, their heads are raised.

  Their fierceness and their claws come to the fore,
and when upon the highest roofs they climb,
from deep down in the mud to stars they soar.

  Their cruelty is such a paradigm,
not pleased to make our deaths most violent,
as they inflict great pain, they take their time:

  at first they break our bones, then they relent;
they push us, drag us, and when death does come,
it's always much more slow-paced than we want.

  Rather than see a son of mine succumb,

chi vìdiri un spettaculu di chisti
in qualchi figghiu meu, mentr'eu sù viva!

   Ahimè! quali accurtizza mai risisti
d'iddi a l'insidii, quann'anchi durmennu
tramanu novi inganni e novi acquisti?

   Nè sonnu è chiddu so, pirchì sintennu
appena un peditozzu, aprinu l'occhi,
e adaciu adaciu si vannu spincennu.

   Si sù guardati, fannu li santocchi;
ma quannu'un si cci avverti, di la casa
ciorìanu li 'gnuni e li crafocchi;

   e intenti sempri a fari la sua vasa,
s'informanu di tuttu, e da la 'ntrata
passanu sinu all'àstrachi la rasa.

   La carni d'ogni specii c'è grata;
la mancianu ammucciuni e arraggiatizzi,
però la cruda d'iddi è chiù gustata;

   la guardanu in effettu allampatizzi,
si la vidinu in àutu, e prestu o tardi
ci juncinu cu astuzii e scaltrizzi.

   Ci sù cani, a lu spissu, chi riguardi
ànnu a la carni, e regginu custanti
a li tentazioni chiù gagghiardi,

   e ci stannu indefessi pri davanti

and act before my eyes in such a play,
I hope God takes my eyes and strikes me dumb!

   Poor me! What watchfulness can stay
their cunning art, when even in their sleep
a plot for new deceits and gains they lay?

   Nor could one call their sleeping sound or deep,
for as they hear the noise of steps, they wake
and slowly stand all ready for the leap.

   If watched, pure saintliness they'll fake,
but when you pay no mind to them, each hole,
each hiding place to smell they'll undertake,

   and, always aiming toward their only goal,
they will observe all things in their domain,
from door to attic to maintain control.

   They find that meat of every kind's germane;
they hide to eat it growling with vexation;
raw and uncooked flesh is their favored strain.

   They gaze at it in utter fascination
if they can see it out of reach, too high.
Sooner or later every aspiration

   will be fulfilled, for they are clever, sly.
Oftentimes dogs will be more resolute:
though liking meat, they will not gratify

   their powerful temptations, but stay put

259

senza mancu tuccarla; anzi fidili
da li granfi la salvanu di tanti;
  ma li gatti, di geniu sempri vili,
vidennula anchi pinta ntra lu muru,
squagghianu pri disiu comu cannili.
imici a li viventi, odianu puru
la propria specii, ed anchi sgranfugnannu
fannu l'amuri. Chistu è cori duru!
  Nzumma è na razza nata a fari dannu:
ma lu peju qual'è? Chi ntra l'aspettu
nun ci si sapi leggiri l'ingannu.
  Guardativi, vi dicu chiaru e schettu,
da chisti mansuliddi comu pani;
criditi a cu vi parra per affettu!
  E nuddu nescia mai da li soi tani,
si prima 'un sciogghi sta prighera, e dici:
Giovi, scànzanni a tutti, anchi a li cani,
  da l'orribili trami di sti mici!"

*****

before it steadily, not touching it,
nay, faithfully defending it, to boot.
  But cats will melt like candles that are lit
if they just see it painted on a wall
because their mean streak is near infinite.
 Hating the living and their kind, they'll maul
each other even when they copulate:
that's what sure proof of their cold heart I'd call!
  Cats are a race born havoc to create.
But what's the worst of it? That you can't see
their treachery. They seem naive and straight.
  Look out, I say with great sincerity,
for those who seem to be meek as a lamb.
Believe one who speaks out of empathy!
  Let all stay in their nests, snug as a clam,
and only come out when you've said this prayer:
O Jove, please spare us from the lethal sham
  of such a scheming, mean and dreadful slayer!"

*****

LXV
LU CANI E LU SIGNU

Un gentilomu avìa
na vigna, e si lagnava
chi fruttu 'un ni vidìa,
la vurza ci sculava,
lasciandulu dijunu,
curatulu importunu.

Lu Vecchiu era presenti,
lu libru sfugghiau,
ed opportunamenti
un simili truvau
casu, ch'è chistu appuntu
ch'eu, già traduttu, cuntu.

Un cani avìa aducchiata
tra un'àrvulu sublimi
na viti carricata,
attorta tra li cimi;
saziavisi a guardari,
ma 'un ci putìa acchianari.

Vidennu chi pirdutu
era lu tempu indarnu,
pinsau circari aiutu
d'unu, chi siccu e scarnu,
agili appiccicassi,
e ci la vinnignassi.

Vidi na vulpi in tana
nisciuta pri mità;
ci dici: "Veni, acchiana
chidd'àrvulu ch'è ddà,
guarda comu sta china
la cima di racina".

La vulpi, chi acchianari
ddà supra 'un si la senti,
ci dici: "Lassa stari,
amicu, 'un vali a nenti,
ci appizzu la fatia,
è agra, 'un fa pri mia".

Lu cani però gira
di ccà, di ddà circannu;
a un signu poi ammira,
ch'incontra trippiannu;
cridi chi sarìa chistu
per iddu un bonu acquistu.

Affabili ci accosta,
dicennu: "Tu sì in oziu;
t'aju circatu apposta

LXV
The Dog and the Monkey

A gentleman possessed
a vineyard and complained;
indeed, he was depressed,
to see his purse so drained
without an ounce of gain:
his work just seemed in vain.

The Old Man who was there
leafed through his book and lo!
a case he could compare
soon found quite a propos,
a tale he did translate;
the same one I'll relate.

A dog had chanced to see
a rich abundant vine
on top of a tall tree
with branches intertwined.
He watched it longingly,
but could not climb that tree.

And knowing it was vain
to stare and waste his time,
help tried he to obtain
from someone who could climb,
a lean and agile beast
to help him start his feast.

He saw a fox's snout
halfway outside his lair
and said to him: "Come out!
Come climb that tree up there!
Look how the top's replete
with sweet grapes we could eat."

The fox who did not see
himself up on that tree
replied: "Oh, let it be,
Friend, it's not worth my fee.
My toil for naught would be.
They're bitter! Not for me!"

The dog kept going round
and looking everywhere.
A monkey then he found,
saunt'ring without a care.
With him, he came to feel,
he could strike a good deal.

He spoke to him this way:
"I sought you out to ask,
as you don't work today,

pri dariti un nigoziu.
Si tu cu mia voi stari
c'è viviri e manciari.

Sarrà la tua incumbenza
di appiccicari a un'ulmu,
duvi racina immenza
pendi da lu so culmu;
tu cogghi e jetti a mia,
jeu poi ni dugnu a tia".

Cunsenti a un tali invitu
lu signu, e di cuncertu
si avvianu a lu situ,
già consaputu e certu;
arrivanu, e d'un sàutu
l'unu è a li cimi in àutu.

La viti era provista
cu frundi e frutti tantu
chi ci spirìu di vista.
Lu signu trisca intantu
chiusu tra l'abbundanza,
manciannu a crepa-panza.

Di quann'in quannu alcuna
rappa purrita o virdi
la jetta e l'abbanduna;
lu cani grida: "Oh spirdi!
chi purcarìa chi jetta!"
e cu pacenzia aspetta.

Doppu chi saturatu
si fu lu furbu, scinni,
dicennu: "Sù arrivatu
pri fina tra l'intinni,
ma fradici e corrutti
truvai li rappi tutti.

Chisti chi ti jittai
ni sù la 'mmustra, e avverti,
li megghiu ti scartai...
M'aju li rini aperti!
È un jornu chi a lu stagghiu
dijunu, ohimè, travagghiu!"

L'afflittu cani in attu
quasi di santiari:
"Ver'è, dici, lu pattu
di dàriti a manciari;
ma jeu cridia sicuru,
ch'avìa a manciari puru

Comu jiu jiu lu 'mbrogghiu,
jeu sù razza onorata,
ed adempìri vogghiu

that you perform a task.
And if my terms you meet,
there's much to drink and eat.

Your task requires you
to climb upon a tree,
on which there is a slew
of grapes you'll throw to me.
You pick and let them fall,
then we'll share the good haul."

Accepted the invite,
the monkey without phlegm
proceeded to the site
which was well known to them.
Once there, with a quick hop,
he climbed up to the top.

There was such wealth of fruit
and foliage on that vine,
the dog lost sight of it.
But hidden in that mine,
the monkey ate such a glut,
enough to bust a gut.

Once in a while he'd throw,
some green or rotten grapes,
that is, he just let go.
The dog cried out: "What ape!
What crap he's throwing me!"
and waited patiently.

After he'd had his fill,
came down the cunning beast
and said: "I climbed until
I could no more. A waste!
I found that every grape
was rotten or dried up.

These bunches that I threw
are a sure proof. What's more,
I picked the best for you.
A true back-breaking chore!
I worked the whole day long
for the proverbial song!"

The disappointed beast
was near to curse. "It's true,"
he said, "I acquiesced
to give some food to you,
but I thought in this pact,
I too would eat, in fact!

This sham now matters not.
But I'm of a proud breed
and I feel that I ought

la mia parola data:
Va' sfunna! Ti cunsignu
stu restu, e mi la sbignu".
*****

to keep the promise made.
Take all! To hell with you
and I will beat it too!
*****

LXVI
LU CASTORU E AUTRI ANIMALI

Un castoru elogii senti
di una vulpi celebrari:
cui lodava li talenti,
cui li soi maneri rari.
  Dici a chiddi: "In preggi tanti,
chi mi aviti decantati,
pirchì 'un sentu misi avanti
bona fidi e probitati?
  Sù li primi chisti tali,
e senz'iddi 'un vannu un cornu
l'àutri preggi, anzi chiù mali
fannu a tuttu lu contornu".
  Ddocu vitti chi ammuteru;
iddu torna a lu so tonu:
"Lu talentu è pri mia zeru,
si lu cori nun è bonu".
  *****

LXVI
The Beaver and Other Animals

One day a beaver heard
the praises of a fox:
some of his talents purred,
some praised the way he walks.
  "Among the qualities,"
he said, "that you have sung,
why are integrity
and honor left unsung?
  These are our greatest worth,
without them, I suggest,
the others will bring forth
more evil to the rest."
  When silent they had grown
he said in the same tone:
"Talent's not worth a sou,
if the heart's not good, too!"
  *****

264

LXVII
L'INSETTI MARITIMI DI LI SPONZI

Tra tanti e tanti sponzi chi sù in mari,
da migghiara d'insetti populati,
duvi ci ànnu li casi e li sulari,
ciumi, ponti, curtigghi, chiazzi e strati,
pri vidìrni una, e stàricci na picca,
lu spiritu di Esopu sicci ficca.

E in virtù di la sua potenza innata,
vidi non vistu, e gira, e, senza scala,
scinni e acchiana ogni loggia; allurtimata
penètra in una specii di sala,
duv'eranu in consessu radunati
l'insetti li chiù saggi ed accimati.

Si ferma, ed eccu senti recitari
d'unu d'iddi un discursu, unni si prova
chi l'universu cunsisteva in mari
duvi la sponza, o munnu so si trova
(sponza si chiama munnu tra sti banni,
nun avennu àutra idia di cosi granni).

Agghiunceva dicchiù, chi falsamenti
avevanu l'antichi soi cridutu,
ch'un munnu sulu ci fussi esistenti;
mentr'iddu da na specula vidutu
ni avìa, cu novi soi strumenti esatti,
multi àutri in gran distanza accussì fatti.

"Benchì nun si distingui, poi soggiunci,
si chisti tali fussiru abitati,
lu miu strumentu a tali signu 'un junci;
ma, si grata udienza mi accurdati,
m'ingignirò, signuri, di pruvarlu,
ma nun mi fidu poi di a vui mustrarlu.

Pri criari stu munnu da lu nenti
ci vosi na potenza àuta, infinita;
e a un'Essiri Infinitu, Onnipotenti
tant'è creari un munnu e darci vita,
quant'è crearni centu miliuni:

LXVII
Marine Insects living in Sponges

There are many large sponges in the seas
on which a thousand bugs live or much more
who make their homes in them, their factories,
with courtyards, bridges, streams, with streets and
    squares.
The ghost of Aesop thought it was worthwhile
to visit one of them and stay a while.

And owing to his native might and flair,
he could see things without his being seen,
climb up and down all loges with no stairs.
He went into a kind of hall, wherein
the wisest bugs — those sporting eminence —
had been assembled for a conference.

He paused to listen to a pompous speech,
pronounced by one of them in which he claimed
the universe consisted of a sea in which
the "sponge," or world, is found (the world is called
"sponge" by those living in and round that "land"
for they knew nothing larger or more grand.)

The insect further claimed the ancient ones
had been in error when they all believed
that there existed but one world alone,
for through a looking glass he had perceived
— it was a more precise, new instrument —
more worlds like theirs, in the far firmament.

He added, "Though it's difficult to tell,
if these worlds are inhabited at all
—my instrument does not reach out that far—
I will attempt to show you that they are,
my Lords, if you will grant me audience,
although I can't produce the evidence.

This world of ours from nothing to invent
required a power infinitely great
and such a Being who's Omnipotent,
a hundred million worlds can then create
as easily as breathing life in one,

Giovanni Meli

ddocu vi lasciu, bonciornu patruni".

  Lu spiritu di Esopu tra sè dissi:
"È l'omu pri rapportu all'universu
picculissimu insettu, comu chissi,
tra un restrittu orizzonti chiusu e immersu;
l'atmosfera è lu mari, ed è lu munnu
sponza, chi fluttua di stu oceanu a funnu".
*****

And here I say goodbye. My case is won!"

  The ghost of Aesop to himself declared:
"Man is a tiny insect just like these
when to the universe he is compared,
immersed, restricted to his narrow views.
The sea's our atmosphere, a sponge the world,
that at the bottom of the sea is hurled.
*****

LXVIII
SURCI, GIURANA E MERRU

C'è statu sempri tra surci e giurani
un mari vecchiu, un'odiu radicatu,
sin da quannu lu figghiu a Rudi-pani
ci fu da Guncia-tempuli annigatu:
d'unni surgìu na guerra sanguinusa,
chi tra na trumma risunau famusa.

Finìu di poi chi Giovi truniannu,
li granci armati di duri curazzi
di li giurani in succursu marciannu,
a li surci spilaru li mustazzi,
truncaru gammi e cudi cu tinagghi;
tra na parola, ci dettiru l'agghi.

Di allura insinu a nui nun c'è mai stata
tra sti dui specii nessuna azioni
chi fussi digna d'essiri nutata;
ma o sia pr'istintu o pri prevenzioni,
di cui li testi ci ristaru guasti,
nun s'incontranu mai senza cuntrasti.

Dunca un jornu a la ripa di un pantanu
un surci avvicinannusi, scrupriu
vinìri na giurana di luntanu,
chi senza diri bonciornu nè addiu,
d'una punta di juncu lu vrazz'arma,
poi dici: "Trasi, si ti basta l'arma!"

Ripigghia l'àutru: "Nesci e ven'in terra,
sugnu ccà, pruviremu cui chiù vali,
nun manciu filu, veni caniperra..."
ed idda: "Sollennissimu jacali,
si di valuri e curaggiu ti vanti,
a 'ncugnari unni mia pirchì ti scanti?"

"E tu, ripigghia l'àutru, pirchì timi
a viniri ccà 'nterra, putrunazza?..."
Ma mentri cu l'inciurii ognun'esprimi
chiù assai chi nun farrìa cu spata e mazza,
si senti un gaddu ddà 'ncostu cantari,
ed àutri chiù luntanu replicari.

LXVIII
Mice, Frogs, and Blackbird

Twixt frogs and mice there has forever been
bad blood and heartfelt animosity,
and dating back to when Bread-Nibbler's son
was drowned by Swollen-Cheek's mean perfidy.
From this event a bloody war began
which was made famous by a worthy pen.

The thundering great Jove, to bring an end
to the dispute, crabs armed with hard, thick shells
to march against the mice, was forced to send,
and these the mice's whiskers soon began to pull,
chopping with their sharp claws their legs and tails;
in other words, they knocked them on their heels.

And to this day, there never has occurred
between these species any deed or act
that was in any way deserving to be heard.
Be it because of instinct or the fact
the text was damaged or left incomplete,
these species always quarrel when they meet.

And so one day, upon the shore of a bog,
a mouse approached the water with some care,
when from a distance there appeared a frog
who saying not "Good morning," nor "beware!"
and brandishing a reed's tip in the air,
burst out: "Come in the water, if you dare!"

The other one replied: "You come on land!
I'm here. We'll see who is more valiant then.
So come, you ugly beast! For here I stand!"
He answered: "What a rotten specimen!
Of courage and great daring, oh why brag
when you're afraid to come near to a frog?"

"And why are you afraid," the other cried,
"to come here on dry land, you lazy slob?"
The two more harm kept threatening in stride
than could have been inflicted with a sword or club,
when suddenly a nearby rooster crowed
and others soon replied from down the road.

Un merru ch'avìa 'ntisu li cuntrasti,
grida: "Nun chiù, zittìtivi un momentu,
sintìtivi sti gaddi, e tantu basti:
ogn'unu in casa sua valipri centu,
e a stu cricchiutu oceddu lu cumparu:
canta ogni gaddu tra lu so puddaru".
*****

A blackbird heard the quarrel and cried out:
"No more! For just a moment, please, be still!
Be glad to listen to the roosters' bout.
Each one is worth one hundred on his hill.
And I compare him to this crested bird:
inside his coop each rooster is a lord!"
*****

LXIX
LI CRASTI, L'API E LU PARPAGGHIUNI

Diversi crasti a forza di curnati
un gran fasceddu fracassaru d'api,
e lu meli e li vrischi sprannuzzati
si persiru tra vrocculi, acci e rapi.
Vidennu farni sta mala vinditta
l'apuzzi si chiancevanu la sditta.

Un parpagghiuni dissi: "Nun è nenti;
fabbricamuli arreri, l'opra mia
jeu puru mittirò, stati cuntenti".
Rispusir'iddi: "Va' pri la tua via
qualunqui bestia è bona pri guastari,
ma nun è poi di tutti lu cunzari".
*****

LXIX
The He-Goats, the Bees, and the Butterfly

A few he-goats, with their strong horns destroyed
a large beehive and honeycombs and bees
together with the honey were deployed
among the turnips, broccoli, and celery.
On seeing such destruction, the poor bees
began to weep upon their miseries.

A butterfly exclaimed: "You need not sob!
Let's build them back again. Be of good cheer!
I'll be right glad to help you do the job."
They answered him: "Please, go away from here!
all animals can pick or tear apart
but to repair things, not all know the art."
*****

LXX
LI PORCI

Un rumitoriu, quasi clausuratu
da macchi e da spini, da rocchi e fussati,
multi porci si avevanu furmatu
ntra un voscu chi avìa ghiandri in quantitati.
L'istitutu si cridi da Epicuru:
Oraziu l'assicura, eu nun ci juru.

Si eliggi ogn'annu lu chiù grossu e grassu
e veni fattu Patri guardianu;
l'àutri sù eletti poi di passi in passu
resta fratellu cu' è chiù siccu e nanu;
e pri alcuni soi punti nun decisi
fannu conclusioni in ogni misi.

Nesci un gran varvasapiu a disputari,
lu multu reverennu Anghi-ammulati;
nesci poi lu Priuri ad impugnari,
lu reverennu fra Commoditati:
lu primu sputa, e poi 'ntunatu e sodu
'ntavula l'argumentu di stu modu:

"Precettu è in nui lu viviri e manciari;
precettu nun lu negu è ancora l'oziu;
l'unu nun divi all'àutru ripugnari:
dunca, manciari è oziu in negoziu".
Ripigghia l'àutru: "Patri, chistu è sbagghiu
manciannu si fa motu, ergo è travagghiu.

La nostra saggia regula è funnata
supra un precettu di putrunaria;
atqui facennu lunga masticata,
la vucca cu ddu motu si fatìa;
ergo manciari pri puri alimenti,
e dipoi stari senza fari nenti".

Dissi l'àutru: "Ritorciu l'argumentu:
s'è travagghiu pri vui lu masticari,
pirchì la vucca fa ddu movimentu,
ergo è travagghiu ancora parrari,
ergo vui, tantu d'oziu zelanti,
argumentannu siti già in fraganti".

Ddocu un comuni applausu di 'nguì 'nguì
interrumpìu lu cursu a la disputa,
chi comu tutti l'àutri accussì
finìu senza conchiudiri...Ma sputa
un purcidduni, chi avìa la zimarra

LXX
The Pigs

A herd of pigs had fashioned for themselves
inside a wood where acorns did abound,
a sort of hermitage, set off by shelves
of rock, thick bushes and uneven ground.
This institute dates back to Epicure,
Horace asserts, though I am not so sure.

The fattest and the largest of the swine
was chosen Father Guardian each year.
The rest, in turn, had their own chance to shine.
But dwarfs and skinny pigs had no career.
For some unclear and still unfathomed trait,
each month they gathered to deliberate.

A large Wiseacre moved to take the floor.
The reverend Sharp-Molars was his name.
Brother Commodity, who was the Prior,
was charged to voice the opposition's claim.
The first one spit and in firm, vibrant tones,
expressed his argument along these lines:

"For us to eat and drink is a precept;
a precept, too, I know, is not to work!
Therefore, the two of them we should accept,
to wit: 'to eat is otium at work!'"
The other said: "My Father, that is wrong!
For eating's work: I cannot go along.

Our guiding principles have their foundation
on precepts of complete poltroonery:
whereas, the mouth engaged in mastication
is open to fatigue and drudgery,
we should eat only for our nourishment
and as for work, remain quite abstinent."

The other said: "I turn the argument
on you. If chewing is considered work,
because the mouth in moving is intent,
then speaking, too, must be considered work.
Therefore, one who would otium exalt,
by arguing so much is found at fault!"

A general applause of many oinks
at that, cut short the hot porcine debate
which ended like all of the other ones,
without achieving anything ...But wait!
A big fat hog who wore a robe of mud

di crita e fangu, nesci in menzu, e parra:
  "Oh reverenni, finirannu insumma
sti quistioni di lana caprina?
Pirchì ntra vostri vucchi nun rimbumma:
  Multiplicati la razza purcina?..."
Sautàru allura tri vecchi maiali,
dicennu: "Chiudi ssa vuccazza, armali!"

  Si la moralità mi ricircati,
vi dicu chi la favula è istruttiva,
e chi cunteni na gran veritati,
di cui ni avemu esperienza viva:
chiù d'unu adatta la religioni
a la sua dominanti passioni.

  Dici un'avaru: Sobriu sù abbastanza
pri aviri (ccà a mill'anni) all'àutra vita
ntra li beati una sicura stanza;
purrìa fari na tavula squisita;
ma poi nun ci starrìa beni in cuscenza;
piaci multu a lu Celu l'astinenza.

  Lu prodigu si fida chi 'un à avutu
nè a beni, nè a dinari attaccamentu;
da l'impacci tirreni s'à sciugghiutu,
nè lassa liti tra lu tistamentu;
cu stu confortu opera quantu pò
a fari chi lu so nun fussi so.

  Mi staju in chiesa, dici lu putruni,
e casa e figghi raccumannu a Diu.
L'arma 'un allorda, dici lu manciuni
chiddu chi trasi in vucca, anzi è ricriu;
ma quannu la vucca si tramanna,
dici lu testu, li nostri almi appanna.

  Alliga lu lascivu: È un gran precettu
natu cu l'omu lu multiplicari,
a li codici antichi mi rimettu.
Finalmenti aju'ntisu perorari
anchi un'mbrugghiuni, chi acchiappa pri
            scutu:
Aiùtati, Diu dici, ch'eu t'aiutu!"
                    *****

and clay, stood in their midst, spit once and said:
  "Reverend Fathers, when, alas, will end
this pondering of hard and woolly cases?
Why is it that you never recommend?:
  'Go on and multiply your porcine race?'"
On hearing that, jumped up three agèd hogs,
and cried, "Oh, shut your mouth, you filthy pig!"

  If you should ask me for the moral sense,
this fable is instructive, I will say,
for it's about our own experience,
containing truth to stand the light of day.
Many a man religion will adapt
to make his dominating passion fit.

  A man who's avaricious just declares:
"I'm sober enough to earn among the blessed
a room in heaven, in a thousand years!
And I could set a table with the best,
but then my conscience would not feel at ease:
in Heaven abstinence is a great prize.

  The spendthrift is quite confident that he
is not attached to money and such frills.
From earthly bonds he sets himself quite free,
leaving no grounds for quarrels in his will.
With this consoling thought his best he does
to see that what was his, no longer is.

  "I'll stay in church," will say the lazy man,
"and place my kids and home in God's own hands."
"What goes in through the mouth the soul won't stain,"
the glutton says. "In fact, it's sustenance.
What really tarnishes our souls, instead,
is what comes out of it, as the Text said.

  The lustful man claims that to multiply
ourselves is a great precept that's innate,
and for the proof on ancient codes relies,
and finally, I've heard a scoundrel state
as a defense and shield for all his frauds:
"So help yourself, that I will help, said God!"
                    *****

Giovanni Meli

LXXI
LU GATTU E LU GADDU

Meravigghiatu un gattu di li tanti
provi di omaggiu e ossequiu chi un puddaru
prestava a lu so gaddu dominanti,
sicci avvicina, e dici: "Amicu caru,
fammi a parti di tua saggia politica,
giacch'iu mi trovu in circustanza critica.

Li gatti, pri lu chiù, da mia nun 'ncugnanu;
mi chiamanu a jinnaru...accostu, e arràzzanu;
tra d'iddi 'un fannu lega, si sgranfugnanu,
s'arròbbanu a vicenna e s'amminàzzanu;
'nzumma nun c'è nè capu, nè unioni,
e si campa tra guerri e quistioni.

Viju a l'incontru poi stu to puddaru
regulatu con ordini eccellenti,
e tu chi ci passii cu fastu raru,
comu un'Imperaturi d'Orienti;
appena gridi, tutti ti obbediscinu,
e inginucchiati l'ordini eseguiscinu".

Lu gaddu gravi ci fa sta risposta:
"Tu vidi sulamenti li vantaggi
di lu miu statu, e 'un sai quantu mi costa
di firnicii, di curi e di disaggi!
Sta fidi di li mei, st'attaccamentu,
è ricompensa, e nun è complimentu.

Jeu sù chi quann'occurri di cummàttiri
cu qualch'armali a lu puddaru infestu,
lu pettu espognu, e micci mettu a bàttiri;
jeu vigghiu a la custodia, eu manifestu
l'ura di l'arrisbigghiu, ed eu rivelu
li vicenni di l'aria e di lu celu.

Jeu dugnu avvisu a stàrisi guardigni,
o 'ntanarisi dintra li pagghiari,
si scopru un nigghiu in aria, o in terra signi
aju di cui ci veni ad assaltari;
lu pisu è miu, sù l'organu efficaci
di la saluti publica e la paci.

Jeu, si trovu pri terra un cicireddu,
o un cocciu di frumentu, minni privu
di fàrinn'usu pri miu vureddu,
ma chiamu a tutti fistanti e giulivu,
lu mustru ad iddi, e lu cedu cu grazia,

LXXI
The Cat and the Rooster

A cat who was surprised to see a group
of hens display great homage and esteem
for the rooster who was master in their coop,
approached and said: "Dear friend, what wise regime,
do you adopt, what norms political?
Please tell me, for my case is critical.

For the most part, with me cats will not bother.
They call me in January, but they soon withdraw;
we never get along, we scratch each other,
we steal, we're ready to extend our claws.
We simply have no unity nor head,
and live with quarreling and war, instead.

In contrast, then, your chicken coop I see,
governed with rules most excellent and fair,
and you who walk about in majesty
just like an oriental emperor.
No sooner than you cry out, they will scoot
and kneeling, all your orders execute."

The rooster then replied quite seriously:
"All the advantages of my high post
are visible to you, but you don't see
the worries, cares, and hardships that they cost.
Their loyalty, their strong attachment's meant
as recompense. It's not a compliment.

It's I who when the need arises for a fight
against a beast that's harmful to the rest,
bareing my chest, expend all of my might;
it's I who stay on guard, make manifest
when it is time to rise, and it is I
who tell of changes in the air and sky.

When they must stay alert, alarms I sound,
or when they should seek refuge in hay stacks;
if hawks I see high in the air, or ground,
I've ways to say who's coming to attack.
Mine are all the responsibilities.
I'm a sure tool of public health and peace.

If I should come across a "ceci" bean
upon the ground, or just a grain of wheat,
I go without, and calling everyone,
I cheerfully invite them to go eat,
forsaking my own stomach in good grace

272

e lu vidirli sazii mi sazia.

    Jeu ci scegghiu li lochi chiù opportuni
pri fàrisi li cuvi e li ciuccati;
ci staju a li talài da campiuni,
pri 'un essiri, figghiannu, disturbati;
poi, fattu l'ovu, iu lu miu cantu sparu
pri darni avvisu a tuttu lu puddaru.

    Jeu sugnu chi mantegnu l'armunia
in tutti quanti, e si qualchi gaddina
o fa la capizzuta o s'inghirria,
jeu curru, e cu severa disciplina,
abbìa di pizzuluni e corpa d'ali,
c'insignu li doveri sociali.

    Amicu caru, chistù è lu segretu
per esseri acclamatu e pri rignari:
ti lu confidu, pirchì sì discretu,
e da bravu allegatu poi guardari
da baddottuli e vulpi stu puddaru,
chi sù pri nui flagellu aspru ed amaru".

*****

for seeing them well-fed, that is my price.

    I choose the place that is most opportune
in which to lay the eggs and make them hatch.
And as their champ, lest hens be importuned
while laying eggs, I always mount a watch.
Then when the egg's been laid, I shout it out
to spread the news to everyone about.

    I am the one who keeps the harmony
within the chicken coop and if a hen
behaves unseemly or too haughtily,
I run and through severe, swift discipline,
with many pecks and blows from wings galore,
I teach her to maintain social decor.

    So my dear friend, this is the secret feat
through which you can become acclaimed and reign.
I'm telling you because you are discrete
and as a good ally you can maintain
this coop safe from beasts who are dangerous:
weasel and fox: a bitter scourge for us."

*****

LXXII
LA CURSA DI L'ASINI

Multi vespi e muscagghiuni
scuncirtavanu la testa
a li scecchi e a li stadduni,
pri poi fàrinni la festa.

Chisti, troppu insuperbuti
di la propria asinitati,
da ddi bestii punciuti,
intunarunu: Libertati!

E cu sàuti a muntuni,
e cu càuci senza fini,
li zimmìli e li varduni
si scucciaru da li schini.

Freni rumpinu e tistali;
cui chiù reggiri li pò?
Già si cridinu l'armali
chi lu munnu è tuttu so.

Scioti e liberi sfirrannu,
la città n'è desolata,
cui pò diri, ohimè! lu dannu,
chi appurtau sta gran scappata?

Tutti currinu a migghiara,
l'unu all'àutru 'mmesti e ammutta,
lu patruni, si 'un si para,
si lu chiàntanu di sutta.

Jennu tuttu a divastari,
cu li vespi sempri addossu,
poi si vannu a sdirrupari
tutti quanti dintra un fossu.

Testi e gammi fracassati
sparsi sù tra terra e fangu,
e li vespi ddà appizzati
sinni sucanu lu sangu.

A sta nova chi ricivi
lu patruni, ch'è climenti,
pri succurriri li vivi
sàuta e vola prestamenti.

Ni cacciau li vespi feri,
chi sicc'eranu appizzati,
e a ddi poveri sumeri
li succurri e li cumpati.

Puru (cui lu cridirìa!)

LXXII
The Donkeys' Race

Many wasps and fierce mosquitoes
the heads buzzed of some poor beasts
— some proud stallions and jackasses —
as a prelude for the feast.

When those beasts who were so proud
of their asininity
were attacked by that fierce crowd,
they cried out, "Oh, liberty!"

They kept jumping like he-goats
and the haversacks and packs,
through their endless kicking spree,
they removed right off their backs.

Then they broke their stays and headgears.
Who could have restrained those beasts?
They began to think the world
for their use had been released.

Once their fetters were removed,
the poor city suffered woes.
Who could count, alas, the damage
and debris their race did cause?

They all ran, — a thousand beasts —,
crashing into walls, pell mell.
If their master had been careless,
they'd have trampled him as well.

With the wasps still on their backs,
and destroying all in sight,
the beasts fell into a ditch,
ending there their brief, wild flight.

Broken heads and limbs were strewn
on the ground, in the dark mud,
while the wasps were still attached
and were busy sucking blood.

Once the owner — a good man —
of the fall had heard the news,
to go rescue the survivors
quickly ran, indeed, he flew.

Having chased the wasps away,
who were sucking on each sore,
those poor donkeys he then succored,
and their health tried to restore.

Yet some asses in the ditch

274

tra lu stissu pricipiziu
c'è chiù d'unu chi caucìa,
pri nun perdiri lu vizziu.

Lu patruni, a sti maligni,
a sti bestii tradituri,
fa tagghiàricci l'ordigni,
d'unni surgi lu viguri.

Poi cu forti capizzuni,
'nfrena l'àutri e sinni va:
"Da li scecchi e li stadduni
sempri arrassu si ci sta".

*****

— who would have believed as much? —
kept on kicking, as some said,
not to lose their so-called "touch".

So the owner then disposed
to cut off the instrument
whence those traitorous, sly beasts
get their vigor and their strength.

He tied up the rest with heavy
and strong ropes and went his way:
"From a stallion or jackass
always stay ten feet away!"

*****

LXXIII
L'ASINU RUSSU E L'ANIMALI

Cumparsi na jurnata un sceccu russu,
pirchì s'àvìa stricatu tra lu taju,
e lu coddu, l'oricchi, testa e mussu,
e tuttu in brevi era ntra sauru e baiu,
e na crusta indurita anchi ci avìa
canciata tutta la fisonomia.

L'animali in vidirlu si allarmaru,
cridennulu un gran mostru novu e stranu,
e tutti spavintati s'intanaru.
Iddu, a lu scantu d'iddi, unciatu e vanu
si critti cosa granni, e pigghiann'anza,
isa la testa e s'inchi di baldanza.

Passìa pri ddi campagni cu gran fastu,
comu ni fussi assolutu patruni,
nuddu 'ncuntrannu chi ci dassi 'mmastu;
ma poi per isfogarisi lu pulmuni
apri la vucca, etta un'arragghiu, ed eccu
chi si duna a conusciri pri sceccu.

Chiddi chi prima timidi e scantati
s'avìanu 'ncrafucchiatu tra li grutti,
di l'equivocu cursi e nichiati,
ci fannu trattamenti strani e brutti.
Giustamenti lu saggiu addunca dissi:
"Parrami prima, acciò ti conoscissi".

Quanti, chi nui videmu cu gran tubba,
chini d'insigni e di ornamenti rari,
o chi, adorni di toga e lunga giubba,
fannu a la vista li genti trimari,
chi, parrannu, non ragghi di sumeri,
ma caccianu carteddi di fumeri!

*****

LXXIII
The Red Donkey and the Animals

An ass appeared one day with a red hide
because he had been rolling in some clay.
His neck, his ears, his snout and head were dyed
as though he'd been a Saurian or Bay,
and furthermore, a hardened crust had he
that altered his appearance totally.

On seeing him, the other animals
became alarmed, believing him to be
a new, strange monster, and quite scared, they all
sought hiding places. When he saw them flee,
the vain and puffed-up ass, thought he was grand,
considering himself Lord of the Land.

With majesty he walked the countryside,
believing he was master of all things,
meeting no one who ever even tried
to bother him. But then, to clear his lungs,
he opened up his mouth and loudly brayed,
and thus his asininity displayed.

The others who before had run to hide
in caves, out of timidity and fear,
upset and worried by their loss of pride,
acted toward him in ways strange and severe.
The wise man justly coined this phrase, therefore:
"Speak up, so I may know just who you are!"

We see so many people with top hat,
dressed up in regal clothes and lengthy cloaks,
wearing rare medals like a diplomat,
whose sight alone engenders fear in folks,
and who, when speaking, not hee-haws emit,
but veritable piles of pure horseshit.

*****

LXXIV
LI SURCI E LU GATTU VECCHIU

Un surci era malatu. Li parenti,
l'amici e li vicini si aggiuntaru
pri scigghìricci un medicu eccellenti;
ma tra la scelta poi nun si accurdaru:
"Chistu, dicìanu, è musciu, è 'un parra nenti;
chidd'è millantaturi munsignaru;
chistu 'un sta 'mmenzu, nun è ricittanti,
chiddu 'mmesti azzardusu e ammazza tanti".

Mentri sù 'mmarazzati, irrisoluti
veni unu, e dici: "Lessi in certu avvisu,
chi è vinutu da parti sconosciuti
un surci assai di medicina intisu,
chi à rusicatu li libra saputi
d'Ippocrati e Galenu pri distisu;
'mpasta l'oturi antichi e li moderni,
e di la vucca ci nescinu perni.

Ma pri lu rangu so nobili e graBnni,
e pirchì ancora è multu facultusu,
nun si abbassa a jiri a tutti banni
visitannu malati 'nsusu e gnusu.
Ma cui d'iddu à bisognu ni dumanni
unni vidi l'avvisu. Chistu è l'usu
di li paisi granni: Persia, Eggittu,
Francia, Germania. E ccà finiu lu scrittu".

A sta notizia tutti allegri vannu
a la locanna, unni lu scrittu stava,
lu malatu cun iddu carriannu,
nell'ura quannu ogn'umu ripusava,
sutta la porta jènnusi ficcannu,
tràsinu...Ddocu appuntu l'aspittava
lu gattu vecchiu cu pacenzia e flemma,
ch'era l'auturi di lu stratagemma.

Quannu già vidi la vasa sicura,
dici: "A guarirvi d'ogni infirmitati
la mia ricetta corrispunni allura,
anzi vogghiu chi tutti la pruvati..."
Dissi, e poi sfoderannu l'armatura,
jetta c'un sàutu, scàrrica granfati,
e tra un gràpiri e chiudiri di vucca,
lu malatu pri pinnula s'ammucca.
*****

LXXIV
The Mice and the Old Cat

A mouse was ill. Each relative and friend,
together with the neighbors all agreed,
they wanted the best doctor to attend
to him, but on the choice they disagreed.
"This one's too dull," they said. "He hardly talks;
that one's a braggart and an awful liar;
this one is weird: he won't prescribe for folks;
that one takes chances, many have expired!"

While they were troubled by this quandary,
someone arrived and said: "Somewhere I read
that from a distant land a prodigy
has come, a mouse who has a brilliant head
for medicine because he nibbled all
Hippocrates and Galen's learnèd pages.
He mixes modern medicine with old,
and from his mouth you hear the best of sages.

But since he ranks so high and has no peer,
and also for the fact that he is wealthy,
he won't stoop down by going there and here,
and everywhere to cure those who're not healthy.
If you need help, ask where this sign you see.
That seems to be the custom they adopt
in such great countries: Persia, Germany,
Egypt and France. And there the writing stopped."

On hearing the good news, all full of glee,
— and at the time when every man's asleep—
and carrying their sick friend eagerly,
under the door they slipped or through a peep
to read the notice on the tavern wall.
However, th' author of the stratagem,
an old cat armed with patience and with gall,
was waiting there to welcome each of them.

When he was certain that the trap had sprung,
he said: "My own prescription's sure to cure
every infirmity for old and young;
in fact, you all should try some...to make sure!"
This said, he then unsheathed his armament
and pounced, and with sharp claws he struck to kill.
His mouth he opened, shut, with no time spent
and the sick mouse he swallowed like a pill.
*****

LXXV
DIRI E FARI

Eranu un tempu amici Diri e Fari,
anzi fratuzzi, e a filu duppiu uniti.
Poi lu primu alzau catrida a insignari
l'arti chi tessi di paroli riti.

Appi in Ateni e in Roma pri sculari
l'omini chiù insigni ed eruditi,
ed oggi è risu numi tutelari
di li curti, li pulpiti e li liti.

Quannu si vitti denti, corna, ed ugna:
"La forza, dissi, è l'unica chi regna,
e regnari cu socii repugna.

Di miu frati lu nomu si trattegna
'mpizzu a sta lingua, ch'ogni cori espugna;
iddu, però, unni sugnu eu nun vegna".

*****

LXXV
Saying and Doing

Saying and Doing were once quite close friends;
indeed, like brothers bound with a double knot.
Then the first one a Chair erected whence
the art that weaves a net of words he taught.

He formed a school in Athens, then in Rome,
attended by most wise and learnèd men
and now he's a divinity whose home
is forums, pulpits and litigious citizens.

When he saw in himself horns, teeth, and nails
he said: "The only thing that counts is force;
to reign with partners is repulsive, vile.

And let my brother's name be held, of course,
at the tip of my tongue, that every heart can chain,
but he should not come near to where I reign."

*****

LXXVI
LI VULPI

Avennu avutu rastu di gaddini,
na vulpi cu la figghia, coti coti,
attraversannu prati, orti e jardini,
pri viiuleddi incogniti e remoti,
s'incrafucchiaru tra frascàmi e ddisa,
aspittannu la notti a fari prisa.

Vinuta già la notti, impazienti
la figghia d'aspittari, nesci, e scurri
cu nasu, occhi ed oricchi tutti attenti,
e s'incammina versu d'una turri;
ma a lu passari pri certa nuàra,
vidi na testa e subitu si para.

Vota, torna a la matri, e cunta tuttu;
la matri dici: "Aspittamu un pocu;
la quatela nun noci". Pri un cunnuttu
doppu un pezzu si avvianu a ddu locu:
"Eccula ddà, grida la figghia, osserva
la testa, ch'è curcata supra l'erva!"

La matri attenta, e squatra d'ogni latu;
vidi chi nun si movi e 'un dici nenti,
s'anima di coraggiu e pigghia ciatu;
poi dici: "'Un ti scantari, teni a menti,
e a sti paroli mei lu senziu aguzza:
Testa chi 'un parra, si chiama cucuzza".
*****

LXXVI
The Foxes

Once they sniffed hints of chickens near at hand,
fox and her young daughter traveled through
orchards and gardens and wide open land,
and crossing little paths nobody knew,
beneath some leafy branches went to lay,
awaiting nightfall to go hunt for prey.

When darkness came, the daughter ventured out,
impatiently, and she began to scour
with bright eyes, perked-up ears and sniffing snout.
She started walking toward a big old tower,
but when she chanced to cross a melon patch,
she saw a head and frightened stopped to watch.

Turning around, the fox ran to her mother
and told her everything. The mother thought:
"Let's wait a while. Precautions are no bother."
Later, through pipes, they went to the same spot.
"That's where it is," the daughter cried. "Look there!
There's the head lying on the grass. Beware!"

The mother looked with care from every side,
and saw it did not move or make a sound.
Relieved, she breathed more easily, and sighed:
"Fear not! Recall this when I'm not around.
Inside your brain these words you must imbed:
'One who can't speak is just a pumpkin head!'"
*****

279

LXXVII
LU LUPU E L'AGNEDDU
(Traduzioni di la prima favula di Fedru)

Arsi di siti un lupu ed un'agneddu
eranu capitati, tutti dui
in un tempu, ad un stissu ciumiceddu:
lu lupu stava supra, ed assai chiui
sutta l'agneddu, situatu arrassu,
unni lu ciumi discinneva abbassu.

Lu latru, chi, aducchiandulu tra un lampu,
gargiuliari la gula s'intisi,
un pretestu di liti misi in campu,
acciò putissi vèniri a li prisi,
e dissi in tonu bruscu e nichiatu:
"Birbu! pirchì m'ài l'acqua intorbidatu?"

Chiddu, trimannu, rispusi: "Vossia
mi scusi, e comu mai lu pozzu fari?
È l'acqua sua chi veni ccà unni mia,
lu ciumi scinni, nun va ad acchianari!"
'Nsaccatu a sti ragiuni ddu farfanti,
subitu nàutru strunfu metti avanti,

dicennu: "Ora pri biru mi suvveni,
chi tu, sù circa sei misi arreri,
di mia nun ni parrasti troppu beni".
Rispunni ddu mischinu: "E comu veri
ponnu essiri sti culpi, quannu natu
nun era allura e mancu siminatu?"

"Ah, fu to patri, certu, ripigghiau
lu lupu, chi di mia ni dissi mali";
e in dittu e in fattu cursi, e lu sbranau.
Quant'omini ci sù a stu lupu uguali,
cui pretesti nun mancanu e strumenti
pri opprimiri li deboli e innocenti!
*****

LXXVII
The Wolf and the Lamb
(A Translation of Phaedrus' First Fable)

Driven by thirst, a wolf and a young lamb
chanced to arrive at the same rivulet
at the same time. The wolf was far upstream;
the little lamb, whose feet were not yet wet,
was standing far away near to the place
where the small stream began its downhill race.

The thief the lamb immediately did spy
and felt a gurgling sound rise from its throat,
and with a false pretext he thought he'd try
to start a brawl his aims thus to promote.
"Why did you foul my drinking water, Knave?"
he thundered with a voice both vexed and grave.

"Oh, Sir," replied the other tremblingly.
"Excuse me, how could I have done this deed?
It is your water that comes down to me.
The stream flows down, uphill it will not speed!"
That thieving scoundrel, foiled by this reply,
another false pretext went on to try,

saying, "I really do remember now
that it was you, about six months ago,
who did not speak too well of me, somehow."
The wretched lamb replied. "That can't be so!
How could I have committed such a crime,
when I was neither born nor bred at the time?"

"Ah...Ah! It must have been your father, then,
who said mean things of me," the wolf replied.
This said, to slaughter the poor lamb he ran.
How many men can stand by this wolf's side,
men who possess pretext and instrument
to persecute the weak and innocent!
*****

LXXVIII
SURCI E GATTI

Spissu pri riparari a qualchi mali,
o pri dari a un delittu la sua pena,
si cummetti la cura a certi tali,
a cui chiù di rei feti la lena.

Si nni vidi un'esempiu naturali
tra un contrapostu chi si metti in scena
di gatti e surci, e tra na favulicchia
ch'a propositu trasi tra sta nicchia.

Li surci fannu guastu; e chistu è veru.
Dunca mittemu gatti? È chiù dammaggiu;
si lu surci fa un vadu a lu formaggiu,
lu gattu si lu mancia tuttu interu.

Lu surci è latru, ma nun è poi feru;
fui quann'è scuvertu, e nun fa oltraggiu;
lu gattu è tradituri ed è sarvaggiu,
e a li stritti, si avventa pri daveru.

Lu surci ci pens'iddu pri li tozza;
lu gattu, ultra chi arrobba a tutti banni,
a tavula è lu primu chi s'intozza.

Putrìa suppliri a stu svantaggiu granni,
quannu, cu pleggi, e a pena di la crozza,
si obblighi risarciri intressi e danni.
*****

LXXVIII
Mice and Cats

To remedy an evil or to mete
a proper punishment for a vile crime,
quite often we entrust the care of it
to someone worse than those whom we would blame.

A true example, natural, concrete
can be observed in the contrasting claims
of cats and mice, and in this little tale
which fits our circumstance like two dove tails.

It is quite true that mice some damage cause.
Shall we get cats? The harm is greater now,
for if a mouse a hole makes in the cheese,
a cat through the whole thing will surely plow;

A mouse is thieving but he is not vicious.
Surprise him and he'll run. He won't attack.
But cats are traitorous and quite ferocious,
and if they're cornered, they will not hold back.

A mouse will not complain about stale bread.
But cats, aside from stealing everywhere,
are first at the table begging to be fed.

They could make up for this if they would swear
or pledge, on pain of giving up their heads,
that the harm done with int'rest they'd repair.
*****

281

Giovanni Meli

LXXIX
LU REGNU DI LI VULPI

Un vulpi era timutu, rispettatu
da tutta la sua specii, a tali signu
ch'Esopu ni ristau meravigghiatu:
"Quali meritu, dissi, lu fa dignu
di ossequii tanti?" Rispus'unu a latu:
"Tra lu regnu e dominiu vulpignu,
malizia summa, frodi, astuzii e inganni
sù li scalini ad àuti posti e granni".

*****

LXXIX
The Realm of Foxes

A fox was so respected and so feared
by every member of his foxy kind
that Aesop thought it strange and almost weird.
"What special merit in him can one find
to make him worthy of so much regard?"
"In realms where foxes reign," a neighbor whined,
"great malice, fraud, deceit, and craftiness
are stepping stones to notable success."

*****

LXXX
LU SIGNU E LU CANI

Spissu fannu a li grandi impressioni
chiù li preggi apparenti, chi li veri;
chiù la tustizza e l'ostentazioni,
chi li virtù e li meriti sinceri;
n'è na prova stu fattu ch'eu vi dicu
tali quali truvai tra un vecchiu arcivu.

Un signu aveva apprisu ad imitari
pochi lavuri e cosi burginsàtichi;
dipoi fu in curti, e misi a contrafari
li curtiggianarii li chiù fanatichi;
e cu sti mimarii, stu bistiuni
si attirau l'occhi di lu so patruni:

chi a cridirlu arrivau forsi staccatu
da la specii feroci di li signi,
e spissu spissu si lu misi allatu,
e lu trattava quasi cu carigni,
e ci avìa tanta fidi e deferenza.
chi ci detti a curari na dispenza.

Ci misi, è veru, allatu un cani braccu,
forti e capaci; ma la sua fidanza
era supra lu signu; e stu vigghiaccu
nun facìa chi abusarni cu baldanza;
lu cani ci vulìa sotari addossu,
ma pri digni rispetti nun s'è mossu.

Stava un jornu lu cani addurmisciutu
supra lu limmitaru di la porta;
lu signu, pazzu, e forsi insallanutu,
e ch'a forza e pri jugu lu supporta,
scippa un piruni di la megghiu stipa,
e pri suppostu a chiddu ci lu 'ntipa;

e cu tanta mastria, chi nun s'intisi
lu cani di st'estraniu chi trasiu
o pri la sprattichizza nun comprisi
sta nova specii di vinditta o sbiu,
nè pri lu so darreri suspittava,
sapennu ch'era porta ch'un spuntava.

Trasi fratantu lu patruni, e trova
la stipa senza vinu nè piruni;
cerca l'auturi di sta bella prova,
ma lu signu ci dici a l'ammucciuni:
"Vuliti (ma in sigillu) provi veri?

LXXX
The Monkey and the Dog

Often apparent merits will impress
the mighty a lot more than will real worth,
pure ostentation and sheer brazenness
more than true virtue and a sincere heart.
A proof of this is in this ancient tale,
gleaned from an old archive in all details.

A monkey had learned how to imitate
several chores and things that farmers do,
then when at court he tried to duplicate
the most fanatical of court yahoos,
and with his mimicries, this worthless beast,
attracted the attention of his master,

who went as far, it seems, as to believe
that he was from wild apes a breed apart,
and let him often cling onto his sleeve,
treating him with affection and with heart.
The farmer felt such trust and deference
for him, he placed his pantry in his hands.

He put a capable, strong dog, it's true,
next to the monkey, but nevertheless,
the ape was trusted more. This scoundrel, though,
abused his master's trust with brazenness.
The dog kept feeling that he should attack.
To show respect, however, he held back.

While the poor dog was sound asleep one day
upon the threshold, by the pantry's door,
the crazy ape, whose brain had gone astray,
for whom the dog was like a yoke he wore,
removed a cork from the best barrel there
and stopped with it the dog's derriere.

The dog felt not —such was the ape's diligence —
the strange, new object going into him,
and, due to his sore inexperience,
of this new type of vengeance or strange whim
knew nothing, nor could he suspect his ass,
aware it a was a dead-end street, alas!

Meanwhile the master came and, having seen
the barrel without cork and without wine,
looked for the author of so fine a scene.
The monkey sought the master's ear to whine:
"(In strictest confidence!) D'you want to find

Guardaticci a lu cani lu darreri.

St'armali pati assai di stitichizza,
nonostanti chi mancia e mancia beni,
e si licca li pratti a stizza a stizza,
suca lu grasciu di cui va e cui veni:
truvannusi lu stomacu indispostu
si misi lu piruni pri suppostu.

Jeu menn'addunai tardu, e nun putìa
stàricci a frunti; è grossu lu 'nnimicu;
ma pri truvari a vui di già vinìa
pr'essiri libiratu da st'intricu;
jeu chiù d'iddu fidarimi nun pozzu;
sfrattatilu, e a pietà daticci un tozzu".

A lu patruni parsi raggiunevuli
e equitabili insiemi lu cunsigghiu,
multu chiù chi fu dittu cu amurevuli
tonu di vuci, e cu piatusu cigghiu;
quannu lu signu ci proposi e dissi,
appruvannu, lodau, si suttascrissi.

Cussì lu saggiu e lu fidili cani,
ultra lu cunsaputu cumplimentu,
ch'appena ci lassau l'ingrispi sani,
vinni sfrattatu, e sin da ddu momentu
ristau in cura ad un pazzu la dispenza:
Tant'opra tra stu munnu l'apparenza!

*****

the surest clue? Look at the dog's behind.

This animal to constipation's prone,
despite the fact he eats and eats, alas,
licking the plates clean, chewing every bone,
and gobbling up what's thrown by those who pass,
finding his stomach not so honky-dory,
he put the cork in as suppository.

I noticed it too late: nothing to do!
So strong an enemy I could not face.
But I was on my way to fetching you,
so you could free me from this tangled maze.
I cannot really trust him from this day.
Give him a bone and send him on his way!"

His master thought that this advice was fair
and reasonable, too, and even more,
because it was pronounced with love and care,
as though his very plan he did deplore.
Whatever said the monkey, all he'd shown,
was by his master praised, approved, and done.

Therefore, the wise and faithful hound,
beside the compliment we spoke about,
which left his inner folds but barely sound,
was thus evicted, and from that day out,
the pantry has remained in a fool's care;
appearance in this world such deeds prepares.

*****

LXXXI
L'ALLEANZA DI LI CANI

Tra Concu e Capu di Bona Spiranza,
e in tutta l'Etiopia ci sù cani
salvaggi e feri assai, ma chi allianza
hannu tra d'iddi da antichi Spartani,
eserciti furmannu e battagghiuni,
d'affruntari li tigri, ursi e liuni.

Lu jornu vannu a caccia squatrunati,
facennu predi di qualunqui sorti,
poi tornanu a li tani carricati
d'animali in guerra o prisi o morti,
e cu esattu economicu bilanciu
si spartinu, e fannu lu so ranciu.

Or'avvinni (pri quannu lu Vicchiuni
tra lu tarlatu miu libru truvau)
chi di sti cani ci nni fu un squatruni,
in cui la gran catina si smagghiau,
pri l'abbusu di avirsi postergatu
lu publicu vantaggiu a lu privatu.

Pirchì turnannu cu la preda ogn'unu
sinni ammucciava deci e vinti parti,
e dicchiù si spacciava pri dijunu,
pri dumannari l'àutra chi si sparti;
perciò la preda nun putìa bastari
pri tutta la gran chiurma saturari.

Circau riparu a stu sconcertu
tutt'obbligannu a li riveli esatti,
ma nun pigghiaru, pri essiri scuvertu
lu cuntrabbannu, li misuri adatti
pirchì tutti sti liggi e sti misuri
l'avìanu impostu li contravventuri.

Si agghiuncìa chi li dazii da pagari
eranu ripartuti tantu a chiddi
a cui l'abbastu vineva a mancari,
quantu a cui supricchiàvacci pri middi:
l'unu pagava a costu di la panza,
l'àutru menu di un'esimu chi avanza.

Sta cosa chi purtau? Chi l'osservanti,
li debbuli, li vecchi, e li malati,
cu li ventri ristavanu vacanti,
e li forzi vinevanu mancati;
parti murianu di consunzioni,

LXXXI
The Dogs' Alliance

Between the Congo and Cape of Good Hope,
and throughout Ethiopia, there live
wild and ferocious dogs who fight in group,
like ancient Spartan armies and they give
no quarter to their prey. They even dare
a tiger to attack, a lion and a bear.

In daytime they go hunting in large packs,
preying on animals of every breed;
then, with the beasts they killed in their attacks,
or else found dead, to their lairs they proceed.
After precise accounting, they then share
the daily booty and their chow prepare.

It happened that among the dogs, one pack
(as far as the Old Man could ascertain
in my moth-eaten book) went off the track,
and managed to break up the social chain,
through the abuse of placing private good
above the interests of the brotherhood.

Thus every dog returning with its prey,
a tenth or twentieth part would put aside.
What's more he'd claim he'd fasted the whole day,
to get a part of what they would divide,
and that is why the daily prey was found
not large enough to feed that many hounds.

They tried to put a stop to this abuse,
obliging everyone to be exact,
but all their measures never could reduce,
or yet discover contraband. In fact,
each regulation, measure, every clause
was made by those who contravened the laws.

And add to this that duties to be paid
were split among the ones who did not have
enough to eat and those who had parleyed
a thousand times more than they'd ever crave:
one group paid at the cost of stomach pains,
the other got an 'nth of the remains.

What was the end result? Those who'd obey
the laws, those who were weak, or old, or ill,
with empty stomachs were condemned to stay,
which sapped in turn their strength and will.
A number of the dogs wasted away,

285

parti a la guerra 'un eranu chiù boni.
  L'uni pri fami, l'àutri pri l'eccessu
di lu manciari abbuttati e gravusi,
nun putevanu curriri d'appressu
a l'imprisi chiù forti e chiù azzardusi;
eranu 'nzumma li pochi ristati
li chiù infirgardi e li debilitati.
  La conseguenza fu chi a un primu attaccu
foru, in locu di battiri, battuti:
li lupi e l'ursi ni ficiru smaccu.
Pozza st'esempiu so fari avviduti
tutti li societati di dd'armali,
chi vantati si sù razzionali.
*****

others became too frail to hunt for prey.
  Because of hunger the first group, the second one
because excess had made them ponderous
and slow, that breed of dogs just could not run
after the strongest and most dangerous
of preys. The few dogs that were left, at last,
were just the lazybones and the downcast.
  As a result, upon their first attack,
instead of victory, they saw defeat.
The bears and wolves destroyed the sorry pack.
May this example make much more discrete
all those societies of animals
who've boasted of their being rational.
*****

LXXXII
LA VACCA E LU PORCU

"Mi pari porcu a la fisonomia,
ma so chi la tua specii è grassa e grossa:
tu sì siccu! patisci d'ettisia?"

"Ti meravigghi ch'eu sù peddi ed ossa;
sacci chi nun mi tocca in nutrimentu,
chi l'erva sula, e chista a summu stentu.

Mi la vaju abbuscannu tra rampanti,
ccà un filu, nàutru ddà, sempri stintannu.
Li tempi nun sù chiù ch'eranu avanti,
comu sintìa cuntari da me nannu,
quannu li porci avevanu a munseddu
ghiandri e manciari ad uffu tra un tineddu.

E chi dui misi avanti di la scanna
li passavanu a tavula di favi,
chi ci sapìanu chiù di meli e manna.
Cu sti boni preludii li nostr'avi
murennu, lu tributu ànnu pagatu
all'omu, chi l'avìa ben nutricatu.

Chiddu, l'agghiandri e favi chi ci dava,
pri meccanica e chimica maggia,
tutti poi carni e lardi li truvava,
e macellannu un porcu s'arricchia;
ma in nui ci trovan'ossa da liccari,
e pri li suli cani diffamari.

Si allura centu porci di un cantàru
diffamavanu un populu, di sicchi
pri diffamarlu nun basta un migghiaru,
ancorchì d'ossa fussiru assai licchi.
Eccu lu sfrangu di la nostra razza,
chi va a finiri pri sta genti pazza!"

Dici la vacca: "Tra lu stissu casu
nui semu e tra l'uguali circostanzi;
pascemu tutti tra un tirrenu rasu,
e di ristucci l'induriti avanzi;
e preni, e strippi, e magri a lu maceddu
tutti quanti ni portanu a munseddu.

Tralasciu quannu sentu raccuntari
di li costumi di paisi saggi:
chi l'armali chi si ànnu a macillari
li nutricanu prima a grassi erbaggi;
ci dann'anchi simenza di cuttuni,

LXXXII
The Cow and the Pig

"A pig you seem to me in physiognomy!
For being big and fat your kind is known,
but you're so thin. Consumptive can you be?"
"You are amazed to see me skin and bones!
Know that as nourishment I get just grass,
and not without great hardship, too, alas!

I earn it for myself as I explore
steep hills, a blade here, there, another one.
It's hard! Times are not what they were before,
when as my grandpa said, in tales he spun,
a pig could eat at will inside their trough
and of acorns he had more than enough.

And that two months before the slaughter day,
the hogs were fed with fava beans galore
which more than manna they seemed to enjoy,
or honey. And with such preludes, therefore,
in dying our ancestors paid their due
to man who'd nourished them so well thereto.

The acorns and the fava beans man bought,
through natural and magic chemistry,
all into meat and lard on pigs was wrought,
and slaughtering just one a man would be
enriched. In us, though, bones are all you'll find
which are just good enough for dogs to grind.

If then a hundred pigs that weighed a ton
sufficed to feed a nation, in our own,
it would require a thousand skinny ones,
provided men were fond of chewing bone.
That is the dreadful wasting of my kin
that's bound to perish with such crazy men."

The cow replied: "We're living your same case,
and are by the same circumstances bound.
We graze upon some stubble in a space
where only hardened stalks stick from the ground,
and pregnant, sterile, and thin, with no thought,
all to the slaughter house in droves we're brought.

I will not even mention what I hear
regarding customs of a wiser folk,
who before slaughtering a pig or steer,
with thick, rich grasses feed the chosen stock;
they even give them lots of cotton seed

e ci feddanu rapi a battagghiuni.

E ccà stissu l'antichi costumavanu
abbiari tra feudi e tra riservi,
e nutricavani beni ed ingrassavanu
lu voi, la vacca cu li chiù megghiu ervi;
ma li Don Nìnnari, omini d'aguannu,
pirchì l'ànnu fattu àutri nun lu fannu.

Nun so spiegari sta fatalitati,
modi frusteri riguardanti a lussu
in capitari ccà sunn'abbrazzati;
però la moda e l'usu ch'ànnu influssu
all'utili o vantaggiu di li Statu
si lodanu e si mettinu di latu".

*****

and slice of turnips more than they would need.

In our land, too, the ancient farmers sent
their stock to the reserves and lordly fiefs,
providing the best grass as nourishment,
fattening oxen, cows to make good beef.
But all the farmer Browns, men of today,
won't copy others who did it that way.

I can't explain this strange fatality!
When foreign fashions of great luxury
arrive to town they are embraced with glee,
but fashions and the customs that could be
useful and advantageous to the State,
are praised and then all quickly put aside."

*****

LXXXIII
LA TIGRI TRA NA GAGGIA DI FERRU

Tra na gaggia di ferru carcerata
una tigri frimìa. Lu so custodi
ci dissi: "Scatta ddocu, scelerata;
    tu chi tra sangu e straggi trischi e godi
diri osi chi la vita a sosteniri
àutri menzi nun trovi ed àutri modi?

    Ma pirchì sazianduti a doviri
la tua ferocia crisci, e a varia e a nova
straggi ti porta sempri a incrudeliri?

    Chista è certu, certissimu, na prova
chi godi in fari mali, e sinni approva.

    E ci scummettu chi tra stu sticcatu
di ferru, unni ti trovi, stai pinsannu
di squartari e sbranari ogn'omu natu.

    Nun lu fai pirchì ostaculu ti fannu
li ferrati ben forti: 'un ti lagnari
dunca si ddocu dintra stai penannu".

    Ci rispunni la tigri: "Rinfacciari
nun ti vogghiu li straggi e crudiltà
chi soli l'omu all'àutri specii fari,

    nè chiddi chi a la propria specii fa;
ma ti parru di chiddi sulamenti
chi teni occulti tra la voluntà,

    pirchì nun pò spiegari apertamenti,
comu mia, stannu chiusa tra firrati,
tra liggi cioè ch'avi presenti.

    Chistu si divi chiaru a li nuttati
ch'iddu impiega pri leggiri o vidiri
li fatti atroci di li scelerati,

    chi sù fatti suggetti di piaciri
tra li teatri, unni li morti antichi
risurginu pri vidirsi moriri,

    pri vidirni li palpiti e li dichi,
sintìrinni li làstimi e lamenti,
e di li sceleraggini l'intrichi.

    Autri vannu piscannu st'argumenti
tra li fatti chiù atroci e sanguinusi
di la chiù vecchia istoria, o la currenti,

    comu vuturi, chi a li chiù fitusi
carogni vannu in cerca a disfamari
li brami soi crudili e schifiusi..."

*****

LXXXIII
The Tiger in a Steel Cage

A tiger was imprisoned in a cage
of steel and writhed. Her guardian exclaimed:
"You bloody beast,—may you burst from sheer rage—
    who live and who enjoy to kill and maim,
that for your kind there are no other deeds
through which you can survive, how can you claim?

    So why when you have satisfied your needs
at will, does your ferocity grow more,
and on increasing cruelties just feeds?

    This surely is a proof that at the core
you are most evil and degenerate,
rejoicing in your awful acts. What's more,

    I bet that now behind that iron gate
where you are caged, you're thinking how you'd slay,
how every human being you'd mutilate.

    You do not do it 'cause your iron stays
are much too strong: so then, do not complain
if you are suffering inside that bay."

    The tiger answered him: "I will not deign
to name the slaughters and the cruelties
that man on other species will ordain,

    nor those against the species that is his,
but I'll speak only of those that are found
well hidden in his secret strategies

    because on them he clearly can't expound,
as I can, held inside this iron fence,
considering the laws by which he's bound.

    Of this we have the clearest evidence
when he spends nights to read or yet to see
some histories of awful truculence,

    turned into objects of sheer revelry
in theatres, where men long dead and gone,
yet live to see themselves die finally,

    to hear their palpitations and their moans,
to know their suffering and all their woes,
and for their evil acts the plots they've drawn.

    To find these subjects other men propose
to look among the most atrocious deeds
of ancient history, or yet of those

    of our own day, like vultures who will feed
on carcasses quite smelly, decomposed,
to sate their cruel and disgusting needs..."

*****

LXXXIV
LU CODICI MARINU

Conosciuto è in Sicilia l'anticu
nomu di Cola-pisci, anfibbiu natu
sutta di lu secundu Fidiricu:
omu in sustanza ben proporzionatu,
pisci pri l'attributu singulari
di stari a fundu cu li pisci in mari.

Scurrennu li gran pelaghi profunni,
facìa lunghi viaggi, e rappurtava
li meravigghi visti sutta l'unni,
e multi di sua manu li nutava.
Mi è capitata, tra li tanti, chista
scritta di propria sua manu, e rivista.

In fundu di lu Balticu, e a li spaddi
di na muntagna in mari sprofundata,
cuverta di un vuschittu di curaddi,
vitti na turba granni radunata
d'insetti molestissimi forensi,
chi trattava un processu tra sti sensi:

Si truvau divoratu un grossu tunnu,
e pri st'accusa foru processati
pochi sarduzzi ritruvati a funnu,
supra d'un'ossu cu li mussi untati.
Lu Fiscu, ch'è un strumentu chi vi frica,
ci apriu di tunnicidiu la rubrica.

E tantu ddi sarduzzi chi liccaru,
quannu chiddi ch'in bucca avìanu grasciu,
tantu chiddi chi appena lu cioràru,
tutti foru cumprisi tra lu fasciu
dicennu: "Ccà nun c'è ossu, nè spina,
foru coti in fraganti, è prova china.

La nostra liggi parra tunnu e chiaru:
'Lu pisci grossu mancia lu minutu';
ccà li minuti lu grossu manciaru,
l'ordini di la liggi ànnu sburdutu,
d'una liggi ch'è in nui fundamintali,
dunca sù rei di pena capitali".

Di li poveri esclama l'avvocatu:
"Pri st'infelici la difisa è chiara:
lu scheretru di l'ossa è smisuratu,
lu tunnu, almenu, era di tri cantàra;
tutti sti sardi 'nzemmula assummati

LXXXIV
The Marine Code

The ancient name of Nick-the-Fish is known
in Sicily as an amphibian,
born under Frederick — the second one! —
who was, in fact, a well proportioned man,
endowed with special gifts, a prodigy,
who lived with fishes at the bottom of the sea.

The ocean's great expanse he thus would roam,
journeying far and wide, and he'd relate
the marvels that he'd seen beneath the foam.
Many a tale he wrote and then collated.
Among the many written and revised
by him, this one I want to verbalize:

Deep in the Baltic Sea, against a cliff,
which had sunk deep into the ocean's shroud,
and which was covered by wild coral reef,
he spied the gathering of a large crowd
of very noxious insects of the forum,
who were a case debating with decorum.

A heavy tuna fish had been devoured,
and for this crime, they had accused sardines
who had been seen as they the bottom scoured
with greasy mouths from chewing on some bones.
Taxation——vexing tool in people's side—
indicted the sardines for tunacide.

And the sardines who simply licked the fish,
as well as those whose mouths were slick with fat,
and even those who'd entertained the wish,
were all included in the bunch, in that,
they said, "It's so. No ifs or buts about it!
Red-handed they were caught. So there's no doubt.

Our law is unmistakable and clear:
'The large fish eats the little one. That's so!'
The little fish the larger one ate here,
subverting thus the orders of the law,
a law that's fundamental for us, hence,
they're guilty of a capital offense.

The wretched fish's attorney simply cried,
"For my poor clients the defense is clear.
The skeleton is very long and wide.
The tuna weighed at least three tons, for sure,
and all of the sardines, if weighed at once,

nov'unzi nun ci sù, si li pisati;
    si scàpulanu chiù di li nov'unzi
(comprisi anchi l'entragnos tutti quanti,
cu li squami, li reschi, peddi e 'nzunzi)
'mpinnitili, e livatili davanti;
ma, si 'un ponnu nov'unzi scapulari
stu tunnu unni si l'àppiru a ficcari?"

    Ripigghia lu Fiscu: "Li misuri
e li pisi nun sù punti legali,
servinu sulu pri li vinnituri;
ccà si tratta di causa capitali,
nè na rubrica di cui vinni e spenni
putrà smuntari na liggi sollenni;
    e datu chi nun fussiru li ardi
rei tunnicidi, è puntu stabilitu
ch'unni mancia lu grossu nun azzardi
nemmenu di liccari lu minutu..."
"Concedu, dici l'àutru, chista è curpa;
ma ccà si tratta d'ossu e non di purpa".

    Si sbattìu di ccà e di ddà citannu testi
in gerghi girbunischi oltramarini,
e si citaru codici e diggesti,
commentati da cernii e da 'mmistini;
purtaru fatti, e tantu scarruzzaru
chi lu puntu mattanti lu sbraccaru.

    Sidevanu da judici li granchi,
lu presidenti era un granciu fudduni;
tutti a dui vucchi, acciocchì l'una manci,
l'àutra addrizzi buggii, torcia raggiuni,
e cu ottu pedi a croccu, a dritta e a manca,
trasevanu di chiattu e di fajanca.

    Nun ànnu accessu a sti divinitati
salvu chi li supremi sacerdoti,
cioè li compatroni e l'avvocati;
li curiali un pocu chiù rimoti
curunanu li vittimi di ciuri,
mentri vannu sucànnucci l'umuri.

    Tuttu lu restu è populu profanu,
nè tra stu santuariu metti pedi;
o si ci trasi, tra un locu stramanu
s'agnuna, e guarda la suprema sedi,
chi di la vita disponi e di tanti
aviri e facultà di tutti quanti.

    Doppu chi sessionaru un lungu pezzu,

will not amount to more than a mere nine ounces.
    And if they happen to exceed that weight,
(including all internal organs, skin,
together with the scales, the bones and fat)
hang them! Just take them out and do them in!
But if they won't exceed a full nine ounce,
where could they've put the tuna's other pounds?"

    The Tax Department took the floor to yell:
"Measures and weights do not make legal sense.
They're useful only for the folks who sell.
We're trying here a capital offense,
and no defense for those who sell and spend
our solemn law will ever foil or bend."
    Even if the sardines were all decreed
of tunacide not guilty, it is known
to everyone that where the mighty feed
should be off limits to the little ones."
The other said: "I grant you that's a crime,
but they licked bones, not meat. It's not the same!

    They haggled back and forth, reciting texts
in weird, dark languages from far away,
citing some legal codices and law extracts,
on which beasts of the sea and groupers had their say.
They quoted facts, but they went off the track,
and to the main point they could not get back.

    The crabs were sitting in the judges' seat,
a soft-shelled one was chosen to preside;
all had two mouths: they used the first to eat,
and with the other raised objections, lied.
And with eight hook-like feet, both left and right,
they always moved in crooked ways, not straight.

    No one has access to these deities,
except for the supreme, official priests,
that is, the lawyers and their endorsees.
The lawyers who're a bit removed, at best,
will crown the victims with some flower buds,
while they continue sucking on their blood.

    All of the rest is populace, profane,
and won't set foot inside that holy place,
or if they do, it's likely they'll remain
timidly hidden in some darkened space,
looking at the supreme high seat which rules
the lives, the properties, and acts of all.

    After a long and difficult debate

291

da una parti e da l'àutra l'avvocati,
e lu Fiscu a li straggi sempri avvezzu
ni vulìa 'mpisi e ni vulìa squartati,
li judici gridaru: "Fora tutti!"
E s'inchiusiru suli tra li grutti.

Chisti dunca spusannu a la prudenza
li riguardi e li proprii fortuni,
consultanu lu codici, ma senza
dari un'occhiata a lu senzu comuni,
nun vulennu avvilirisi a pinsari
comu pensanu tutti li vulgari.

Dicevanu dicchiù: "Si s'apri strata
a consultari la raggiuni un pocu,
la Curia tutta quanta è ruinata,
nè lu foru legali avi chiù locu,
e qualunqui idiota o strafalariu
trasirà tra lu nostru santuariu.

Si circamu cui effettivamenti
si divurau lu tunnu, ni tiramu
l'odiu di l'immistini oggi potenti;
basta ch'in chisti un qualch'esempiu damu:
o liccaru, o cioraru fu sempri un casu;
sunnu senzi ugualmenti e vucca e nasu".

Cu sti riflessioni santi e giusti,
mittennusi lu testu avanti l'occhi,
scrissiru, cu li spini di lagusti,
la sintenza, racchiusi tra crafocchi,
chiusa c'un "ita quod" per appendici,
ch'in gran parti la sburdi e contraddici.

"Si assolvanu li sardi di la morti,
ita quod nun putissiru campari.
A st'oggettu, li squami ed ogni sorti
di grassu e 'nzunzi e peddi devorari
si li diva lu Fiscu; e in spiaggi ingrati
li rimasugghi sianu confinati".

Sta sintenza, riguardu a lu fatali
codici, parsi d'equità vistuta;
però certuni dissiru chi mali
l'equità fussi stata compartuta;
ch'in canciu di distinguiri, cunfunni
li ciauraturi e li licchiabunni.

Tra un'annu intantu di fricazioni,
di carceri, stritturi e assaccareddi,
va trova sardi chiù! Di porzioni

among the lawyers from opposing parts,
and the Tax Bureau, ready to create
carnage, that wanted sardines torn apart,
or hanged, the judges yelled: "Get out! Outside!"
and found a cave, they shut themselves inside.

These judges then consulted the old codes,
marrying prudence with their high esteem
for their own fortunes. However, they bestowed
no thought to common sense, just not to seem
that they to such low depths would ever sink
to think whatever common people think.

And furthermore they said that, "If the road
to reasoning is opened just a bit,
the Curia will surely be destroyed,
the legal forums will no longer fit
a need, and any fool or feather brain
will be free to intrude in our domain.

By seeking those who actually did slay
and ate the tuna, we'll have cause to fear
from those who are the mightiest today.
All we need do is set examples here!
Whether they licked or smelled is a good case,
because the mouth's a sense, and so's the nose."

With these reflections which seemed holy, sane,
and having put the text before their eyes,
they wrote the sentence with a lobster's spine,
— still hidden in their holes — with *so as*
included as appendix which, at best,
undid and contradicted all the rest.

"From death we now acquit all the sardines,
insofar as they shouldn't go on living;
and to this end, the scales, with all the skins,
with every bit of fat, must be given
to the Tax Bureau to consume. Moreover,
scatter on distant beaches what's leftover."

Considering the fatal code, it seemed
the judgment had been equitably done,
but there were certain fish who had not deemed
that even-handed treatment had been shown,
for rather than distinguishing the two,
smellers and lickers threw into a stew.

After a year of thievery had passed,
meanwhile, of hardships, worries in a jail,
good bye, sardines! Nothing remained, alas,

nun ni ristau chi sula resca e peddi;
l'àutra mitati sfumau pri la strata
da l'insetti fiscali divurata.

    Pri riguri di codici, st'insetti
nun putìanu li sardi devorari;
ma lu ritu, in virtù di soi ricetti,
fa tuttu impunementi, fari e sfari;
pertantu cui stu ritu oggi professa
si metti supra di la liggi stessa.

    Cola proposi sta difficultati:
"Si ccà la forza è chidda chi prevali
pirchì inventari sti formalitati,
judici, foru e codici legali?"
Chista da Cola a un trigghiu fu proposta,
ed eccu qual'è stata la risposta:

    "Li granci avvezzi a perdiri jurnati
tra l'oziu, insidiannu li pateddi,
nè avennu forza, lena e abbilitati
di assicutari vopi ed asineddi,
idearu un sistema di sta sorti,
e poi l'insinuaru a li chiù forti;

    dimustrannunni l'utili e profittu,
chi quannu cu la forza hannu de fattu
cunvinìa chi l'avissiru di drittu
autenticatu in codici e contrattu:
e li niputi, pocu o nenti bravi,
di li vantaggi godanu di l'avi.

    Chiddi chi li soi figghi e li niputi
si vidinu pri drittu assicurati,
sunnu ad autorizzari divinuti
li granci cu li vucchi scancarati,
e d'unanimi votu si proponi
fidarni ad iddi l'esecuzioni.
Stu codici li granci esaggerannu,
mustraru ad evidenza lu vantaggiu
di li potenti, e lu minuri dannu
possibili pri l'àutri. E tantu saggiu
parsi a la vista da la scorcia in fora,
chi fu abbrazzatu, e si osserva tutt'ora".

    *****

excepting a few bones, some skins and scales.
The other half had vanished on the way.
The Fiscal insects had consumed their prey.

    These bugs, if by the code were to abide,
to eat sardines were not at liberty.
But owing to its recipes, the Rite
makes and unmakes, acts with impunity.
In the meantime, those who profess it's so,
have simply placed themselves above the law.

    So Nick-the-Fish proposed this argument:
"If brute force is here the prevailing mode,
why must you such formalities invent
as judges, courts, as well as a legal code?"
These thoughts to a red mullet were addressed,
and this is the reply that was expressed:

    "The crabs who are accustomed to waste days,
lying in wait for limpets, as they've shown
to have no strength, ability, nor ways
of catching porgies with means of their own,
a system of this kind devised and then
whispered it to the strongest specimen.

    The gain and the utility they showed
to try obtaining by sheer force of right,
— confirmed by contracts and the legal code —
what they already had by force of might,
so that the nephews, with or without brains,
could then inherit the ancestors' gains.

    Once they had seen their nephews and their sons
assured, made safe by right, the mightiest,
who had into authorities then grown,
proposed unanimously to entrust
to those old crabs who had two crooked jaws
the swift administration of the laws.
The crabs, exaggerating the new code,
with clarity did demonstrate the gains
for the most powerful, and also showed
the minor losses for the rest. So sane
appeared the code, seen from the surface out,
it was embraced and it's observed throughout."

    *****

LXXXV
LU GRIDDU E LA LUCERTA

Un griddu era pusatu
tra na chianura aperta.
Ci accosta na lucerta,
ed iddu chiù calatu
si metti. Cridi chidda
soggezioni d'idda.

Anza perciò pigghiannu
di stuzzicarlu 'un lascia.
Ma chiddu, mentri abbascia,
li gammi sbalistrannu,
cu' un càuciu la ribbutta,
sàuta e la sbota sutta.

Nun vi fidati troppu
cu l'apprittari a chiddi
calati e mansuliddi;
qualchi cattivu intoppu
ni avriti. St'allerta
pinsati a la lucerta.

*****

LXXXV
The Cricket and the Lizard

A cricket was at rest,
low on a little hill.
A lizard near him pressed
and he sank lower still.
The lizard was convinced
he saw the cricket wince.

So bolder he then grew,
harassing him some more.
But as the cricket drew
close to the ground, he soared,
and turned, with a strong kick,
the lizard on its back.

Don't be too confident
when teasing those who're meek,
who walk with their brows bent.
Your future may turn bleak.
So then stay quite alert!
Recall the cricket's hurt!

*****

LXXXVI
LU SCECCU, LU PATRUNI E LI LATRI

"Sàuta, ci dissi, ca vennu li latri",
a lu so sceccu càrricu, Chiruni.
"Forsi, lu sceccu replica, li latri
mi chiàntanu chiù grossu lu varduni?"
"Oh, no: lu stissu càrricu li latri
ti mittirannu." "E beni, me patruni,
sautati vui, pri mia m'importa un ficu
cu' di li dui m'incoccia lu viddicu".

*****

LXXXVI
The Donkey, His Master, and the Thieves

"Run, quick...the thieves!" said Chiron to his ass,
who was quite burdened with a heavy pack.
The donkey answered him: "These thieves, alas,
will they increase the load upon my back?"
"Oh, no, the load you'll bear will not surpass
the one you're carrying right now." "Well, Jack,
you'd better run, for I care not a whit
which one of you will make me bite the bit."

*****

Giovanni Meli

LXXXVII
LU VOI E LA MUSCHITTA

Mentri un voi lavurava, na muschitta
a pusari ci jiu supra un cornu;
poi pretisi la sira essiri ascritta
tra li lavuratura di lu jornu
e dumannau la paga. Lu burgisi,
di sta pretenzioni sinni risi.

Ma non ridinu in nui certi baruni,
anzi paganu beni e profumati
li tanti parassiti muscagghiuni
chi si fannu vidìri affaccinnati
e usurpanu lu lucru tuttu interu
di chiddi chi fatiganu daveru.
*****

LXXXVII
The Ox and the Gnat

One day an ox was working when a gnat
upon one of his horns came down to rest.
When night arrived, the gnat pretended that
she had worked too, and issued a request
for pay. The farmer thought it was a game,
and therefore laughed at her pretentious claim.

But certain barons in our land don't cry
with laughter. They, in fact, pay well and smile
at all the parasitic winery flies
who make believe they're busy all the while
as all the profits they usurp and steal
from those who labor hard, long, and for real.
*****

LXXXVIII
L'ETIOPU E LA NIVI

Un'Etiopu nigru comu pici
pritindia farsi biancu strufinannu
la nivi tra la facci. Un saggiu dici:
"È tempu persu, lèvati d'affannu,
purrà tua facci la nivi anniriri
ma non già chista tua facci imbianchiri".
*****

LXXXVIII
The Ethiopian and the Snow

An Ethiopian who was inky black
pretended he could whiten his black face
by rubbing snow on it. "You're off the track,"
a wise man said. "Yours is a hopeless case!
Your black face may the white snow turn to black
but snow can't whiten your black face, alack!"
*****

LXXXIX
LA MUSCA E LU LIUNI

Na musca si pusau supra un liuni,
e vidìa chi l'armali tutti quanti
scuprennu ad iddu stavanu a li 'gnuni,
nè ardianu cumpariricci davanti;
  "Dunca, dissi, eu nun sù di la comuni
giacchì degna suffrirmi..." L'ignoranti
nun cumprindia chi pri dda testa altera
tra l'essiri criati, idda nun c'era.
*****

LXXXIX
The Fly and the Lion

Upon a lion came a fly to rest
and noticed that all animals would stay,
on seeing him, against a corner pressed,
and none of them dared move or even sway.
  "Since I'm allowed so near, I must be blessed
with special gifts," the fool went on to say.
The fly knew not that he did not exist
in the proud lion's creatures master list.
*****

XC

Un certu surciteddu arditu arditu
pri lu disiu di liccuniari
niscìu da la sua tana, ed attrivitu
tutti li 'gnuni misi a firriari.
Ciàura ccà... licca ddà... junci ntra un situ,
senti un'oduri e metti a naschiari,
pirchì ad un nasu (dicinu) surcignu
lu furmaggiu è lu ciàuru lu chiù dignu.

S'accosta e vidi tra firrati e sticchi
penniri certa cosa bianculidda
eccu ci fa la gula nnicchi-nnicchi:
"O beni meu! n'avissi na scardidda!"
Dissi, e affilannu li soi fauci licchi,
s'alliffa tuttu e movi la cudidda,
ed accumincia a fari passagagghi,
circannu un'apirtura ntra ddi 'ngagghi.

La guarda e squagghia, la cuntempla e smiccia,
e si nni senti jiri duci duci.
Ogni difficultà chiù lu 'ncapriccia,
nè si cueta si nun s'introduci;
trasi a la fini, tasta, si scapriccia;
ma ntra lu megghiu, chi la fera luci,
senti un scrùsciu, si jetta a manu manca
e lu stomacu, ohimè! si ci sbalanca.

Curri di ccà, di ddà, cerca scappari,
e vidi chiusi tutti li spiragghi;
torna a vidiri, ritorna a tentari,
ma 'un trova menzu comu si la sgagghi;
na negghia all'arma si senti calari,
presagiu infaustu di li soi travagghi;
passia, e lu furmaggiu disiatu
ci sbatti mussu mussu, e 'un è 'nningatu.

C'è passata la fami e lu pitittu;
lu furmaggiu ci pari cantunera;
si mai lu 'mmesti, vota, o tira drittu,
senza mancu guardarlu tra la cera;
poi sclama: "Libertati e pani schittu,
oh chi turnassi ad esseri com'era!

XC

A brazen little mouse who felt an urge
to gourmandize went out from his safe lair,
and he began with daring and with brashness
to search for food in every hiding place.
Whiffing and smelling with his nose in air,
he recognized a most familiar scent.
So he sniffed harder, for a mouse's nose
they claim, knows of no sweeter smell than cheese.

As he approached, he saw a whitish thing,
just hanging there inside a fence of sorts
made with some sticks. His mouth began
to water. "My delight! If I could have a bite!"
he said, while sharpening his greedy fangs.
He moved his little tail and stroked himself,
and back and forth around the fence he went
to find an opening through some small vent.

He looked adoringly at it, he gazed
with such great longing that he nearly swooned.
The obstacles increased his eagerness,
nor did he rest until he was inside.
He finally got in. He had a taste,
but when he'd reached the summit of delight,
he heard a noise, ran to the left, alas
and his poor stomach emptied out *en masse*.

He ran in all directions, here and there;
he tried to flee but every crack was sealed.
Again he looked, again he tried, but found
there was no way through which he could escape.
He felt a fog descend upon his soul:
an evil omen of his sharp travails.
He paced, but he ignored the longed-for cheese
which was in reach and begging to be seized.

He'd lost his hunger and his appetite.
The cheese appeared to him as hard as bricks.
If he ran into it, he turned away
or went straight on, without a glance at it.
He cried: "Ah, to be free on bread and water!
I wish I were just as I was before.

Chi mi servi la piatta dilicata?
La vucca di lu stomacu è attuppata.

Miseru, ohimè! Pr'un pezzu di furmaggiu
aju persu la cosa la chiù cara!
A lu so gustu, appena chi l'assaggiu,
quantu c'è di livaricci di tara?
Si masticassi un carduni sarvaggiu
nun avirrìa la vucca accussì amara;
arrinegu li gusti e li sapuri,
libertà, libertati e tozza duri".

Mentri l'afflittu pensa a li soi guai,
tant'àutri surciteddi a lu so rastu
sunnu arrivàti e stannu a li talài;
innamurati di ddu bellu pastu,
fannu lu cannarozzu longu assai,
pirchì la porta chiusa c'è d'immastu;
e intantu a lu scuvertu allampatizzi
stannu a lu ciàuru e apparanu li sbrizzi.

Unu ci passa e spassa pri davanti,
nàutru tenta la porta, o la suffitta
cui si cuntenta tuccarlu un'istanti
cu la cudidda pri na 'ngagghia stritta;
cui licca li muddichi di li canti,
cui s'increpa e bestemmia la sua sditta;
c'è cui suspira, c'è cui spinna e mori;
c'è cui guarda cu l'occhiu di lu cori.

Poi vidennu vicinu a lu tumazzu
stari un surciddu cu lu mussu asciuttu:
talè, dicianu, chi gramagghiunazzu!
Fa badagghi e lu beni arresta tuttu!'
Nàutru dicìa: "S'in locu di stu pazzu
fuss'iu di lu furmaggiu accussì 'ncuttu,
oh chi bella scialata! Ntra stu casu
mi nni vurrìa jittari pri lu nasu".

Ripigghiava poi nàutru a vuci forti:
"Diascacci! sti belli cugninturi
sù pri li babbi e pri li juga-torti!
Pr'iddi sù fatti li megghiu sapuri!
E a mia nudda di chissi? Oh sorti! oh sorti!

What need have I for tasty, dainty food?
My stomach's hardly in a working mood!

Ah, wretched me! For just a piece of cheese
I lost the dearest thing that I possess.
As soon as one bites into it, what tare
will he have to subtract from its true taste?
If I had chewed upon wild prickly plants,
my mouth now would not taste such bitterness.
All tastes and flavors I renounce with dread.
Freedom, liberty and hard stale bread!"

While the afflicted mouse reflected on
his troubles, many other little mice
followed his scent and were there looking in,
enamoured of that beautiful repast.
Their gullets from sheer longing were outstretched
because the closed door barred their way. And so
out in the open, hungry and wide-eyed,
they sniffed the smell and they remained outside.

One started pacing back and forth in front;
another tried the ceiling or the door;
one seemed content to touch it for an instant
by stretching its long tail through a small gap;
another licked the crumbs right from the sides;
some bristled and with disappointment cursed;
and others sighed; some mice did pine and die,
while others looked at it with their heart's eye.

Then when they saw a little mouse who stood
right by the cheese with such a dry, sad puss,
they said, "Look there, look what a nincompoop!
He's yawning while that goodness stays intact!"
Another said: "If it were I, instead
of that dumb fool, who stood next to the cheese,
oh, what a ball I'd have, for in that case,
I'd gorge myself. I'd really stuff my face!"

Another one continued very loudly,
"By Jove, these marvelous occasions are
for swindlers and for fools. The best of flavors
are all reserved for them. And what of me?
Nothing like that for me? Ah, bitter fate!

Nun pozzu aviri mai di tia un favuri?
Nun distingui né meriti, né ranghi,
duni viscotta a cui nun avi ganghi!"

Never am I to have a treat from you?
Merit and rank mean nothing to your eyes.
Hard candies you hand out to toothless mice!"

Nàutru diceva: "Unn'iddu avi li pedi,
disiiria d'aviricci la facci;
nun conusci la gioia chi possedi
st'armali e 'un sa godirni li procacci;
avi tantu chi fari, ed iddu sedi!
S'iddu nun pò, mi dici almenu: Vacci:
ch'è tintu! ch'è sdiserramu! e mandruni!
Mancu conusci li boni vuccuni!"

Another mouse then said: "Oh, I would like
to put my face where he has placed his feet.
That beast knows not the joy that he possesses.
He has so much to do and he just sits,
and does not know how to enjoy its goodness.
If he can't do it, let him say to me: 'It's yours!'
He's lazy, mean: a really stupid cad!
A good thing he can't tell from one that's bad!"

Ripigghia nàutru: "Va' rùsica l'ervi,
ca sti boni vuccuna 'un sù pri l'orvi
cu' avi la cugnintura e 'un si nni servi,
nun trova cunfissuri chi l'assorvi.
Chi ci aduri tu ora? chi cunservi?
Sparagni pri li cani, o pri li corvi?
Giacchì tu nun lu 'nninghi, né ci dici,
almenu fanni parti pri l'amici!"

Another one began! "Go chew on grass,
for these good morsels aren't for the blind!
Who has the chance and makes no use of it,
won't find a priest to give him absolution.
What are you waiting for? What are you saving?
Are you reserving it for dogs or crows?
But since for it you show indifference,
at least you could just share it with your friends!"

Lu surci, chi si senti dari liti,
pri mettiri a chidd'àutri tra l'affanni,
ci dici: "Stu furmaggiu, chi viditi,
mi lu sparagnu pri li festi granni;
del restu, si vuatri ni vuliti,
iti avanti; circati a tutti banni;
si viditi casuzzi cu firrati,
trasiticci e sarriti cunsulati".

The mouse who felt the brunt of such harassment,
to give the others troubles of their own,
replied to them: "This cheese you see right here,
I'm saving for myself for holy days.
But if you want a bit of it, go on,
go search in every place, and if you find
small houses with a fence, go right inside:
I am convinced you'll be most satisfied."

Li surci n'accattaru di ssa stuppa,
e 'mpanniddaru filici e fistanti;
vannu ntra nàutra stanza tutti a truppa
unni c'era na trappula a li canti.
Ora vennu a lu pettini li gruppa;
eccu chi lu chiù sgherru si fa avanti:
già trasi, vidi, tasta, resta prisu
e lu destinu so eccu è decisu.

The mice all bought the story eagerly
and with some shrieks of joy, excitedly
into another room rushed as a group,
and there they found a trap set in a corner.
The time for retribution had arrived.
The most defiant moved up to the snare,
walked in and saw, he tasted and was caught.
His destiny thus was completely wrought.

Attentanu a lu scrusciu l'àutri attornu,
e vidennu calari un catarrattu,
si mettinu a gridari: "Cornu! cornu!
Di stu furmaggiu 'un ni vulemu affattu;

When they heard noise, the others' ears perked up
and when they saw the gate come crashing down,
they started screaming, "Spare us, spare us, please!
We do not want this kind of cheese at all!

chi s'avi a stari prisi notti e jornu,
senza mancu spiranza di riscattu?
Furmaggiu, sarrai duci e bellu assai;
ma a stu gran prezzu certu nun ci vai".

   Cussì li surci pensanu: ora vui
si truvati st'idei sciocchi ed improprii,
diciti qual'è megghiu di li dui:
"Mparari a spisi d'àutru, o a spisi proprii?
Nun c'è bisognu ch'iu mi spieghi chiui;
ogn'unu si la pensi e si l'approprii;
e vija, s'avi flemma e avi coraggiu,
di stari prisu allatu a lu furmaggiu".

           *****

Are we to stay in prison day and night
without the hope of ever being rescued?
O cheese, you may be very sweet and nice,
but you are certainly not worth the price!"

   That's how the mice reflected: now, if you
find these ideas foolish or improper,
decide which is the better of the two:
"to learn at the expense of other beings
or at one's own? I need explain no further.
Let everyone reflect and make it sink.
And if he has the courage and the nerve,
let him next to the cheese in prison serve."

           *****

This long fable (XC) was part of Canto X (octaves 43 to 58) of the *Don Chisciotti and Sanciu Panza*. It is significant that Meli chose to let Sanciu recite the fable. This can be seen as a demonstration of his increased status in the poem. He is no longer the ignorant and illiterate squire. He has grown in stature and he is now able to share the wisdom he has acquired through suffering and experience. He appears to take on the role of the popular philosophers of the past, such as Aesop, so greatly admired by Meli, foreshadowing the fact that when Sanciu dies he will spent his time in the Elysium in the company of philosophers. I included the fable here even though it was not part of the *Moral Fables*.

Miscellanea

I
LU CHIANTU D'ERACLITU

Spelunchi, avvezzi sulu a riferiri
l'aspri lamenti di li svinturati,
chi nasceru a lu munnu pri patiri;
    fantasimi, ch'infausti guvirnati
pri menzu di l'orruri e lu spaventu,
sti locali a la mestizia cunsagrati,
    eccu ch'in olocaustu iu vi presentu,
teatru orrendu di miseria umana,
chista, chi vita chiamanu, ed è stentu.
    Stendu li vrazza a la spiranza vana,
ma poi m'avviju ch'è la sula pena
chi nui da lu non essiri alluntana;
    chi si un lampu serenu luci appena,
di un subitu svanisci a lu pinsari
chi affannu e morti chiudinu la scena.
    Omu superbu, e ardisci chiù vantari
lu pinseri, la menti e la ragiuni,
ddi tiranni chi t'ànnu a turmintari?
    Sutta un giugu di ferru a strascinuni
lu bisognu ti umilia e l'avveniri
ti pisa supra comu un bastiuni.
    D'unni a li mali toi, d'unni poi aviri
riparu e scampu, si cu punta ascuta
la menti stissa ti veni a firiri?
    Invidiirai la stupidizza bruta,
chi licca lu cuteddu chi l'ocidi,
e mori comu vampa chi s'astuta.
    Miseru, ohimè! si chianci; ohimè! si ridi,
miseru forsi chiù, chi o cecu o pazzu,
l'infinita miseria nun vidi.
    Quali fannu di tia vili strapazzu
li passioni, venti impetuusi,
da cui sì spintu, e nun vidi lu vrazzu!
    L'ambizioni, ohimè! t'attacca e cusi
ntra un angulu di sala, e alliscia e indora
li pinnuli cchiù amari e 'ntussicusi.
    L'intressu di lu cori caccia fora
li doviri chiù santi, e listi listi
l'odiu ti sbrana dintra e ti divora:
    ora a lu beni d'àutru ti rattristi,
ora godi d'un mali, ora ti penti,

I
The Crying of Heraclitus

Caverns accustomed only to report
the harsh lament of poor, unhappy folk
who came into this world to suffer pain,
    ill-omened ghosts who govern these locations
all consecrated to sad desolation
through means of horrors and through frightful deeds,
    let me present as in a holocaust
the horrid play of human misery,
this thing called life that is adversity.
    I stretch my arms before me toward hope,
only to realize that suffering
alone is what keeps us from non-being,
    for as soon as a flash of peace does glow,
it quickly disappears when you well know
that struggle, death the curtain will then close.
    O haughty man, do you still dare to praise
your thought, your mind, your rationality,
those tyrants that torment you constantly?
    Beneath a yoke of steel, prostrated low,
poverty humbles you and future years
like a huge bastion weigh upon you so.
    Where can you find a shelter or relief
for your harsh suffering, if your own mind
with sharp attacks goes on inflicting grief?
    You'll grow to envy brute stupidity
that licks the knife that's causing him to die,
and fades out like a candle out of wax.
    Wretched, alas, if you laugh, if you cry
perhaps more so, for either mad or blind,
you cannot see the endless misery.
    Ah, how your passions, those impetuous winds
that drive you on, will cause you endless wear,
and you won't even realize they're there!
    Ambition then attacks you and behold,
you're stuck in corners, while it flatters you,
coating the bitterest of pills with gold.
    Self interest most sacred duties chases
out of your heart and hate tears you to pieces,
devouring you. You're sad for the success
    of other folk; in evil you rejoice;
you feel remorse, but then you will repent

torni a pintirti poi ca ti pintisti.

    la gilusia t'agghiazza; in peni e stenti
Amuri ti fa scurriri la vita;
l'ira in bestia ti cancia, e l'oziu in nenti.

    A middi eccessi gioventù t'incita;
t'abbatti e stolidisci la vicchiaia,
ch'è di tutti li mali calamita.

    Ora l'orrenda povertà t'impaia
sutta la smunta fami, e pri chiù luttu
l'asinu ti quacia, lu cani abbaia.

    Ora infangatu e in middi vizii bruttu,
piaciri 'un c'è chi a tua lascivia basti,
quasi d'umanità spugghiatu in tuttu.

    Miseru! In quali abbissu penetrasti
cu respirari l'auri di la vita!
Ahi! quantu caru l'esseri cumprasti!

    Complessu miserabili di crita,
unni regna la barbara incertizza,
chi spargi di velenu ogni ferita.

    E chistu è l'omu?... Ahi! nenti, ahi stupidizza,
assurbiti di mia sinu a lu nomu,
o canciatimi in ciumi d'amarizza.

    C'è lagrimi, chi bastanu pri l'omu?

the fact that you repented once again.

    Jealousy chills your bones, and love will make
you live your life in suffering and pain;
wrath turns you to a beast, and sloth to nothing,

    youth spurs you to commit a thousand follies,
old age, which is the magnet for all ills,
will batter you and turn you to a fool.

    Now horrid poverty will burden you
beneath pale hunger, and for greater woe
the donkey kicks at you and the dogs howl.

    Now sullied in the mud of many vices,
no pleasure ever satisfies your lust,
devoid completely of humanity.

    Ah, wretched man! In what abyss you fell
by breathing in this atmosphere of life!
How dearly you have paid just to exist!

    O worthless mixture of the humblest clay
where barbarous uncertainty is queen,
spreading its poison over every wound!

    And this is man? Ah, stupid nothingness,
absorb my being and my name as well,
or change me to a stream of bitterness.

    Have we sufficient tears to weep for man?

The three Heraclitus Elegies I include here were written probably during the poet's stay in the town of Cinisi where he had been engaged as a physician. They were published in the first edition of his *Opere* in 1787 and again in 1814. The profound pessimism displayed in these elegies is expressed through the voice of Heraclitus, a Greek philosopher (VI-V century BC) and reflects a moment of deep discouragement experienced by the poet. To avoid the possibility of censure, Meli felt obliged to add that Heraclitus was speaking of the "infinite vanity of things" because he had been born before the "Revelation". But the feelings expressed in this poem and in the other two on the same subject are Meli's and they are expressed in other poems such as "The Mirror of Disillusionment, that is, the Mockeries," included in this anthology.

Giovanni Meli

II
SU LU STISSU SUGGETTU

Nivura malincunia, tu chi guverni
cu lu to mantu taciturnu e cupu,
l'immensi orruri di li spazii eterni,
    a tia ntra li deserti urla lu lupu;
pri tia la notti lu jacobbu mestu
di luttu inchi la valli e lu sdirrupu.

La scura negghia di cui l'alma vestu
mi strascina pri forza e mi carrìa
a lu to tronu orribili e funestu.

L'umbri caliginusi, amaru mia!
unni sedi la morti e lu spaventu,
sù la mia sula e infausta cumpagnia.

Purtatu supra l'ali di lu ventu,
murmura 'mmenzu l'arvuli e li grutti
di l'afflitti murtali lu lamentu.

Fatta centru a li lastimi di tutti,
l'infelici alma mia, china d'affannu,
lu tristi amaru calici s'agghiutti.

Chist'atomi ch'eu staju respirannu,
sù li suspiri di tanti mischini,
chi stannu a st'ura l'anima esalannu;

    sti terri, ch' eu scarpisu sularini,
sunnu (oh vicenni infausti e lagrimusi!)
sù di regni e citati li ruini;

    st'ervi, sti pianti, st'arvuli frundusi
su cadaveri d'omini e di bruti,
cu terra ed acqua 'nzemmula cunfusi.

Ci stannu attornu friddi e irrisoluti
l'umbri, cumpagni antichi; e li scuntenti
sù cundannati a stari sempri muti.

Volanu intantu l'uri, li momenti,
e ognunu d'iddi porta supra l'ali
straggi, ruini, guai, travagghi e stenti.

L'origini qual'è di tanti mali?
Lu sensu, ohimè! lu sensu, chi repugna
d'unirsi a corpi fragili e murtali;

    cussì tirannu, l'omu vivu incugna
a un cadaveru putridu, ed unisci
carni a carni, ossa ad ossa, ed ugna ad ugna.

    Si lu sensu a li Dei si riferisci,
quali fatalità barbara e ria

II
The Crying of Heraclitus

Gloomy disheartenment, you who rule over
the massive horrors of eternal space
that lies beneath your dark and silent cover,

    for you the wolf out in the desert howls,
for you at night the gorges and the dales
resound with echoes of the mournful owl.

The somber fog with which I clothe my soul
is dragging me by force against my will
before your horrible and fatal throne.

The indistinct and obscure shades, poor me,
where death and terror make their residence,
are my sole and ill-omened company.

Carried aloft upon the wings of wind
the lamentations of afflicted mortals
are heard throughout the caverns and the trees.

Placed in the midst of everybody's woes,
my own unhappy soul, most breathlessly,
the sad and bitter cup now swallows whole.

These atoms that I'm breathing are the sighs
emitted by a multitude of souls
who at this time are taking their last breaths.

    These solitary lands on which I tread
are what (oh doomful, tearful destinies!)
of kingdoms and of cities still remains.

    These grasses and these plants, these robust trees
cadavers are of animals and men
that earth and water blended into one.

Around them, cold and wavering, there are
shadows, old comrades, and the wretched souls,
are sentenced to remain forever silent.

Meanwhile the hours and the minutes fly
and each one carries on its wings travails,
massacres, ruins, struggles, pain, and misery.

What is the origin of all these evils?
The sense, alas, the sense that finds it hard
to join with frail and mortal human bodies;

    it's so tyrannical that living man
it edges close to a putrescent corpse
and joins flesh onto flesh, bone onto bone

    and nail to nail. If sense refers to Gods
what barbarous and guilty destiny

a stu signu l'umilia e assuggettisci?

    Piaci forsi a li Dei la tirannia?
forsi si dirrà chi chiù potenti
d'iddi lu Fatu e lu Destinu sia?

    Forsi è in pena di l'omu sconoscenti?
Ma pirchì ni participa lu brutu
e ogni animali simplici e innoccenti?

    Innatu a la materia o so attributu
forsi è lu sensu? Ma pirchì guastannu
l'ordini in idda, lu sensu è finutu?

    Forsi esisti da se? Ma unn'era quannu
l'ordini di lu corpu e l'armunia
nun era ancora jutasi furmannu?

    È forsi parti di l'Eterna idia?
Di la Causa Increata? E s'idda è eterna,
pirchì fu in tempu l'esistenza mia?

    Lu pinseri, chi s'aggita e s'interna,
nun discerni chi tenebri ed orruri,
da cui resta abbagghiatu e si costerna.

    Forsi st'abbissu d'umbri cussì oscuri
è l'infinitu limitu fatali
situatu tra l'omu e lu Fatturi?

    Indarnu umana menti azzanna
l'ali dintra di sta caligini profunna,
chi a penetrarla la sua forza 'un vali.

    Chistu è lu sagru velu, chi circunna
la Prima Essenza, centru, comu un sassu,
di li diversi circuli di l'unna;

    chi presenti in ogni opra, in ogni passu,
penetra, avviva ed occulta a lu sensu
la manu, lu disignu e lu cumpassu.

    Oh tu, Causa, Principiu eternu, immensu,
ntra li tanti attributi 'un sarrai bonu?
E infelici nni voi senza compensu?

    Lu mali è gloria a lu to eccelsu tronu?

humbles it and subjects it to this sign?

    Are Gods perhaps amused by tyranny?
Or can we say that Fate and Destiny
are much more powerful, perhaps, than they?

    For man's ingratitude is this the price?
But why do innocent, pure animals
and brutes participate in this as well?

    Is sense perhaps innate in matter or
an attribute of it? But why then will
sense vanish when its order is no more?

    Does it exist alone, perhaps? But where
was it when the body and its harmony
had not yet quite begun to take its form?

    Is it a part of the Eternal Concept
perhaps? Of Non-created Cause. And if
it is eternal, why was it once my life?

    The thought that stirs and penetrates deeper,
cannot discern but shadows and sore strife,
which leave it apprehensive, in distress.

    Perhaps this somber, shadows-filled abyss
is the unending, fatal boundary
that stands between mankind and its Creator?

    The human mind will stunt its wings in vain
inside this fathomless obscurity:
its strength is not sufficient to see through.

    This is the sacred veil that goes around
the Primal Essence at its center, like a rock
creating different circles of the wave,

    which, present in all works, in every gait,
just penetrates, gives life and hides from our
senses the hand, the compass and design.

    O Cause, o endless Principle, immense,
is goodness not an attribute you own?
And want us wretched without recompense?

    Is evil glory to your mighty throne?

III
SU LU STISSU SUGGETTU

Notti, chi rendi a li terreni oggetti
lu veru aspettu so nivuru e tristu,
di cui la luci n'impidia l' effetti,

    ceca sì tu, nè l'àutri globbi ài vistu
in tia dispersi e tra lu primu nenti,
gemellu to, comu sarà di chistu.

    Sta fraggili mia spogghia già cadenti
sutta di li corvini toi grand' ali
sarà turnata a soi primi elementi.

    Lu pinseri però, raggiu immortali
di eterna luci, spetta a lu so tuttu,
a la sfera suprema originali.

    Intantu, mentri chi cu peni e luttu,
'intressi di stu massu di sustanza,
da la terra sburzatumi, jeu scuttu,

    quantu stu alloggiu di terrena stanza,
quantu caru mi custa! Oh enormi usura
pr'una pinusa, efimera tardanza!

    Appena chi n'impresta la natura
lu so tirrestri fangu, oh quanti mali
manna missaggi a rimburzarlu allura!

    Cuvi, frevi, varoli, ed àutri tali
malanni e infermità tormentatrici,
pri cui stu munnu è all'occhi mei spitali!

    Chiddi ch' 'un ànnu addossu sti nimici
sunnu da li passioni turmintati,
frutti di la fangusa sua radici.

    Quasi fussiru pochi l'espressati mali,
chi all'omu manna la natura,
quant'àutri lu so funnu n'à scuvati!

    L'odiu tinaci, la smorta paura,
lu tradimentu, chi si teni forti
a la silenziaria congiura;

    la vinditta, ch'av'armi di ogni sorti;
la guerra, chi di l'utili metalli
ni à furmata la fàuci di la morti,

    porta di appressu e tra li soi intervalli
la zarca fami e smunta caristia,
e la pesti chi colpu mai nun falli;

    la spogghia orfani e vidui ippocrisia,
chi spissu à 'nsanguinatu e tempii e otari;

III
On The Same Subject

O Night, you who reveal the gloomy, mean,
real look of earthly objects whose effects
in the bright light of day could not be seen,

    are blind, nor have you seen the other globes
dispersed in you, and in the primal void,
your own twin, as will occur with this one.

    This fragile body, whose fall's imminent,
beneath your blackbird like, great wings
will be returned to its first elements.

    The thought, however, an immortal ray
of everlasting light, belongs completely
to the original, supreme array.

    Through mourning and through suffering, meanwhile,
the interest for the substance that the earth
has given me, for such a little pile,

    is very high. How dearly I must pay
for lodging on this earth. What usury
for so ephemeral and painful stay!

    As soon as nature lends its earthen mud
to us, how many woeful notes it sends
demanding reimbursement! Teething pains,

    fevers, and mumps and other similar
misfortunes and sore maladies for which
the world a hospital appears to be.

Those who are not oppressed by all these foes
tormented are by passions and by woes,
emerging from their earthly muddy roots.

    As though the list of evils Nature sends
to man was not enough, how many more
has he uncovered deep inside his core!

    Undying and persistent hate, pale fear,
betrayals that hold tightly onto plots
silence-driven that will never disappear,

    vengeance which brings all sorts of arms to bear;
warfare that out of useful metals makes
weapons that represent the scythes of death

and carries in its wake, and in between,
miserable hunger and haggard famine
and pestilence that never fails to strike.

    Hypocrisy that orphans, widows robs,
that temples, altars often has made bloody;

l'invidia, chi li cori camulìa;
l'ambizioni idropica, astutari
chi mai pò la sua siti viiulenta
di appropriarsi celu, terra e mari;
  e l'avarizia magra e macilenta,
chi a filu duppiu unita a lu suspettu
vigghia l'intera notti ed arriventa.
  Tra un cori di sti rei aliti infettu
putrà mai la saggizza, lu costumi
e la giustizia aviricci ricettu?
  Ma comu sti fangusi, infetti fumi
ponnu essiri in contattu, e tormentari
stu chiaru raggiu di celesti lumi?
  Ccà mi perdu! Iddu stissu rischiarari
nun pò stu gruppu oscuru e portentusu,
unni si vennu sti essiri a toccari;
  nè lu motivu sa pri cui sta 'nchiusu,
e vidi 'ncatinata la sua sorti
da un sovranu Decretu imperiusu.
  Benchì fraggili sianu li porti
chi chiudinu stu lucidu balenu,
nuddu pò aprirli, salvu chi la Morti!
  La Morti? Ma quantu orridu è lu trenu
chi l'accumpagna! Oh misera, oh scuntenta
umanità! Lu carceri terrenu
  ti affliggi, e lu scapparni ti spaventa!

envy which like a moth eats out the hearts;
  bloating ambition that can never satisfy
its raging thirst to gain possession of
all of the land, the oceans, and the sky.
  And gaunt, emaciated avarice,
which to suspicion with a thick line's bound
and wakes the whole night tossing, turning.
  Can wisdom, justice and good manners find
ever a good reception in such minds
that are infected with ill-boding breaths?
But how can these infected, muddy fumes
come into contact with and then torment
this limpid beacon of celestial light?
  This is where I get lost! The light cannot
shine on this gloomy and portentous knot
where all these beings come to be involved,
  nor can it know the motive why it's locked
and see its destiny so tightly blocked
by a supreme and irresistable Decree.
  Although the gates wherein this shiny flash
is held are frail, nobody has the power
to open them, no one, excepting Death.
  Death? But how horrid is the train behind
of it? Oh wretched and poor humankind!
The earthly prison causes you distress,
  and running from it frightens you no less.

Giovanni Meli

AVVERTIMENTI MORALI E POLITICI

Moral and Political Advice

A tempi chi la Grecia ciuria d'omini granni,
intenti a coltivari
lu bon costumi e la filosofia,
un Saggiu, avennu 'ntisu celebrari
la fama d'àutru Saggiu, e ben sapennu
chi a stu munnu c'è sempri ch'imparari,
e multu chiù da l'omini di sennu,
(chi di la specii umana a lu vantaggiu
li proprii lumi vannu diffunnennu)
pri truvarlu intraprenni lu viaggiu;
e, arrivatu, un dialogu s'intessi
di san'idei tra l'unu e l'àutru Saggiu,
in chisti sensi pressu a pocu espressi:

- Lu distintivu (dimmi tu, ch'ài lumi)
d'omu saggiu qual'è? - Lu bon costumi.
- Tra li saggi lu primu quali scegghiu?
- Cui parra beni e pocu, ed opra megghiu.
- Qual'è la scola chi forma li Saggi?
- Esperienza, studiu e disaggi.
- Bastanu da se suli liggi boni
a regolari Stati e Nazioni?
- Senza costumi li liggi eccellenti
sù, senza mastri, l'ottim'istrumenti.
- Mi sapristi tu diri cosa sia
chidda chi nui chiamamu ippocrisia?
- È lu censu d'omaggi e di tributi
chi lu viziu paga a la virtuti.
- Tra l'idoli, ch'in terra sunnu e foru,
cu' avi chiù cultu e chiù seguaci? - L'oru.
- Chista vita zocch'è? - Jocu di scacchi;
finitu, re e pidini entranu in sacchi.
- Qual'è l'omu a lu munnu chiù felici?
- Cui sicci cridi. - E cui lu chiù infelici?
- Cui sicci cridi. - E cui mentr'in dinaru
abbunda, è poverissimu? - L'avaru.
- Mi sapristi tu diri cui ci sia
chiù riccu in terra? - Cui menu disia.
- È coraggiu tra guai non avvilirsi?
- Ma è chiù tra l'augi non insuperbirsi.
- Cos'è la nobiltà? - Zeru, ma cunta

When Greece was flourishing with learned men
intent on cultivating good traditions
and studies of philosophy, a Wise man
who had heard praises of the reputation
of yet another Sage and knowing that
in this world there is always an occasion
to learn and more from men of intellect
who spread their learning wide to benefit
all human kind, decided he would start
a journey to find him, and so he did.
The two wise men engaged in conversation,
exchanging rational and healthy notions
that more or less were spoken in this fashion:

-Enlightened man, please tell me, what's the trait
that sets apart a wise man? - Good behavior.
-Among wise men whom would you choose? -The
[one
who speaks well, not too much, and acts much
[better.
-What is the school that will make a man wise?
-Experience, study and great suffering.
-Are the good laws sufficient by themselves
to regulate a nation and a state?
-Without good conduct even good laws are
excellent tools without an artisan.
-Could you explain to me what is that vice
that everyone knows as hypocrisy?
-It is the wealth of homage and tribute
that wickedness to virtue pays. -Among
earth idols, past and present, which one has
a greater following and cult? -Gold does.
-What is this life we lead? -A game of chess.
When over, kings and pawns go in a chest.
-Who is the happiest man here on earth?
-He who thinks so. -Who's the unhappiest?
-He who thinks so. -And who while he's awash
with money, thinks he's poor? -The greedy man.
-Can you tell me who is the richest man
on this our planet? -He who desires least.
-It's brave twixt troubles not to get depressed?

310

da deci in deci a meriti s'è junta.
- Cos'è l'onuri? - È di virtù l'impronta,
ch'in mancanza di chista oggi si appronta.
- Senza li grazii comu cridi e chiami
tu la biddizza? - L'isca senza l'ami.
- Cui da l'amuri grati frutti cogghi?
- Cui non gilusu ama la propria mogghi,
e chi o cridi a la ceca, o è ben fundatu
essiri da la stissa riamatu.
- Di un omu comu l'indoli svelari?
- Mettilu in libertà di fari e sfari.
- Cui si valuta chiù di quantu vali,
ch'impressioni all'àutri fa? - D'armali.
 - Cui l'amicizii attacca e fa durari?
- L'ugual'induli e modu di pensari.
- La conseguenza di quant'ora dici
dunca qual'è? - Chi nui saremu amici. -

Yes, but it's braver to stay meek upon success.
-What is nobility? -A zero, but it counts
from ten to ten in merit if it's added.
-What's honor? -It's the mark of virtue: lacking
the latter, now the former is made ready.
- What do you think of beauty without grace?
Have you a name for it? -Bait without hook.
-Who's able to obatin good fruits from love?
-The man who loves his wife without jealousy
and he who thinks quite blindly, or who has
good evidence that he is loved by her.
-How can one know a man's true character?
-Grant him the freedom to do as he wants.
-He who believes he's worth more than he is,
what image does he cast? -That of an ass.
-What makes good friends and makes them last?
-Same dispositions, thinking the same way.
-Therefore, what do you think the consequence
will be for what you said? -That we'll be friends.-

Dissiru, e s'abbrazzaru tutti dui,
l'unu di l'àutru sodisfattu. Intantu
vannu suprajuncennu sempri chiui
l'odituri, chi aspiranu a lu vantu
di apprenniri la bona saviizza,
ch'in chiddi tempi era stimata, oh quantu!
(Tempi felici!) ogn'unu cu ducizza prega
lu Saggiu a sediri e parrari
di la scienza, chi li cori addrizza,
ed iddu cussì metti a perorari:

The two of them so spoke and then embraced
each other, both completely satisfied.
Meanwhile new listeners arrived in greater
numbers, all of them wishing to acquire
wisdom and knowledge, which in the old days
was held in great esteem, (oh happy times!).
Each person sweetly begged the wise old man
to sit in comfort and to speak about
the science that men's hearts can straighten out,
and thus he started to expound as follows:

"O tu chi fari voi vita decenti,
e li scogghi scanzari di l'erruri,
osserva sti precetti esattamenti:
   Primu adempisci cu lu Creaturi
a tutti l'importanti toi doviri,
poi cerca tra lu munnu a farti onuri.
   Di li talenti nun t'insuperbiri;
cedi a la verità, nè ti ostinari
pri amur propriu, o pri pompa di sapiri.
   Autri chi onesti genti 'un frequentari,
cun iddi accorda li toi sentimenti,
cerca in iddi d'apprenniri e imparari.
   Quannu intraprenniri un affari tenti,

"O you who want to live a decent life,
and to avoid the hindrances of errors,
be sure to follow these precepts with care.
   First, your important duties satisfy
toward the Creator, and then you should try
to earn respect in matters of this world.
   Do not grow arrogant for your good skills,
give way to truth, nor be inflexible
for love of self or showing off your wit.
   Don't frequent anyone save honest folk,
and harmonize your feelings with their own,
attempt to learn from them and understand.
   When you're about to start a novel venture,

chiddu chi pò avvinirni ti schera
a la tua fantasia tuttu presenti.
    Cerca di dipurtariti in manera
da essiri pri li meriti esaltatu,
non pri maneggi o via pocu sincera.
    Lu to discursu sia sempri adattatu
a chiddi cu cui parri, e teni cura
di nun nesciri mai di siminatu.
    Tra li discursi toi risplenda pura
la verità. Sinceru, a l'occhi mei
lu facchinu da nobili figura:
    e da vili figuranu, e plebei,
li magnati si sù finti e buggiardi:
fidanu supra la buggìa li rei.
    Chista li cori fa vili e codardi,
lu decoru di l'omini sfigura,
e li porta a lu fossu o prestu o tardi.
    Di non smentiri cu li fatti cura
la lingua tua: s'impegni la parola
sia chista inviolabili e sicura.
    Prima però chi da la vucca vola
zoccu prometti, masticalu beni,
riflettilu e profitta di sta scola.
    Un gratu abbordu e affabili susteni,
non già familiari, ma decenti,
e francu cu qualunqui chi ti veni.
    A l'improntu 'un decidiri mai nenti,
ma prima a la valanza appenni e pisa
raggiuni e circustanzi esattamenti.
    Ama, ma senza intressu, ed ogni offisa,
senza puntu avviliriti, perduna,
cussì un'anima granni si palisa.
    Cu chiddi chi produssi la furtuna
a li gradi eminenti, sii summissu
senza bassizza vili ed importuna.
    Teniti in gustu a tutti, chi a lu spissu
qualchi pitrudda servi da maramma,
e trovi in qualchi amicu àutru te stissu.
    Liti non intraprendiri, chi ciamma
ti attiri in casa tua, chi la divora;
e s'àutru perdi un vrazzu, tu na gamma.
    Cura l'intressi proprii, nè fora
intricàriti a scopriri e sapiri
l'interni affari di qualch'àutru ancora.

let your imagination visualize
before your eyes whatever can occur.
    Try to behave in such a way that you
will be exalted for all your good deeds,
not for your deft moves or your crooked ways.
    Your speech should always be adapted to
the folks who stand before you, and beware
of ever straying from the beaten path.
    Let truth straightforward shine through your discourse.
The lowly porter, if he is sincere,
presents a noble figure to my eyes,
    and fake and vulgar will tycoons appear
if they are liars and deceitful men;
those who are evil put their trust in lies.
    And these make their hearts cowardly and low,
destroying men's decorum, driving them
sooner or later, to their sorry grave.
    Take care not to let facts negate the truth
of what your tongue declares; if you then give
your word, let it be sure, infrangible.
    Before your promise flies out of your mouth,
however, chew it well, reflect on it
and try to gain some profit from this school.
    An affable and kind rapport maintain,
not so familiar, but decent and dignified
with anyone that you may chance to meet.
    Never decide a thing right on the spot,
but first hang motives and all circumstances
upon the scale and weigh them with precision.
    Love, but without interest, and forgive
all insults, without feeling low at all;
that's how a great soul manifests its worth.
    With those whom fortune raised to high positions,
submissive be, but without cowering
or groveling quite inappropriately.
    Be in good terms with everyone, for often
a little grease is good to oil the gears,
and find another you in some good friend.
    Don't start a quarrel, for you will attract
a fire inside your house that will devour it;
an arm they'll lose, but you may lose a leg.
    Mind your own business and out of it
don't try to meddle in or yet discover
the innermost affairs of other men.

'Mpresta, ma senza frutti, e fa piaciri;
ma 'mpresta cu giudiziu e cu prudenza;
favuri fanni a tuttu to putiri.

Si ti obliga un doviri, ricumpenza
cu bona grazia, e sempri nobilmenti:
cussì cui è gratu e generusu penza.

Bilancia entrati e spisi esattamenti,
e pensa chi lu prodigu e l'avaru
l'unu mori, autru campa da pizzenti.

Nun ti mustrari singulari e raru,
nun figurari mai nè chiù nè menu,
ma chiddu chi tu sì dimostra chiaru.

Li vani desiderii teni a frenu,
sacci chi lu chiù riccu di lu munnu
è chiddu chi desidera lu menu.

Cumpatisci li miseri, chi sunnu
oppressi da disgrazii, e cu l'amici
sii veru amicu di lu cori in fnnnu.

Supporta d'iddi li difetti, e dici
dintra te stissu: Eu puru aju li mei;
semu tutti macchiati di na pici.

Si provi traversii, disastri rei,
nun t'avviliri, ma fatti coraggiu,
nè sfugari cu l'àutri li nichei.

Duvi regna discordia tu da saggiu
porta la paci: nun ti vindicari
chi cu li beneficii di ogni oltraggiu.

Riprendi senza asprizza, e si a lodari
lu meritu t'invita, la tua lodi
sempri luntana sia da l'adulari.

Ascuta compiacenti, e ridi e godi
di l'onesti motteggi e li toi sali
sianu decenti, naturali e sodi.

Riguarda ogn'omu quasi originali
tra lu so impiegu, e pri ostentazioni
nun criticari mai, nè diri mali.

Sii lu modellu di li cori boni gratu
a li benefizii, e li toi detti
paga, si n'ai, senza dilazioni.

Preveni di l'amici toi diletti
li bisogni, e sparagna a li mischini
la pena di scopriri li soi petti.

Da, ma nun dari pri secunni fini,
nè pri fama di splendidu acquistari,

Lend money, but without a gain, and do
as many favors as your means allow,
but lend judiciously and with discretion.

If you are bound by obligation, pay
the recompense with grace and dignity:
a grateful, generous man thinks this way.

Balance your income and expense with care
and think of the spendthrift and greedy man:
the first one dies, the other lives as scrooge.

Don't try to show you are unique and rare;
don't ever seek attention markedly,
but demonstrate quite clearly who you are.

Your futile longings keep under control;
know that upon this earth the wealthiest
of men is he who craves for things the least.

Have pity for the poor who are oppressed
by sore misfortunes and with your own friends
be a real friend, deep in your heart and soul.

Accept all their defects and then admit
to your own self that you too have your flaws;
we are all tarnished by the same black tar.

If you encounter adverse winds and sore
disasters, don't be downcast. Be brave
and don't take out on others your despair.

Where disagreement reigns, be the wise man
who brings the peace; don't seek revenge, except
with benefits for each offense against you.

Rebuke without asperity, and if
you're called by merit to give praise, let then
your praise be ever far from adulation.

Listen contentedly, laugh and enjoy
the honest anecdotes, and let your own
be decent, natural, in moderation.

Consider each man an original
in his own trade, and do not criticize,
or speak ill ever out of ostentation.

The model be for the good-hearted men,
grateful for benefits, and pay your debts,
if you have any, without procrastination.

Anticipate the needs by your close friends
and spare the wretches the humiliation
of opening their hearts before your eyes.

Give, never for ulterior motives though,
nor to acquire a splendid reputation,

nè ch'oltrepassi mai li toi confini.
Ma guardati però di rinfacciari
in jocu o in seriu mai li complimenti,
a l'amici comuni confidari.
Si ti scomponi na bili nascenti,
frenanni li trasporti; e 'un diri mali,
multu menu di cui nun è presenti.
Campa sobriamenti, e in modu tali
regula li toi entrati chi ti avanzi
pri l'infortunii qualchi capitali.
Di lu Governu e di li soi finanzi
nun t'impicciari; bada a dari assettu
a la tua casa ed a li toi sustanzi.
Ossequia, loda e tratta cu rispettu
qualunqui omu, ch'in arti o tra scienzi,
tra saggizza s'è risu perfettu.
Nun ti tenti l'invidia, e si tu penzi
di superarni alcunu, li toi fatti
lu dimustrinu, e non li maldicenzi.
Cu li servi ducizza e boni tratti,
confidenza non già, sgarbi ni abbuschi;
allisciati sgranfugnanu li gatti.
L'intressu tra lu jocu nun t'offuschi,
sempri serenu e placidu discurri,
nè sianu l'occhi a li doviri luschi.
Pensa aggiustatu, e parra quannu occurri
lacconicu, benignu e senza ingannu;
gradisci tuttu, e quannu poi succurri.
Segretu granni in ogni pena e affannu
è di lu guardu sutta tia fissari,
e non in chiddi chi supra ti stannu.
Li debbituri non tiranniggiari,
usacci boni modi. Si un segretu
t'è confidatu, nun lu rivelari.
Tra lu trattari sii sempri discretu;
nun ti vantari di li preggi toi,
li sannu o nun li sannu, sta cuetu.
Scanza da lu to cori quantu poi
li forti ed inquieti passioni,
chi fannu naufragari anchi l'eroi.
Tra l'andamenti toi, quantunqui boni,
guardati da l'estremu viziusu:
sta tra lu menzu la perfezioni.
Si acquista la virtù sulu cu l'usu:

nor let the deed be known outside yourself.
And do refrain from ever holding anything
against someone in jest or seriously,
or yet confide it to your common friends.
If an emerging bile is making you upset,
restrain the anger; and do not speak badly,
especially of those who are not present.
Live soberly and act in such a way
to regulate your income so you'll have
a bit of cash for any accidents.
Don't be concerned about the government
and its finances: worry just to mend
your own household and your own property.
Pay homage, praise and treat respectfully
any man who, in science and the arts
or through his wisdom has perfection reached.
Let envy not entice you, and if you
believe you have surpassed someone, your deeds
will show it, not your gossip or hearsay.
With servants use sweet ways and be polite,
never familiar though, for you'll be slighted:
when cats are stroked, they turn around and scratch.
Let interest in gambling not blind you;
ever serenely speak and evenly,
nor turn your eyes to fraudulent affairs.
Speak suitably and only when you need,
laconic, caring, and without deceitfulness.
Accept all things and when you can, give aid.
The greatest secret for each care and woe
is to regard the folks who are below,
and not the ones who stand above yourself.
Your debtors do not tyrannize, but treat
them with good manners. If someone
tells you a secret, do not make it known.
Dealing with others, always be discreet.
Don't boast about your worthiness, be cool,
whether they know your qualities or not.
Purge from your heart as much as possible,
the strong and restless appetites that make
even the heroes sink below the waves.
In all your acts, as good as they may be,
from vices of excess you ought to flee:
perfection always stands half-way between.
Virtue can be acquired only through its use.

perciò cu sti precetti anchi ci voli,
pr'essiri un omu saggiu e virtuusu,
chi adoperi chiù fatti chi paroli".

Therefore with these precepts you also need,
so as to be a wise and worthy man,
to utilize just fewer words, more deeds."

LU SPECCHIU DI LU DISINGANNU SIA LA CUGGHIUNIATA

Oh! vera inclita matri di li Dei,
basi e sustegnu di l'illustri eroi,
scinni, ti prego, ntra li versi mei,
Cugghiuniata, cu li grazii toi.
Pri tia sunnu spassi li nichei,
lu spusu abbrazza li figghi non soi,
la summa di li cosi è in tia appujata,
e 'un si rispira chi cugghiuniata.

Oh! ch'è beddu lu munnu cuncirtatu,
oh! chi machina immenza, oh! chi stupuri,
l'omu! Oh poi l'omu è privilegiatu,
ogni cosa è criata in so favuri.
Benissimu. Vossia ha chiacchiariatu?
Vossia mi dica: Nn'ha avutu duluri?
Vicchiaia, camurria, nn'ha mai pruvata?
Provi è poi vija, s'è cugghiuniata.

Oh! la gran primavera, oh! comu ridi
fra ciuri ed ervi la campagna tutta!
L'estati ohimè, lu càudu nni ocidi,
la terra ciacca, ogni riconca è asciutta;
l'autunnu poi di frutti nni providi;
l'invernu nni sequestra a stari sutta;
'nzumma di beni e mali crapiata,
passau l'annu: chi fu? Cugghiuniata!

Oh! ch'è beddu lu mari, oh! l'orizonti
comu vagu si pinci ntra l'alburi!
Eccu lu carru chi guidau Fetonti!
Eccu la bedda stidda di l'amuri!...
Ohimè si turba! Ohimè! comu sù pronti
li turbini, chi apportanu l'orruri,
ohimè, comu di ventu un rufuluni
la navi s'agghiuttiu! Cugghiuniuni!

È prena, figghia, e l'omu picchiannu
nasci, poi fa lu cuntu, poi si smamma,
poi cuva, poi valori e ogn'àutru affannu,
di poi va sulu e dici pappa e mamma,

The Mirror of Disillusionment, that is, Mockery

True worthy mother of the godly race,
of heroes of renown, base and support,
descend upon my verse with all your grace,
descend, o Mockery, you I exhort!
Because of you a groom may yet embrace
children of others: woes for you are sport.
The sum of things is in your custody,
and nothing else exists but Mockery!

The world's arranged in such a lovely way!
What wondrous thing is man! What complex brain!
And man is privileged in every way!
All things have been created for his gain!
Oh, very well! Now that you've had your say,
please tell me, Sir: have you felt any pain,
known gonorrhea and old age? You'll see,
when you have tried them, if it's Mockery!

Oh, how the fields do smile in time of spring,
with grasses and with flowers everywhere!
Alas, the summer kills us with its sting,
the ground's completely cracked, each pool is bare;
the autumn then her fruit for us does bring,
but winter keeps us in its frigid snare.
With good things and with bad, then, finally,
the year elapsed. What was it? Mockery!

How lovely is the sea! Oh, how at dawn
horizon's rim is painted with delight!
The chariot behold of Phaeton!
Behold, the lovely star of love's in sight!
Alas, the weather's changed. How quickly spawn
the whirlwinds that leave horror in their flight.
Alas, that sudden burst of wind at sea
swallowed a ship! Oh, what great Mockery!

She's pregnant, she gives birth, and wailing, man
is born. He stammers, then he's weaned, anon
cuts his first teeth; small pox comes next, and then,
come woes of every kind; he walks alone,

316

poi crisci e va li donni assicutannu;
gira, viaggia, acquista; già la gamma vacilla,
è vecchiu, mori e in tri assaccuni
la scena già finiu, cugghiuniuni!

Oh! Chi bedda picciotta! Oh ch'è sciacquata!
Oh chi sangu! Oh chi vezzi! Oh chi attrattiva!
Ah! mi la vogghiu tèniri abbrazzata,
ah! lu so alitu stissu mi ravviva:
mettiti bona, figghia nzuccarata,
proi ssu labbru... Apri ssi cosci... oh! viva!
Moviti, stringi... Oh estasi biata!
Ticchi, ticchi, finiu... Cugghiuniata!

Chi pezzu d'omu bonu! Chiesa e casa,
criditimi na pagghia nun ci pisa,
ogni santuzza chi vidi la vasa
e 'un si la tocca chi cu la cammisa.
Ah! mariolu, è fatta già la vasa,
avi chiù impieghi mmanu ch'un ci pisa
e l'orfana e la vidua c'è affidata,
la chiù chi frutta è sta cugghiuniata!

Cugghiunia Furtuna, chi a l'avaru
pri sua felicità mustra un tesoru.
Natura cugghiunia, chi a lu capraru
prumittennu ci va l'età di l'oru.
Cugghiunia lu cori, ch'avi caru
posti, ricchizzi, dignità e decoru;
sù sfilocchi di cutra a chiddi dati,
chi vonnu essiri chiù cugghiuniati.

Si dunca cugghiunianu l'aria e lu mari
e la natura e tutti l'elementi,
oh! nobil'arti di cugghiuniari,
oh! eterna e prima liggi di li genii,
oh! eroi di dui culuri chi a puntari
la vinisti a sti spiaggi espressamenti,
tu lu Cunfuciu sì, tu lu Maumettu,
tu vera stidda, tu profeta elettu.

Sarà, sarà a li seculi futuri
sagr'un *Cugghiuni* to supra l'altari:

---

says wawa, mommy; women chases when
he's grown; he travels, roams, and earns his own;
his leg is weak, he's old, the comedy
is over in three gasps: what Mockery!

Oh, what a pretty lass! What prodigy!
What spirit and what charm! What winning way!
Oh, how her very breath rekindles me!
Oh, how I want her in my arms to stay!
Oh, sugar-coated child, do lie with me!
Give me your lips... your thighs expose... hurray!
Strive now... hold tight... o wondrous ecstasy!
In-out... in-out... It's over: Mockery!

What a fine man! All church and home he is!
Believe me, feathers do not weigh him down.
He kisses every female saint he sees,
and he won't touch himself but with a gown.
The scoundrel's busy with conspiracies.
He handles everything without a frown.
He's made of orphans, widows a trustee,
but all his scheming ends in Mockery!

Thus fortune mocks all avaricious men,
by showing treasures as true happiness;
and nature mocks all simple shepherds when
to bring the Golden Age she does profess;
Alas, the heart is mocking you again,
when it holds dear decorum, wealth, success,
and pride. These are pall threads against those
            [stocked
who want to be, alas, more greatly mocked!

If then the air is mocking us, the sea,
nature, and elements of every kind,
o truly noble art of Mockery,
o first eternal law of all mankind,
o hero of two shades who purposely
came to our shore to give it to our kind,
Confucius and Mohammed, too, you are,
the chosen prophet, and the truest star.

In future centuries, upon a shrine
one of your balls will be a holy sight.

317

Dall'arsa zona, e dall'ursa minuri
d'unni Febu tramunta, e d'unni appari
lu pilligrinu *Cugghiuniaturi*
virrà stancu lu votu a sodisfari
notannu di lu tempiu a li lati
tra brunzi e marmi li *Cugghiuniati*.

From where Apollo rises and declines,
from Minor Bear and from the parched-out site
will come the weary Mocker peregrine
to realize a vow he made: to write
along the temple's walls, within a frieze
of marble and of bronze, his Mockeries.

This poem was probably written in Cinisi. It was recited by the poet during Carnival in 1779 in the home of Baron Lombardo, a friend of Meli, and it was published with this title in Pisa in 1805. It was inspired by the same feelings of discouragement that the poet felt when he wrote the Heraclitus Elegies. See the introduction.

Ditirammu Sarudda	**Dithyramb: Sarudda**

Sarudda, Andria lu sdatu e Masi l'orvu
Ninazzu lu sciancatu,
Peppi lu foddi e Brasi galiotu
ficiru ranciu tutti a taci maci
ntra la reggia taverna di Bravascu,
purtannu tirrimotu ad ogni ciascu.
E doppu aviri sculatu li vutti,
allegri tutti misiru a sotari
ed abballari pri li strati strati,
rumpennu 'nvitriati
ntra l'acqua e la rimarra,
sbrizziannu tutti ddi genti
chi jianu 'ncuntrannu
E intantu appressu d'iddi
picciotti e picciriddi,
vastasi e siggitteri,
cucchieri cu stafferi,
decani cu lacchè
ci jianu appressu, facennuci olè.

Allurtimata poi determinaru
di jiri ad un fistinu
d'un so vicinu, chi s'avia a 'nguaggiari,
e avia a pigghiari a Betta la caiorda,
figghia bastarda di fra Decu e Narda;
l'occhi micciusi, la facciazza lorda,
la vucca a funcia, la frunti a cucchiara,
guercia, la varvarottu a cazzalora,
lu nasu a brogna, la facci di pala,
porca, lagnusa, tinta, macadura,
sdiserrama, 'mprisusa, micidara.

Lu zitu era lu celebri ziu Roccu,
 ch'era divotu assai di lu diu Baccu:
nudu, mortu di fami, tintu e liccu;
e notti e jornu facia lu sbirlaccu.
Eranu chisti a tavula assittati
cu li so amici li chiù cunfidati;
ntra l'autri cunvitati
c'era assittata a punta di buffetta
Catarina la Niura,
Narda Caccia-diavuli,

Sarudda, Andrew the flop, and Tom the blind,
Lame Tony, Crazy Joe, and Con-man Blaise
had eaten chow,
all paying their own ways,
inside the royal tavern of Bravascu
creating wild turmoil with every flask.
And after they had drained the barrels dry,
all mighty "high," they started leaping
and dancing in the street,
breaking windows,
jumping in pools of water and in mud
and splashing every "bud"
they chanced to meet.
Behind them grew a crowd
of children and young men,
porters, supporters of chairs,
coachmen and footmen,
deacons and lackeys,
cheering them on and crying "Olè!"

At last they all agreed
to join the feast
of their fast friend who was engaged to wed
Narda and brother Degu's bastard daughter
whose name was Lizabeth the Slob.
Watery eyes had she, an ugly dirty face,
a mushroom mouth; her forehead was spoon-like.
Half blind, her chin was a protruding ledge,
a flat pug nose, a shovel for a face,
she was a slimy, grimy, mean, foul wench,
lazy and crazy, murderous and whining.

The groom was the most famous uncle Ruckus
who was devoted to the old god Bacchus.
Dying of hunger, poor, mean and voracious,
he led a most ungracious bum's existence.
These folk were sitting at the banquet table,
together with their closest friends and kin.
Among the other guests,
sitting right at the table's edge,
were Catherine, black-skin,
Devils-chasing Narda,

Ancila Attizza-liti,
E Rosa Sfincia 'Ntossica-mariti.
Eranu junti a la secunna posa,
cioè, si stava allura stimpagnannu
lu secunnu varrili,
ch'era chiddu di dudici 'ncannila,
ben sirratu,
invicchiatu,
accutturatu,
e pri dittu di chiddi ch'annu pratica,
era appuntu secunnu la prammatica.

Quann'eccu a l'improvisu chi ci scoppanu,
e, comu corda fradicia, si jettanu
sti capi vivituri, li chiù 'nfanfari,
chisti sei laparderi appizzaferri,
chi sgherri sgherri dintra si cci 'nfilanu;
vennu ad ura ed appuntu, anzi l'incappanu
cu lu varrili apertu, e si cci allippanu.

Primu di tutti Sarudda attrivitu
stenni la manu supra lu timpagnu,
e cu un imperiu d'Alessandru Magnu,
a lu so stili, senza ciu nè bau,
a la spinoccia allura s'appizzau.

Poi vidennu dda 'ncostu na cannata,
di vinu 'mpapanata,
cu un ciauri chi pareva na musia,
la scuma chi vugghieva e rivugghia,
l'agguanta, e mentri l'avi ntra li pugna,
grida: "Curnuti, tintu cui c'incugna!
Tolama, tolama
sciallaba, sciallaba,
tumma, tumma, tumma,
cori cuntenti, e tummamu cumpa'!
Cannati, arci-cannati, anzi purpaini,
tumma, tumma, cumpagnu, a trinch-vaini,
chi cu na 'nzirragghiata di sciroppu
si campa allegru e si vinci ogn'intoppu,
e ci fa fari sauti, comu addaini.

L'avirrò pri un sollenni cacanaca,
erramu, tintu, putrunazzu e vili,

Angel Troublemaker,
Rose Dumpling who choked husbands for a song.
They'd reached the second stage;
that is, they had uncorked
the second barrel,
and one that cost more than a carol,
which had been gauged,
correctly aged,
to shine on any stage,
and which to hear men who should know
was made according to the rule of law.

When suddenly there popped in there,
just like a rotten rope whose threads have snapped,
six peerless master drinkers,
six good-for-nothing parasites,
who entered quickly and without fanfare,
at the right time, and catching them in fact
with barrel open, got into the act.

Sarudda shamelessly was first,
extending his right arm up to the spout
without a word, commandingly as though
he'd been a lord, another Alexander,
attached his mouth rght to the spout.

Then when he saw a mug of wine
filled to the brim,
exhaling a perfume that was divine,
covered with foam that bubbled on the rim,
he grabbed it and began to shout:
"Cuckolds! Woe to the man who dares approach!
Now lift it high, and gulp it down,
imbibe, guzzle, slosh it all down.
Let us drink, brothers,
and without a frown!
Bring mugs, bring jugs, and barrels too,
trinken, my brothers, *trinken wein*,
for if you sip this syrup through clenched teeth
you live with cheer and overcome all fear;
besides it gives us strength to jump like deer.

The man who won't get soused with us tonite,
who will not burst beside the ladle,

cui di nui chista sira 'un s'imbriaca,
e chi nun crepa sutta lu varrili.
Scattassi lu diàntani,
chi vogghiu fari un brinnisi
a Palermu lu vecchiu, pirchì in publicu
piscia e ripiscia sempri di cuntinu
ntra la funtana di la Feravecchia;
e pisciannu e ripisciannu
lu mischinu chiù s'invecchia.

Jeu vivu in nomu to, Vecchiu Palermu,
pirchì eri a tempu la vera cuccagna;
ti mantinivi cu tutta la magna,
cu spata e pala, cu curazza ed ermu;

ora fai lu galanti e pariginu,
carrozzi, abiti, sfrazzi, gali e lussu,
ma ntra la fitinzia dasti lu mussu,
ca sì fallutu, ohimè! senza un quatrinu.

Oziu, jocu, superbia 'mmaliditta
t'ànnu purtatu a tagghiu di lavanca:
tard'ora ti nn'avvidi e batti l'anca;
scutta lu dannu, pìsciati la sditta.

Ma vajanu a diavulu
st'idei si malinconici;
d'ora 'nnavanti in cumpagnia di Baccu
vogghiu fari la vita di li monaci,
quali cantannu, vivennu e manciannu,
campanu cu la testa ntra lu saccu.

Quannu di vinu
eu fazzu smaccu,
tutti li cancari,
tutti li trivuli
li pistu e ammaccu.
Sorti curnuta, m'ài sta grazia a fari,
chi cantannu e ciullannu, comu un mattu,
pozza tantu cantari, e poi ciullari,
pri fina chi, facennu un bottu, scattu.

Di stu gottu, chi pari na purpania,
mentri lu vinu in pettu mi dilluvia,

is nothing but a solemn parasite,
a mean lowlife who shits inside his cradle!
Now let the devil burst,
but I want to propose a toast
to old Palermu, 'cause it pees in public
with peeing that's continuous
inside the fountain of the Old Marketplace,
and as it does, the wretched cuss
is getting ever older with each piss.

I drink to your name, Old Palermu,
because you were the land of plenty once.
You lived in splendor and magnificence,
with armor and with helmet, sword and spade.

Now you're gallant, quite a *Parisien*,
carriages, wasteful spending, pomp, brocades.
This time your rump has fallen in the slime,
for you are bankrupt, and without a dime.

Idleness, gambling, and accursed pride
have brought you the edge of doom:
too late you tried to change your ways, alas;
so pay the piper now, pay through your ass.

But these depressing thoughts let's ban to hell!
From this day forward
I just want to dwell
like monks in Bacchus' company,
who keep their heads forever in a sack,
singing and drinking, munching on a snack.

When I consume
a lot of wine,
all of my cares,
all of my gloom,
just fade in air.
Grant me this wish, ungracious fate:
that I may sing and dance like mad
and that my songs and play would be so great
that in a loud bang then I may explode.

From this wine goblet looking like a pit,
while wine is pouring in my breast,

eu sentu, amici, na calura strania,
chi dintra va sirpennu cùvia cùvia.

Ed intantu li so effluvia
a la testa sinn'acchiananu;
mi gira, comu strummula,
mi va, comu un animulu,
mi fa cazzicatùmmula
lu beddu ciricòcculu;
li mura mi firrianu,
li porti sbattulianu,
lu solu fa la vòzzica,
lu munnu ohimè! s'agghiommara,
li tetti già trabballanu,
tavuli e seggi pr'alligrizza ballanu.

Sàrvati, sarva;
chi tirribiliu!
guarda, guarda, chi stravèriu.
Sinni vinni lu dilluviu!
Giovi à già sbarrachiati
catarratti e purticati!
L'àutu Empireu purpurinu
chiovi vinu: allerta tutti,
priparati tini e vutti.

Crisci la china,
ohimè! unni scappu?
Dintra na tina,
trasu pri tappu;
no, nun è tina,
pigghiavi sbagghiu,
è un quartaloru
senza stuppagghiu,
chi cula e chi pircula
l'ambrosia biata
dintra sta sollennissima cannata.

Dammi, o cannata
nàutra vasata ...
Chista è guarnaccia,
chi cui la tempira,
merita in faccia
sarrabbutì.

I feel, my friends, a warmth that's strange,
at best, snaking its way around inside my chest.

Its vapors now are rising,
they're going to my head
that's spinning like a top,
and running like a spindle;
my noggin
is aknocking,
it's doing somersaults.
The doors slam shut and open,
the vault swings back and forth,
the world grows tangled up,
the roofs seem to be shaking;
tables and chairs appear to dance for joy.

Take care, beware;
Oh what a mess!
Look out, look out, oh what distress!
The flood is coming!
Jove has flung open
flood gates and exits!
The High Empireum is raining
purple wine! Awaken everyone,
get barrels and get steins.

Alas, the flood has grown,
poor me, where shall I run.
I'll hide inside a vat,
and use myself as cork.
Oh no, that's not a vat.
Too bad it will not work,
it is a quarter tub
that does not have a cork ,
which seems to leak and perk
this blessed ambrosia
inside this fine carafe.

Give me, Carafe,
another little kiss ...
This is Vernaccia wine
that you must not dilute,
unless you want a boot
to travel up your ass.

L'acqua 'un fu fatta no pri maritarisi;
l'acqua fu fatta pri starisi virgini,
ntra lu mari, o ntra ciumi, o ntra nuvuli,
ntra laghi, o ntra puzzi, o ntra funtani,
pri li granci, li pisci e li giurani;
si l'ogghiu ci junciti, si sta sùvuli,
mmiscata cu la terra, fa rimarri,
mmiscata cu lu vinu fa catarri.

Dunca a menti tinitilu
stu muttu praciribili,
chi l'acqua mali fàciri,
e vinu cunfurtibili.

Cui disia di stari allegru,
viva sempri vinu niuru,
vinu niuru natu in Mascali,
chi pri smorfia signurili,
si disprezza in un barrili;
poi si accatta, comu archimia,
'mbuttigghiatu,
'ncatramatu,
siggillatu,
da un frusteri, tuttu astuzia,
chi ci grida pri davansi:
Tringh-lansi, vin de Fransi.

Pri la monaca racchiusa,
ch'avi sempri ostruzioni,
facci pallida e giarnusa,
isterii, convulsioni,
viva, viva a tuttu ciatu,
muscatu di Catania, o Siragusa;
nun è cura radicali,
ma minura li soi mali.

A li schetti affruntuseddi,
chi sù timidi e scurtisi,
Calavrisi
li sbulazza,
e li fa nèsciri in chiazza.

Li cattivi, li mischini,
chi su scuri e 'ngramagghiati,

Water was not intended to be wed;
water was made to keep its maidenhead,
unsullied, in the sea, in streams or clouds,
or in a fountain, in a well or in a bog,
for crabs, for fish and even for a frog;
if you add oil to it, it stays on top,
if you mix soil with it, it will make mud,
but water mixed with wine, will chill the blood.

This pleasing thought imbed
inside your head,
that water can do harm,
but wine has soothing charm.

If you want to live in joy,
drink black wine throughout your life,
the black wine that's made in Mascali
which when sold out of a stein
will be looked on with disdain,
but it's bought as an elixir
when it's bottled,
well tarred and sealed,
by a clever foreigner
who comes barking
in the square:
"Drink, my friends, this wine's from France!"

For the nun stuck in a convent,
who is suffering obstructions,
whose complexion's pale and jaundiced,
who's convulsive and hysterical,
Muscatel is the right juice
from Catania or Syracuse.
As a cure it is not radical,
but it will reduce her woes.

Single people who are shy,
who are timid and uncouth,
if they drink Calabrian wine,
it will make them want to fly,
and come to the public square.

As for widows, wretched folk,
who are mourning dressed in black,

e ànnu l'occhi sempri chini
di li tempi già passati,
pri nun aviri chiù filati e baschi,
durmissiru la notti cu dui ciaschi.

who have eyes filled with old things
that belong to their lives past,
they should rest next to two flasks
to get rid of their sad masks.

Maritati, chi o li siddi
o la scura gilusia
v'à livatu l'alligria,
e vi à risu laschi e friddi
si vui tummati malvacia di Lipari,
'nfurzati e quadiati, comu vipari.

Married folks, if you have lost
all your cheer because of worries,
or if sorry jealousy
has made you both cold and slack,
drinking Malvasia from Lipari
will put you right back on track.

Pri chiddi debuli,
chi ntra lu stomacu
ci ànnu lu piulu,
chini di viscidu,
di flemma e d'acitu,
cu facci pallida,
cu carni sfincida,
divinu viviri
lu Risalàimi,
ch'è sanatodos,
anzi è lu làpisi
di li filosofi;
e si vivennulu,
e rivivennulu,
nun si sollevanu,
nè si ristoranu,
torninu a biviri
a buttagghiuni
varrili e ciaschi,
finchì abbuluni
ci nescia pri l'oricchi e pri li naschi.

Folks who are weak,
who languish listlessly,
whose sour stomachs
are filled with phlegm,
who have heart burn
and acid churning,
who have no color,
whose skin is clammy,
must drink a lot
of Risalàimi,
a cure for all:
indeed, the stone of the philosophers.
If they drink it the first time,
and they drink it once again,
if their ills are still not cured,
or don't show much of a gain,
then they must drink a lot more.
In their gullets let it pour,
from the barrels and the flasks
till the wine will just explode
from their ears and from their nostrils.

Pri qualchi malinconicu mischinu,
ch'àvi l'occhi 'nfurrati di prisuttu,
e ntra un munnu, di beni e mali chinu,
lassa lu bonu e s'applica a lu bruttu,
chi sta mestu e distrattu ntra un fistinu,
e ntra làstimi poi s'applica tuttu;
vinu di li Ciacuddi lu quadia,
e lu guarisci di la sua fuddia.

For a fellow who's depressed
whose eyes see, but only dimly,
who where good and bad abound
chooses bad instead of good,
who mopes at parties, draping walls,
but complains in bitterness,
Ciacuddi wine will warm his soul
and will cure him of his madness.

Si qualchi bàcchiara,

If some *chubbette*,

simplici e tennira
senti ntra l'anima
qualchi simpaticu
vermi, chi rusica,
e prova spasimi,
sintomi e sincopi,
granfi di màtiri
cu affetti sterici,
ed àutri strucciuli
ntra ventri ed uteru,
si la voli poi 'nzirtari,
e scacciari
sti fantastici virmazzi,
viva Guarnaccia di li Ficarazzi.
Trinchi, tummi la Guarnaccia,
ch'un diavulu a nàutru caccia.

Bisogna conveniri, amici cari,
tutti li vini sunnu beddi e boni,
sunnu la vera ambrosia di li Dei;
ma in bona paci, dittu sia tra nui,
(sacciu chi parru cu li mastri mei)
lu vinu chiù eccellenti e prelibatu,
a miu pariri, è chiddu accutturatu.

Chistu vinu accussì finu,
chi da dami e cavaleri,
da magnati e da frusteri,
cu lu mussu strittu e 'ncuttu,
è chiamatu vinu asciuttu.

Li francisi 'nnamurati
vonnu vini delicati:
vonnu a Cipri ed a Firenza,
a Pulcianu ed a Burgogna,
a Sciampagna ed a Burdò;
jeu dirria, cu sua licenza,
ch''un sù vini chisti tali,
ma sunn'acqui triacali.

E si lu Inglisi si vivi la birra,
è signu incuntrastabili
chi ntra li soi ricchizzi è miserabili;
nui, chi vivemu vini spirdatizzi,

simple and tender,
feels in her soul
a worm-like squirming,
pinching inside her
and she feels throbbing
symptoms and cramps,
biting her womb,
causing hysteria,
and other trifles,
twixt womb and uterus,
to chase these awful worms
of her imagination
she can't go wrong
if she drinks Vernaccia from Ficarazzi.
Trinken Vernaccia, gulp it down:
one devil kicks the other out.

My dearest friends, we all agree
that wines are beautiful and fine.
They are the very nectar of the gods.
But without argument, let me just say
(I know I'm speaking to my teachers here!)
that the most excellent, the finest wine,
I will opine, is wine that's aged.

This wine's so very fine
that dames and knights,
nobles and foreigners,
with lips all puckered tight,
will call it a "dry wine".

French people who're in love
want their wines to be most delicate;
Wines from Cyprus or from Florence
from Pulciano and from Burgundy,
from Champagne and from Bordeaux;
But to me, excuse my gall,
these are not good wines at all,
they are waters spiced for show.

And if Englishmen drink beer
it is surely a true sign
that in wealth they're poor, indeed.
We who drink cheap, hearty wines

semu chiù ricchi di li soi ricchizzi.

Oh Casteddu vitranu, beni miu!
Ciamma di lu miu cori, vita mia!
A pinsaricci sulu m'arricriu,
lu gran piaciri, ch'eu provu di tia.

Oh Carini, Carini! Oh nomu! Oh idia,
chi mi trapana l'alma di ducizza!
Oh Alcamu! Oh Ciacuddi! Oh Bagaria!
ricettu di la vera cuntintizza!

Chiova sempri lu suli a vui d'intornu
l'influssi a li magghioli chiù propizii,
nè mai vacca ci arraspi lu so cornu,
nè ci accostinu mai merri e malvizii.

Oh Baccu allegra-cori,
straviu di li murtali,
ntra gotti e cantamplori
annei tutti li mali.
Pri tia lu munsignaru
dici la veritati;
lu pigru fai massaru;
scacci la gravitati.

Pri tia lu sangu tardu
rivugghi tra li vini,
pri tia si fa gagghiardu
cu' è debuli di rini.

La gilusia tu scacci,
asciuchi tu li chianti,
tu levi di la facci
l'affruntu di l'amanti.

Tu l'estru in testa attizzi
nun sulu a li poeti,
m'anchi a lu vulgu 'mmizzi
d'Apollu li segreti.

Bench'iu sia cuticuni,
avvezzu a li taverni,
un sulu to vuccuni

are far richer than they are.

O Castelvetranu, my own pride!
Flame of my heart, my life!
I'm in heaven when I think of you,
what great pleasure you provide!

O Carini, just your name, your thought
my soul drenches with delight.
O Alcamu, Ciacuddi, Bagheria:
you're a refuge of real happiness.

Let the sun rain all around you
the most propitious influences;
let no cow her horns come scratch,
let no crow or fowl approach.

O Bacchus, bringer of cheer,
soother of mortals,
with your goblets and your mugs
all our troubles disappear.
Those who lie, because of you,
will say only what is true;
lazy men will work hard too;
all grave thoughts just go skiddoo.

Because of you slow blood
starts boiling in our veins;
because of you a weakling
will grow daring in a flash.

You dark jealousy will chase,
every tear you cause to dry,
you take from a lover's face
all the blushing of the shy.

You the genius inspire
not only of the poets,
but to plain folk you conspire
to reveal Apollo's secrets.

Although I am uncouth,
accustomed more to pubs,
with just one sip of you

326

mi fa spacciari perni.	pearls will pour out of my mouth.

Vogghiu cantari,
vogghiu ballari,
vaja sunatimi
li scatagnetti;
vajanu a cancaru
corni e trummetti.
Nun vogghiu cimmalu,
nè viulinu,
mancu salteriu,
nè minnulinu;
chisti mi piacinu,
però mi spiranu
certu pateticu
chi fa addurmisciri!
E catàmmari, catàmmari
mi fa jiri in visibbiliu.

Si vuliti ch'eu canti na canzuna
vogghiu sunata la napulitana,
c'un tammureddu chinu di cirimuli,
cu lu liutu e la citarra chiana.

Amuri mi fa in pettu ticchi-ticchi;
lu senziu va pri l'aria ab hoc e abbacchi,
la bedda fa a la gula nicchi-nicchi;
ahimè!, ca scattu comu un tricchi-tracchi!

Veni, ca ti farrò salamilicchi;
ssi toi biddizzi quantu sù vigghiacchi!
Bedda cannata mia, tu fai li ricchi,
veni fammi a la gula tracchi-tracchi.

Caspita! caspita!
Mi pigghia sincupa,
nun pozzu chiù.
Già mi pricipitu,
cumpari Brazzitu,
tenimi tu.

Ahi, chi sintomu, ahimè!
Chi motu di riversu, ch'eu mi sentu!
Prima ch'eu mora ccà, comu un stè-stè,

I want to sing,
I want to swing,
come on and play
the castanets;
the hell with trumpets,
the hell with horns.
I want no fiddles,
or harpsichord,
not even psalters,
or mandolins;
although I like them,
they strike in me
a certain urge
to fall asleep
and willy nilly
I just go reeling.

If you want to hear me singing,
play for me a tune from Naples
with small bells on tamburines,
with the lute and flat guitar.

Love in my heart just goes ba-boom ba-boom,
my senses fly in air from here to there.
I see a beauty and I go a-voom, a-voom,
I think I'll burst like crackers in midair.

I'll kneel to you, "salam alecum," if you come.
Your beauty is too treacherous to bear.
You make the rich, my fair carafe, my plum.
Pour down my gullet and just go glo-glum!

Gracious, good gracious,
I'm kind of nauseous,
I'm gonna fall
on my calcaneus!
Dear brother Brazzitu,
please hold me up.

Ah, what are these symptoms!
What backward motion is what I feel!
Before I die here like an ass, my friends,

sintiti, amici, lu miu tistamentu.	please witness my last will and testament.

When my soul bursts, I want to be baptized
inside a monastery in the presence
of Lombard tavern keepers as a pack,
holding carafes and barrels on their backs.

Quannu mi scatta l'arma e lu battisimu,
vogghiu chi vegna in locu di cunventu,
cu li carrabbi in manu e vutti in coddu,
tuttu tuttu l'interu lummardìsimu.

I want these bones of mine to rest inside
a vat filled to the brim with wine so fine
that even a king's palate will be satisfied.

Vogghiu chi l'ossa mei stassiru a moddu
dintra na tina, china a tinghi-tè
d'un vinu, chi pò vivirni lu re.

I don't want to be laid out on the ground,
but in a warehouse, within city walls.
I want you to construct a mausoleum,
three feet in height or more above the floor,
three casks upon each other and me on top.

Nun vogghiu essiri espostu supra terra,
ma ntra lu Burgu, dintra un magasenu,
vogghiu chi si facissi un musuleu,
àutu tri canni, e chiù, di lu tirrenu,
di stipi supra stipi, e supra jeu.

And on that day, in memory of me,
let them break goblets, mugs, and jugs
give all the taverns and the quater casks
the task of sounding off my farewell dirge.

Si spezzinu ddu jornu in mia memoria
gotti, carrabbi, carrabbuni e ciaschi;
sunassiru li tocchi e li martoria,
li quartalori e tutti l'incantini.

Each tavern and each keeper with full mouth
must sing aloud and help to glorify
the practice of grape-stomping and must-bottling,
never allowing their mouths to go dry.

A vucchi chini, taverni e facchini
ànnu a cantari ed ànnu a celebrari
l'offiziu di vinu pistammutta,
senza ristari mai cu vucca asciutta.

I leave you, friends, in company of wine;
the only peerless secret that exists,
that happiness can hand upon a plate,
in spite of unpredictable, mean fate.
And when you reach a blissful drunken state,
this world replete with troubles, filth and woe,
will have become a stage of pure delights
as though a magic art had made it so.

Vi lassu ntra lu vinu, o cari amici,
l'unicu gran segretu imparaggiabili,
pri cui putiti farivi felici
ad onta ancora di la sorti instabili;
e quannu arriviriti a 'mbriacarivi,
stu munnu, tuttu guai, 'mbrogghi e spurcizii,
a modu di portentu ed arti magica,
divintirà teatru di delizii.

Vainly, so vainly
many fanatics
blow empty smoke,
pumping with bellows,
building up pressure
in retorts and alembics
filled with strange mixtures,
to find the universal medicine,

'Mmàtula, 'mmàtula
tanti spargirici,
tutti s'affumanu,
ciusciannu mantaci,
fannu premiri,
chini d'inchiastri e intrichi,
li storti e li lammichi,
pri circari a tanti mali

lu lapis, midicina univirsali.

Jeu nun negu chi si dìi;
ma nun sta ntra li burnii,
ntra li stipi e ntra l'armarii
di affumati aromatarii;
lu truviriti,
si giririti
di li lummardi taverni e facchini,
li stipi, vutti, quartalori e tini.

A li 'nnimici mei, pri camulìrisi
li civa di li corna, eu tutti lassu
ddi pinseri chi sfrattu, e mannu a spassu:
si smiduddàssiru,
sfirniciassiru
circa l'origini
di munnu e d'omini,
di venti e grandini.
Pri quali causa
nun pò firmarisi
un mulu, un asinu,
na petra in aria?
Pirchì producinu
nuàri ed orti
longhi li vrocculi,
chiatti li cavuli,
russi li fràuli,
citrola torti?
Pirchì lu vinu
dintra li fauci
nni punci e mùzzica,
gattigghia e pizzica,
titilla e stuzzica?
E l'acqua si nni cala
locca locca, muscia muscia!

Jeu sti dubbii, sti pinseri
nun li sciogghiu nè indovinu,
ma l'annegu, tutti interi,
ntra na ciotula di vinu.
Viju li genti a quattru a quattru! Ohimè!
Sta nuvula ntra l'occhi, chi cos'è?
La testa pisa assai ... chi cosa ci aju?

a cure for woes, the magic stone.

I don't say we should not look for it,
but it cannot be found in the glass jars
or inside the drawers
of smoke-filled perfumeries.
You will find it,
if you go look
in taverns and in Lombard pubs,
in barrels, casks, in vats, and tubs.

So to my enemies, so they may gnaw
the marrow of their horns,
I leave behind all worries
that I banish and send walking;
let them just rack their brains;
let them go nuts
to find the origins
of earth and men,
of winds and hailstones.
What is the reason
a mule or ass,
a simple stone,
cannot be stopped while in the air?
Why do the orchards
and melon patches
produce long broccoli,
flat cabbages,
red strawberries,
and bent cucumbers?
And why does wine
inside our gullets
tickle and bite,
stimulate and sting?
While water smooth and soft
pours down your throat?

All these worries and these doubts
I won't solve or guess about.
I'll just drown them as a whole
in a bowl of hearty wine.
I see folks in groups of four, ahi, ahi!
What's this cloud inside my eye?
My head is heavy, what is wrong?

Giovanni Meli

Li gammi nun annervanu!. .. chi fu?	My legs are rubbery, what can it be?
Jeu ca ... eu ca ... eu caju...	I'm going to fall, I'm ... falling ... down ...
Tenimi ... ajutu ... ivì! Non pozzu chiù!".	Hold me up! Help me! Jesus, I am blitzed!
Cussì lu su Sarudda	So uncle Sarudda,
'mmenzu la fudda lascu s'abbanduna,	surrounded by a crowd, let himself go
cu l'occhi 'nvitriati,	with glassy eyes,
li vrazza sdillassati;	and arms relaxed.
lu pettu mantacìa,	His chest is heaving,
parra già cu li naschi, e tartagghìa ...	he's talking through his nose, while stuttering ...
Abbucca ... fa un gran sforzu, e si ripigghia ...	He falls upon his head, gets up again,
Camina un pezzu ad orsa ... cimiddìa.	he walks a bit bear-like, and bending down,
Poi pigghia un stranfuluni ...si ricupa	then pulls himself up with a mighty effort.
gira ... sbota ... trabballa ... allurtimata	He stands, he turns, he twists, he dances for a bit,
bùffiti 'nterra na strimazzunata.	and finally he plummets to the ground.
Cursiru allura li cumpagni amati,	His loving comrades, each one in worse shape
tutti 'ngriciati ancora peju d'iddu;	than he was, quickly ran to offer aid;
lu spincinu esi-esi a cuncumeddu;	slowly into a squatting pose he was parlayed
poi ntra li vrazza, comu un picciriddu,	and then they lifted him just like a child,
si lu purtaru a cavu-cavuseddu.	and crossing their arms they carried him away.

This poem was written probably n 1786 and it was published in the first edition of his *Opere* in 1787. Many regard this poem as one of Meli's masterpieces. Other Melian poems in which the power of wine is exhaulted are "The Bacchantes," "In Praise of Wine," and "Hymn to Bacchus," all ncluded in this anthology.

Don Chisciotti e Sanciu Panza
Canto V

**Illustrations by
Beppe Vesco**

Giovanni Meli

CANTU QUINTU

Argumentu

L'Accidenti l'Eroi guida e proteggi,
facennu pr'iddu insoliti prodigi;
di pernottari in rumitoriu eleggi
Sanciu, e veni c'un monacu a litigi.
Don Chisciotti d'un magu a li dispreggi
dà ad un giganti e un vausu trafiggi;
dipoi cu Sanciu per un sbia-sonnu
si dannu pugna e cauci quantu ponnu.

1. Soli ingerirsi tra l'umani affari
un certu non-socchì, figghiu putenti
di la Fortuna, solitu scherzari cu tutti,
ed è chiamatu l'Accidenti:
chistu in jochi di sorti esercitari
soli l'imperiu so, li soi portenti;
e tannu godi e nn'avi cuntintizza,
quannu lu jucaturi chiù si stizza.

2. Regna ancora a lu nasciri di tutti;
iddu fa li vassalli e li patruni;
cui fa nasciri in tetti e cui fra grutti;
cui bassu, cui mircanti e cui baruni;
iddu forma li beddi, iddu li brutti;
perciò a li voti un'erramu jippuni
fa chiù fracassu, chiù gala e chiù scrusciu
di lu chiù riccu e sfrazzusu cantusciu.

3. Benchì è fraschetta, non ostanti è tali,
chi affari di rimarcu e d'impurtanza
li ruina c'un ciusciu, e a tantu vali
chi scoti ad Astria stissa la valanza;
mai si previdi, d'improvisu assali;
pirchì s'ammuccia in qualchi circustanza,
l'armi soi sù impalpabili, invisibili,
nun si cci bada e puru sù terribili.

4. Perciò spissu è fatali, pirchì sgridda,
ammucciatu ntra baddi di scupetta;
ora s'occulta dintra na faidda

CANTO V

Summary

Performing novel wonders for the Hero,
Accident guided and protected him.
Then Sanciu spent the night inside a cloister,
but there he came to quarrel with a monk.
A sorcerer's contempt made Don Chisciotti
battle a giant, but he struck a cliff.
Then he and Sanciu, just to pass the night,
each other kicked and punched with all their might.

1. A certain "don't know what," the mighty son
of Fortune, who is known as Accident,
is wont to play with all, and likes to meddle
in human enterprises and concerns.
He exercises his portentous hold
and his dominion over games of chance,
and only then he's satisfied and pleased
when gamblers to hot anger he has teased.

2. It's he who reigns supreme when we are born;
he makes of us a vassal or a lord;
he lets some come to life beneath a roof
or in a cave; he makes us merchants, short,
or barons. Ugly he fashions us or fair.
That's why at times, an old beat-up trench coat
can make a greater splash, gain more renown,
than the most opulent and rich silk gown.

3. Although he's flighty, still he can destroy,
quite weighty matters and important deals
by blowing air on them; he is so mighty
that he can even shake Astraea's scales.
Because he's wont to hide in circumstances,
he's not predictable, he strikes abruptly.
His weapons can't be felt or even seen;
you pay no mind to them, but they are mean.

4. He's often fatal for this very reason:
he secretly pops out of shotguns' pellets.
At times, he hides inside a little spark

e fa tuttu ddu dannu ch' 'un s'aspetta;
ora s'agnuna dintra na pupidda
d'un maritu gilusu, e si diletta
li contrabanni scopriri e li 'mbrogghi
di la fidili ad àutru, amata mogghi.

5. Stracanciatu di notti soli jiri;
s'ammuccia ntra purtuni e cantuneri;
cu vacabunni ci mustra piaciri
poi lu so sbiu sunnu li sumeri,
li proteggi e li pigghia a ben vuliri,
li tratta pri parenti e amici veri;
siccomu ancora è n'amicu viraci
di li bizzarri, capricciusi e audaci.

6. Infatti di l'audacia e bizzarria
di l'Eroi nostru s'era innamuratu;
tra periculi gravi l'assistia,
indivisibilmenti c'era allatu;
perciò vittoriusu nni niscia
da tant'imprisi in cui s'avìa ficcatu;
né criditi chi ancora moribunnu
lu lassi stari di lu ciumi a funnu.

7. Ntra li visceri alpestri di lu munti
per occulti canali e obliqui vini
trapilavanu l'acqui, chi poi junti
ntra li cavi voragini a la fini,
sbuccanu impetuusi, e fannu frunti
a vausi e grutti e a forza di ruini
s'annu incavatu ntra la rocca dura
na strata suttirrania ed oscura.

8. Incognita a lu munnu e a li viventi,
scurri un gran trattu l'unna in cechi grutti
poi a pedi di lu munti li soi argenti
mustra in facci lu suli e avviva a tutti;
bagna l'aperti campi a passi lenti
fecondanduli d'erbi, ciuri e frutti;
cadi in vaddi, entra in silvi e s'incamina
cu murmuriu suavi a la marina.

9. Di la cava voragini a lu funnu,
unni ciecu lu ciumi scaturia,

and causes damage one would not expect.
At other times, he will conceal himself
inside the pupil of a jealous husband,
and take delight to show the plots and strife
caused by his loved, to others-faithful wife.

5. At night he likes to roam alone disguised,
hiding in corners or in alleyway,
and he enjoys the company of bums.
However, donkeys are his real diversion.
He dotes on asses and protects them,
treating them as true relatives and friends
because he truly is a friend, I'm told,
of folk who are bizarre, capricious, bold.

6. In fact, he'd come to love our Hero's daring
and his eccentric ways, protecting him
in the most perilous of enterprises
and staying indivisibly by him.
That's why the Knight emerged victoriously
from many troubles that entangled him.
That on a river bottom he could leave
our dying Hero, you should not believe.

7. The waters seeped through underground canals
through crooked veins within the mountain's deep
alpine entrails and after filtering
through hollow chasms impetuously burst
inside large caverns and steep cliffs at last,
and there right through the walls of solid rock
they hollowed with their harsh, erosive force
a dank and lightless, subterranean course.

8. Within blind caves, the river flowed at length
unknown to living beings and the world.
Then at the mountain's base, its silver waves
emerged to face the sun, and give new life
to all; the open fields were slowly moistened
making the grasses, fruits and flowers grow.
Flowing through dales, it made sweet harmony
while crossing woods and streaming toward the sea.

9. Since he had fallen in the hollow chasm
from which the unseen river had its birth,

già cadutu l'Eroi, l'aggira 'ntunnu
lu vortici, chi strepita e firria;
ma l'Accidenti, ch'è sempri fecunnu
di menzi, pri cui teni in sua balia,
lu solleva e a chidd'unna lu cunsigna
chi scurri sutta placida e benigna.

the Hero had been struggling hard against
a swirling, noisy vortex of dark water.
But Accident, who's always most resourceful
and has the means forever within reach,
lifted him up and placed him on a wave
which gently flowed downstream inside the cave.

10. Ntra un lettu accussì morbidu sdraiatu
l'umidi passi di l'acqui assecunna;
pallidu, semivivu e rilassatu
cu nenti cibu e viviri ch'abbunna;
cussì scurriu gran trattu l'incavatu
suttirraneu canali, e quannu l'unna
a pedi di lu munti sbuccau fora,
sbuccau cun idda don Chisciotti ancora.

10. Reclining on so soft a bed, the Knight
flowed down along the water's humid course.
He was quite pale, relaxed, and half alive
with nothing much to eat and lots to drink.
He flowed for quite a while within that deep
and hollow, subterranean waterway.
The wave emerged below the mountain's base
and Don Chisciotti flowed from that same place.

11. A lu sbuccari detti un sammuzzuni
s'attuffau sutta e visitau lu funnu
senza siti tummau chiù d'un vuccuni
poi vinni supra, lassu e moribunnu
eccu nun ciata chiù, né lu pulmuni
da l'aliti magnanimi a lu munnu
lu sangu 'un gira, l'anima è sopita
ntra na vera parentisi di vita.

11. When he emerged, he did a somersault.
He dove and lingered for a while below.
Though without thirst, he drank more than one gulp,
then he came up again, worn out, near death;
alas, he breathed no more; upon this earth
his lungs sustained his noble breath no more
his blood stopped flowing; he seemed free from strife
in such a true parenthesis of life.

12. E manu e testa e gammi e coddu e vrazza
sù senza senzu, di l'unna in balia
l'unna li movi, l'unna l'arrimazza,
l'unna li gira, l'unna li carrìa
finalmenti lu 'mbrogghia e lu 'mbarazza
ntra junchi e cannizzoli, e si 'un juncìa
unu chi ddà vicinu aveva l'ortu
a la surda e a la muta sarrìa mortu.

12. His hands, his legs, his arms, his head and neck
were limp and at the mercy of the waves.
The waves made them revolve and beat them down.
The waves transported them, and dragged them far,
until they finally entangled him
in a cane brake among the reeds. Had not
a man arrived whose land was near the stream,
his death might yet have been a silent scream.

13. Lu sulitariu Sanciu afflittu e mestu
allatu ia di lu ciumi, pinsirusu:
"Quantu, diceva, ohimè! sfumanu prestu
li speranzi di l'omini ccà ghiusu!
O chi munnu 'mbrugghiatu e senza sestu!
Beatu cui in sua casa sta oziusu!
Chiù chi si cerca e chi si gira 'ntunnu,
chiù 'mbrogghi e guai si scoprinu a stu
       [munnu.

13. The lonely Sanciu walked along the river.
Sad and depressed he was and so he mused:
"Alas, how quickly fade men's hopes down here!
Oh, what a troubled and disordered world!
How very fortunate is he who stays
inside his home in idleness! The more
you seek on earth, the more you go around,
the greater are the woes there to be found.

14. Sempri aju avutu, ohimè! sti sentimenti!

14. "Alas! I've always had these sentiments.

Ma lu patruni e li soi gran librazza
m'ànnu insaccatu, ohimè! ca sti saccenti
sù armali e nun discurrinu capazza!
Stu grand'omu chi struggi 'ncantamenti
chi spila a li giganti li mustazza
chi raddrizza li torti a manu franca,
pirchì 'un addrizza a mia lu nasu e l'anca?

15. Quantu ni paghirìa si lu vidissi!
Chi sfogu vurrìa fari contra d'iddu!
Oh li soi libra 'mputiri l'avissi!
Certu 'un ci farrìa sentiri chiù friddu!
M'ammagava cu chiacchiari e promissi!
E m'infasciava comu un picciriddu!
La duttrina e valuri eu mi cridìa
ch'eranu boni cosi e sù pazzia.

16. Quali beni a lu munnu ànnu fruttatu
la duttrina e valuri di li genti?
Liti, guerri, omicidii, pri cui è statu
oppressu lu bon cori e l'innoccenti;
tanti librazza chi s'ànnu stampatu,
ànnu fattu lu munnu chiù clementi?
Chi fors'ora 'un s'arrobba e puddtrìa,
comu un tempu senz'iddi si facìa?

17. Chi forsi sannu chiù di mia taluni
chi ànnu sfugghiatu librazza e scritturi?
Chi 'un fui presenti quannu lu patruni
argumentava cu quattru dutturi?
Cui trattava lu suli d'un putruni,
chi stava fissu e sodu di tutt'uri,
cui dicìa chi girava comu un mattu;
'nzumma nun si cunchiusi nenti affattu.

18. Ch'aju bisognu di la sua duttrina,
pri godiri l'invernu di lu suli?
Senza l'anatomia e la medicina,
chi 'un aju fattu puddtreddi e muli?
Dunca a chi servi di sira e matina
sfasciarinni la testa suli suli?
Tutti li librarii ammuntuati
sunnu civa di corna allammicati".

My master, though, with his big, worthless books
completely blinded me. These learned men,
being so dumb, don't make much sense at all!
This great man who can vanquish magic spells,
who can pull hairs from the moustache of giants,
who rights all wrongs with such apparent ease,
why can't he mend my thigh and my poor nose?

15. Oh, how I'd make him pay if he were here!
Oh, how I'd vent my wrath against him now!
And if I had his books within my grasp,
I would make sure they'd never feel the cold!
His talk, his promises enchanted me;
he wrapped me round his finger like a child!
Doctrine and valor were good things, I thought,
now I believe they're things of madness wrought.

16. What good has ever come upon this earth
out of the people's worth and erudition?
Only harsh quarrels, murders, and great wars
that have oppressed good hearts and innocence!
Has this poor world been made more merciful
for all the worthless books that have been printed?
Perhaps, today the people don't have fun
or steal, as once without the books was done?

17. Can it be said some men know more than I,
for having leafed through rotten manuscripts
and books perhaps? Was I not there when Master
debated with four pompous Ph.D.'s?
One fellow called the sun a lazy bum
who never moves, and stays forever still;
madly the sun revolves, another preached.
But no agreement ever could be reached."

18. Have I need of his learning to enjoy
the warm sun on a cold and wint'ry day?
Have I not gotten little colts and mules
without Anatomy and Medicine?
So then whatever purpose can be served
to rack our brains both night and day alone?
The most renowned and greatest libraries
are distillations of brains' mockeries."

19. Cu sti riflessi aggiustati e maturi
(ch'è l'unicu vantaggiu e lu reali,
chi ni procaccia lu viaggiaturi
ntra coddu e gammi rutti ed àutri mali),
Sanciu jeva pinsannu a l'avventuri,
e conchiudeva ch'era statu armali;
ma supra tuttu poi l'amareggiava,
ca troppu tardu, ohimè! si nn'addunava.

19. With these reflections, timely and mature
(which are the only real advantages
the traveler receives together with his
worn legs, stiff necks, and other common pains),
Sanciu his past adventures thus recalled,
concluding that he'd been a dumb jackass.
What saddened him the most about his fate
was that he'd realized it far too late.

20. Junci duvi lu ciumi, in dui spartutu,
lasciava 'mmenzu un'isuletta asciutta
e un ponti vecchiu, e quasi già cadutu,
grida pietati all'acqua chi c'è sutta;
un rumitoriu simplici e spirutu
tra cersi antichi e frassini s'ingrutta:
"Ccà, dici, d'alluggiari aju spiranza,
si lu ponti ntra l'acqua 'un mi sbalanza".

20. He reached a place wherein the river forked
and left a little island in the middle.
There was an ancient bridge about to crumble
which asked for mercy of the waves below.
A simple, unassuming hermit's hut
he saw among the ash and old oak trees:
"The night inside this shack I'll spend, I think,
if that old bridge won't toss me in the drink."

21. Passa a gran stentu all'àutru latu
e scinni ntra l'isula, unni trasi
e s'incamina. Lu mischinu, in guardarla,
si sovvinni di chidda, chi cridìa tantu vicina:
"Lu meu serviri, ohimè! stu premiu ottinni!
Qual'isula lu Celu mi destina!
Uni sunnu li trummi e li tammuri
pri fari omaggiu a lu Cuvirnaturi?

21. After much struggle he made it across,
Stepped on the island and began to walk.
The wretched fellow, as he looked about
recalled the other isle he deemed not far.
"This is the prize my service has obtained!
This is the isle the gods reserved for me!
Where are the trumpets, say, where is the band
to greet the Governor to his new land?

22. Chi bedda gala chi portu cu mia!
Li scarpi rutti, un cileccu sfardatu,
na càusa chi tutta pinnulia,
un'anca zoppa e lu nasu tagghiatu!
E certu chi vol'essiri risia
truvari alloggiu e 'un essiri pisciatu:
oh vicenni di munnu! Oh stravaganza!
Nun c'è ntra li pizzenti cui m'avanza".

22. I am arrayed in elegant, fine clothes!
Old broken shoes, a worn out, ragged vest,
baggy old trousers, a poor crippled thigh,
a nose that's sliced in half! Nevertheless,
I should regard myself most fortunate:
I found this lodge and no one peed on me!
Oh, weirdness! Oh, vicissitudes of life!
The poorest man does not endure such strife!"

23. Trasi ntra un'urticeddu assai restrittu
d'insalati diversi e pitrusinu
c'è l'amenta, chi smovi lu pitittu,
mastrozzu, matricala e gersuminu;
dui rumiteddi cu lu mussu afflittu,
discurrennu, sidevanu vicinu;
Sanciu s'accosta e cu li manu 'mpettu
s'inchina dumannannucci ricettu.

23. He walked inside a narrow little orchard
where parsley grew and salads of all kinds.
There was mint there, to stir one's appetite,
and jasmine, bitter plants and watercress.
There were two hermits with turned-down, sad mouths
who sat by one another as they talked.
Sanciu approached with hands upon his chest,
he knelt and made for shelter a request.

24. "D'unni veni? Cui sì? Chi vai facennu?"
unu di ddi rumiti ci addimanna.
Sanciu rispusi: "Patri rivirennu,
jeu vegnu d'una rustica capanna;
aju giratu pri comprari sennu
di ccà, di ddà ramingu in ogni banna;
finalmenti 'mmiscatu cu lu fangu
truvàinni un pocu, ma mi custa sangu.

24. "Where are you coming from?" One hermit asked.
"Who are you? What's your business here?"
"Reverend Father," Sanciu then replied,
"I'm coming from a rustic peasant hut.
I've roamed the world, I've traveled everywhere
in order to acquire knowledge and wisdom.
At last, I found a bit, mixed with some mud,
but it cost dearly, for I paid with blood.

25. A costu d'anchi rutti e nasi muzzi,
d'affanni, di travagghi e di spaventi
di suspiri, di lagrimi e sugghiuzzi,
di fami e siti ed àutri patimenti,
aju vistu e tuccatu cu manuzzi
chi mai ci foru in munnu chiù potenti,
chiù granni, chiù sollenni e famusuni
asini, quantu mia e lu meu patruni.

25. And I have come to learn through first hand
                          [knowledge
by having paid the price with severed noses
and broken thighs, with toils and frightful scenes,
with sighs and tears and never ending sobs,
with famine, thirst, and many other pains
that there has never been upon this earth
such a renowned, more solemn, greater pair
of asses as myself and Master were!

26. Era longu, era siccu e assimigghiava
tuttu scurciatu a vostra riverenza;
a lu parrari li genti ammagava,
ed ogni sua palora era sentenza;
jeu cu la vucca aperta l'ammirava,
ma 'un c'è bugiarda chiù di l'eloquenza;
cosi chi 'un si putìanu imaginari
vi li faceva vidiri e tuccari.

26. He was quite tall and lanky and he looked
the very picture of Your Reverence!
The people were entranced by what he said,
for full of wisdom were the words he spoke.
I used to gaze at him with mouth agape
but there's no liar worse than eloquence.
He made you feel and touch with your own hand
those things that others hardly could invent.

27. Si fussi iddu ora ccà a lu nostru latu,
vui sarrissivu un magu in carni e 'nnossa;
un colpu 'ntesta 'un vi sarrìa mancatu,
o una scorcia di coddu grassa e grossa;
lu viditi stu nasu ch'è tagghiatu?
Iddu mi lu tagghiau dintra na fossa;
e fratantu 'un criditi ca jucava
si poi spiati ad iddu, mi stimava.

27. And if he'd been right here beside us now,
he would have seen you as a real magician.
A blow upon your head you'd have received
or yet a solid chop upon your neck.
Look, can you see this severed nose of mine?
He was the one who cut it in a pit.
Meanwhile, believe me, this was not a game.
To love me, if you asked him, he would claim.

28. Aveva un primu motu bestiali,
ma a trattarlu era poi n'apa di meli;
tinìa massimi eroici e reali
e ntra lu cori so nun c'era feli;
cu tuttu ciò patìa d'un certu mali
ch'essennu 'nterra si cridìa a li celi;
mendicu, si crideva un signurazzu;

28. His first reaction was quite violent,
but afterwards he was a honey bee.
He spouted regal and heroic maxims,
but in his heart he held no bitterness.
A certain malady possessed him, though:
being on earth, he thought he was in heaven;
being a beggar he believed he was a lord;

dijunu saziu, 'nzumma era un gran pazzu".

29. "Ni menti pri la gula, anima ingrata",
lu rumitu gridau comu un liuni;
'chist'è la fidi chi tu m'ài jurata?
cussì si parra di lu to patruni?
S'in canciu di la mia tagghienti spata
nun mi truvassi cintu stu curduni
e si tu fussi un pari miu, a stu puntu,
di zoccu ài dittu mi darissi cuntu."

30. Sanciu ristau na statua di marmu,
trasiculatu, e pri lu gran spaventu
lu mancu mancu appi a scurzari un parmu,
tantu si rannicchiau ntra ddu momentu;
tali na pasturedda di poc'armu,
chi mentri sta scippannu da un sarmentu
na rappa di racina, vidi in chidda
un scursuni, chi d'ira ardi e sfaidda.

31. Intantu umili e mestu s'inginocchia;
a lu patruni so caru e timutu
vasa li pedi, abbrazza li dinocchia;
ci addimanna perdunu e poi fa vutu
chi si videva na ficu, un'aprocchia,
un cavulu di ciuri arripuddutu,
duvìa sempri parrari beni d'iddu,
pri lu timuri ch'iddu 'un fussi chiddu.

32. Cu lu talentu so lucidu e nettu,
ma nell'antichi scoli coltivatu,
don Chisciotti accettau dd'attu imperfettu,
pirchì partia da un'omu limitatu;
cussì l'abbrazza e si lu strinci in pettu;
l'assicura d'avirlu perdunatu
e l'incoraggia poi cu vuci amica
di riturnari a la saggizza antica.

33. "Ah Sanciu! Sanciu! ah ingratu, ci dicìa,
quantu ti trovu, ahimè! quantu diversu!
Comu scurdasti la cavallaria!
L'anticu zelu, ahimè! comu l'ài persu!
Comu ti trovu senza pulizia,
ntra tanti erruri sprofundatu e immersu!

not having eaten, full. In short: out of his gourd!"

29. "You're lying through your teeth, ungrateful soul!"
One of the hermits like a lion roared.
"Is this the oath that you have sworn to me?
Is this the way you talk about your master?
If I were not still girded with this cord
which I exchanged for my sharp sword before,
and if you were my peer, a well-bred knight
you'd have to answer me for this great slight."

30. Sanciu was so dumbfounded he became
a statue made of stone. He was so scared
he truly must have shrunk at least a palm!
He wished to sink into the ground to hide
just like a timid shepherdess who sees,
on reaching for a bunch of tasty grapes,
the head of a black snake inside the vine
seething with anger and with eyes that shine.

31. Meanwhile, with sadness and humility,
Sanciu before his loved-feared master knelt.
Kissing his feet, embracing then his knees,
he begged forgiveness and he made this vow:
If ever he would see a fig, a nut,
a cauliflower withered and dried up,
he'd feel obliged to speak respectfully
for fear that each might Don Chisciotti be.

32. But Don Chisciotti, whose intelligence
was keen and sharp, and in the old schools trained,
accepted patiently that flawed behavior:
it came from one who had his limitations.
So he embraced him, and he held him close,
of his full pardon thus assuring him.
And then encouraged him with friendly tone
the wisdom to regain that was his own.

33. "Ah, Sanciu! How ungrateful you've become!"
he said." Alas, my Sanciu how you've changed!
How could you have forsaken chivalry?
How you have lost the ancient zeal, alas!
I've found you without cleanliness, immersed,
nay, in so many errors deeply sunk!

Ah! nun cridìa chi mi siccava in ciuri
sta pianta chi adacquai cu li suduri!"

Ah, never would I have believed the broom
I nurtured with my sweat would die in bloom!"

34. "Signuri, è tempu già di disingannu,
già ci aju vistu a li cosi lu funnu,
dicìa Sanciu, chi jamu firriannu?
Chi nni spiramu chiù da chistu munnu?
Quali acquisti nni jamu lusingannu?
Si pri nui siminati nun ci sunnu!
Sta terra 'un sapi daricci àutri frutti
chi disgrazii, amarizzi, ed anchi rutti.

34. "Master, it's time now to come down to earth.
I have already seen the bottom line,"
Sanciu replied. "What are we searching for?
What more can we expect from this our world?
What acquisitions can we hope to make?
Nothing's been planted here that bears our names!
This earth another fruit cannot supply,
save woes, misfortunes and a broken thigh!

35. Qual'isula mi resta chiù a spirari
da una sorti accussì cruda e nimica?
Chi sempri, ahimè! mi porta a sdirrupari
e chi di mali in pessimu m'intrica?"
"Anzi di chistu stissu ti a' preggiari,
l'Eroi ripigghia, bon'è ca 'un t'è amica;
la sorti è donna e a lu peju s'appigghia,
e l'asini e li bestii alliscia e strigghia.

35. What island can I still expect to get,
with such unfriendly, cruel destiny
that always leads me toward the edge of doom,
entangling me in things that go from bad
to worst?" "You should be proud of this, in fact,"
the Hero said, "it's good Fate's not your friend.
She is a woman and the worst she aids.
Asses and beasts with care she grooms and braids.

36. La sorti è pazza, ed è di geniu vili,
chi nun accorda mai li soi favuri
chi a li genti chiù infami è chiù crudili,
a latri, ad usurarii e tradituri;
lu veru eroi con animu virili
li doni di la sorti l'à in orruri;
pri mia lu miu triunfu chiù bizzarru
sarrà di strascinarla a lu miu carru".

36. Inclined to cowardice, insane is Fate
who never grants her favors but to those
who are the meanest, most disgraceful men,
to thieves, betrayers and to usurers.
The truly daring, virile-hearted knight
regards the gifts of Fate with utter dread.
The most fantastic triumph I may gain
will be to drag her bound behind my train."

37. Sanciu, doppu chi metti a mussiari,
dici: "Sti cosi sunnu beddi e boni,
cioè quannu s'avissiru a stampari
dintra un poema o ntra un'orazioni;
ma no quannu nni manca lu manciari,
o quannu la miseria nni scomponi;
si si camina cu sorti cuntraria,
virtù e valuri sunnu botti all'aria".

37. Sanciu began to twist his mouth in doubt,
and said: "These things are beautiful and fine
if they are meant to be in print; that is,
as poetry or figurative speech,
but not when we don't have enough to eat!
Or when we are beset with poverty!
If with opposing Fate one must contend,
virtue and valor one need not expend."

38. L'Eroi prorumpi: "Ohimè! chi cosa sentu!
In bucca d'un'allevu miu sti senzi!
Cui dunca in tantu miu travagghiu
e stentu m'à salvatu sin'ora? Cui ti pensi?
Cui dunca da l'orrendu incantamentu,

38. The Hero blurted out: "What's this I hear?
My pupil's mouth is uttering such words?
Who has protected me until today
in my ordeals and toils? Whom do you think?
Out of that fierce and horrid magic spell,

da pelaghi profunni e abissi immensi
mi purtau vivu a sti parti sicuri?
Cui fu? La mia virtù, lu meu valuri.

39. Cun iddi allatu intrepidu e costanti
vegnu di visitari nàutru munnu;
ddà nascinu li gioi e li diomanti,
ddà li mineri preziusi sunnu;
mi assaltau la disgrazia a l'istanti,
ma nun mi potti cacciari a funnu;
un torrenti m'agghiutti, ma poi sanu
mi salva la pietà d'un'ortolanu.

40. Ma tralasciannu li gran meravigghi,
ch'eu vitti ntra ddi pelaghi profunni
(sia tua gloria, virtù, chi sempri vigghi
pri aiutari a li toi, nè ti cunfunni,
doppu d'aviri scursu tanti migghi,
jeu vinni sanu e salvu supra l'unni;
ma però sarrìa mortu intirizzitu,
si ddà a casu 'un juncìa certu rumitu.

41. Chi, unitu all'ortolanu pietusu,
mi portanu a la sua cedda vicina:
ddà mi sfigghianu l'elmu ruginusu,
l'autr'armi e la corazza suprafina;
mi spogghianu di susu fina jusu,
m'asciucanu e m'annettanu la rina;
e pirchì 'un c'eranu àutri vistimenti,
in abitu ristai di penitenti".

42. "Signuri, dici Sanciu, eu timu assai,
chi la sorti di nui si nni diverti;
ammunsiddannu va guai supra guai,
tutti reali, tutti veri e certi;
e la felicità nun mustra mai,
chi ntra sonni, chimeri e cosi incerti;
senza vidirla curremu a tantuni,
ed idda sfui comu parpagghiuni.

43. Già nni pari pusata vascia vascia,
e nui ci jamu calati calati;
già già si pigghia, già s'afferra ed ascia,
ma poi strinciti e nenti v'attruvati:

out of the deepest ocean's wide abyss,
who carried me to these safe shores alive?
My virtue and my worth made me survive!

39. With them right at my side, intrepidly
and with unshaken faith, I visited
another world where gems and diamonds
have their beginning, where rich mines are.
I was assaulted quickly by misfortune,
but she could not make me sink to the bottom.
A torrent swallowed me, but safe and sound,
thanks to a peasant's mercy I was found.

40. The many marvels that I saw below
among those oceans' depths let's now omit.
(O Virtue, let the glory be all yours
because untiringly you help your own!)
So after flowing for so many miles,
I came up safe and sound above the waves.
I would have died a freezing death, alas,
had not a hermit by there chanced to pass.

41. Together with the merciful old peasant,
he brought me to his cell which was nearby,
and they unfastened there my rusty helmet, my
other arms, my breastplate superfine.
From head to toes they then undressed me;
they cleaned from me the sand and dried me off.
And since there were no other garments there,
I wore what penitents are wont to wear."

42. "Master," said Sanciu, "I am most afraid
that Fate is toying with the two of us.
She keeps on piling sorrows that are real,
and true, and certain, over other woes,
and never shows us any happiness,
except in dreams, in vain and doubtful things.
Although we see her not, we grope her way,
but like a butterfly, she glides away.

43. She seems to have alighted very low
and we on tiptoes try to capture her.
She's just beyond our reach, she's in our hands,
but then when we unclasp, there's nothing there.

si mustra arreri, ni tenta e ni 'nfascia,
e nui scurdannu li burli passati,
turnamu ad idda; poi lu ciatu manca,
apremu l'occhi e ni battemu l'anca.

She shows herself again, and coyly tempts us;
and we, forgetting her past mockeries,
resume the chase. Our breath gives out again
and we're left disappointed and in pain.

44. La sorti a miu pariri si assimigghia
a lu turnaru, e nui semu lignami;
ni fa strùmmuli d'unu, d'àutru brigghia,
d'àutru ghiummina, o fusi pri li dami;
lu fusu trova sempri cui ci vigghia;
la strùmmula firrìa pri la fami;
lu ghiumminu s'intrica tutti l'uri;
brigghiu e trastullu di li criaturi.

44. I think the operator of a lathe
resembles Fate and we are like the wood.
It makes a top of me, of you a skittle,
of others plummets, or spindles for the ladies.
The spindle never lacks for company;
the top forever spins with hunger pains,
the plummet gets entangled all the time,
and skittles are a joy for a child's game.

45. A mia m'avi pri brigghiu e ci scummettu
pirchì si nn'à sbìatu a crepa-panza;
a pinsari di vui nun mi ci mettu,
ma criu ca nun vi tratta cu crianza;
ni teni 'mpedi, ma 'un è tuttu affettu;
ni pigghia 'mmanu, ma poi ni sbalanza;
e forsi ancora sazia 'un è di nui
e avirrà robba assai pri tutti dui.

45. I bet that Fate considers me a skittle.
It has amused itself to bust a gut.
I will not even think about your case,
but I don't feel it treats you with respect.
Fate holds us up, but it's not all affection;
it takes us in its hands, then flings us down.
Perhaps, it's not entirely satisfied;
more woes for us, I fear, it will provide.

46. Pirchì cu' è natu pri fari la strùmmula,
gira e firrìa, ma sempri è a na banna,
in ch'è tisu e in chi fa cazzicatùmmula;
cui pri brigghiu la sorti lu cunnanna,
la testa si farrà bùmmula bùmmula;
ma non pri chistu la sorti tiranna
si placa o cedi o cancia di pinseri;
e si lu spinci, è pri ghittarlu arreri".

46. The man who's born to be a spinning top
will spin forever always in one place.
One moment he'll stand straight, the next he'll fall;
the man whom Fate as skittle has condemned,
will always have a head that's full of bumps.
But tyrant Fate will not be soothed for this,
nor will it yield, or change, its harsh attack;
for if it pushes, it's to push man back."

47. "Ah sceleratu! don Chisciotti esclama,
ah turcu cani, fidi di Maumma!
Tu cridi chi la sorti è qualchi dama
d'altu putiri e d'autorità summa?
Sorti da li filosofi si chiama
lu resultatu, o siasi la summa
chi da lu nostru liberu operatu
cu l'ostaculi fisici assummatu".

47. "Ah, scoundrel!" Don Chisciotti then exclaimed,
"You Turkish dog, believer in Mohammed!
Do you believe that Fate's a high-born Dame
who has supreme authority and power?
Philosophers know Fate as the result,
that is, the total that's obtained by adding
each physical impediment we meet
to things our own initiatives complete."

48. "Siasi 'nzoccu sia, rispusi Sanciu,
una cosa è sicura ed evidenti,
ch'eu s' 'un travagghiu e si nun sudu, 'un

48. "That may be as you say," then Sanciu said.
"One thing is sure and evident, that is,
if I don't work and sweat, I do not eat,

manciu,
ed àutru sedi, mancia e sta cuntenti;
e st'ostaculi stissi, si nun scanciu,
chi vi parinu a vui cosa di nenti,
fannu un muru di brunzu e forsi chiui,
ch'è situatu tra la sorti e nui".

but others sit and eat contentedly.
These same impediments, if I'm not wrong,
that seem so insignificant to you, in truth,
a wall made out of bronze create,
and maybe more, between ourselves and Fate."

49. Don Chisciotti fratantu era vutatu
cu l'occhi a la muntagna e riflittìa...
Quann' eccu un gran giganti smisuratu,
chi pri ddà costa rapidu currìa;
er'àutu chiù d'un migghiu e aveva allatu
na mazza (com'ad iddu ci parìa)
chi a na calata sula era bastanti
a scafazzari un tauru o un'elefanti.

49. Meanwhile, Chisciotti had begun to gaze
towards the mountain and was deep in thought.
Behold! An awesome giant soon appeared
running so ever rapidly across
the mountain slope! Much taller than a mile
he had a club with him (or so it seemed)
which was enough with just one single blow
to smash an elephant or buffalo.

50. D'un gloriusu ardiri eccu s'accenni
e grida: "All'armi! Olà, vegna la spata,
vegna la lancia. L'autr'armi tremenni;
addiu, tonica e vita arripusata!"
Sanciu, chi lu motivu nun comprenni,
resta sturdutu, comu si pitrata
avissi avutu 'ntesta; poi ripigghia:
"E mali, forsi, chistu chi vi pigghia?

50. A glorious daring then raced through his veins.
He cried: "My arms! Ah, quickly bring my sword!
My lance, my other dreadful weapons bring!
Goodbye, my tunic, life of rest, goodbye!"
Sanciu, who saw no motives for his cries
was stunned as if a rock has struck his head.
But then he asked, to solve the mystery:
"Is this another kind of malady?

51. Chi vi abbinni? Chi fu?" "Guarda, rispusi,
ddu giganti, chi curri ntra dda costa!
Comu avanza li rocchi machinusi!
Comu a gran passi versu nui si accosta!"
Sanciu a li primi accenti si confusi,
poi cu la facci pallida, ma tosta guarda
ed osserva l'umbra, chi ghittava
un grossu nuvuluni, chi passava.

51. What has come over you? What is the matter?"
"Look at that giant, running on that slope,"
said he, "how easily he overcomes
those rocky cliffs, how quickly he approaches."
When Sanciu heard that first account, he was
confused, but then—his face quite pale, but straight—
he looked intently at the shadow cast
by a big cloud which was just blowing past.

52. S'arrisetta lu sangu e respirannu:
"Chi semu miserabili! poi dissi;
quant'omini si vannu inquietannu
pri nuvuli e per umbri uguali a chissi!
Si cirnemu e si jamu esaminannu
li causi di li coluri e li rissi
truvamu chi sti mostri e sti giganti
sunnu nuvuli ed umbri tutti quanti.

52. His blood stopped racing. Taking a deep breath,
he then exclaimed: "How wretched can we be!
How many men grow restless and upset
for shadows and for clouds the likes of these?
If we but sift, and carefully examine
the causes of all riots and vexations,
we'll find these monsters and these giants are,
in truth, just clouds and shadows, nothing more!

53. Cu sti riflessioni veri e giusti

53. I am aware I'm wiser than the rest

sù saviu chiù di l'àutri, già lu viu,
ma saviizza, ahimè! quantu mi custi!
St'avanzi si sù fatti a costu miu!"
L'Eroi fratantu cu l'armi robusti,
tuttu spiritu, focu, arduri e briu,
va girannu la spata e sfida a morti
lu mostru, chi parìa superbu e forti.

54. Cussì ntra primavera lu sirpenti,
lasciata già la vecchia spogghia nuda
superbu di la nova ed insolenti,
mustra tri lingui e sta supra la cuda.
Sanciu ci dici: "E via cu st'armamenti,
chi vi criditi di pigghiari a Buda?"
Ma l'Eroi risolutu grida forti:
"Ccà nun c'è menzu: o fama eterna, o
  [morti".

55. Eccu s'abbia versu lu giganti
e mustrannu ch'è mastru di la guerra,
isa lu scutu di la testa avanti;
ora s'inquarta, ora si abbassa a terra,
ora stenni lu vrazzu fulminanti,

for these reflections are both true and right,
but, wisdom, how I've paid for you, alas!
Such progress has been made at my expense."
Meanwhile the Hero with his mighty arms
was full of daring, zest and eagerness;
he whirled his sword and challenged that great freak
who did appear quite strong and hardly meek.

54. Chisciotti looked exactly like a snake,
which having shed in springtime its old skin
shows its three tongues and stands upon its tail,
with insolence and pride in its new hide.
Sanciu exclaimed: "Enough with armaments!
Do you think Buddha you're about to catch?"
But loud the Hero screamed with all his breath:
"No middle ground: eternal fame or death!"

55. Behold! He started moving toward the giant,
and showing he was master of warfare,
he raised his shield up high before his head.
At first he parried, then he bent quite low,
then he extended that most dreadful arm.

ora si scopri tuttu, ora si serra,
ora s'affretta, ed ora fa li passi,
comu si appuntu l'ova scarpisassi.

56. Cussì lu gaddu d'India, quannu abbeni
lu cani, chi camina lentu lentu,
sbrogghia la 'nnocca, lu contempla beni,
dipoi va unciannu, comu un'utri a ventu;
stenni lu coddu, 'nzaia e poi si teni,
avanza un passu e poi si para attentu;
si concerta superbu e pitturutu
poi sbruffa pri li naschi un gran stranutu.

57. Tali lu nostru Eroi, tra l'armi chiusu,
s'avanza arditu cu la spata in autu,
e da guerreru espertu e cautelusu
cerca lu so vantaggiu e marcia cautu;
scopri di lu nimicu machinusu
lu ciancu disarmatu, e jetta un sautu;
eccu disigna na gran botta dritta...
Ma ci trasi ntra l'occhi na muschitta.

58. Sta muschitta, chi intattu lu so onuri
pensau di conservari, jia fuennu
un muscagghiuni, chi d'impuru amuri
ardia per idda, e la vinìa strincennu
già già la junci cu trasportu e arduri;
idda, vicina a lu gran passu orrennu,
trasi ntra l'occhiu e eleggi lu so giru
pr'onestu reclusoriu e ritiru.

59. Però chi certi istorici accurati
vonnu chi ntra stu fattu singulari
ci fussi intelligenza di li Fati
e chi si vosi apposta cuncirtari;
jeu lassu a locu so la viritati,
pinsativilla vui, comu vi pari;
'nzumma l'insettu, benchì vili, è tantu
chi l'Eroi nun po' teniri lu chiantu.

60. Tu chianci, don Chisciotti! Ah già
       [comprennu,
chista è la parti machinali e bassa;
pirchì l'insettu è dintra e va puncennu,

He left himself wide open, but recovered.
At times he'd rush, and then he'd raise his legs
and walk as if the ground were paved with eggs.

56. As when a turkey who begins to walk
extremely slowly when it sees a dog,
then stares at it, unfurling its red crest,
puffing itself like a goat skin in wind,
stretching its neck to test, then holds it back,
advances by one step and halts intently
prepares itself with proud, inflated chest
and sneezes through its nostrils with great zest.

57. Clad in his suit of armor, thus our Knight,
advanced with boldness and with sword upraised,
and sought, as would an expert cautious fighter
such as he was, to gain the upper hand.
Discovering the unprotected flank
of his portentous foe, he made a leap.
A huge straight lunge he tried to improvise,
but a mosquito pierced one of his eyes.

58. Intending to preserve her virtue whole,
this insect was then fleeing from a fly
that lusted after her with love unchaste.
The fly was drawing dangerously near
to capturing its prey with burning ardor.
But when she was at that horrendous pass,
the roundness of his eye she chose to treat
as her own honest prison and retreat.

59. Some well-informed historians maintain,
however, that this singular event
betrayed the art and cunning of the witches
who had arranged it all for their own goals.
I'll leave the truth in its own rightful place.
You're free to think about it as you please.
Though the mosquito was a lowly bug,
it made the Hero's face a tearful mug.

60. You weep now, Don Chisciotti! Yes, I know!
This is the vulgar and mechanic part,
  because the insect is inside and bites
and if you press the eye, the liquid flows.

si premi l'occhiu e lu licuri abbassa;
ma sti lagrimi, ohimè! pirchì nun vennu
quannu a la menti Dulcinia ti passa?
Quantu, dimmi, na lagrima di chissi,
quantu ntra dd'uri, quantu paghirissi!

But why, alas, don't all these tears stream down
when Dulcinea passes through your mind?
How much for one such tear as this, oh say,
how much in those long hours, would you pay?

61. Apri fratantu l'occhiu lagrimusu,
ed eccu, benchì appena ci vidìa,
vidi lu gran giganti portentusu,
chi all'àutru latu già passatu avìa;
e cu lu sbraccu so meravigghiusu
scurri di munti in munti, anzi passìa;
cu gesti l'amminazza e lu disfida;
s'accendi pri la stizza e dipoi grida:

61. Meanwhile he opened up the tearful eye,
and suddenly, although he barely could,
he saw the giant who portentously
had crossed already to the other side.
And with his marvelous great strides he trod
from mount to mount; indeed, he seemed to stroll.
Burning with wrath, Chisciotti challenged him
and threatened him with signs, and with a scream.

62. "Aspetta, pirchì fui? Sì grassu e grossu,
ài tuttu stu vantaggiu e pati appagnu?
E di cui timi, dimmi, o gran colossu?
D'unu chi nun t'arriva a lu calcagnu?
Pruvirai cu tua pena sinu all'ossu
ddu vrazzu, chi a lu munnu 'un à cumpagnu";
dissi, e cu summu ardiri e gran baldanza
e di vàusu in vàusu si sbalanza.

62. "Wait, there, why do you flee? You're big and
        strong,
you've got such great advantage and you're scared?
Tell me, whom do you fear, my great Colossus?
One who can hardly come up to your heels?
You'll feel with your own pain, down to the bone,
 this arm that has no peer upon this earth,"
he cried. And with audacity, indeed,
from cliff to cliff he hurled himself with speed.

63. Quantu voti cadìu, quantu s'alzau,
quantu contusioni in vrazza e rini,
quantu macchi o piraini affruntau,
quantu detti la facci ntra li spini,
quantu voti la carni si sfardau,
quantu sangu chiuviacci da li vini
cui si fida cuntarli, pò cuntari
li stiddi in celu e l'unni ntra lu mari.

63. So many times he fell and rose again,
so many bruises on his arms and sides,
so many thorns and brambles in his path,
so many times on thorns he scratched his face,
so many times his flesh was torn apart,
and so much blood rained out of his poor veins!
If you think you can count them all, then try
to count the waves, or stars up in the sky.

64. Ma la sorti purtau chi giustu appuntu
mentri stava passannu pr'un vadduni,
si trova anchi a passari ntra ddu puntu
l'umbra di chiddu o d'àutru nuvuluni.
Tuttu allegru esclamau: "È juntu, è juntu
l'ultimu to momentu, o gran putruni":
isa dda spata, chi 'un si torci o stocca,
e jetta un colpu orribili a na rocca.

64. But Fate decreed that at the time
he passed through a ravine, the shadow
of that cloud or of another one that was as big
chanced to pass, too, above that very spot.
He cheerfully exclaimed: "You lazy bum!
Your final moment now at last is here!"
That sword that does not bend or curve he raised
and on a rock a mighty blow he blazed.

65. Nun cadi accussì forti a Muncibeddu,

65. Never inside Mount Etna did the hammer

345

mentri Vulcanu teni la tinagghia,
di Steropi e di Bronti lu marteddu
supra lu tronu, chi ddà si travagghia,
comu la spata chi cadi a liveddu
contra lu vausu, e in pezzi lu sparpagghia:
e foru li sfrantumi tanti e tali,
chi parsi chi lu vàusu avissi l'ali.

of Sterope and Bronte fall so hard
with Vulcan holding the great pliers firm,
upon the thunderbolts they shaped in there,
as did the sword that fell against the cliff.
It was so hard it simply broke apart.
There were so many broken chips and things
it seemed as if the cliff had sprouted wings.

66. È fama (ed è attestatu unitamenti
da tutti li sculari di Turpinu)
chi a lu colpu terribili e potenti,
tantu li pezzi ficiru caminu
chi a una certa città di l'Orienti
chiuveru petri pr'un misi cuntinu.
E a n'ebreu, chi bivìa cu facci babba
na petra ci rumplu mussu e carrabba.

66. The legend says the blow had been so strong
it sent small fragments everywhere,
(this was confirmed in unanimity
by every Turpin scholar), and in fact,
upon a city of the Orient
it kept on raining stones for a whole month.
And to a Jew, enjoying a good quaff,
a stone broke both his mouth and his carafe.

67. A la trimenna botta un porcu spinu,
ch'era sutta ddu vàusu agnuniatu
sgridda e scocca li dardi da vicinu
e l'impanna da l'unu a l'àutru latu...
Quattru foru tra gargi e cuddarinu,
unu a lu nasu, nàutru a lu palatu,
dui ntra li gigghia prossimi di l'occhiu,
unu a la gamma, nàutru a lu dinocchiu.

67. At that tremendous shot, a porcupine
jumped out in haste from underneath the cliff
where it was hiding and shot his bristles
against poor Don Chisciotti at close range.
Four darts hit home between his cheeks and neck,
one on his nose, another in the palate
two hit between the brows, next to the eye,
one on his knee, another on his thigh.

68. L'Eroi pri lu duluri sbalurdìu;
poi rivinutu abbampa di russuri
cerca lu so nimicu, ma spirìu;
vidi li dardi e ni senti l'arduri;
"Ah! dici, Negromanti infami e riu
chi canci formi e muti li figuri;
finciti comu voi, deformi e sporcu,
nun ti timu giganti e mancu porcu".

68. The pain was such the Hero was struck dumb.
When he recovered, though, he blushed with shame.
He sought his enemy but it had vanished
He saw the bristles, and he felt their sting.
"Ah, guilty and disgraceful sorcerer,"
he said, "who can disguise yourself at will
take on the form you wish, deformed, foul swine!
I feared you not as giant nor as porcupine!"

69. Sanciu intantu (era cosa veramenti
chi v'arristava l'occhiu pri guardari)
pri lu suverchiu ridiri, li denti
tutti si ci putevanu cuntari;
si strinceva li cianchi fortementi
timennu di 'un avirisi a cripari,
e affirrannusi forti ad una rama
si turciunìa comu na ligama.

69. Sanciu meanwhile was laughing with such glee—
quite an amazing and amusing sight —
that you could easily identify
all of his teeth and count them one by one.
With all his might he held his sides for fear
he might explode and croak. But finally
he hugged a tree as though he were a vine
and writhed so much he seemed to have no spine

346

70. Di tantu in tantu ci gridava: "Evviva,
ammazzatilu! Forti! Forti ad iddu!...
Ecculu ddà ntra dd'arvulu d'oliva!
Ah, cani! comu sàuta! Ch'è griddu?"
Sti paroli a finirli nun arriva,
chi ridi e 'ngùscia comu un picciriddu;
dipoi conchiudi chi sutta la luna
nun si pò dari cosa chiù buffuna.

71. Si ci fa incontru e dici: "Via, signuri,
aviti assai sudatu sutta l'armi;
sta vota vi facistivu d'onuri
la cosa è digna di brunzi e di marmi;
asciucativi un pocu lu suduri,
doppu aviri mitutu tanti parmi;
ora conosciu, appettu a sti giganti,
chi voli diri Cavaleri erranti".

72. "No, rispusi l'Eroi, nun sarà veru
ch'eu ceda a la fatiga e a la stracchizza;
stari in traficu sempri, pirchì speru
purtari lu miu nomu a granni altizza".
Sanciu, ch'è di natura assai sinceru,
nun teni di sirragghiu, e già si stizza:
"Dunca, dici, 'un permettinu l'Eroi,
chi passi un'umbra pri l'affari soi?

73. Dunca lu celu nun è chiù patruni
di cacciari li nuvuli unni voli?
E chi mancu a li vàusi e a li ruccuni
lu starisi cueti chiù ci coli?
Dunca sti stravaganzi e sbariuni
sunnu lu fruttu di li vostri scoli?
S'è chissu, li dutturi e saputazzi
sunnu l'antesignani di li pazzi".

74. L'Eroi placidamenti ci rispusi:
"Sanciu, ti cumpatisciu e ti pirdunu:
L'occhi di la tua menti sunnu chiusi;
fora di l'umbri nun vidi a nessunu;
li stissi senzii mei sunnu confusi
pri fariti cumprendiri opportunu
lu modu comu vennu sti portenti
e 'un trovu espressioni confacenti.

70. From time to time he yelled to him: "Hurray!
Kill him, hit hard! Come on! Oh let him have it!
There he is now, up on that olive tree!
Oh, darn! How he can jump! Is it a cricket?"
He was unable to complete these words,
for like a child he laughed enough to choke.
Then he concluded that beneath the moon
nobody could come close to that buffoon.

71. He then approached him saying: "Come, Master,
You have perspired much in this war game.
This time your laurels you have truly earned.
This deed should be preserved in bronze or marble;
but having reaped so many palms, it's time
to stop and dry your perspiration off.
Now that I've come to see such giants' might,
I've learned the meaning of an 'Errant Knight!'"

72. The Hero answered: "No, it shall not be
that I desist because of weariness
or of fatigue. Forever will I strive
for I will lift my name to greater heights."
But Sanciu, who by nature was sincere
and quick of trigger, was already vexed
and cried: "Who said that heroes can deny
a cloud to freely travel in the sky?

73. So then the sky's no longer free to drive
the clouds wherever it may want? The cliffs,
the boulders that just mind their own affairs,
cannot be left alone, all to themselves?
These awful blunders, your extravagance
are the results of all your education?
If so, the doctors and the know-it-alls
are the forerunners of the greatest fools!"

74. The Hero placidly replied to him
"Sanciu, I will excuse you and forgive you
The eyes to your own intellect are closed,
and but for shadows you don't see a soul.
My very senses are a bit bewildered,
as I attempt to make you understand
how these great portents actually take place.
I cannot find the words to state my case.

75. Del restu pruvirò na paritati:
Figurati ca sì ntra na chianura,
e ddocu 'ncontri ntra li matinati
un cacciaturi chi dici e assicura
chi ddà 'ncostu ci sù lebbri agghiazzati;
tu guardi afflittu ntra dda sua drittura
a lu chiù vidi un fumu, né l'apprenni;
chistu è assai, pri cui è pratticu e comprenni.

76. Ora, comu una picciula fumata,
chi esala da na troffa, all'omu espertu
ci duna signu di lepri ammucciata,
e senza chi la vida già n'è certu
cussì eu canusciu a certa maniata
tutti l'incanti, e cridimi ca 'nzertu;
ci voli menti, studiu e suduri
a conusciri incanti e incantaturi.

77. Tu ti nni ridi e puru n'ài na prova
ntra stu fattu passatu chiara chiara:
vidisti un'umbra, e nun è cosa nova,
quannu la negghia lu suli arripara;
ma pirchì mannau dardi, comu chiova?
E pirchì l'umbra, ch'è di corpu avara,
si muta in porcu chi si vidi e tocca?
Ed è in un tempu ed umbra e porcu e rocca?"

78. "Signuri, via, finemula, 'un sia chiui:
sù persuasu, è cosa manifesta;
fu veru incantu, basta a dirlu vui;
anzi pens'iu chi si v'afferra 'ntesta
di cridiri 'ncantati tutti nui
cu l'isula, lu ponti e la foresta,
cu tuttu chi di chistu 'un ci nn'è ciàuru.
farriti vui lu jocu di lu tauru.

79. Addunca ripusativi per ora
e poi pinsamu a fari lu viaggiu".
"Riposo il Ciel non mi concede ancora,"
ci rispusi l'Eroi prudenti e saggiu:
"jeu vogghiu esercitarimi ccà fora
li forzi, lu valuri e lu coraggiu,
comu facìanu appuntu li Romani
ntra li circuli massimi e li chiani.

75. At any rate, a simile I'll try:
imagine that you are out on a plain
and early in the morning you encounter
a hunter who claims, nay, who guarantees
that there are hares in hiding there about.
Upset, you look in the direction shown.
At most, you'll see a meaningless smoke puff,
but for the practiced eye that's quite enough.

76. Now then, just as a little puff of smoke
that rises from a bush can give an expert
a clue that there's a hidden hare about
and without seeing it he can be sure,
so I can recognize all magic spells
by scent alone! Believe me, for, I can!
You need to study hard and long and well
to know magicians and a magic spell!

77. Go on and laugh! But in this past event
you had the clearest, brightest proof of it!
You saw a shadow. Nothing new in that!
It happens when the fog blocks out the sun.
But why did it shoot darts as sharp as nails?
How could a shadow that's bereft of body
change to a living, solid porcupine
and be at once a shadow, rock, and swine?"

78. "Come, Master, stop! Let's talk no more of it.
I am convinced, it's very clear indeed!
It was a magic spell, if so you say!
In fact, I do believe that if it comes
into your head to think that we, this bridge,
this forest and this isle are all spell-bound
though there is not a shred of evidence,
you'll be an angry bull inside a fence.

79. So for the moment rest and afterwards
we'll think about the journey to be made."
"The heavens will not grant me rest as yet,"
the prudent and wise Hero answered then.
"My strength, my courage and my worthiness
I want to exercise out in the open,
as Romans used to do when they would train
in grand arenas or in a small plain.

80. Ma nun essenducci àutru chi tia
ntra st'isula, benchì fussi scuderi,
jeu t'abilitu a mettirti cu mia,
pirchì è na prova e nun sù cosi veri;
tra li primi esercizii, sceltu sia
la lutta, ch'a li seculi 'nnarreri
fici onuri a l'atleti tutti quanti
e doppu ancora a Cavaleri erranti.

81. Cu lu spissu battirisi, l'azzaru
si rendi assai chiù splendidu e chiù duru;
la ginnastica in Grecia ebbiru a caru
chi furtifica l'omu comu un muru;
tali nell'arti mia, nun c'è riparu,

80. Since on this island there's nobody else
but you, I grant you leave, though you're a squire,
to stand against me in this test of strength.
It's not real fighting, only exercise.
And so let us choose wrestling as first trial;
for in the centuries gone by, it brought
all athletes wide acclaim and much delight.
It was the same for every Errant Knight.

81. Steel can be made more splendid, harder, too,
by being pounded with more frequency.
They loved gymnastics a great deal in Greece
 because it made men sturdy as brick walls.
There's no avoiding it, my work is such

bisogna esercitarimi, e tu puru;
chi quannu lu scuderu è un gran putruni,
e macchia chi s'estendi a lu patruni.

82. Orsù, coraggiu! Sanciu, via, da bravu,
ch'eu pri l'amuri e stima chi ti portu
mi scordu di me stissu, e quasi un schiavu
chi tu mi stassi a pettu oggi supportu;
tu sì un piliddu, ed iu ni fazzu un travu;
gradiscinni l'affettu e a drittu o a tortu
li pugna e vastunati di sta sciarra
di la mia stima sianu la caparra".

83. "Si chista è stima odiarmi e avirmi a mali
vi pregu, 'un è pri mia sta lezioni;
nun sù vappu e sfurzari un naturali
mi pari propria un'indiscrizioni;
pazzii n'aviti fattu originali
ma chista è grossa assai, c'è lesioni;
lu nasu... l'anca... 'nzumma... vui di mia
n'aviti forsi a fari anatomia?"

84. "Sanciu pri carità, si mi voi beni,
dissi l'Eroi, nun ti mustrari vili:
pri quantu lu miu onuri a caru teni,
cerca ostentari un'animu virili;
la mia gloria si reggi e si susteni
anchi supra di tia; infatti è stili
chi pri sapiri un'omu chi arti fa,
si osserva cu cui prattica e unni va.

85. Orsù, sbrazzati e lassa li riguardi
dovuti da lu servu a lu patruni;
ti permettu li pugna chiù gagghiardi,
li gargi, li tistati e l'ammuttuni;
usa l'arti e la forza, 'un sianu tardi
li vrazza né li gammi; un bastiuni
sia lu to corpu, ed iu da l'àutru latu
usirò l'arti mia ch'aju 'mparatu".

86. Sanciu, alluccutu di sta nova dosa
di pazzia, dici: "E stativi cuetu;
jocu di manu cu qualch'àutra cosa,
criditilu di mia, ca vannu a fetu".

that it demands much exercise, yours, too!
For when the squire is a real disaster,
the stain will soon extend onto the master.

82. Come, Sanciu, be a good, brave fellow now!
And since I feel regard and love for you,
I will forsake my worth, and like a slave,
today, I'll let you fight me man to man.
You're a small fry, I'm making you a giant!
Accept this sign of caring, right or wrong.
My punches and my blows you may well deem
a pledge or token of my great esteem."

83. "If you express esteem this way, please hate
or wish me ill! This test is not for me.
I'm not a he-man and in my opinion
forcing our nature is an indiscretion.
Unique insanities you have committed,
but this one takes the prize: you've spilt some blood!
My nose, my thigh! I wonder, could it be
you're studying anatomy through me?"

84. "Oh, Sanciu, if you love me, please," replied
the Hero then, "don't act so cowardly!
If for my honor you have some regard,
try to exhibit a more virile heart.
My glory rests and it depends on you
as well. In fact, it is traditional
that to find out what a man's job may be,
with whom he goes and where, one needs to see.

85. Come now, roll up your sleeves and put aside
all the respect a servant owes his master.
You're free to punch as hard as you can punch,
and you may even butt, and scratch, and shove.
Use all your skills and strength; don't let your legs
and arms move slowly; let your body be
a bastion, while from the other side,
with all the skills I've learned I will abide."

86. Sanciu, astonished by this novel dose
of madness, said: "Please, Sir, behave yourself!
Rough play, believe me, leads to playing rough
especially when other things are added."

350

Ma don Chisciotti intantu nun riposa;
L'aguanta e dici: "Un fari lu discretu;
orsù, viguri, armu, distrizza, o Sanciu
e chidda chi nun servi ti la canciu".

87. Accussì dittu, scarrica c'un pugnu,
chi 'ntunau ntra li spaddi strepitusu.
"Ddocu chi 'un ci sta nuddu? Eu chi 'un ci
[sugnu?
dissi Sanciu, o pruvati lu dammusu?
Basta... nun chiù... lu nasu vi lu scugnu...
No, nun vuliti starivi?... A tia pusu!..."
Ci abbia na tistata ntra li ganghi,
poi 'ntipa forti ad iddu, tinghi e tanghi.

88. S'accicciaru tra d'iddi a signu tali,
chi parìa di dui corpi un corpu sulu;
Sanciu d'ira è na bestia, un'animali,
dava tistati e cauci, comu un mulu.
Lu nostru Eroi gridava: "O beni o mali,
jeu certu nun sugn'omu chi arricculu":
dissi, ed un pugnu ntra li costi affunna;
Sanciu intantu una tempula ci ciunna.

89. S'imbrogghianu li gammi e testi e vrazza,
chi 'un si conusci di cui sunnu chiui;
ora un pugnu, ora scinni na gargiazza,
né si sa da cui vinni ed a cu' fui;
cui sgranfugna, cui duna, cui amminazza,
sù accicati da l'ira tutti dui;
li vastunati chiovinu a timpesta,
e ni risona l'aria e la foresta.

90. "Ancora avi a resistiri! dicìa
tra se stissu l'invittu don Chisciotti,
l'antica forza ch'è già morta in mia?
Un tintu servu reggi a li mei botti?
Pri pietà, nu lu saccia Dulcinia!"
Sanciu fratantu, comu megghiu potti,
sciogghi na manu e 'ntesta ci ribumma
na botta tali chi parsi na bumma.

91. Sturdìu l'Eroi e tanti stiddi e tanti
ci passaru pri l'occhi a jornu chiaru;

But meanwhile Don Chisciotti did not rest
and grabbed him saying: "Don't be so polite!
Sanciu with vigor, heart, dexterity,
do all you can, you'll get no less from me."

87. Having this said, he let go of a blow
that echoed loudly from poor Sanciu's back.
"You're knocking at a door where no one lives?
Am I then not at home? You're listening
for echoes?" Sanciu asked. "Enough. . .no more!
I'll rearrange your nose! You won't stay still?
Beware!" His jaw he butted with great might,
then climbed all over him from left and right.

88. Then they became so closely intertwined
that their two bodies were like one instead.
Sanciu's great anger made a beast of him,
an animal who butted with his head,
and kicked mule-like. "For better or for worse,
our Hero yelled, "I'm not a man to turn
and run." And sank a punch in Sanciu's side
who scratched in turn a chunk of his old hide.

89. Legs, heads, and arms had gotten so embroiled
you could not tell which limb belonged to whom.
A punch was thrown; a scratch was the reply.
'Twas hard to know the puncher from the punched!
They had become so blinded by their rage
that they kept scratching, hitting, screaming threats.
Indeed, the blows sprayed down like drops of rain
echoing through the forest and the plain.

90. The yet unvanquished Don Chisciotti said
within himself: "He's still resisting me!
The ancient vim's already spent inside?
A lowly serf can yet withstand my blows?
I pray, let Dulcinea never know!"
Sanciu, meanwhile, had managed to untie
one of his hands and on his head he drummed
a blow that left Chisciotti nearly numbed.

91. The Hero was quite dazed and many stars
paraded right before his eyes in plain daylight.

fu di cadiri in forsi ma a l'istanti
li spiritazzi soi lu rispigghiaru;
li sguardi sù di focu fulminanti:
"Guardati, Sanciu, ohimè! cerca riparu!"
Sanciu, chi già previdi la timpesta,
si ripara cu l'ùvitu la testa.

92. Comu da un tenebrusu nuvuluni
prima si senti in aria lu bisbigghiu,
poi cadennu li grandini abbuluni,
tinta dda matri chi ci avi lu figghiu
sbuccanu pri la china li vadduni,
tuttu lu mummu si vidi in scumpigghiu,
li turbini e li trona fannu guerra,
e s'impasta lu celu cu la terra;

93. tali l'Eroi tra l'ira sua trimenna
fulmini e focu da li naschi sbruffa;
si sgarra un colpu, lu difettu emenna,
torna a dari di novu e l'accutuffa.
Sanciu fratantu cu na furia orrenna
lu so patruni pri li cerri acciuffa;
ma pirchì di capiddi n'era spanu,
si nni vinniru allura ntra li manu.

94. Circau mettirci un pedi pri traversu,
'mpiddugghiarlu, e poi darci un'ammuttuni,
ma l'anca zoppa nun ci jeva a versu
e l'afflittu frimia comu un liuni;
finalmenti pinsau persu pri persu
l'espedienti chiù prontu e communi,
e li spiranzi, comu megghiu potti,
ntra li causi funnau di don Chisciotti.

95. Passa un vrazzu pri sutta e ci l'aguanta,
li tirau forti e ni rumpìu la cinta,
cala la tila e scopri tutta quanta
la mappa cu la sfera ben distinta;
vidi lu so vantaggiu e si nni vanta,
Sanciu, gridannu: "La battagghia è vinta!
La breccia è rutta e apertu è lu vadduni
pri fina dintra di lu pavigghiuni".

96. Don Chisciotti avvampannu di russuri

He was about to faint, but in an instant
his old, undaunted heart was re-awakened.
His looks became a searing flashing flame.
"Sanciu, look out! By God, defend yourself!"
Sanciu the storm already had foreseen
and with his elbow tried his head to screen.

92. As from a tenebrous, vast cloud, at first
you hear a murmuring up in the air,
then hailstones fall in buckets to the ground
– pity the mother whose poor son is caught
within the storm– and gorges overflow,
and the whole world appears to be upturned
as lightning, thunder, in harsh conflict vie,
and earth is kneaded into one with sky,

93. so was our Hero who with dreadful wrath
was snorting fire and lightning from his nostrils.
If he but missed a blow, he made amends,
returning to the fray and thrashing him.
Sanciu, meanwhile, with dreadful violence
grabbed hold of his own master by his locks.
However, since he was so scarce of hair
off in his hands it came and left him bare.

94. He tried to put a foot in front of him
to trip him up and then to push him down,
but his lame thigh inhibited his plan
and the poor fellow seethed like a caged beast.
But, finally, believing he was lost,
he came up with a common stratagem,
one that was near at hand: he took a chance
and sank his hopes inside Chisciotti's pants.

95. Sanciu then slipped his arm right under them
and pulled so hard he broke the Hero's belt.
The curtain fell, disclosing the whole map,
leaving in view the globes in sharp outline.
Seeing his own advantage, Sanciu yelled
with boastful pride: "the battle's mine. I've won!
I've made a breach and open lays the gorge.
Inside the far pavilions I can forge."

96. Chisciotti, who was blushing from the shame,

ci strinci li gariddi fortementi;
Sanciu spatedda l'occhi e a lu duluri
si torci tuttu e zurrichìa li denti;
era già quasi juntu all'ultim'uri,
si 'un s'appigghiava a certu espedienti:
stenni la manu e cu distrizza immenza
di don Chisciotti turciunìa l'essenza.

97. Attaccatu chi fu stu contrafocu,
l'Eroi vacilla e la sua forza stagghia;
va cadennu in deliquiu, e appocu appocu
già quasi manca, s'abbanduna e quagghia:
fra tantu sunnu cursi ntra stu locu
a lu fracassu di sta gran battagghia,
un'omu, chi zappava na nuara,
un rumiteddu ed una lavannara.

98. L'unu si ci fa avanti cu la zappa,
dicennu: "Via, spartemu sta discordia";
L'àutru cu la pacenzia e la cappa
grida: "Fratelli mei, paci e cuncordia";
la fimmina in scupriricci la chiappa,
esclama: "Chi sfrinzia! Misiricordia!"
'Nzumma pri menzu di sti boni genti
foru divisi sti dui cummattenti.

99. Mentri l'Eroi si accommoda li càusi,
lu rumiteddu cu l'occhi modesti
tessi un sermuni cu dovuti pàusi
riccu di boni frasi, auturi e testi,
pruvannu chi l'Infernu ni fa sàusi
di chiddi chi sù torbidi e molesti;
e chi fu vistu un jornu Farfareddu,
chi ni purtava quattru a Muncibeddu;

100. e ch'è na quinta vucca sta muntagna
pri cui si scinni jusu a casa-càuda
e chi Bolena di la gran Brittagna
ci fu purtata e s'abbruscau la fàuda;
e chi nuddu castiu si ci sparagna,
pirchì fu mariola e fu rifàuda;
e poi conchiusi: "Sulu veni ammisu
l'amicu di la paci in Paradisu".

began to squeeze the glands on Sanciu's neck.
The pain was such that Sanciu started writhing,
rolling his eyes and grinding his poor teeth.
Already he was nearly out of breath
when he came up with this expedient:
with his free hand, with great dexterity,
he wrung the Hero's masculinity.

97. The Hero, when attacked by this cross fire
began to vacillate and lose his strength.
Already he felt weak and bye and bye
he was beginning to give up and swoon.
Attracted to this place by the loud noises
of such war games, there came along a laundress,
a man who worked inside a melon patch,
and a poor hermit: all with great dispatch!

98. The man came forward with his hoe and said:
"Come on, let's settle this dispute!" The hermit,
who wore his patience like a cape exclaimed:
"My brothers, let's have peace and harmony."
"For shame! That is disgusting, Oh, have mercy!"
the woman said on seeing his behind.
At last, as these good people did their part,
the two combatants were soon pulled apart.

99. As our poor Hero tried to fix his pants
the hermit, glancing modestly about,
a noble sermon then began to weave
complete with proper pauses and quotations,
with authors, texts, and goodly words to prove
hell made minced meat of men who're troublesome.
In fact, he said, one day the devil Farfarel
was seen on Etna leading four such types to hell.

100. And that this mountain's truly a fifth mouth
through which you could descend to the Hot-house;
and that Boleyn of Britain was brought there
wherein her skirts were singed. She was not spared
her punishment because she truly was
a naughty and disgraceful wench. He then
concluded: "No one enters Paradise,
unless as friend of peace he qualifies."

101. "Patri, dissi l'Eroi, da pari vostru
lu sermuneddu è statu ben tissutu:
ma nun è adattu pri lu casu nostru,
la guerra in nui nun è fururi, è vutu;
comu vui vi spusati cu lu chiostru,
eu spusu pri la paci spata e scutu,
pri la paci cummattu, e st'eserciziu
fu fattu pri addestrari stu noviziu".

101. "Father, your little sermon was well spun,
as I'd expect from you," the Hero said,
"but inappropriate for this our case.
Warfare in us does not derive from hate,
but from a vow. As you the cloisters wedded,
I've married both the shield and sword for peace.
I fight for peace: that is my very office!
This exercise was meant to train this novice!"

102. "Patri, ripigghia Sanciu, in santa paci
n'avemu ruttu e grattatu la facci,
e pacificamenti a taci-maci
n'avemu datu cauci, comu macci:
nun sacciu si chist'arti a vui vi piaci;
si vuliti vidiri li procacci,
eccu lu nasu e lu sangu, chi chiovi
da chist'àutri firiti frischi e novi.

102. "Father," continued Sanciu, "we have scratched
and torn our faces in great harmony,
and each in his own way, but peacefully,
has kicked the other one just like a mule.
I know not if you like this art of ours,
but if you want to see what we have gained,
look at my nose, look at this blood that rains
out of these painful, freshly opened veins!

103. E zoccu aviti vistu, e chi viditi,
è statu un passa tempu veramenti
pirchì tra nui nun ci sù stati liti
e ni vulemu beni estremamenti;
st'eserciziu ni ammazza; ma dirriti:
mòrsiru pr'ammulari li strumenti;
chi vita saggia! Chi bellu campari!
Diciti, patri miu, chi vi nni pari?"

103. And what you saw before and see right now
has truly been a past-time, for between
the two of us there's been no quarreling.
In fact, we love each other very much.
This exercise will kill us, but, you'll say:
'they died while sharpening their instruments!'
What a wise life! What a nice way to live!
Speak, Father, please and your opinion give!"

104. Ripigghia don Chisciotti: "Boni genti,
avissivu, 'nzamai, qualchi molestia
di qualchi magu o Ciclopu insolenti?
Di fieru dragu o di salvaggia bestia?
S'aviti rastu ccà d'incantamenti?
O folletti, chi stannu cu smodestia?
Dicitilu, e 'nsignatimi la via,
ch'eu vi li sdugnu; chista è l'arti mia".

104. But Don Chisciotti spoke again: "Good folk,
have you had any trouble with magicians,
or maybe with a Cyclops who's ill-mannered,
with haughty dragons or some savage beast?
Is there a hint of magic spells about?
Are there sprites that behave indecently?
Say so, show me the way and say adieu.
I'll rid you of them all! That's what I do!"

105. "Pri mia, ripigghia Sanciu, si sapiti
unni fussi un ripostu o na 'ncantina,
un porcu sanu cu tutti li 'nziti,
o un stufatu di carni sarvaggina
vi pregu pri pietà chi lu diciti,
pirchì mi trovu na fami canina".
L'astanti tutti tri s'insalaneru
si guardaru ntra l'occhi e si nni jeru.

105. "As for myself," said Sanciu, "If you know
where I can find a tavern or a nook,
a pig that's whole, with all its bristles still,
or a good wild game stew, I beg of you,
for pity's sake, to tell me now because
I am so hungry I could eat a horse."
The three spectators nearly went berserk,
exchanged a glance and went right back to work!

Notes

1-6: See my introduction for a discussion of Meli's pessimism.

3: Astraea: Daughter of Zeus and Themis, goddess of justice. She lived among men in the Golden Age, but when their wickedness increased, she withdrew and was placed among the stars as the constellation Virgo, who is represented as a woman holding a scale.

15: I would make sure they'd never feel the cold: Sanciu is hinting that he would burn the books, as was done with Don Quijote's library (Part 1, Chapter VI).

14-18: In these octaves Sanciu voices Meli's belief that bookish knowledge without experience is more harmful than ignorance. In the "Vision", written in 1813 and added to the 1814 edition of the *Don Chisciotti e Sanciu Panza*, Meli returned to the same concept, making it one of the objectives of the poem (octaves 42-43 and 48). See the introduction.

It may be interesting to point out that Meli's assertions that he intended to write a satire of pseudoscientists who offered too facile a solution to difficult and insoluble problems (octave 48, the "Vision") may have been responsible for Francesco De Sanctis' condemnation of the Don Chisciotti as out of tune with its time. In the famous paper read at the University of Palermo in 1875, De Sanctis compared Meli's poem to the Cervantian novel by saying: "...but Cervantes' novel is immortal and Meli's, although extremely lively and full of imagination, is forgotten. Cervantes' poem represents the end of the Middle Ages; it is the birth of the modern world, a cosmic concept, a milestone in the history of the world. Meli's is but a little concept, designed to strike against the charlatans of science, its Don Quijotes, those whom Napoleon called ideologues: a little concept which could be the base of a chapter, too inadequate for a poem. In addition it was behind the times, because what interested that century was the greatness of science which was mastering the world, not a caricature of it, a farce." (My translation) (From *Saggi Critici*, a cura di Luigi Russo, Bari: Laterza, vol. 3, pp. 202-3). De Sanctis did not appreciate the poem because he understood it as an attack on science. His deeply positivistic attitudes colored his judgment. While a desire to satirize the pseudo-scientists of his day was present in Meli, it would be erroneous to consider it the sole objective or the justification of the poem, as I pointed out in the introduction. The expressed desire of Cervantes to rid the world of chivalric poems, has in the final analysis little to do with the huge success of his novel. Similarly, even if we were to accept De Sanctis' characterization of Meli's "concettino" (little concept) as the guiding principle of the poem, it would not follow that it would have to be a failure or out of tune with its time. In addition, to consider Meli as anti-scientific is erroneous and misleading. As a physician and as a professor of chemistry at the studio of Palermo, he subscribed to modern principles of scientific investigation. De Sanctis' article was a milestone in Melian criticism. It established the parameters of future debate and influenced the direction of Melian studies for many decades. His dismissal of the Don Chisciotti as something of a failure was undoubtedly responsible for some of the negative criticism voiced about this work.

22: Sanciu was referring to the island promised him by Don Chisciotti as reward for his service.

26: Meli's Don Chisciotti retains the same physical appearance as the Spanish Don Quijote.

49-79: The adventure with the cloud-giant recounted in this long episode must have struck Luigi Pirandello as a particularly Quijotic tale. While writing his essay on Umorismo Pirandello suffered an interesting mental lapse. As he analyzed the differences between El Cid and Cervantes' Don Quijote, he unconsciously quoted a Melian episode —precisely the episode narrated in these octaves — believing it to be a Cervantian reminiscence. The paragraph in question reads as follows:

"Ma Don Quijote? Coraggio a tutta prova, animo nobilissimo, gamma di fede; ma quel coraggio non gli frutta che volgari bastonate; quella nobiltà d'animo è una follia; quella gamma di fede è un misero stoppaccio ch'egli si ostina a tenere acceso, povero pallone mal fatto e rappezzato, che non riesce a pigliar vento, che sogna di lanciarsi a combattere con le nuvole, nelle quali vede giganti e mostri, e va intanto terra terra, incespicando in tutti gli sterpi e gli stecchi e gli spuntoni, che ne fanno strazio, miseramente."

(But Don Quijote? He had undaunted courage, a very noble soul, and burning faith. That courage, however, begot for him only vulgar beatings. That nobility of soul was a folly; that burning faith was a miserable rag that he obstinately kept lit, a poor, badly made and patched up balloon which could not hold the wind, who dreamed of fighting against clouds, in which he saw giants and monsters, and meanwhile he moved low along the ground, stumbling into every stump, and twig and crag that wretchedly tore him to pieces.)

55: This octave is patterned after Ariosto's *Orlando Furioso*, I, 55.

65: Mount Etna: The poet used "Muncibeddu," another name for the volcano, derived from "Mons" (Latin for mountain) and "gebel" (Arabic for mountain). Thus 'Muncibeddu' might be translated as "Mountain of Mountains".

Mount Etna is the volcano in which Vulcan, the blacksmith of the gods, had his shop, and where he manufactured Jove's lightning bolts with the help of the Cyclops Sterope and Bronte, according to the legend.

66: Turpin: See notes to I, 12.

81-97: This episode vaguely recalls Don Quijote's lashing of poor Sancho Panza for delaying the self-punishment that according to Merlin was required to break the magic spell binding Lady Dulcinea (Part 2, Chapters XXV-XXVI). In reality, the two episodes reflect the differences between the two works. In Meli, the two men fought a battle which resulted in Sanciu's technical victory achieved by grabbing Don Chisciotti's genitals. The fact that Sanciu was able to withstand Don Chisciotti's blows testifies to the new stature of the squire.